Cultural Sustainabilities

Cultural Sustainabilities

Music, Media, Language, Advocacy

Edited by Timothy J. Cooley

Foreword by Jeff Todd Titon

UNIVERSITY OF
ILLINOIS PRESS
Urbana, Chicago, and Springfield

Publication supported by a grant from
the Division of Humanities and Fine Arts,
University of California, Santa Barbara.

Library of Congress Control Number: 2019935628

ISBN 978-0-252-04236-2 (hardcover)
ISBN 978-0-252-08415-7 (paperback)
ISBN 978-0-252-05120-3 (e-book)

For Jeff Todd Titon, a quiet voice of reason
for sound ecology.

Contents

Foreword

JEFF TODD TITON

SUSTAINABILITY DIDN'T BECOME a vogue word until early in the twenty-first century. It had first gained attention in the Brundtland Report of 1987, where sustainable development was defined as "development that meets the needs of the present without compromising the ability of future generations to meet their needs" (World Commission on Environment and Development 1987). Later, sustainability entered the energy discourse over fossil fuels, recycling, and finite versus renewable resources. Now it is ubiquitous, whether about development, energy, climate change, economic and social justice, species extinctions, or sustainability of life on planet Earth: go green, recycle, eat local, plant trees, reduce your carbon footprint. Sustainability isn't confined to science and technology; the humanities have entered the discussion, generating new fields such as ecojustice, environmental philosophy, religion and ecology, and the environmental humanities. Cultural sustainability themed the 2013 conference of the American Folklore Society (AFS), while sustainability guides the Sustainable Futures music cultures project (Schippers and Grant 2016). Music and sound may not at first appear essential for survival, yet animal behavior depends on sound communication, and no human society lacks music. This volume on music, culture, and sustainability is therefore timely, and it's gratifying to see contributions from colleagues, many of whom studied with me—some recently, some as many as forty years ago.

Tim Cooley suggested that I write self-reflexively about my intellectual life and participation in the sustainability discourse. Leitmotifs here will be conservation, public folklore, applied ethnomusicology, activism, ecology, and the power of sound. My sustainability epiphany came in 2004 when the Common Ground Country Fair sponsored by the Maine Organic Farmers and Gardener's Association (MOFGA) invited me to bring friends and neighbors to demonstrate

an old-time string band jam session. MOFGA advertises this event, which at-
tracts eighty thousand visitors, as a "celebration of sustainable living." Our music,
which we play at home for our own enjoyment, is a renewable resource. Every
year since 2004, we've demonstrated it there alongside the livestock, produce,
and crafts exhibits. Besides, in most years since 1981 I've grown a large organic
vegetable garden and apple orchard. Organic gardening is all about building
and sustaining the soil, and whether it's garden soil, cultural soil, or life itself,
the ecological principles are pretty much the same. In that epiphany I realized
sustainability might offer advantages over conservation as a way to think about
the future of music and of culture.

My approach to folklore, ethnomusicology, and sustainability is, broadly
speaking, ecological, and it grows out of an activism that extends back to my high
school days, in Atlanta, when in the name of equal justice under law I supported
the civil rights demonstrations, lunch-counter sit-ins, and school integration.
Ecology per se had to wait until college: I interned on a medical ecology project
and took an experimental morphology course with Oscar Schotté. Schotté was
an eminent embryologist whose scientific lineage descended directly from Ernst
Haeckel (Neurotree 2016). Haeckel founded ecology, in 1866 coining the word
and defining it as "the comprehensive science of the relation of the organism to
the environment" (Egerton 2013, 226). Knowing my disappointment that Am-
herst College didn't offer an ecology course, Schotté helped me to understand
Eugene Odom's *Fundamentals of Ecology*, organized around energy exchanges
within ecosystems.

After I entered graduate school at the University of Minnesota in the fall of
1965, I became active in the anti–Vietnam War movement and, at the end of the
decade, in the burgeoning environmental movement. Exploring conscientious
objection with my political science professor, Mulford Q. Sibley, a Quaker and
campus radical, helped further my understanding of the role of conscience in
making a just and peaceful society. Having learned guitar in high school—my
father was an amateur jazz guitarist—I continued playing in college, and in
graduate school I joined a blues band led by Lazy Bill Lucas. While making
music with Lucas and his friends, I promoted their careers at home and abroad,
producing two albums for them in France and publishing interviews in blues
fan magazines in England. My advocacy was born of friendship and a desire
to give something back to the people who were giving so much to me. Our
band performed in bars and at concerts, festivals, and events for civil rights
and related activities. I never will forget my role in a theatrical piece called *Dat
Feelin'*, written by Milton Williams, a black historian, performed at the Guthrie
Theatre in Minneapolis in 1970. I was in Lucas's band playing blues in a slave
hut, the only white person in the cast. During rehearsal I asked Williams why
we were in a slave hut when music historians thought blues began late in the

nineteenth century. "You mean to tell me slaves didn't have the blues?" he replied. I learned how narrow music history could be when confined to musical form and structure, and I learned a lesson about the blindness of Eurocentric academic hegemony.

As an undergraduate I had pursued both the sciences and the humanities. I loved learning and wanted to make a life out of it. In graduate school while earning a master's degree in English and a doctorate in American studies, I also took courses in history, music, sociology, and cultural anthropology. My anthropology professor, Pertti Pelto, adopted a cultural ecology approach, offering me another way to think about ecology. Ethnomusicologist Alan Kagan joined the Minnesota faculty in the fall of 1966; I took every graduate course he offered. Ethnomusicology at the time was defined as the study of music all over the world, in its cultural context. American studies was the interdisciplinary study of American culture, past, present, and future. An American cultural approach to blues, employing methods from ethnomusicology and American studies itself, struck me as an appropriate dissertation topic. Blues writers had always been anxious about the genre's future because they thought commercial forces debased it and threatened its destruction. As a member of a blues culture, however, I sensed that blues was resilient. Ecosystem ecology confirmed my experience of blues as a dynamic cultural system; I didn't share the other writers' worries. While studying ethnomusicology I read William K. Archer's seminal essay, "On the Ecology of Music" (1964, 28–33). As far as I know, he was the first to connect music with ecology in print. Archer conceived of music within its cultural context as an information system. But his idea of music as an information system did not seem ecological. It was remote from the cultural ecology I had learned from Pelto. Besides, nowhere in his article did he use the term *ecosystem*, nor did he discuss ecological science per se. Information systems did not seem to be true ecosystems, governed as ecosystems are by the flow of energy within ecological communities. Information appears static in its relations, whereas an ecosystem is dynamic. I didn't realize then that cybernetics involved the dynamic flow of information in complex systems.

Upon finishing my dissertation in 1971, I accepted a position in the English department at Tufts University, teaching freshman composition, folklore, American literature, and twentieth-century poetry. I continued to be active in the peace movement and became an informal adviser to students opposed to the ongoing Vietnam War. In 1974 on released time from English, I started teaching ethnomusicology in the music department, revised my dissertation for publication (Titon 1977), and began ethnographic studies of the power of sound, space, and sacred language within traditional religious communities in the United States, studies that continue to this day. In the 1970s and 1980s, I also was a consultant for the public folklore infrastructure being established, first in

Washington, DC, and then throughout the United States, in arts organizations, museums, and other extra-academic settings. Arising from a progressive political stance, public folklore was established with a mandate to conserve and encourage folklife among the cultural groups that comprise the United States' full ethnic mosaic. I worked for the Smithsonian Folklife Festival and as a member of the National Endowment for the Arts' Folk Arts Panel, serving along with indigenous panelists from those cultural groups such as Beatrice Medicine and Charlotte Heth (Native Americans) and Robert Garfias (Hispanic). Heth and Garfias were ethnomusicology professors at UCLA; Garfias was also a powerful voice on the National Council on the Arts, advocating on behalf of cultural equity for artists from American minorities.

From the 1950s through the 1980s, it was uncommon for academic folklorists, and practically unheard of for ethnomusicologists, to do applied work in public folklore or ethnomusicology. The elders in both fields had established their bona fides inside universities. Musical and cultural conservation work outside the academy might be well and good, these leaders thought, but was it professional? Applied folklore and ethnomusicology smacked of amateurism, of the folk music revival, of the "song and dance" societies associated with UNESCO's International Folk Music Council. Besides, recalling that Nazis and Communists used folklore for propaganda, cultural purification, and ethnic cleansing, these elders distrusted social engineering in public folklore and applied ethnomusicology (Titon 2015a, 19). Nonetheless, I and other younger academics whose idealism was nourished and whose political, musical, and environmental activism was forged in the 1960s carried few such reservations into our work in the following decades, as we sought to work as advocates for and in partnership with community scholars, elders, and practitioners in the music cultures we were studying.

In 1977 I taught a summer session at Indiana University and became acquainted with anthropologist Alan Merriam, one of the founders of the Society for Ethnomusicology (SEM) in 1955. Committed to ethnomusicology as an objective, social-scientific study of music, he wanted to discuss music's relation to culture. I expressed my view that once one separated the two—into music "and" culture or music "in" culture—it was impossible to bring them back together. We agreed it was better to think of music as culture, that is, as a cultural system in itself. I couldn't interest him in ecology, but later that year as I mused further on the topic of our conversations, it came to me that music—today I would say sound—is the energy that flows to connect, integrate, and disconnect and disintegrate various dynamic components within a music culture. A music culture "can be regarded as an ecological system," I wrote in 1978 for the first chapter of the first edition of a new textbook in ethnomusicology, *Worlds of Music* (Titon and Slobin 1984, 9). In light of later critiques of my work (e.g.,

Keogh 2013; Keogh and Collinson 2016), it should be understood that I did not think of ecology solely as a metaphor, and neither had Archer fourteen years earlier. Instead, Archer conceived music in its cultural context to be an information system, and I conceived music cultures to be dynamic ecological systems, not merely to be like them.

In the mid-1970s I started two ethnographic projects on the power of sound in performed language, one with the African American preacher Rev. C. L. Franklin, the other with a mountain church in Virginia's northern Blue Ridge. In *Powerhouse for God* (Titon 1988), I discussed the cultural and natural ecologies of mountain farming in that region. I proposed that in the practices of husbandry could be found the adaptations and traditional connections among family, farming, and belief. The people's religious folklife was an inherited tradition and not, as other scholars had claimed, a pathological response to modern life. In the early 1980s I co-founded Tufts's American studies program and tried out some of those ideas in a team-taught course titled "History and Ecology in America." Although I didn't think that this collaborative academic project would garner public attention, the Powerhouse documentary recording was discovered by music critics Dave Marsh and Greil Marcus and featured on National Public Radio, while news about the in-progress Powerhouse documentary film attracted Ted Koppel's attention (Titon and George 1982; Dornfeld, Rankin, and Titon 1989). An ABC-TV special *Koppel Report* contrasted televangelists with the pastor of the Powerhouse church, Brother John Sherfey (Koppel 1988).

In 1986 I moved to Brown University as a professor of music and director of the PhD program in ethnomusicology. Four years later, I spent a semester at Berea College and began visiting with Old Regular Baptists in southeastern Kentucky. Their melodically elaborate, unaccompanied singing is the oldest English-language religious music in oral tradition in the United States (Titon 1999, 2005). Most had grown up in the mountains of central Appalachia, coal-mining country. They say that sounds have a "drawing power" and connect them with the natural world, with one another, and with the divine. Charles Shepherd recalled a time when a group met for a memorial in a cemetery: "I heard my daddy singing 'Amazing Grace.' I never heard a more beautiful sound in my life. Seemed like the trees was just carrying that sound up and down the valleys, and it did something to my heart" (Shepherd in *Songs of the Old Regular Baptists* 1997, track 13). Elwood Cornett added, "It seems to me that there's something innate about the sound that we have in the way that we sing. There's some kind of a special connection between, I think, a human and somehow that's released by that sound" (Cornett in *Songs of the Old Regular Baptists*, vol. 2 2003, track 17).

Cornett, the moderator (elected leader) of the Indian Bottom Association of Old Regular Baptists, asked for my help in conserving their oral tradition of lined-out hymnody. We worked together on a music documentation project, making recordings and producing cassettes to distribute throughout the membership. Over the next twenty years, this project in applied ethnomusicology snowballed into two Smithsonian Folkways CDs and demonstrations of the church members' singing at the Kentucky Folk Festival, the Smithsonian Festival of American Folklife, and two conferences on "line singing" at Yale. In 2015 the recordings were chosen for preservation in the National Recording Registry. Convinced of the value of their musical traditions, the Old Regular Baptists are intent on sustaining it. As Elder Cornett said, when interviewed by an Appalshop reporter about eight years ago, "It would appear to me that this way of singing is much more accepted right now than it was a few years ago and I think the interest of Jeff [Titon and some others] has made a lot of difference in that, and then our people have begun to say, 'Hey, we've got something here pretty special.' The Smithsonian [published] a couple of CDs of our singing, and all of that has caused our people to say, 'Hey, we need to, we want to hang on to this way of singing'" (Cornett 2007).

In the 1990s applied ethnomusicology moved closer to the SEM mainstream. In 1989 as program chair for the annual SEM conference, I convened a special session on applied ethnomusicology and invited several of my colleagues from the NEA Folk Arts Division to speak on it. In 1989 I also accepted an invitation to edit SEM's journal, *Ethnomusicology*, and made that conference session the basis for a special issue on "Music and the Public Interest" (vol. 35, no. 1, 1992), now recognized as a turning point for applied ethnomusicology within SEM. An SEM Committee on Applied Ethnomusicology was established in 1997, and the committee became a section in 2002; in 2007 the International Council for Traditional Music (ICTM) established a study group on applied ethnomusicology. A scholarly literature on theory and practice has emerged; a bibliography is maintained on the SEM Applied Ethnomusicology Section's web page (https://tinyurl.com/yavcggxz). Today, the Applied Ethnomusicology Section is SEM's third largest, with three hundred members. Activist and community-engaged ethnomusicology is on the rise.

During a sabbatical in 2004–5, I researched sustainability in developmental anthropology, economics, ecology, and the environmental movement. I began speaking publicly on musical and cultural sustainability in 2006: in the Nettl Lecture at the University of Illinois; at the annual AFS conference, and in a session on musical and cultural sustainability I had organized for the annual SEM conference (Titon 2006a, 2006b, 2006c). Papers from the 2006 SEM session evolved into a special issue of *the world of music*. In it, I put forward four principles of an ecological approach to music and sustainability in an article bearing that title:

1. Cultivating diversity, and fertilizing the cultural soil rather than targeting interventions chiefly at cultural monotypes such as individual expressive genres.
2. Stewardship rather than ownership, holding music and culture in trust for the present and future.
3. Recognizing limits to growth, whether in communities, economies, eco-systems, or even in persons.
4. Interconnection and interdependence among all beings, which has always been ecology's fundamental tenet (Titon 2009).

An ecological approach to sustainability does not imply restoration to some stable golden age characterized by a "balance of culture." Individuals, social groups, and political, economic, and environmental conditions were, and are, always responsible for innovations and disturbances that result in continuous cultural and musical change. In more recent publications, I take the position that sustainability and continuity require a strategy of resilience and adaptive management (Titon 2015b; 2016b). Adaptive management need not rely on instrumental consciousness or inappropriate technology; even deep ecologists practice a kind of adaptive management. Meanwhile, following the example of my colleague Kiri Miller, in 2008 I started a research blog as a place to lodge ideas for a possible book project. This *Music and Sustainability* blog (http://sustainablemusic.blogspot.com) proved so popular that since 2010 I have been aiming it at a general audience.

I made my sound ecology project public in 2012 when I began speaking on Thoreau and sound and issued an appeal for a sound commons for all living beings (Titon 2012, 2015c). It is an ecomusicological inquiry into sound experience as a basis for being in, knowing, and acting in the world (Titon 2012). My experiences as a musician, teacher, writer, outdoors observer, and organic gardener center this project, while my research in phenomenology and animal sound communication, acoustic and soundscape ecology, community sociology, ecological economics, conservation biology, and behavioral ecology underpins it, and my earlier ethnographic research into the power of sound and space informs it. I begin with sound, rather than with texts (as humanists tend to do) or objects (as scientists tend to do). Sound connects. From a scientific viewpoint, sound consists of vibrating molecules that travel in longitudinal waves, through a medium such as water, air, and beings—including, of course, human beings. Sound signals presence and connects beings viscerally through mutual vibration. This interconnection is experienced as co-presence. Sound connections suggest an intersubjective ontology and epistemology, rather than an objective relation between a thinking subject and external objects, including texts. From a sound co-presence among beings follows community, a sound economy based in reciprocity, and a sound ecology based in a social, not a self-ish genome interacting with other beings and the environment. In the spring of 2016 I delivered four public lectures summing up this project to date: one on sound experience, one on sound community, one on sound economy, and the last on sound ecology (Titon 2016a).

Unifying these two projects—sustainability and sound ecology—I approach an ecomusicological conclusion: a sound ecology teaches that all beings, human and otherwise, are interconnected. If so, then all beings are related. All beings are our relatives. A sound ecology points us toward an ethic of responsibility toward all beings, the common good, the commonwealth of nature and culture, and the sustainability of life itself.

References

Archer, William K. 1964. "On the Ecology of Music." *Ethnomusicology* 8 (1): 28–33.

Cornett, Elwood. 2007. Interview by Josh Noah, Appalshop Community Correspondence Corps, WMMT-FM, Whitesburg, KY.

Dornfeld, Barry, Tom Rankin, and Jeff Todd Titon, producers. 1989. *Powerhouse for God.* Documentary film, 58 min. Distributed by Documentary Educational Resources, Watertown, MA. Also streaming on www.folkstreams.net.

Egerton, Frank. 2013. "History of Ecological Sciences, Part 47: Ernst Haeckel's Ecology." *Bulletin of the Ecological Society of America* 94 (3): 222–44.

Keogh, Brent. 2013. "On the Limitations of Music Ecology." *Journal of Music Research Online* 4. http://www.jmro.org.au/index.php.

Keogh, Brent, and Ian Collinson. 2016. "'A Place for Everything, and Everything in Its Place': The (Ab)uses of Music Ecology." *MUSICultures* 43 (1): 1–15.

Koppel, Ted. 1988. "The Billion-Dollar Pie." *The Koppel Report*, ABC-TV, broadcast May 12. http://www.tcm.com/tcmdb.

Neurotree. 2016. Neuroscience Academic Family Tree. http://neurotree.org/beta/tree.php?pid=6459. Accessed November 18.

Schippers, Huib, and Catherine Grant. 2016. *Sustainable Futures for Music Cultures.* New York: Oxford University Press.

Songs of the Old Regular Baptists: Lined-Out Hymnody from Southeastern Kentucky. 1997. Smithsonian Folkways CD SFW40106, compact disc.

Songs of the Old Regular Baptists: Lined-Out Hymnody from Southeastern Kentucky. Vol. 2. 2003. Smithsonian Folkways CD SFW50001s, compact disc.

Titon, Jeff Todd. 1977. *Early Downhome Blues: A Musical and Cultural Analysis.* Urbana: University of Illinois Press.

———. 1988. *Powerhouse for God: Speech, Chant and Song in an Appalachian Baptist Church.* Austin: University of Texas Press.

———. 1999. "'The Real Thing': Tourism, Authenticity and Pilgrimage among Old Regular Baptists at the 1997 Smithsonian Folklife Festival." *the world of music* 41 (3): 115–39.

———. 2005. "'Tuned Up with the Grace of God': Music and Experience among Old Regular Baptists." In *Music and American Religious Experience*, edited by Philip V.

Bohlman, Edith L. Blumhofer, and Maria M. Chow, 311–34. New York: Oxford University Press.

———. 2006a. "Sustainable Music." Bruno and Wanda Nettl Lecture, presented at the School of Music, University of Illinois, Urbana-Champaign, March 6.

———. 2006b. "Theorizing Sustainable Music and Culture." Paper presented at the annual meeting of the American Folklore Society, Milwaukee, WI, October 18–22.

———. 2006c. "Theorizing a Sustainable Music." Paper presented at the annual meeting of the Society for Ethnomusicology, Honolulu, HI, November 16–20.

———. 2009. "An Ecological Approach to Music and Sustainability." *the world of music* 51 (1): 119–38.

———. 2012. "A Sound Commons for All Living Creatures." *Smithsonian Folkways Magazine*, Fall–Winter 2012. https://tinyurl.com/yaxwazx5.

———. 2015a. "Applied Ethnomusicology: A Descriptive and Historical Account." In *The Oxford Handbook of Applied Ethnomusicology*, edited by Svanibor Pettan and Jeff Todd Titon, 4–29. New York: Oxford University Press.

———. 2015b. "Sustainability, Resilience, and Adaptive Management for Ethnomusicology." In *The Oxford Handbook of Applied Ethnomusicology*, edited by Svanibor Pettan and Jeff Todd Titon, 158–96. New York: Oxford University Press.

———. 2015c. "Thoreau's Ear." *Sound Studies*, 1 (1): 144–54.

———. 2016a. Sound, Experience, and Understanding: Spring 2016 Basler Lecture Series. Presented while holding the Basler Chair of Excellence for the Integration of the Arts, Rhetoric, and Science, January– June, East Tennessee State University, Johnson City. https://etsucfaa.wordpress.com/2016/01/12/sound-ecology-titon-lectures/.

———. 2016b. "Orality, Commonality, Commons, Sustainability, Resilience." *Journal of American Folklore* 129 (514): 486–97.

Titon, Jeff Todd, and Kenneth M. George. 1982. *Powerhouse for God*. University of North Carolina Press 0–8078–4084-X, two 12" LPs with booklet. Reissued in 2014 by Smithsonian Folkways Recordings SFS60006, compact disc.

Titon, Jeff Todd, and Mark Slobin. 1984. "The Music-Culture as a World of Music." In *Worlds of Music: An Introduction to the Music of the World's Peoples*, edited by Jeff Todd Titon, 1–11. New York: Schirmer Books.

World Commission on Environment and Development. 1987. *Our Common Future*. New York: Oxford University Press.

Acknowledgments

THIS BOOK BEGAN as a conversation between Gregory Barz, Jeff Todd Titon, and me. Greg and I wanted to celebrate Jeff for achieving professor emeritus status at Brown University, where Greg and I met as graduate students under Jeff's mentorship. We coauthored an encomium for Jeff that we presented when he was given an honorary membership by the Society for Ethnomusicology at its 2014 annual meeting in Pittsburgh, where we also announced our plans for this volume. While the book is a festschrift of sorts, our desire was to honor Jeff not with flattering stories but by engaging critically his core contributions to scholarship and activism. Though Greg Barz ultimately had to withdraw from coediting this volume for pressing personal and professional reasons, his signature wisdom and clarity of thought influenced much that is good in this book. Greg also provided valuable feedback on early chapter drafts by a number of the authors, including the introduction and my own chapter. It is a much better book for his considerable efforts. Thank you, Greg.

A volume such as this is a profoundly collaborative effort. I am personally very grateful for the patience of each and every author as I pressed them to meet deadlines and make revisions. To the individual they were a pleasure to work with, and every one of them taught me something important about sustainability and resilience. I owe a debt of gratitude to each and every author for putting up with my editorial nudging and nagging and for teaching me so much along the way. At moments when I was struggling with some aspect or another of the book manuscript, individual authors provided an idea, a suggestion, or an encouraging word that made all the difference. Jeff Titon was always available to answer questions and provide much-needed advice and encouragement, though from the beginning he let Greg and me run with our own ideas and vision. I suspect that most if not all of the authors of this book know this to be a quality of Jeff's wise mentorship. Thank you all.

As we were putting the final touches on this volume, my home institution, the University of California, Santa Barbara (UCSB), hosted a mini-conference to bring together as many of the authors as could come and join us. This enabled many of us to collectively and in person thank Jeff Titon for the inspiration and encouragement he has given us and to make minor final adjustments to the book and strategize about how to use our efforts to encourage the humanities to further engage questions of sustainability and ecology. Thank you, David Pellow (Environmental Studies), Janet Walker (Film and Media Studies), and Mary Hancock (Anthropology and History), all colleagues involved with UCSB's Environmental Humanities Center and all of whom helped me organize the mini-conference. A special thanks to Ruth Hellier Tinoco (music, theater, and performance studies), who was the primary co-organizer of the conference. The conference was cosponsored by UCSB's Departments of Music, Anthropology, Film and Media Studies, and Environmental Studies and by the Center for the Interdisciplinary Study of Music. The conference was also generously supported with grants from UCSB's Interdisciplinary Humanities Center and the College of Letters & Science. Finally, we gratefully acknowledge John Majewski, Michael Douglas Dean of Humanities and Fine Arts, University of California, Santa Barbara, for a subvention that helps keep the purchase price of this volume at a minimum.

Sadly, during the production stage of this volume, Burt Feintuch, the author of chapter 16, "Cultural Integrity and Local Music in Cape Breton and New Orleans," died accidentally while being treated for cancer. One of Jeff Titon's closest colleagues for decades (Jeff described their relationship as "simpatico"), and similarly loved and respected by the many authors of this book who knew and worked with him, Burt is greatly missed. We are very grateful to Burt's long-time partner Jeannie Thomas, professor and department head of English at Utah State University, who, even in her grief, stepped in to see a number of Burt's projects to completion. She assures me that to the end, Burt sustained his spirit with conviviality and active musicking among a tight community of friends.

Sustainability, Resilience, Advocacy, and Activism

Introduction

TIMOTHY J. COOLEY

SUSTAINABILITY IS SOCIAL ACTION, cultural practice, and relationships with other people, other living beings, and the environment. Sustainability is not a competition, a marketable brand logo, something one can outsource, a growth model, or even a new green technology. Yet efforts at cultural and environmental sustainability need to account critically for all of these as human behaviors with intended and unintended impacts on ecosystems. And sustainabilities of all sorts call for resilience, advocacy, and activism.

The chapters in this volume are driven by the proposition that environmental and cultural sustainability are inextricably linked. The authors represented in *Cultural Sustainabilities* join a growing chorus of voices calling for profoundly integrated efforts to better understand sustainability as a challenge that encompasses all living organisms and ecosystems. While ecological scientists do inevitably engage humans, their focus nonetheless has tended to prioritize a conception of nature separate from human intervention (Boyle and Waterman 2016, 26). When ecologists do include humans in their studies, human impact is often interpreted as detrimental. The contributors to this volume, on the other hand, embrace human engagement with ecosystems and even celebrate it, though with a profound sense of collective responsibility born from the emergence of the Anthropocene. If life systems on earth are to be sustained, we who study human systems need to do our part. This volume contributes to the field of environmental humanities, which sees environmental crises as fundamentally social, political, ethnical, and cultural questions (Heise 2017, 2). These are the sorts of questions that anthropologists, folklorists, musicologists, ethnomusicologists, ethnographers, and documentarians are well suited to address.

A primary unifying factor of this book is each contributor's response to the inspiration and provocations of the ongoing lifework of Jeff Todd Titon, who for decades has called for ecological approaches to cultural sustainability, not only as metaphor but also as a means to understand, for example, that musical practices are ideally ecosystems themselves. Titon is well positioned to offer holistic approaches to cultural sustainability by dint of his lifelong efforts to blend ecological, philosophical, musicological, and practical approaches in his research, teaching, musicking, advocacy, and documentary work. Beginning with an education in American studies, Titon was fascinated by philosophical traditions that foreshadowed ecology (see Titon 2015a) and attracted to the musical practices of peoples on the fringes of dominant and dominating society. Informed by early scientific ecology when he was a university student, he created his own implicit synthesis of folklore, ethnomusicology, and environmental activism. Titon was an early adaptor of new technologies for communicating and disseminating ideas (see, for example, Dornfeld, Rankin, and Titon 1989; Titon 1971, 1991, 1992, 2003), but his research interests tend toward distinct music-cultural practices of communities that may appear to have been left behind by modernity but that are self-sustaining and resilient against all odds. The odds those communities and practices face tend to be the product of industrial capitalism, which deems them unprofitable, yet, as Titon explains in the foreword to this volume, those communities still maintain music-cultures that are "dynamic ecological systems." Such ecological cultural systems, he concludes, remind us "that all beings, human and otherwise, are interconnected," and they provide models for sociocultural changes that are resilient and sustainable.

Titon's path toward a concern for cultural resilience has led him increasingly from a focus on musical sounds and toward sound more broadly, something he calls "sound ecology" or "soundscape ecology," a concept that he links back in time through Steven Feld's "acoustemology" (1990, 2015) and Murray Schafer's "soundscapes" (1980) to Henry David Thoreau's attention to sound as experience in the environment (Titon 2015a). Thus Titon has moved from music to environmental and ecological concerns generally. Titon's sound ecology model avoids the objectifying acquisitive/collector impulse of earlier models of salvage folklore and ethnomusicology and develops new approaches based on resilience, advocacy, and activism. His work encourages communities to actively value, renew, and sustain their particular cultural practices, whether it be bringing senior blues players to new audiences (and renewed careers) on college campuses in the 1970s or documentary work with the inherited traditions of hymnody, husbandry, agriculture, and religious folklife of several rural regions in the Appalachians. This integrated and applied approach to research subjects led Titon to influential consulting work with the National Endowment for the Arts when it was establishing public folklore programs. Titon continues to be a leading proponent of applied folklore and ethnomusicology internationally, promoting such engagement as a form of moral obligation for reciprocity with the human subjects and communities we engage (see Hellier-Tinoco 2003) as well as a culturally sound practice.

I and the other contributors to this book respond to Titon's work by looking anew at our own areas of expertise with an eye toward cultural sustainability as a crucial part of ecology. Similar to Titon's own move beyond music studies, our discussion has been prompted by the challenges of sustainability to expand beyond music-focused fields even as musicking finds its place in most of the chapters. We are compelled to join our colleagues in the sciences, especially ecologists, in an effort to move toward a "third culture" in which humanists and scientists are co-investigators (Allen and Dawe 2016b, 5). Many of the contributors are actively doing collaborative work with scientists in their own projects, though such cooperative efforts are not the focus in this volume. Instead here we seek to speak together as humanists from various sister disciplines to highlight what we contribute to the study of environmental and cultural sustainability. Indeed, the scientific community agrees that human activity is having a deleterious impact on global environmental and ecological systems, yet human societies—especially those that prioritize wealth over welfare—resist the changes needed to mitigate this impact. Changing human behavior is as much a cultural question as scientific one. We join other humanists (e.g., Heise, Christensen, and Neimann 2017) in claiming that our work must address issues of ecological and environmental sustainability. We believe that humanists are also well positioned to step outside the academy to engage private- and public-sector policy makers—and many of the contributors have made this a significant part of their vocation (e.g., Baron, Dornfeld, Hufford, MacDougall, Post, and Summit).

Our collective approach to cultural sustainability does not mean that we believe all human cultural practices are sustainable or even should be sustained. On the contrary, as Aaron Allen details in this volume, a "sustainability-maintain" model of human cultural behavior is ultimately destructive—it leads to a deleterious Anthropocene. The point is to change human cultural behavior—Allen's "sustainability-change" model—if we are to redress the harmful impact humans are having on environmental ecosystems globally. This sustainability-change model shares much with Titon's resilience work, and several chapters provide case studies of how cultural practices have incorporated change with some success (Guy, Cavicchi, Tucker, Summit), though some communities that have historically been nimble at adapting are now struggling due to the scope of climate change (DeWitt, Feintuch, Post). Other authors suggest that some cultural practices are harmful to ecosystems and should be abandoned (Cooley, DeWitt, Hurley-Glowa, Kisliuk), while some chapters focus intently on the sustainability of cultural practices, using environmental ecology as metaphor (Cavicchi, Feintuch, MacDougall, Rankin, Samtani, Summit; see also Perlman 2012). Thus the volume as a whole is about cultural sustainabilities broadly, and most chapters, though not all, link this inextricably to ecology and environmentalism.

The Conversation

Cultural Sustainabilities does not propose revolutionary new ideas for environmental studies, though we wish to encourage humanistic scholars and activists working with broadly performative traditions to seek connectivity with environmental studies. We are decidedly contributing to the vital new discipline of environmental humanities and providing a bridge to other scholars working with human cultural practices. This volume does not focus on ecojustice (for this subject, see Pellow 2018), though some of the chapters address issues of environmental justice (Allen, DeWitt, Guy). It does not seek to define or critique emerging fields such as ecomusicology, though several of the key founders of that field are featured here: Aaron S. Allen, Jennifer C. Post, Denise Von Glahn, and Jeff Titon all have chapters in the seminal *Current Directions in Ecomusicology* (Allen and Dawe 2016a); Nancy Guy (2009) is the author of a much-cited article, "Flowing down Taiwan's Tamsui River: Towards an Ecomusicology of the Environmental Imagination," which appeared in the journal *Ethnomusicology*; and Tom Faux and Mark F. DeWitt have both published articles in "Music and Sustainability," a thematic issue of *the world of music* edited by Jeff Todd Titon (2009). Neither is this a volume devoted to applied ethnomusicology, even as several authors address this field (Faux, MacDougall, Nitzberg and Bakan, Titon; see also Pettan and Titon 2015). Our ultimate goal is to encourage by example all readers to ask how their own professional and advocational skill sets might be employed to respond to the Anthropocene—to imagine their own communities' cultural practices as part of a sustainable, mutually supportive ecosystem.

As *Cultural Sustainabilities* was in production, other volumes emerged that join this conversation. Huib Schippers and Catherine Grant's *Sustainable Futures for Music Cultures: An Ecological Perspective* (2016) is a collection of essays by different authors, each examining the resilience of distinct musical cultures. While that volume was inspired by Titon's work as well (Schippers and Grant 2016, ix, 5), it differs from the present volume in its systematic comparative approach and exclusive focus on music. Similar to Grant's 2013 contribution on "Music Sustainability" for the Oxford Bibliographies series and her 2014 book, *Music Endangerment*, the contributors to *Sustainable Futures for Music Cultures* use "ecology" as a metaphor for music cultures but do not engage the ecology of the biosphere as many of the authors do here. We also commend to our readers David Ingram's book on ecocriticism in American popular music (2010), two books by professor of communications and anthropology Mark

Pedelty (2012 and 2016), and musicologist Denise Von Glahn's 2013 book, *Music and the Skillful Listener: American Women Compose the Natural World*. All published in the decade in which this volume was written, these works and others have established a critical mass of scholarship on performative human cultural practices to which the present volumes contributes.

Cultural Sustainabilities also joins other urgently needed studies of ecosystems from humanistic perspectives that call for advocacy and activism. While appealing for informed activism, we must be careful not to replicate the very unsustainable cultural practices that we seek to critique. For example, many of the contributors to this volume are from the Global North, and our claims for diversity must be modest. While several of the authors critique colonialism and advocate for indigenous rights, indigenous voices are lacking in the roster of authors. Susan Hurley-Glowa, Jennifer C. Post, Timothy J. Cooley, and Joshua Tucker locate significant examples of indigenous activism, but do we succeed in avoiding a Western, colonial, top-down interpretive approach? As Tucker asks in this volume: "Should we perhaps look for indigenous activism outside the narrow realm of party politics—in, say, the realm of cultural sustainability?" We leave it to readers to determine if we are learning from and honoring our indigenous interlocutors or yet again colonizing their best ideas. The question needs to be asked and will not return stable answers. While acknowledging the limited perspectives represented in this book, we add that authors from the Global North may have a special responsibility to ask hard questions about our own cultural practices more urgently than others do since our societies are putting the greatest strain on the earth's resources. Thus we write with humility, in awe of the earth that sustains us, as we try to undo our own habits of Cartesian dualism (Hufford, this volume) that separate us from other living organisms, human and more-than-human.

Organization

Cultural Sustainabilities is organized in five parts. Each part contains four or five deliberately short chapters that we encourage you to read as thematic discussions contributing to the larger questions of the book as a whole. Part 1, "Thinking, Writing, and Musicking about Sustainability," suggests critical approaches to the tensions inherent in any effort to expand the discussion of sustainability beyond disciplinary conventions. As Robert Baron and Thomas Walker explain in their coauthored chapter, "Sustainability Clashes and Concordances," cultural sustainability is often at odds with environmental sustainability, yet they share a lexicon. In considering metaphors found in discourses of environmental and cultural sustainability, they show that they ultimately "affect how we perceive and act in the world." This, in turn, drives the social agency of a sort probably unique to the human species that demands advocacy on behalf of environmental and cultural sustainability. Mary Hufford picks up the theme of language in chapter 2, "Dialogues All the Way Down." Drawing substantially from traditions of semiotics, philosophy, and American pragmatism and grounded in her own ethnographic fieldwork with participants in a community-based science monitoring project, Hufford shows what we gain from folklore studies in integrating ecological and social sciences with the humanities. More to the point, she demonstrates how speech genres help us to engage reflexively beyond our own species. In chapter 3, "Radical Critical Empathy and Cultural Sustainability," Rory Turner calls for radical empathy in which people sustain culture "from underneath" with the understanding that sustainability must be mutual. Cultural sustainability is, as he puts it, "an intersection of well beings: of well beings for the sustaining biosphere, human systems, and coexisting individuals." Chapter 4, Aaron S. Allen's "Sounding Sustainable," engages Titon's work directly and challenges his focus on human-cultural sustainability while addressing environmental issues only by analogy. The Enlightenment idea of a nature/culture dichotomy still dogs us, Allen notes, and privileging human culture over nature (from whence our human metaphor for "culture" comes in the first place) endangers the sustainability of all cultures, human and otherwise.

Part 2, "Responding to Anthropogenic Change," addresses the issues presented in part 1 with five case studies interpreting widely divergent ways that humans are grappling with ecological and environmental challenges by engaging in expressive culture. In chapter 5, "Garbage Truck Music and Sustainability in Contemporary Taiwan," Nancy Guy takes us to that densely populated tropical island to show us how music is integral to successful strategies for dealing with waste, literally orchestrating daily choreographies of waste management, on the one hand, while the melodies linked to garbage collection are resounded in popular music, on the other. Taiwan's successful waste management, including some of the highest recycling rates in the world, was initiated by grassroots protests and citizen activism. Musical practices associated with a "garbage consciousness" are part of the efficacy of Taiwan's waste-reduction policies and practices. Transporting us to a very different ecosystem, Jennifer C. Post asks us in chapter 6, "Climate Change, Mobile Pastoralism, and Cultural Heritage in Western Mongolia," to learn from seminomadic herders some of the ways they have managed to live, dance, and make music sustainably in their biologically diverse environments—environments now threatened by climate change. She shows how these historically resilient societies—whose responses to ecological, economic, and political changes can be measured in their musicking, material arts, and ceremonial gatherings—are increasingly vulnerable.

Mark F. DeWitt, Susan Hurley-Glowa, and Denise Von Glahn respectively illustrate how ecological and cultural balance was long ago compromised if not lost in three distinct American locations: the humid wetlands of Louisiana; America's coldest city, Fairbanks, Alaska; and key inland waterways of America's East and West. DeWitt and Hurley-Glowa both consider musical responses to economic and environmental disasters resulting from humans' thirst for oil. In particular, DeWitt in chapter 7, "Singing for *la Mêche Perdue*," shows that in South Louisiana, where the economy is dominated by oil production, human cultural sustainability does not always coexist with environmental sustainability. In chapter 8, "Alaska Native Ways of Knowing and the Sustenance of Musical Communities in an Ailing Petrostate," Hurley-Glowa presents contrasting case studies of two very different musical communities that share the same space: a university concert hall in Fairbanks, Alaska. Drawing from Titon's writings on resilience, she documents how Alaska Native musical practices have adapted to changing social, economic, and environmental contexts, while the Fairbanks Symphony Orchestra may prove to be unsustainable as oil revenues decline in the state. Water, not oil, is the natural resource for which humans were willing to deface the landscape in chapter 9, Von Glahn's "*The New River* Updated." Here Von Glahn links Charles Ives's 1921 song, "The New River," and what she calls his involvement in proto-environmentalist initiatives, with earlier American transcendentalism (also influential in Titon's work). Ives realized a century ago that human artistic endeavors were best understood as interrelated with social, economic, and environmental concerns and that balance must be achieved.

Mimicking the ways that ecologists (sometimes reluctantly) show that any given sustainable system needs to take into account human involvement, part 3, "Musics, Sustainability, and Media," illustrates why we must better understand the role of media in sustainable cultural practices. The case studies in this section note that various forms of media from audio recording, film, photograph (Dornfield, Rankin, and Tucker), and the internet (Hutchinson) to the popular recording industry itself (Cavicchi) can be tools for sustainability. As all five chapters explain, media's role in cultural sustainability is not confined to documentation—though documentation has been shown time and again to be essential—but new media also generate new ways of being culturally expressive in the first place.

Daniel Cavicchi's "Fandom's Remix," chapter 10, picks up Ian Scoones's argument that sustainability is doing "boundary work" connecting diverse groups (Scoones 2007) but asserts that environmentalists and sustainability studies rarely touch popular culture (exceptions in music studies include Ingram 2010; Pedelty 2011, 2016; and Cooley, DeWitt, Dornfeld, and Guy in this volume). He then goes on to argue that while fan culture is more about creating community than celebrating capitalist consumption, it can also create "a wider ecology of listeners," which can be a case of music sustaining people. Barry Dornfeld asks how the scholarship of music has been aided by media and mediated representations of music culture in chapter 11, "Music, Media, and Mediation." He concludes that media allow us to interact with musical practices in new and rich ways and in many cases sustain the life of musical moments and experiences. In chapter 12, "Photography, Memory, and the Frail Instant," documentary photographer Tom Rankin, who worked with Barry Dornfeld and Jeff Titon on the film *Powerhouse for God*, asks how photography can be an act of reflection. This in turn sustains community identities as well as personal community-based memory. In "'Tis the Company," Chapter 13, Patrick Hutchinson notes that the social virtues of neighborliness, connectedness, participation, and humility are at the core of the Irish piping tradition in which he participates. He then asks how one sustains this tradition in the digital age, when a surprising amount of music sharing is "stuffed down a wire." Hutchinson concludes that the Internet expands sociability, and that to survive, traditions must change—a notion consistent with Titon's writings on resilience and Allen's "sustainability-change" model (this volume). The final chapter of the section, Joshua Tucker's "Sustaining Indigenous Sounds," brings together media, advocacy, activism, and indigenous cultural survival. The story he tells involves homemade and field recordings replayed at crucial moments, and an all Quechua-language radio station that—over time and through deliberate interventions—supported the very idea of indigeneity in Peru. The very concept of indigeneity there is bundled with language and musical expressions to sustain identities that government policies had sought to minimize or even eliminate.

Part 4, "Voice, Language, Trauma, and Resilience," builds on key themes in Tucker's chapter, especially that very human obsession with voice and language, and the ways in which they are tied to notions of place. How do we sing, chant, and speak our world into existence? Does our use of voice and language—seemingly central to human self-realization and cultural survival—help or hinder cross-species and hence ecological sustainability? What do the ways that we sing, chant, speak, and structure language reveal about how we engage ecosystems? Can we use language to help us engage more sustainably the land, sea, other living organisms, and traditions that, in turn, sustain us?

Rabbi and ethnomusicologist Jeffrey A. Summit starts the conversation in chapter 15, "Digital Technology, Chanting Torah, and the Sustainability of Tradition." Reminding us that musicking is about more than sound, Summit shows how sustaining musical practices (in this case, the profoundly contextual practice of chanting Torah at one's bat or bar mitzvah) with new technologies is enabling resilience in Jewish expression and identity at a time when institutional structures of Jewish cultural life may be waning. Summit interprets this phenomenon as an expression of Titon's idea that "resilience recognizes that perturbation, disturbance, and flux are constant characteristics of any complex system" (2015b, 193). Folklorist Burt Feintuch asks how music might be integral to a good life and emblematic of a kind of wholeness in local cultures in chapter 16, "Cultural Integrity and Local Music in Cape Breton and New Orleans." He develops a concept that he calls "cultural integrity" and relates it to how some environmental and ecological scholars use the concept of integrity. Rupturing that integrity becomes the question in chapter 17, Michelle Kisliuk's "BaAka Singing in a State of Emergency." Interweaving deeply personal stories with global crises, she asks how understandings that bridge the sciences, the humanities, and the arts might lead to action that preserves individual, family, nation, and planet. Drawing from decades of sharing with BaAka people living in Central Africa, she notes that they have developed sustainable practices, knowing how to sing and live with the forest and with one another. How might what BaAka know be shared to save the planet? Pioneering Russian musicologist and cognitive ethnomusicologist Margarita Mazo asks what laments for the dead can do to help us sustain life. In chapter 18, "Lament and Affective Cardiac Responses," she brings together earlier ethnographic studies of Russian lament and new empirical research measuring the affective heart-rate response to lament to ask how lament sustains people in times of grief. Moving through a few human lifecycle events from bar and bat mitzvahs to death and laments, the chapters in part 4 also take us to moments of human and environmental crisis as well as those of joy to remind us that everything is cyclical and we would do well to live gently.

Part 5, "Applying Sustainable Practices," joins Titon's highly influential work establishing and promoting applied ethnomusicology and speaks directly to the themes of advocacy and activism. Engaging medical ethnomusicology—another emerging field that bridges the humanities and science—Dotan Nitzberg and Michael B. Bakan take up Titon's challenge to consider cultural resilience before sustainability since a resilience model "offers a strategy, a means toward the goal of sustainability" (Titon 2015b, 158). In chapter 19, "Resilience and Adaptive Management in Piano Pedagogy for Individuals with Autism Spectrum Conditions," Bakan works with coauthor Nitzberg, an Israeli concert pianist diagnosed in childhood with Asperger's syndrome, to ask how people with this and other autism spectrum conditions achieve resilience through creative strategies of adaptive management. In chapter 20, "The Fiesta de la Bulería of Jerez de la Frontera," Roshan Samtani, argues that song, music, and dance are often central in the active processes of creating traditions and identities necessary for oppressed communities to engage their larger society in an essentially ecological process of survival. In Chapter 21, "Fiddle-icious," ethnomusicologist Thomas Faux explores how a Maine tradition-bearer exemplifies the American community music school movement's role in cultural and community sustainability. He concludes that face-to-face relationships are a more effective means of sustaining culture than many well-meant bureaucratic efforts. Also working in Maine, historian, folklorist, and anthropologist Pauleena M. MacDougall asks how doing research—especially fieldwork among the practitioners of intangible cultural heritage—can be a vital component of cultural sustainability. In chapter 22, "Discovering Maine's Intangible Cultural Heritage," she argues that cultural life in Maine is intimately connected to the ecosystem. Referencing recent events among representatives of some of the same Native American peoples in Maine that MacDougall works with, as well as other indigenous communities, Timothy J. Cooley suggests in chapter 23, "Song, Surfing, and Postcolonial Sustainability," that colonialism exploits both environmental resources and indigenous peoples together with their cultural practices. Decolonization needs to restructure and heal cross-cultural human interactions as well as human beings' engagement with their shared global environment. He concludes with a hopeful case study of the Hawaiian Polynesian Voyaging Society, which actively links indigenous cultural practices with environmental science to promote the healing of ecosystems worldwide.

* * *

The question of sustainability has driven work in many humanities disciplines since the modern industrial era and the institutionalization of universities. Folklore, comparative musicology, ethnomusicology, and anthropology have all been deeply engaged in activities that we might reinterpret today as addressing cultural sustainability (Grant 2013). Now that the term *sustainability* is on the lips of politicians and industrial leaders for other reasons, we feel it is all the more important that scholars and community activists reassert the significance of cultural sustainability. Scientists, environmentalists, artists, musicians, politicians and policy makers, land developers, and more need to hear what humanists concerned with sustainability have to say—and often more importantly, what our interlocutors engaged around the world during ethnographic fieldwork have to say. People need to hear and listen to one another; people need to hear and listen to their environments. Scholars in the humanities are well trained to facilitate this sort of hearing and listening. In *Cultural Sustainabilities*, we focus on human expressive practices and give careful attention to how social, economic, and environmental changes impact the sustainability of those cultural practices. We also call on all humanists to critique the impact of human cultural practices on our shared biosphere. Our hope is that readers will be encouraged and empowered to add their voices to the call for ecologically engaged sustainability.

References

Allen, Aaron S., and Kevin Dawe, eds. 2016a. *Current Directions in Ecomusicology: Music, Culture, Nature.* New York: Routledge.
———. 2016b. "Ecomusicologies." In Allen and Dawe 2016a, 1–15.

Boyle, W. Alice, and Ellen Waterman. 2016. "The Ecology of Musical Performance: Towards a Robust Methodology." In Allen and Dawe 2016a, 25–391.

DeWitt, Mark F. 2009. "Louisiana Creole *Bals de Maison* in California and the Accumulation of Social Capitol." *the world of music* 51 (1): 17–34.

Dornfeld, Barry, Tom Rankin, and Jeff Todd Titon, producers. 1989. *Powerhouse for God*. Documentary film, 58 min. Distributed by Documentary Educational Resources, Watertown, MA. Also streaming on www.folkstreams.net.

Feld, Steven. 1990. *Sound and Sentiment*. 2nd ed. Philadelphia: University of Pennsylvania Press.

———. 2015. "Acoustemology. In *Keywords in Sound*, edited by David Novak and Matt Sakakeeny, 12–21. Durham, NC: Duke University Press.

Grant, Catherine. 2013. "Music Sustainability." Oxford Bibliographies. http://www.oxfordbibliographies.com.

———. 2014. *Music Endangerment: How Language Maintenance Can Help*. New York: Oxford University Press.

Guy, Nancy. 2009. "Flowing down Taiwan's Tamsui River: Towards an Ecomusicology of the Environmental Imagination." *Ethnomusicology* 52 (2): 218–48.

Faux, Tom. 2009. "Don Roy, Fiddle Music, and Social Sustenance in Franco New England." *the world of music* 51 (1): 35–54.

Heise, Ursula K. 2017. "Introduction: Planet, Species, Justice—and the Stories We Tell about Them." In Heise, Christensen, and Neimann 2017, 1–10.

Heise, Ursula K., Jon Christensen, and Michelle Neimann, eds. 2017. *The Routledge Companion to the Environmental Humanities*. London: Routledge.

Hellier-Tinoco, Ruth. 2003. "Experiencing People: Relationships, Responsibility and Reciprocity." *British Journal of Ethnomusicology* 12 (1): 19–34.

Ingram, David. 2010. *The Jukebox in the Garden: Ecocriticism and American Popular Music since 1960*. Amsterdam: Rodopi.

Pedelty, Mark. 2012. *Ecomusicology: Rock, Folk, and the Environment*. Philadelphia: Temple University Press.

———. 2016. *A Song to Save the Salish Sea: Musical Performance as Environmental Activism*. Bloomington: Indiana University Press.

Pellow, David N. 2018. *What Is Critical Environmental Justice?* Cambridge: Polity Press.

Perlman, Marc. 2012. "Ecology and Ethno/musicology: The Metaphorical, the Representational, and the Literal." *Ecomusicology Newsletter* 1 (2): 1, 15–21.

Pettan, Svanibor, and Jeff Todd Titon, eds. 2015. *The Oxford Handbook of Applied Ethnomusicology*. New York: Oxford University Press.

Schafer, R. Murray. 1980. *The Tuning of the World: Toward a Theory of Soundscape Design*. Philadelphia: University of Pennsylvania Press.

Schippers, Huib, and Catherine Grant, eds. 2016. *Sustainable Futures for Music Cultures: An Ecological Perspective*. New York: Oxford University Press.

Scoones, Ian. 2007. "Sustainability." *Development in Practice* 17 (4–5): 589–96.

Titon, Jeff Todd. 1971. *Lazy Bill Lucas*. Wild 12MO1, 12" LP. Producer and recordist.

———. 1991. Clyde Davenport. Ver. 0.1 thru 0.18. Interactive HyperCard multimedia stack portraying an old-time fiddler and his music. Providence, RI: Self-published. A

simplified version is available online at http://www.stg.brown.edu/projects/davenport/
CLYDE_DAVENPORT.html.

———. 1992. *Clyde Davenport: Puncheon Camps*. 1990 recordings of traditional Appalachian fiddle and banjo music by 1992 N.E.A. National Heritage Award winner.
Recording, editing, mastering, and notes by Jeff Titon. Appalachian Center, Berea
College, cassette recording. Chosen by the American Folklife Center, Library of Congress, for its Selected List of Outstanding Roots Music Recordings.

———. 2003. *Songs of the Old Regular Baptists: Lined-Out Hymnody from Southeastern
Kentucky*, Vol. 2. Smithsonian Institution SF 50001, compact disc. Producer, recordist,
and coauthor of accompanying brochure notes.

———, ed. 2009. "Music and Sustainability." Thematic issue of *the world of music* 51 (1).

———. 2015a. "Thoreau's Ear." *Sound Studies* 1 (1): 144–54.

———. 2015b. "Sustainability, Resilience, and Adaptive Management for Applied Ethnomusicology." In Pettan and Titon 2015, 157–95.

Von Glahn, Denise. 2013. *Music and the Skillful Listener: American Women Compose the
Natural World*. Bloomington: Indiana University Press.

PART 1

Thinking, Writing, and Musicking about Sustainability

CHAPTER 1

Sustainability Clashes
and Concordances

ROBERT BARON AND THOMAS WALKER

CULTURAL SUSTAINABILITY came into being as a field shaped by discourses, practices, and theory from environmental sustainability. Both fields are fueled by moral imperatives and troubled by uncertainties about the future defying predictability. And they also share a lexicon. Cultural sustainability freely borrows metaphors and strategies long employed in movements to protect, restore, and renew the natural world. Metaphors currently and potentially drawn from environmental domains include terms such as *adaptation, intervention, stewardship, conservation, cooperation, competition, ecosystem, ecology, interdependence,* and *resilience.* Metaphors of vulnerability and destabilization employing terms such as *endangerment, catastrophe, invasive, exotic, extinction, perturbance, disturbance, flux,* and *collapse* are also actual or potential elements in the cultural sustainability lexicon. This chapter examines key assumptions of this shared lexicon, employed as rhetorical strategy, across different contexts of use and meaning. We suggest that new knowledge, understanding, and voice are achieved by viewing one field through the lens of another—through what Kenneth Burke aptly calls "perspective by incongruity" (1954, 69).

Thinking about sustainability through metaphor, we attempt to illuminate concordances and symbioses between cultural and environmental sustainability while recognizing differences. Metaphor opens up pathways for understanding both the inchoateness and the tangibility of sustainability. Sustainability is an inchoate subject. It is indeterminate and nonlinear because it cannot really be known what we can sustain (Benson 2015, 112–13). It is a large, looming problem, both tangible and intangible, what Timothy Morton would call a "hyperobject" (2013). Metaphor is a mode of embodied reasoning that enables interpretations of new and unfamiliar ideas by predicating a sign or image from another domain—the primary subject—onto an inchoate object or secondary subject (Fernandez 1974, 120). The primary and secondary subjects of metaphors are both alike and unlike since some but not all meanings or qualities are intended to transfer between semantic domains. As a term from the primary subject is appropriated and redeployed from the primary to the secondary subject, it is reinterpreted in multiple, unpredictable, and contextually sensitive ways. Both terms interact and animate each other through what philosophers call a "semantic twist," with each term viewed in a fresh light (Hills 2012).

We contend that metaphor shapes sustainability in highly tangible ways even as it embodies contradictions, paradoxes, incongruities, and the inchoate. Tracking the appositeness, referents, and applications of sustainability metaphors in this chapter, we begin by discussing binary oppositions of nature and culture that are now increasingly open to question. We then turn to tangible manifestations of sustainability as social action. Human interventions in the environment and culture as heritage are viewed as engaging comparable challenges of endangerment, adaptive management, and the fostering of resilience. Conflicts between environmentalists advocating for endangered species and an indigenous people's cultural rights to hunt dramatize on-the-ground clashes of sustainabilities. Our chapter concludes by exploring strategies and policies for creating sustainable ecologies of cultural heritage. These strategies and policies are both informed by and divergent from those of environmentalists. Throughout our chapter, metaphor is viewed as unavoidable for sustainability thought and engagement.

More than mere rhetorical ornament, metaphor engages epistemological dimensions that critically and subtly affect how we perceive and act in the world. Metaphor can structure our very conceptualizations of culture and environment. Rooted in worldviews, they guide our beliefs and behaviors as well as create discourses and paradigms that establish our scholarly traditions. Cognitive scientists George Lakoff and Mark Johnson (1980) argue that "words alone do not change reality. But changes in our conceptual system do change what is real for us and affect how we perceive the world and act upon those perceptions" (quoted in Princen 2010, 60). Examining key metaphors around sustainability enables us to imagine different possibilities for change and challenge obstacles through a new narrative of resilience (Benson 2015) as a governing framework for adaptive management and intervention.

This volume abounds with examples of adaptive management of cultural resources by vulnerable communities designed to foster resilience in the face of environmental and social change. Alaska Natives draw on adaptive strategies developed over centuries of conserving natural resources and flexibly responding to change. Susan Hurley-Glowa indicates that the Festival of Native Arts and social media contribute to the revitalization of songs and dances nearly lost through disruption of Alaska Native cultures. In Western Mongolia cultural resource sustainability responds to threats to natural resources with textile traditions, musical instruments, foodways, and traditional knowledge of wildlife and animal husbandry resiliently maintained, as Jennifer Post indicates, "during times of social and political adaptation and change" (see also Cooley, Faux, and Tucker, this volume). Resilience of cultural resources is also fostered by applied ethnomusicologists, folklorists, applied anthropologists, and linguists acting in mutual engagement with communities whose traditions are vulnerable and no longer widely practiced (MacDougall, Titon, and Turner, this volume).

Nature/Culture Binaries

Cultural and environmental sustainability are driven by urgency (Allen, Kisliuk, this volume). Intervention from both within and outside vulnerable communities is intended to mitigate and foster adaptation to unstable environments. However, while cultural sustainability is viewed as a moral and social imperative akin to protecting and sustaining the biosphere, equivalences between nature and culture are slippery. Nature/culture binaries can be seen as both self-evident and increasingly open to question. Cultural sustainability scholars tend, however, to focus on equivalences while eliding disjunctions. It is important to note the limitations of analogizing environmental and cultural sustainability, as Daniel Cavicchi acknowledges in this volume in stating that resource and capacity limits are not applicable when viewing fandom as culturally sustainable.

Humans are part of nature, and both culture and nature are cultural constructs—as is the notion of sustainability.[1] An environmental perspective has long held ideologies of nature in metaphors of Mother Nature (Gaia) and Spaceship Earth. But centuries of Western political philosophy entrenched a fundamental distinction between culture and nature as the bedrock of the social world. This distinction is increasingly problematized from a variety of points of view. Stefan Helmreich "presses the nature–culture binary to do a good deal of critical work" in a provocative article on nature, culture, and seawater. He argues that seawater should be considered as both the abstraction or theory and a material reality in the world. "Water," he observes, "oscillates between natural and cultural substance, its putative materiality masking the fact that its fluidity is a rhetorical effect of how we think about 'nature' and 'culture' in the first place" (2011, 132).

The nature/culture dichotomy is also called into question in the current "ontological turn" in anthropology (see Descola 2014). In the new ontology nature is reinvested with agency and culture is seen as constitutive of symbolic and material multispecies networks and interactions. Recent work by Anna Tsing (2015) on the sociology of mushrooms and Eduardo Kohn's *How Forests Think* (2013), among others (Hufford, this volume), have reopened this frontier. New technologies have also eroded long-held divides between what is viewed as "natural" and "cultural." Reproductive technologies, as Marilyn Strathern contends, have altered received models of nature and culture while transforming human kinship and descent (Strathern 1992). The green revolution, genetic modification of plants and animals, and advancements in cloning all problematize received distinctions between nature and culture.

Some argue that we have pervasively shaped our environments to the point where "a natural realm outside the impact of human agency no longer seems to exist" (Heise 2010, 50). This putative "end of nature" in the epoch we have come to call the Anthropocene is itself a rich metaphor of species extinction, endangerment, and loss eulogized in narrative genres of elegy or tragedy. These ecological narratives are concomitant with narratives of cultural modernization, and they often overlap where the "endangerment of culturally significant species" expresses conflict or criticism of modernity (2010, 60). Stories and images of "charismatic megafauna" and indicator species like polar bears, whales, wolves, and spotted owls are metonyms for the endangerment modernity poses to their survival. Catastrophic events like tsunamis and hurricanes are subject to overestimation to dramatize what is at stake in climate change. A similar logic is at play in our overvaluation of aesthetically arresting traditions prioritized for safeguarding and public presentation. A compelling blues song, a virtuosically performed southern Appalachian fiddle tune, or an exquisite Pueblo pot are far more likely to be presented at a folk festival than a proverb, traditional landscaping, or a family musical tradition of limited apparent aesthetic merit. Cultural conservation or safeguarding efforts have likewise been skewed toward the most visible, spectacular, publicly presentable, and aesthetically noteworthy traditions.[2]

In effect, the nature/culture binary is both productive and provocative—good to think with. We argue that metaphoric thinking in its yoking of culture and nature, of humanities and science perspectives, has been similarly productive in thinking about cultural and environmental sustainability, as several chapters in this volume attest (see Allen, Hufford, Turner, and DeWitt, this volume).

Intervention and Resilience

As social action, environmental and cultural sustainability are often in accord but may also conflict with defensible justifications. Intervention is one mode of social action explored in this chapter to illuminate the precarious states and futures of cultural and ecological diversity in need of protection and restoration.

Jeff Todd Titon opened up a new paradigm for ethnomusicology and folklore by employing environmental sustainability as metaphor and model. Turning from conservation and preservation as root metaphors, he speaks of how ecologists and environmentalists rejected these terms in favor of sustainability, resilience, and adaptive management. Confronting issues of how to appropriately intervene in the face of environmental change, they crafted strategies suggestive for sustaining cultural traditions. Titon sees stewardship, resilience, adaptive management, and sustainability as apposite for the protection and revitalization of both nature and culture (Titon 2015). He also views destabilizing forces of "perturbance, disturbance, and flux" as inherent in culture as well as nature (2015, 193). For both nature and culture, human social agency is indispensable, although approaches and strategies differ. Titon's groundbreaking scholarship on cultural sustainability invites further thought—and action—around intervention for keeping traditions alive and dynamic in their communities. It also inspires us to consider other metaphors, applicable to the nascent field of cultural sustainability, drawn from the study and protection of the biosphere.

Folklore—as cultural expression—is emergent by nature, created at the moment of performance. Paradoxically, since it is continuously emergent, folklore has been seen as endangered and in risk of extinction unless recorded or transmitted. While *endangerment* and *extinction* are foundational terms for environmentalists that spur calls to action, speaking of dying traditions touches a third rail of folkloristics for contemporary folklorists impelled to emphasize the dynamics of traditions. In the past, endangerment was viewed as part and parcel of the ontological status of oral traditions. As Roger Abrahams notes, the "eleventh hour tale" recognized by early British folklore collectors who intervened to save traditions by recording tales in writing "matured with the help of modern technological devices." He states that "when texts are recorded from a traditional singer, mortality itself becomes the enemy of tradition; songs and stories in performance only live in their performance, and are therefore always subject to near-death as the informants themselves die, but for the folklorist, recording their dying breath" (Abrahams 1993, 12). The intervention of the folklorist as documentarian was seen as a response to collapse and impending catastrophe, terms that have parallels in the destruction of habitats requiring urgent response by environmentalists.

In the late twentieth century, cultural intervention by American folklorists broadened from archival preservation of individual texts to multiple strategies designed to enable traditions to continue within their communities of practice. Eschewing metaphors of endangerment and extinction, they turned their attention to approaches that include fostering intergenerational transmission, valorizing traditions through public performance within both communities of origin and broader publics, and honoring exemplary tradition bearers through heritage awards. Traditions recorded within local and regional surveys are used as a foundation for public programs highlighting particular traditions. Turning from the prior approach of applied folklore entailing folklorists acting unidirectionally on behalf of communities, public folklore, first conceived in the 1980s, stresses collaboration through dialogic engagement designed to enable communities to interpret, present, and sustain traditions on their own terms (Baron 2010, 2016). A national infrastructure of local, state, and national government and nonprofit programs was also constructed in the late twentieth century. These programs are devoted to sustaining living traditions, avoiding reference to endangerment. *Folklore death* is a term never uttered by folklorists, in contrast to *species extinction*—a term embraced by environmentalists. The rhetoric of living traditions was shaped by, and is consonant with, the shift in the academic folklore discipline from centering on text to defining folklore as situated social interaction (Baron 2016). While the discipline of folklore studies long ago abandoned antiquarianism and shifted from concentration on texts to a more phenomenological approach, it suffers from a distorted public and academic image as a retrograde field. Speaking of endangerment, extinction, and dying traditions is viewed as perpetuating these stereotypes.

Public folklore policy and practice are centered on fostering sustainability, which Titon, with reference to music cultures, sees as the "capacity to maintain and develop its music now and in the foreseeable future" (2015, 157). While public folklore emphasizes maintaining the vitality of traditions, a sustainability focus necessarily entails recognition of endangerment. Titon rejects reticence about endangerment. He points out that while music writ large is a renewable resource, "just as language itself is not endangered whereas individual languages have gone extinct and others are going extinct, certain music—that is, music cultures—and genres and instruments are endangered" (169).

At the instance of its performance, folklore, emergent by nature, is dying even as it is newly enacted. It depends on further performance, transmission, and community support structures to continue as living tradition. A song, narrative, or entire tradition can become extinct if the chains of transmission are broken. Just as a language is lost when the last speaker dies, so may a tradition be lost when its last practitioner dies without heirs.

A key sustainability challenge for folklore lies in enabling transmission and community sustenance while acknowledging endangerment and the possibility of extinction of a tradition. Continuing performance is effected through interventions of revitalization, regeneration, and revival, from both within and outside the community of practice.

Anticipating the concept of cultural sustainability by over three decades, Alan Lomax, in his "An Appeal for Cultural Equity," warned that "in our concern about the pollution of the biosphere we are overlooking what may be, in human terms, an even more serious problem" ([1972] 2003, 285). The burgeoning environmentalism movement of the 1970s provided language for Lomax's proto-cultural sustainability brief. It was published in the same year as the "sudden, noisy awakening" of the environmental movement that had "just been rediscovered by people who live in it" on Earth Day in 1972 (Commoner 1971, 1). Uniquely among folklorists prior to Titon, Lomax was unabashed in speaking about the specter of extinction. Comparing the urgent need to stem the loss of diversity among cultural systems with the loss of natural species diversity, he contended that "today . . . cultural variety lies under threat of extinction" ([1972] 2003, 285). In this influential essay, which reads like a manifesto, Lomax provides examples of success stories that counter a view of "expressive systems as doomed" through intervention to strengthen cultural support systems to bring traditions "back to life," including

> the magnificent recrudescence of the many-faceted carnival in Trinidad as a result of the work of a devoted committee of folklorists backed by the Premier; the renaissance of Rumanian panpipe music when the new Socialist regime gave the last master of the panpipe a chair in music at the Rumanian Academy of Music; the revival of the five-string banjo in my own country when a talented young man named Peter Seeger took up its popularization as his life's work; the pub singing movement of England which involved a generation of young people in traditional ballad singing; the recognition of Cajun and Creole music which has led to the renewal of Cajun language and culture in Louisiana. These and a host of other cases that might be mentioned show that even in this industrial age, folk traditions can come vigorously back to life, can raise community morale, and give birth to new forms if they have time and room to grow in their own communities. (Lomax [1972] 2003, 298)

As Lomax suggests, the resurgence, renewal, and regeneration of traditions come about both within communities of practitioners and through interventions by cultural specialists. They reawaken dormant traditions maintained in memory culture but not actively performed. Kenneth S. Goldstein, writing during the same period as Lomax, elaborated on Carl Wilhelm von Sydow's classic distinction between active and passive bearers of tradition. Goldstein thought that social and aesthetic conditions contributed to dormancy or temporary disappearance and sudden reappearance of traditional expressions (1972). Observation of the adaptability of folklore to contextual and formal change testifies to resilience that counters endangerment.

Similarly, in the field of ecology, the capacity for traditional ecological knowledge (TEK) to adapt to "external changes and internal frictions" has long been a defining feature of ecological system dynamics. Like ethnomusicologists and folklorists who recognize the resilience of community members in safeguarding traditions, a growing body of ethnographic research is providing empirical evidence of the resilience of TEK. Ecologists are shifting their attention away from concern about knowledge loss, disappearance, and recovery (due to various forces of modernity and neoliberalism) to focus more on adaptive responses emphasizing socioecological systems of knowledge distribution, generation, and application to new conditions (Gómez-Baggethun and Reyes-Garcia 2013). In this view, discrete or particular items of traditional knowledge—including expressive culture—and their loss are less worrisome or important than the socioecological or cultural capacities for regeneration of knowledge.

Narratives of endangerment crises, extinction tragedies, and recovery triumphs in environmentalism generally focus on individual *species*. A systemic approach to the adaptation of ecological *systems* is typically elided. The pervasive metaphors involving endangerment and loss of a species in the biosphere reveals parallel features to endangerment, loss, and the urgency of eleventh-hour intervention to sustain cultural traditions. The 1973 Endangered Species Act (ESA), similar to folklore's privileging of genre and item, focuses on the parts at the expense of the whole, missing a "more complex assessment of the resiliency of social-ecological systems" (Benson 2012, 336). ESA deals with the persistence and viability of individual species rather than the dynamics and role of biodiversity in an ecological system. As a legal structure and tool, it relies on the rule of law and litigation to compel compliance. The law acknowledges the importance of the ecosystems on which the endangered species depend and provides for the development of recovery plans, species or habitat restoration, and the avoidance of lawsuits. However, the implicit management model is one of brinksmanship and conservation reliance, which favors interventionist strategies of preservation and restoration over adaptation and prevention or resilience.

An Endangered Species: Sustainabilities in Conflict

Single-minded attention to the individual species springs from the same logic that created scientific forestry and the problem of monoculture in compromising ecosystem resilience. Scientific forestry in eighteenth-century Prussia traded sustainable silviculture yield for the creation of monocultures, engendering the loss of biodiversity as we understand it today. Moreover, according to James C. Scott, "the monocropped forest was a disaster for peasants who were now deprived of all grazing, food, raw materials, and medicines that the earlier forest ecology had afforded" (1998, 19). While Scott refers here to the disappearance of the human institution of the commons—also referred to as "common pool resources"—by their incorporation into state or private property, endangered species and protective enforcement measures by the state exercise no less power over people.

The controversy over the northern spotted owl in the Pacific Northwest is familiar from our own era. During the 1990s the controversy pitted the timber industry against environmentalists, casting timber workers in a pitched drama as the enemy of the spotted owl. The issue was reduced to one of jobs versus owls, eliding what Archie Green observed about the deployment of community imagery by "loggers [who] assert[ed] their need to preserve sawmill towns, while naturalists [saw] old-growth forests as living organisms" (1994, 248). Green suggested that an earlier generation of lumbermen "saw no contradiction between action to improve living standards and commitment to 'reforestation'" (248). From the environmentalist perspective, however, "the owl," according to Benson, "served as a proxy for the forest itself and larger and more complex issues concerning the scale and pace of timber harvest and resource consumption" (2012, 339).

If the public failed to appreciate the occupational culture and traditions of "timberbeasts" (loggers), the decades-long international conflict over whale hunting reached a crescendo in the culture/nature dichotomy with the case of the Makah tribe and its tradition of gray whale hunting that originated over 1,500 years ago. Open conflicts between environmentalists and native notions of cultural sustainability erupted. The whale had been integral to the Makahs' folklife, social relations, and spiritual life, and its meat was a dietary staple until the diminished whale population during the 1920s, brought about in large part by industrial scale hunting, spurred them to suspend their tradition. Although an 1855 treaty granted the Makahs the right to hunt seals and whales and would have exempted them from a 1986 whale-hunting moratorium imposed by the International Whaling Commission, their petition in the 1990s to resume this practice drew worldwide critical attention. In this case, the gray whale became a proxy or metonym used by animal rights and other anti-whaling environmentalists for whom the extinction of the species was at stake. For the Makahs, the whale was a metonym for their cultural identity, and its place in their diet represented indigenous cultural survival. The gray whale was thus the pivot for competing and opposing critiques of modernity and survival.

Widely publicized protests occurred after the tribe was granted permission to resume whale hunts and killed a gray whale in 1999. With lines sharply drawn between pro-whaling tribespeople and anti-whaling animal rights groups and environmentalists, cultural and environmental representations from both sides employed "methods of acculturating nature as embodied in the gray whale" (Martello 2004). Tribal people claimed a connection to the whale based on centuries of living with, hunting, and consuming these animals. The Makah Manifesto asserted, "We Makahs know the whales, probably better than most people. We are out on the waters of the ocean constantly and we have lived with and among whales for more than 2,000 years. We are not cruel people. But we have an understanding of the relationship between people and the mammals of the sea and land" (Johnson 1998). Tribal leaders asserted a right to revive their culture, decimated by assimilationist government policy. This assertion corresponds to the contention of indigenous peoples globally that cultural rights are a human right encompassing collective and group rights in addition to individual rights (Weintraub 2009, 3, 6).[3]

The Makahs had suffered from the scarcity and subsequent endangerment of whales due to industrial-scale whaling for which they bore no culpability. Animal rights activists contested the Makah contention of cultural rights in asserting moral claims in a naturalizing discourse based on human-whale kinship and similarities in the biology and social characteristics of whales and humans. One story characterized Makah hunters during the 1999 spectacle as a "gang of men armed with harpoons and high-powered rifles" ambushing "an unarmed young female whale" (Martello 2004, 272). The metaphor of sexual assault in this instance and widespread criticisms of the Makahs' use of modern technology such as motorized chase boats instead of canoes equipped with the traditional "cedar harpoons and muscle-shell barbs and points" (277) seem intended to degrade Makah culture, impugn the authenticity of cultural claims, and weaken the tribe's rights. To outsider activists, evidence of traditionality was conspicuously absent because it had been replaced with technology and images of modernity that disqualified the Makahs' claims to sustaining cultural heritage. Viewed through another lens, the Makah revival of whaling testified to their cultural resilience and resourcefulness, and to the adaptation of their traditional culture to technological change. The Makahs' indigenous cultural sustainability saw the whale as systemically connected to multiple domains of cultural life, as a kind of keystone species for culture and community.

Dramas surrounding the protection of a single species claim far more public attention than comprehensive, holistic approaches for sustaining an ecosystem through protected habitats, where, as in any habitat, interdependence and predation are both at play. Best practices for national parks, forests, and wildlife refuges focus on the establishment and continued adaptive maintenance of the totality of a habitat.

Ecologies of Cultural Heritage: Strategies and Policies

Folklore and cultural heritage policy and practice rarely focus on cultural analogues to habitat, the totality of the cultural ecosystem. The Cajun revival mentioned by Lomax is an exceptional example of a successful, concurrent revival of language, music, and other dimensions of traditional culture, although some have seen the teaching of standard French in school immersion programs as threatening to the Cajun French historically spoken in the region. More limited and compartmentalized approaches are much more common. Public funding for folklife emphasizes project support, funding for apprenticeships for individual artists, and the cultural brokerage efforts of public folklorists rather than strategically and holistically addressing the folk cultural needs of communities. While the documentation, presentation, and transmission of individual genres and specific traditions are frequently broadly contextualized, larger scale strategies involving sustaining a traditional culture as a whole are generally absent. Such strategies might also incorporate economic and community development.

Carrying out a whole culture strategy is a daunting challenge, beyond the resources of an individual folklorist or ethnomusicologist. In seeking to sustain particular traditions, efforts are targeted to particular, sustainable dimensions. Titon notes that "questions arise over what is to be sustained or restored in a music culture—repertoire, style, performance practice, function and context, feelings and experiences, careers and so forth—and how best to sustain what is to be sustained" (2015, 181).

The 2003 UNESCO Convention for the Safeguarding of the Intangible Cultural Heritage is a large-scale, global policy initiative, but in practice it is also specific rather than holistic in focus. ICH initiatives center on inventorying and recognizing particular cultural traditions, with an emerging interest in fostering transmission. Inventorying and formal recognition of traditions frequently engender economic development efforts like tourism that highlight spectacular, presentable and marketable traditions. Even though UNESCO shifted from creating the list of Masterpieces of the Oral and Intangible Heritage of Humanity to the Representative List of the Intangible Cultural Heritage of Humanity, the traditions selected remain skewed to the aesthetically exemplary, globally unique, and spectacular.

While analogies may be adduced between consciously protected natural habitats and cultural ecosystems, they are vastly different due to human cultural agency and complexities distinctive to cultural systems. Just contemplating the idea of national reserves for cultural traditions modeled on national forests or wildlife refuges evokes the horrific objectification of the human menageries of the Renaissance and the exhibition of live human beings in the world's fairs of the late nineteenth and early twentieth centuries. Proscribing the introduction of traditions of outsiders and limiting interactions generating new traditions suggests creation of a cultural prison. "Habitat" protection for cultural traditions requires bolstering support structures that enable and sustain traditional practices while refraining from limiting social intercourse. Indigenous groups that lack interaction with outsiders, such as those in Amazonia, may warrant a protected cultural ecosystem, but this must occur with the consent of the community.

Living traditions are shaped by exogenous forces and interaction with other cultures, which enliven and reinforce resilience. Emergent and creolized forms, which are increasingly widespread in the contemporary world, come about through cultural creativity and interactions among cultures (Baron and Cara 2011). Illusory notions of cultural purity are lamentably also on the rise, championed by resurgent nationalists advocating shutting borders to immigrants.

Conservation ecology has historically viewed invasive and exotic species as dangers to ecosystems, which require aggressive protection and management. Ecologists are now reexamining this approach, recognizing the inevitable flux of ecosystems due to new species entering over time. Brendon M. H. Larson (2010) and with his colleagues Rene van der Wal, Anke Fischer, and Sebastian Selge (2015) problematize the term *invasive*, viewing it as a militaristic metaphor whose application from cultural domains is inappropriate. While invasive ecologists argue with Larson's view, ecologists agree that natural systems exhibit resiliency in adapting to new species. Management responses to foster adaptation or resistance to new species suggest intriguing comparisons with the curation of culture by applied ethnomusicologists and public folklorists in the face of inevitable cultural change. "Invasive" and exotic species, once universally considered as dangers to be aggressively repelled, are now seen as not necessarily pernicious. They are viewed variously as dangers to ecosystems, justifications for aggressive management, and springboards to resilient responses by ecosystems.

While the flora and fauna of protected natural habitats are managed by human specialists, intervention in cultural ecosystems requires self-determination and control by their human inhabitants along with—when appropriate—assistance by cultural brokers. Titon underscores the distinctions between "'management' [as] an appropriate strategy for conservation biologists" and cultural management that faces pitfalls of top-down control, such as the type that has been practiced by some applied anthropologists and international development specialists (2015, 192). The collaboration of applied ethnomusicologists and public folklorists with communities requires consent, sharing of authority, and dialogical, mutual engagement (Baron 2016). As in a natural habitat, the sustainability of cultural ecosystems entails cooperation and interdependence as well as competition and reconciliation of different interests. Culturally homogenous societies are fading fast in the world, entailing challenges to achieving consensus about sustaining diverse cultures in complex, multicultural human societies. Now more than ever, human cultural identity is not confined to membership in a particular ethnic or national "species." People have multiple cultural identities, frequently identifying with more than one ethnic group or none at all, with other identities based on factors such as occupation, gender, sexuality, and religion.

Mother Nature is too often romanticized as a wise and benign antidote to cultural chaos, instability, and disruption (see Morton 2009). Academic disciplines have uncritically employed naturalistic metaphors, overlooking the play of semantic twists, the concurrence of congruent and divergent meanings characteristic of any term applied from one semantic domain to another.

Victor Turner warns against the

> dangers inherent in regarding the social world as "a world in becoming," if by invoking the idea "becoming" one is unconsciously influenced by the ancient metaphor of organic growth and decay. Becoming suggests genetic continuity, telic growth, cumulative growth, progress, etc. But many social events do not have this "directional" character. Here the metaphor may well select, empha- size, suppress, or organize features of social relations in accordance with *plant* or *animal* growth processes, and in so doing, mislead us about the nature of the *human* social world, *sui generis*. There is nothing wrong with metaphors, or *mutas mutandis,* with models, provided that one is aware of the perils behind their misuse. If one regards them, however, as a species of liminal monster . . . whose combination of familiar or unfamiliar features provokes us into thought, provides us with new perspectives, one can be excited by them; the implications, suggestions, and supporting values entwined with their literal use enable us to see a new subject matter in a new way. (Turner 1974, 30–31)[4]

So it is with cultural sustainability, inspired and metaphorically shaped by environmental sustainability and ecological science but involving a distinctive human social world. Nature and culture are inextricably intertwined—humans are biological entities who are part of nature, nature is a cultural construct of humans, human interventions transform nature, and nature adapts with resil- ience to human interventions. Metaphors currently and potentially employed for both cultural and environmental sustainability illuminate their concordances while pointing to divergences. Cultural sustainability is predicated on activism to counter forces that endanger treasured cultural traditions, as environmen- talism has mobilized to save a threatened planet. However, the conviction of environmentalists of a moral imperative to protect a species seen as endangered may clash with a culture's time-honored beliefs about hunting and ritual use of the same species.

Cultural ecosystems have clear parallels but distinctive contrasts with envi- ronmental ecosystems. Culture requires specific strategies to deal with endan- germent, foster resilience, and respond to inevitable exogenous influences in continuous interaction with cultures experiencing flux and change. Here the ethnomusicologist or folklorist steps in to act as a culture broker and collaborate with human communities who respond with social agency not found in other species. Human interventions decisively shape the planet, in ways both ameliora- tive and disastrous, but humans are also biological organisms subject to the forces of nature. They cannot be disentangled, and their metaphorical entanglement is richly suggestive for the sustainability of both domains, apart and together.

Notes

1. Titon notes that "ecological principals are derived from human constructions of the natural world to begin with" (2015, 178).

2. Anaïs Leblon, discussing the heritization of Fulbe pastoral traditions, states, citing Gaetano Ciarcia, that the "intangible . . . appears understandable only through the mediation of physical goods that render them more easily comprehensible (Ciarcia 2006, 5). Thus, it is difficult in the process of the institutional promotion of heritage to step some distance away from the spectacular and esthetic aspects of the heritage goods" (Leblon 2012, 104).

3. Advocacy for indigenous cultural rights as a human right heightened in the 1990s. The Permanent Forum on Indigenous Issues of the United Nations, established in 2000, was instrumental in developing the 2007 UN General Assembly's Declaration on the Rights of Indigenous Peoples. Andrew Weintraub states that the document included recognition of the rights of indigenous peoples "to maintain and strengthen cultural practices" (2009, 6).

4. Valdimar Hafstein critiques the use of biological metaphors to provide a scientific foundation for folkloristics in the nineteenth and early twentieth century. These metaphors employ terms such as "life, growth, evolution, death, extinction, natural laws, morphology, 'Märchenbiologie' and tradition ecology." He sees them as incompatible with, among other things, "performance as social agency" and a view of tradition as an "achievement rather than a natural fact" (Hafstein [2001] 2005, 407). A folkloristics informed by cultural sustainability could potentially reenvision some of these metaphors. For a critique of the teleological implications of sustainability, particularly in the metaphor of journey and progress, see Milne, Keirins, and Walton (2006).

References

Abrahams, Roger D. 1993. "Phantoms of Romantic Nationalism in Folkloristics." *Journal of American Folklore* 106 (419):3–37.

Baron, Robert. 2010. "Sins of Objectification? Agency, Mediation and Community Cultural Self- determination in Public Folklore and Cultural Tourism Programming." *Journal of American Folklore* 122 (487): 63–91.

———. 2016. "Public Folklore Dialogism and Critical Heritage Studies." *International Journal of Heritage Studies.* 22 (208):588–606.

Baron, Robert, and Ana C. Cara. 2011. "Introduction: Creolization as Cultural Creativity." In *Creolization as Cultural Creativity*, edited by Robert Baron and Ana C. Cara, 3–19. Jackson: University of Mississippi Press.

Benson, Melinda Harm. 2012. "Intelligent Tinkering: The Endangered Species Act and Resilience." *Ecology and Society* 17 (4): 336–43.

———. 2015. "Reconceptualizing Environmental Challenges—Is Resilience the New Narrative?" *Journal of Environmental and Sustainability Law* 21 (1): 99–126.

Burke, Kenneth. 1954. *Permanence and Change: An Anatomy of Purpose.* Berkeley: University of California Press.

Ciarcia, Gaetano. 2006. "La perte durable: Étude sur la notion de 'patrimoine imma-tériel.'" *Les carnets du Lahic*, no. 1. http://www.iiac.cnrs.fr/IMG/pdf/Ciarcia_perte _durable.pdf.

Commoner, Barry. 1971. *The Closing Circle: Nature, Man, and Technology*. New York: Alfred A. Knopf.

Descola, Philippe. 2014. "Modes of Being and Forms of Predication." *Hau: Journal of Ethnographic Theory* 4 (1): 271–80.

Fernandez, James W. 1974. "The Mission of Metaphor in Expressive Culture." *Current Anthropology* 15 (2): 119–45.

Goldstein, Kenneth S. 1972. "On the Application of the Concepts of Active and Inactive Traditions to the Study of Repertory." In *Toward New Perspectives in Folklore*, edited by Américo Paredes and Richard Bauman, 62–67. Austin: University of Texas Press.

Gómez-Baggethun, Erik, and Victoria Reyes-Garcia. 2013. "Reinterpreting Change in Traditional Ecological Knowledge." *Human Ecology: An Interdisciplinary Journal.* 41 (4): 1–9.

Green, Archie. 1994. "Afterword: Raven, Mallard, Spotted Owl—Totems for Coalition." In *Conserving Culture: A New Discourse on Heritage*, edited by Mary Hufford, 245–52. Urbana: University of Illinois Press.

Hafstein, Validmar Tr. (2001) 2005. "Biological Metaphors in Folklore Theory: An Es-say in the History of Ideas." In *Folklore: Critical Concepts in Literary and Cultural Studies*, vol. 4, *Folkloristics: Theory and Methods*, edited by Alan Dundes, 407–35. New York: Routledge.

Heise, Ursula K. 2010. "Lost Dogs, Last Birds, and Listed Species: Cultures of Extinction." *Configurations* 18 (1–2): 49–72.

Helmreich, Stefan. 2011. "Nature/Culture/Seawater." *American Anthropologist* 113 (1): 132–44.

Hills, David. 2012. "Metaphor. In *The Stanford Encyclopedia of Philosophy*, edited by Edward N. Zalta. http://plato.stanford.edu.

Johnson, Keith A. 1998. "The Makah Manifesto." *Seattle Times*, August 23. https://tinyurl .com/y9dxdfn.

Kohn, Eduardo. 2013. *How Forests Think: Toward an Anthropology beyond the Human*. Berkeley: University of California Press.

Lakoff, George, and Mark Johnson. 1980. *Metaphors We Live By*. Chicago: University of Chicago Press.

Larson, Brendon M. H. 2010. "Reweaving Humans and Invasive Species." *Études Rurales* 185: 25–38.

Leblon, Anaïs. 2012. "A Policy of Intangible Cultural Heritage between Local Constraints and International Standards: The Cultural Space of the *Yaaral* and the *Degal*." In *Heri-tage Regimes and the State*, edited by Regina Bendix, Aditya Eggert, and Arnika Pesel-mann, Göttingen Studies in Cultural Property 6, 97–117. Göttingen: Universitätsverlag Göttingen.

Lomax, Alan. (1972) 2003. "Appeal for Cultural Equity." In *Alan Lomax: Selected Writings 1934–1997*, edited by Ronald D. Cohen, 285–89. New York: Routledge.

Martello, Marybeth Long. 2004. "Negotiating Global Nature and Local Culture: The Case of Makah Whaling." In *Earthly Politics: Local and Global in Environmental Governance*, edited by Sheila Jasanoff and Marybeth Long Martello, 263–84. Cambridge, MA: MIT Press.

Milne, Markus J., Kate Keirins, and Sara Walton. 2006. "Creating Adventures in Wonderland: The Journey Metaphor and Environmental Sustainability." *Organization* 13 (6): 801–39.

Morton, Timothy. 2009. *Ecology without Nature: Rethinking Environmental Aesthetics.* Cambridge, MA: Harvard University Press.

———. 2013. *Hyperobjects: Philosophy and Ecology after the End of the World.* Minneapolis: University of Minnesota Press.

Princen, Thomas. 2010. "Speaking of Sustainability: The Potential of Metaphor." *Sustainability: Science, Practice, and Policy* 6 (2): 60–65.

Scott, James C. 1998. *Seeing Like a State: How Certain Schemes to Improve the Human Condition Have Failed.* New Haven, CT: Yale University Press.

Strathern, Marilyn. 1992. *Reproducing the Future: Essays on Anthropology, Kinship and the New Reproductive Technologies.* Manchester: Manchester University Press.

Titon, Jeff Todd. 2015. "Sustainability, Resilience and Adaptive Management." In *The Oxford Handbook of Applied Ethnomusicology*, edited by Svanibor Pettan and Jeff Todd Titon, 157–98. New York: Oxford University Press.

Tsing, Anna Lowenhaupt. 2015. *The Mushroom at the End of the World: On the Possibility of Life in Capitalist Ruins.* Princeton, NJ: Princeton University Press.

Turner, Victor. 1974. *Dramas, Fields and Metaphors.* Ithaca, NY: Cornell University Press.

Van der Wal, Rene, Anke Fischer, Sebastian Selge, and Brendon M. H. Larson. 2015. "Neither the Public nor Experts Judge Species on Their Origins." *Environmental Conservation.* 42 (4):349–55.

Weintraub, Andrew N. 2009. Introduction to *Music and Cultural Rights* 1–18. Edited by Andrew N. Weintraub and Bell Yung. Urbana: University of Illinois Press.

CHAPTER 2

Dialogues All the Way Down

Conversational Genres as Matrices of Cultural and Ecological Renewal

MARY HUFFORD

THE 1987 UNITED NATIONS' Brundtland Report modeled sustainable development as a platform supported by the three pillars of society, ecology, and economy (WCED 1987). Note that this 1987 report is cited by Titon in the Foreword, and by Allen. Hufford is the only one that refers to it in her text solely as WCED. Aaron Allen and Titon refer to it with its full name though Allen often uses WCED. Only in Hufford's references is it called WCED.

This seems like a copyediting task and I am not sure what, if anything, to do about the inconsistency now.

The term *cultural sustainability* has since come into vogue as a way of incorporating a missing fourth pillar: culture (Hawkes 2001). As we engage across disciplinary siloes for sustainable development, this metaphor quickly breaks down. In many respects, culture is not like the other three pillars but rather is the very means needed for integrating them. Positioned as a fourth pillar, culture is strategically a kind of Trojan horse, a means of structuring the much-needed transdisciplinary conversation toward the end that Jeff Todd Titon terms "ecological rationality." As he defines it, "An ecological rationality that turns on the relatedness of all beings is congruent with the fundamental principle of ecological science, namely, that all beings are interconnected, and that a change to any one effects change in every one" (Titon 2017).

Key foundations for ecologically rational, transdisciplinary conversations have been laid over the past two centuries through philosophical projects aimed at undoing Cartesian dualisms. A burgeoning literature in the environmental humanities and social sciences explores the contribution of Mikhail Bakhtin's dialogism, the phenomenology of Maurice Merleau-Ponty, the critical theory of the Frankfurt School, and the pragmatism of Charles Sanders Peirce and John Dewey. As an ethnographic humanity deeply influenced by American pragmatism, public folklore has a unique contribution to make. In what follows, I explore the role that folklore studies can play in the integration of ecological and social sciences with the humanities through the application of performance and genre theory to the transdisciplinary notion of *dialogue* as both object and means of inquiry.

One philosophical trailhead is well marked by environmental philosopher Bryan Norton, who vaunts American pragmatism as a framework for synthesizing transdisciplinary visions and approaches to sustainability. In particular Norton emphasizes the role assigned to culture in Aldo Leopold's conservation aesthetic and land ethic.

> The economics of any society or culture deal with individual values, whether consumptive or spiritual; but economic decisions are bounded by a larger cultural overlay, a multigenerational, living relationship between the land and the people who live on it. Leopold never considered reducing these cultural ideas and the "wisdom" of past cultures to a physical relationship *or* to an economic relationship. It is a cultural one; and the continuities a culture develops with its habitat have a value that transcends individual value; it is value that is stored in the wisdom and practices of multigenerational societies. (Norton 2005, 72)

Indeed, Leopold's *Sand County Almanac* offers one of the earliest and most succinct formulations of culture as a driver of ecological sustainability: "We abuse land because we regard it as a commodity belonging to us. When we see land as a community to which we belong, we may begin to use it with love and respect" ([1949] 1989, viii). With Aaron Allen (this volume), I ask what can it mean to know land as a member of the community? By what mechanisms are the boundaries of the community enlarged "to include soils, waters, plants, animals, or collectively, the land?" (Leopold [1949] 1989, 204) How does "community" shrink to exclude its more-than-human members? In part, the answer lurks in language. "I don't believe we should take trees that are less than 18 inches in diameter," a West Virginia logger told me some years ago. "I seriously think that's robbing the land" (interview, March 11, 1995, Naoma, WV). "Robbing the land" is a notion I heard when I was a child growing up in the Allegheny foothills of Western Pennsylvania. The statement seems to presume that land has rights, and that among those rights are rights of possession.

Invoked by a man who makes his living harvesting and processing timber, the concept of "robbing the land" refuses the separation of a linear time of economic productivity from the cyclical time of ecological reproduction. Probing the language further, we move beyond the notion of land as property possessed by us to recognition of the conditions subtending our own possession *by* the land.

The idea of "robbing the land" figured prominently in Karl Marx's formulation of the sustainability crisis as a "metabolic rift," which anticipated the turn toward cultural ecology by nearly two centuries (Foster, Clark, and York 2011, 66–68). Anticipating the present interest in socio-ecological systems, Marx's notion of *Stoffwechsel* named a process of metabolic exchange between nature and society. This metabolic exchange, foundational in land-based communities, relies on the return of food and animal waste to the soil, where it nurtures the next genera-tion of produce. Marx linked the industrial capitalist mobilization of a work force to the European crisis of soil degradation. When agrarian workers were shifted from the land to become wage laborers in the factories of Manchester, Liverpool, and Birmingham, food produced in the countryside followed them. The waste from this food was then concentrated in urban centers far from sites of agricultural production, which were left exhausted and unreplenished. Justus von Liebig, the German chemist on whose research Marx relied, had decades earlier referred to the geochemical outcome of forced migrations from coun-tryside to city as "robbing the land" (Foster, Clark, and York 2011, 80).

Marx's analysis identifies a relationship between soil condition and social relations that is a proper topic for folklore studies. How has the relationship between soil and humanity become dismantled? *Humus* and *human* are ety-mologically related, of course. But the domains are now so separated that we have forgotten our connection to soil. We forget that soil is not at all the same as dirt. As ethnographers, we know that if dirt is "matter that is out of place" (Douglas [1966] 1979, 7), then dirt must have a place where it would not in fact *be* dirt at all. I once asked mycologist Rosanne Healy: "What is soil?" Healy replied, "Soil is a community." I learned from her that a teaspoon of living soil contains thousands of microbial components, each of which has a place. I said, "You mean, there's no *dirt* there?" "Well, no," she answered, "Not unless it comes into the house on your shoes" (personal communication, July 2003).

The word that commands our attention here is *community*, a term used by ecologists, humanists, and social scientists alike to describe various kinds of collectivities. Complicating the rich discussion of metaphors for sustainability undertaken by Robert Baron and Thomas Walker (this volume), we might ask whether "community" is metaphorical when applied to more-than-human communities? I think not, for on close inspection soil appears to be much more social fact than brute. How can soil be anything but a more-than-human community?

Can it be that patterns of ecological rationality exhibited in soil communities are replicated in human sociality? The possibility is not lost on biologist David George Haskell, who writes: "As in a sandwich shop at lunchtime, much of the soil's life is crowded into the narrow root zone, or rhizosphere. Here microbial densities are a hundred times higher than in the rest of the soil; protists crowd around, feeding on microbes; nematodes and microscopic insects push through the crowd; fungi spread their tendrils into the living soup" (2012, 225). Haskell's rhizosphere teems with performances of calling and responding, propositions made and accepted, permissions sought and granted or refused, functioning for all the world like genres of social communication. Initiating the mycorrhyzal association, "the fungus and the root greet each other with chemical signals, and if the salutation goes smoothly, the fungus extends its hyphae in readiness for an embrace" (225). Strolling across fields, down sidewalks, or through the park, we walk on social communication!

Haskell goes on to describe "the ancient, vital conversation" that establishes mycorrhyzal associations, partnerships among fungi and roots: The root "responds by growing tiny rootlets for the fungi to colonize" and in some cases allowing "the fungus to penetrate the root's cell walls and spread the hyphae into the interior of the cells. Once inside, the hyphae divide into fingers, forming a miniature rootlike network within the cells of the root. This arrangement looks pathological" (2012, 225). Pathological? Haskell is describing what appears to be a healthy, well-functioning community, governed by social contracts undertaken with free, prior, and informed consent. Where's the pathology?

Mycorrhizal associations exemplify the kind of body that Mikhail Bakhtin described as "grotesque"—a body made up of two bodies fused in a productive act. The grotesque body is open to the world, always growing, always emerging, egalitarian, and democratic. Bakhtin opposes the grotesque body to what he calls the "classical body." Epitomized in classical Greek sculpture, the classical body has no openings: it represents perfect symmetry and closure, a fixity of social identity and the hierarchies of class society (Bakhtin 1984, 317)). The classical body is aristocratic. Following Bakhtin, sociologist Michael Bell extrapolates these body types into two kinds of ecology: bourgeois and grotesque. Bourgeois ecologies tend to suppress the messy, "going to seed" stages of gardens and landscapes; grotesque ecologies display all the stages of life: birth, death, decay, going to seed, composting, harboring all manner of creatures, and so forth. Bourgeois ecologies go along with the ideal of the individual as the minimum unit of society, and the protection of individual rights at the expense of communally held values (Bell 1994). Bourgeois ecological aesthetics perpetuate the metabolic rift. Think of the brigades of high-octane leaf blowers that descend each autumn to purge urban and suburban lawns of the leaves needed to replenish rhizospheres capable of nurturing healthy carbon-sequestering, heat-ameliorating canopies. Though humorously intended, Haskell's comment about the pathological appearance of mycorrhizae remains haunted by a bourgeois sensibility that just might take offense at the grotesque interpenetrations of mycelia and roots.

Let's reflect for a moment on the discontinuities undergirding socially stratified ecologies. Bakhtin's distinction between dialogic and monologic forms of communication (1981) mirrors his distinction between grotesque and classical bodies. Dialogism is a problem for class society because, like the grotesque body, dialogue engages reciprocities that undermine class distinction. I argue that there is more than a metaphorical resemblance between conversations in the rhizosphere and those in the semiospheres of sandwich shops along the sides of rivers and roads, for both operate according to the same principles. Dialogues in both spheres structure matrices that nurture relationships foundational to social and ecological renewal.

Subterranean dialogues are structurally recapitulated in human conversations. Consider the similarities to rhizospheric interactions evoked in Merleau-Ponty's depiction of humans in dialogue:

> In the experience of dialogue there is constituted between the other and myself a common ground; my thought and his are interwoven into a single fabric, my words and those of my interlocutor are called forth by the state of the discussion, and they are inserted into a shared operation of which neither of us is the creator. We have here a dual being, where the other is for me no longer a mere bit of behaviour in my transcendental field, nor I in his; we are collaborators for each other in consummate reciprocity. Our perspectives merge into each other and we co-exist for a common world. ([1968] 1992, 354)

Aboveground, as below, what Jeff Titon calls "co-presence" (2016, 487) is achieved through dialogue. In the rhizosphere, chemical greetings initiate a form-giving matrix for the hybrid being of mycorrhizae. Similarly, in human conversations, speech and gestures initiate form-giving matrices in which conversationalists shape common worlds for which they may temporarily coexist. Through the exercise of what Anna Tsing calls "world-making proclivities," (2015, 211) conversationalists in both spheres lend themselves to "a shared operation of which neither . . . is the creator" (2015, 211). This shared operation is in effect a genre of communication—a form of folklore, if you will; an interactional routine that troubles the ideology of individualism to bring selves and others into identity-completing relationships. Functioning as what Merleau-Ponty elsewhere calls the "instituted subject" (1970, 40), the conversational genre dynamically appropriates us, with our consent, into temporary communities of tellers and hearers, tricksters and victims, teachers and students. Think of how we assign an anonymous, appropriating agency to speech when we say that "his name *came up* in conversation" or "rumor *has it* that" or "word *is* to the kitchen *gone*." Or of how we ourselves are appropriated when we "fall into" conversation. The instituted subject, writes Merleau-Ponty, "exists between others and myself, between me and myself, like a hinge, the consequence and the guarantee of our belonging to a common world" (40).

Speech genres of the sort that Charles Briggs calls "historical discourse" (1988, 59) function at the local level to integrate times, spaces, practices, and social identities not only of humans but of a wide range of species and land forms. Conversational genres are blueprints for the sort of reflexivity and meaning making that is foundational to democratic deliberation (Taylor 2009). These blueprints are supple enough to initiate and appropriate field researchers—both cultural and ecological—into the multi-sectoral communities needed for sustainability.

I'll illustrate with examples of conversational genres drawn from fieldwork in the southern West Virginia coalfields, where I participated as a folklorist in a citizen science forest-monitoring project in the mid-1990s. Designed by ecologist Orie Loucks and carried out by field scientists working with volunteers from the region, the research responded to observations of forest species decline by old-timers in West Virginia's Coal River Valley, where land-based community life depends on practices of commoning that include daily conversations about things happening on the land. From the beginning the project sparked a firestorm of criticism from professional foresters, many of them employed by the State of West Virginia as well as by pulp and paper companies (Puckett et al. 2013).

The foresters were not actually critical of the science; rather they were suspicious of research that responded to the talk of mountain people: "rumors," "anecdotes," and "tales" that would surely contaminate the study, while scaring away stockholders. Rumors, anecdotes, and tales are among the many speech genres that function as *matrices* of the land community as a dynamic entanglement of human and more-than-human being. The discourse that the corporate foresters trusted was monologic: passing a litmus test for objectivity by having expunged all traces of subjectivity and reflexivity, suppressing all points of view except for the transcendent perspective, staged, as Donna Haraway puts it, "from everywhere and nowhere" (1988, 58).

On Coal River, speech about the land is dialogic: saturated with what Bakhtin calls "addressivity," double-voicing, reported speech, *and* reported perceptions. Conversational genres like place-name etymologies, aphorisms, scriptural allusions, legends, tall tales, genealogical digressions, and testimonies are means whereby the land community audits itself. In such an ecological rationality, absence of saying can even indicate absence of seeing. "Somebody must have cut those walnut trees down," as one store proprietor told me. "I haven't heard anyone mention them lately."

Over coffee one morning in Sybil's Back Porch restaurant on Route 3 in Naoma, Vernon Williams, a man in his fifties, asked Old Joe Jarrell where two of his ancestors came from. In response, Jarrell delivered a place-name etymology relating himself to his younger interlocutor, simultaneously relating both of them to a place on the land.

vw: *Do you know where Jack and Buzz Williams come from?*
jj: *I don't know where Williams come from, but I know where their grandma*
    come from, 'cause she was my grandpa's sister. Her name was Pliney. I've got
    a hollow up there that's named for her: Pline's Hollow. (interview, October
    4, 1996, Naoma, WV)

Identifying a common ancestor, Jarrell relates himself to Williams and tethers
their relationship to a place named for the shared ancestor: Pline's Hollow.
Through such tiny initiatory rites, names for people, places, and things serve
as inexhaustible touchstones to shared membership in a constantly growing
community of land and people.

Significantly, Jarrell gestures toward Horse Creek and Pline's Hollow when
he says their names. This gesture and its relationship to his words illumine the
site of a third dialogue, a dialogue that anticipates and connects the conversations of humans to the more-than-human dialogues surrounding us. This is the
site of a "mute dialogue of perception" that Merleau-Ponty concluded is both
foundational to, and on a continuum with, speech ([1968] 1992, 154–55). A site
of world making at the interstices of human and more-than-human being, this
perceptual dialogue continually deposits and replenishes what he calls the "soil"
or "flesh" of sensibility. This flesh, for which Merleau-Ponty tells us there had
never before been a term in philosophy, is a lining that gives rise to perceiver
and perceived, subject and object, namer and named, as "interdependent aspects of its spontaneous activity" (Abram 1996, 64). That is to say, perceptual
activity deposits and renews a lining of visibility between the viewer and the
visible, of audibility between the hearer and the audible, of tangibility between
the toucher and the touched, of nameability between the namer and the named,
and so forth. The flesh marks the point at which the sensing "intertwines" with
the sensible, and this intertwining is carnal. "The look," writes Merleau-Ponty,
"envelops, palpates, espouses the visible things" ([1968] 1992, 133).

The flesh or soil of sensibility exemplifies a middle ground, that is, in Val
Plumwood's term, "backgrounded" by the nature-culture split (2006, 119). Merleau-Ponty's account of perceptual activity clarifies sensibility as a vital site of
our co-constitution. For him, perception is not the operation of an active subject
on a passive object. Rather perception is a collaborative, mutually constitutive
activity. Perceiving a tree across a field of visibility, I know myself to be visible,
just as the tree is visible; or on seeing a person, I know that I must be visible as
an object on the other's horizon, just as the other is visible to me. It is because of
this operation, which Merleau-Ponty calls "reversibility" ([1968] 1992, 144–48),
that the completion of my identity becomes possible—I know myself not only
as a subject but as an object in the eyes of another, to whom I must appear as
she appears to me. Merleau-Ponty uses the metaphor of "dehiscence" ([1968]
1992, 123)—the explosive release of seeds leaving a pod with its opening folded

back on itself—to describe the shift in consciousness that changes my sense of self and my relationship to a world for which I and my human and more-than-human others may now coexist.

As a site of metabolic exchange, sensibility is affected by the metabolic rift. Listening to our own speech, we audit what I call the "sensibility rift," making speech itself a site for recovering sensibility.[1] This recovery begins with noticing how what Bakhtin called "living speech acts" engage the mute dialogue of perception. Independently, both Bakhtin and Merleau-Ponty came to espouse the materiality of such speech. As talk that deposits and refreshes sensibility, living speech is material not only because it is physiologically produced, nor just because it implicates and extends perception, but also because of its impacts on what physiologists recognize as the body image or corporeal schema—a phantasmatic structure in which memories of all prior sensations and bodily postures are recorded, and which connects our speaking to the world. The phantom limb provides the most compelling evidence for this structure, which is neither wholly psychological nor wholly somatic (see Grosz 1994, 62–85, for a useful overview).

Merleau-Ponty considered speech and gesture to be in the same relationship to their intended objects ([1962] 1996, 89). The magic of speech is that it brings real things into contact without touching them. "Speech," writes Renaud Barbaras, "has the power to make me—and my interlocutor with me—slip toward the world without the thickness of a living body interposing itself between it and us" (2004, 299). This world toward which we slip implicates our senses. As David Abram argues: "We are unable even to imagine a sensible landscape that would not at the same time be sensed . . . and are similarly unable to fully imagine a sensing self, or sentience, that would not be situated in some field of sensed phenomena" (1996, 66). The speaking, gesturing body of the storyteller hinges us to a sensible world that arouses the storyteller's speech and gestures, which in turn precipitate images in our minds of a world that comes to possess us as it possesses the storyteller (Young 2011). Functioning as what Merleau-Ponty called "instituted subjects," stories continually appropriate humans and more-than-humans into communities. Of this capacity to be possessed by language and perception, Merleau-Ponty noted: "I do not perceive any more than I speak. Perception has me as has language" ([1968] 1992, 190). Relationships that unfold dialogically confer a place not only on human participants but on our historical, biological, and geological others, with whom perceptual activity entangles us. In speech we find enunciated a set of instructions for participating in these entanglements.

On Coal River, for example, a discourse on names and naming illuminates a flesh of nameability. "Each hollow has a name." "Every curve and straight stretch." "Every big rock is named." "Every hole of water's got a name to it. Every little puddle." On Coal River, names of places, not only of side hollows but of camping rocks, holes of water, and curves and straight stretches in the road, elicit dialogues of speech and perception. I asked an elder named Howard Miller about the names of all the side hollows on Drew's Creek. Seated in his living room, Miller gestured toward the location of each in the surrounding hills:

> Each one of these hollers that goes off, they have a different name. To begin with, that first large holler at the end of my land, that's called the Mill Holler, because there used to be a water mill right close there, about where Mabel lives. . . . The creek was ditched through the bottom over there, and that was where they had their mill. And this holler here, in back of my house, is called the Peach Orchard Holler. That undoubtedly had a peach orchard up in there. Then the next one up is School House Holler. There was a schoolhouse at the mouth of it. Then the Bee Light Holler. They would cut out the trees so they could bait bees and see where they went to. Things of that sort is the way they named these hollers. (interview, May 26, 1996, Drew's Creek, WV)

Miller's naming proceeds as a tour of the hollows, through which he moves in his mind, relying on sensory memories of the land to deliver images and names simultaneously. His reflections turn place-names into organs of perception. Images aroused by names offer formulas for proof: one could go to the Mill Hollow to see the remains of the ditch that once accommodated a water-powered gristmill; or to the Bee Light Hollow to understand the use made of the play of light and shadow in order to follow wild bees to their hives; or to Quill Hollow to look for hollow reeds ("quills") that could be installed as spigots for channeling sap from maple trees into buckets.

Conversational storytelling structures the recurring collective experience of a local flesh of sensibility. Reproducing and affirming the collective experience of a flesh of sensibility through conversational storytelling about local things, we refresh the sense of belonging on which Leopold's conservation ethic turns. Miller's story bears the trace of my point of view. His reference to "where Mabel lives"—where I have stayed—incorporates me into his recitation. Conversational storytelling recurrently assembles a collective flesh of sensibility to which Merleau-Ponty alludes as an "intercorporeal perceptual schema."[2] In these conversations, as Molly Hadley Jensen puts it, "multiple selves collaborate and cooperate to form a unified percipience" (2007, 198). When those conversations are about local things, what we replenish, of course, are sensory memories of the species, spaces, and events that tether our shared worlds (Hufford 2015).

So reliable are the sensory components of place-names that Miller concludes there was "undoubtedly" a peach orchard in Peach Orchard Hollow, a move that shifts attention from the place, to its name, and then to the visibility and perceptions of those who named the hollows. When I asked another elder how a tributary named Peach Tree Creek got its name, he said, "When the first white men came into this country, they saw peach trees a-growing here, and called it Peach Tree Creek" (interview, December 13, 1994, Peach Tree, WV). Reaching through time to a landscape created and maintained by Cherokees who hunted and gathered in southern West Virginia, where they planted peach trees obtained through trade with Spanish explorers in the seventeenth century (see Davis 2000, 48–49), the reversibility of speech and perception locates us within a sensibility and a being that is much older than our own operations (Merleau-Ponty [1968] 1992).

The monological discourse of the corporate state opposes the inclusivity of the dialogical discourse of commoning, violently shutting down reciprocities hard-wired into ecologies of social interaction, reciprocities that come to be seen as "pathological." But in a dialogical world, what is pathological is the refusal of dialogue—of the capacity for speech and perception to possess us. Making a virtue of that refusal, the foresters' indignation over the citizen science effort is one small episode in the corporate state's assault on commons (Reid and Taylor 2010), discourses that produce and reproduce land communities (Hufford 2016, 9). This is an assault that expropriates. Thousands of pages on file in offices of environmental protection around the country exemplify what Wayne C. Booth called the capacity of monological discourse both to maim and to conceal its maiming. "Many of the greatest achievements, great when viewed from the perspective of Aristotelian formalism, will . . . appear seriously maimed when we ask whether their forms reflect dialogue or monologue" (Booth 1984, xxi). The "landform complexes" erected in the wake of shattered mountains, touted as feats of engineering, are the material effects of the maiming monological discourse archived by the state. I don't think it a far stretch to suggest that dialogical discourses sustain diversity all the way down, and that diversity suffers when monologic discourses beget such anti-matrixial products as terminator potatoes, chemical fertilizers, hydroelectric dams, nuclear power plants, and mountaintop removal.

Monological discourse is not reversible. Its communications are vigorously scoured of perspective and agency; its subjects lurk under cover of passive voice. Its monocular gaze sees nothing looking back (Dorst 1999, 99). If a subject does appear, it's a version of corporate personhood. Consider, for example, the agency given to "coal mining activities" in the following sentence, taken from a land-use history offered by a coal company in its 1984 permit application to site seven billion gallons of liquid coal waste in the farming community of Shumate's Branch: "Before coal mining activities began in this area, productivity of the land was non-existent" (West Virginia Division of Environmental Protection 1984). In the presence of monologues all the way down, all other perspectives and voices disappear. The facades of post-mining land forms perfectly embody this monologic. Refusing the monologue, members of land communities on Coal River translate its felt impacts into dialogue: "A. T. Massey came in here and said, 'You don't exist.'"

How do dialogically wrought narratives constitute relationships among collectivities? Just as dialogue is a formative medium, enabling two who are subjects to themselves to know themselves as objects from the other's point of view, the collaboratively wrought story absorbs us as subjects in an alternate world, which we inhabit as we inhabit our lived bodies. When this alternate world is the same as our locality, our *place*, the story can open a gap between a locality's lived and object status to complete its identity in relation to other localities. The land ethic, constituted through narratives that undermine class distinction by entangling human and more-than-human being, is key.

My last example of a conversational genre is a scriptural allusion (Briggs 1988) that accounts for the destruction of the land's capacity to speak to us, through us, and for us. In conversation about forest blight with forest researchers and activists, a preacher who worked in the mines reflected: "I'll give you a possible reading on why trees are doing the way they're doing. It says in the Bible that if man don't cry out to God against injustice, the rocks and trees will. Satan knows that, and that's why he's using these companies to destroy them" (interview, April 21, 1995, Drew's Creek, WV).

Set in a conversation fathoming symptoms and causes of forest decline, the biblical allusion gathers forest decline, social injustice, loss of human voice, and ecological crisis into the same frame. Making sense of ecological crisis, the scriptural allusion builds and comments on stories already exchanged. It culminates a struggle not only to define what is happening to trees but also to find a way to talk together about it. The preacher's interpretation grants agency, point of view, and *voice* to rocks and trees. As agents "doing the way they're doing," trees are protagonists, heroes locked in mortal struggle, speaking out despite the perils of advocacy.

The self-referential complexity of the speech genre enables a reversal that brings us to the threshold of "the Leopoldian place," as Jeff Titon puts it, where "if all is connected (by sound waves emanating from the vibrating molecules in every being, organic and inorganic), then all are related, all are kin, and everything and everyone is your and my relative" (personal communication, October 24, 2016). In a metaphor recalling Merleau-Ponty's notion of "dehiscence," Bakhtin locates the poetics of generic form in the reflexive act whereby we see ourselves as objects from the point of view of characters in a story. Taking the point of view of the other, we find "the bud in which slumbers form, and whence form unfolds like a blossom" (Bakhtin 1990, 24–25). When characters in the story are biological and geological others, as in the scriptural allusion, there is an exchange of human and more-than-human points of view. A reversal within the frame of the story shifts the role of storytelling to rocks and trees, who speak on our behalf. This mirroring of our storytelling within the frame of the scriptural allusion triggers a reversal for those of us who are listening, approximating the dehiscence that Merleau-Ponty describes. Seeing ourselves

as rocks and trees might see us, we fleetingly grasp something of what it is to
be *their* environment.

Notes

1. John O'Neill writes, "In any man whose thinking listens to his speaking, there is
founded the soul's city, hearkening to the principles, nature, and laws of mankind. But
to listen to principle and nature is to begin again, to remake sense and sensuousness, to
make of time's body a renaissance of reason and its divine pleasure. This is a communal
birth, and history is its only midwife, for the soul's deliverance is nowhere else than into
this beautiful world" (1974, 37).

2. See Reid and Taylor (2010, 138–42) for a discussion of Merleau-Ponty's notion of the
"intercorporeal schema of perceptuality" and its implications for ecological citizenship.

References

Abram, David. 1996. *The Spell of the Sensuous: Perception and Language in a More-Than-Human World*. New York: Vintage Books.

Bakhtin, Mikhail. 1981. *The Dialogic Imagination*. Austin: University of Texas Press.

———. 1984. *Rabelais and His World*. Bloomington: Indiana University Press.

———. 1990. *Art and Answerability: Early Philosophical Essays by M. M. Bakhtin*. Austin: University of Texas Press.

Barbaras, Renaud. 2004. *The Being of the Phenomenon: Merleau-Ponty's Ontology*. Bloomington: Indiana University Press.

Bell, Michael. 1994. "Deep Fecology: Mikhail Bakhtin and the Call of Nature." *Capitalism, Nature, Socialism*. 5:65–84.

Booth, Wayne C. 1984. Introduction to *Bakhtin: Problems of Dostoevsky's Poetics*, xiii–xxvii. Edited by Caryl Emerson. Minneapolis: University of Minnesota Press.

Briggs, Charles. 1988. *Competence in Performance: The Creativity of Tradition in Mexicano Verbal Art*. Philadelphia: University of Pennsylvania Press.

Davis, Donald. 2000. *Where There Are Mountains: An Environmental History of the Southern Appalachians*. Athens: University of Georgia Press.

Dorst, John D. 1999. *Looking West*. Philadelphia: University of Pennsylvania Press.

Douglas, Mary. (1966) 1979. *Purity and Danger: An Analysis of the Concepts of Pollution and Taboo*. London: Routledge and Kegan Paul.

Foster, John Bellamy, Brett Clark, and Richard York. 2011. *The Ecological Rift: Capitalism's War on the Earth*. New York: Monthly Review Press.

Grosz, Elizabeth. 1994. *Volatile Bodies: Toward a Corporeal Feminism*. Bloomington: Indiana University Press.

Haraway, Donna. 1988. "Situated Knowledge: The Science Question in Feminism and the Privilege of Partial Perspective." *Feminist Studies* 14 (3): 579–99.

Haskell, David George. 2012. *The Forest Unseen: A Year's Watch in Nature*. New York: Viking Press.

Hawkes, Jon. 2001. *The Fourth Pillar of Sustainability: Culture's Essential Role in Planning*. Champaign, IL: Common Ground.

Hufford, Mary. 2015. "Tending Sensibility: Folklore's Narrative Ecology." Paper presented at the Annual Meeting of the American Folklore Society, Long Beach, CA.

———. 2016. "Deep Commoning: Public Folklore and Environmental Policy on a Resource Frontier." *International Journal of Heritage Studies* 22 (8): 635–49.

Jensen, Molly Hadley. 2007. "'Fleshing Out' an Ethic of Diversity." In *Merleau-Ponty and Environmental Philosophy: Dwelling on the Landscapes of Thought*, edited by Suzanne L. Cataldi and William S. Hamrick, 191–202. Albany: State University of New York.

Leopold, Aldo. (1949) 1989. *A Sand County Almanac and Sketches Here and There.* New York: Oxford University Press.

Merleau-Ponty, Maurice. (1962) 1996. *Phenomenology of Perception.* London: Routledge and Kegan Paul.

———. (1968) 1992. *The Visible and the Invisible.* Evanston, IL: Northwestern University Press.

———. 1970. *Themes from the Lectures at the Collège de France, 1952–1970.* Evanston, IL: Northwestern University Press.

Norton, Bryan G. 2005. *Sustainability: A Philosophy of Adaptive Ecosystem Management.* Chicago: University of Chicago Press.

O'Neil, John. 1974. *Making Sense Together: An Introduction to Wild Sociology.* New York: Harper and Row.

Plumwood, Val. 2006. "The Concept of a Cultural Landscape: Nature, Culture, and Agency in the Land." *Ethics and the Environment* 11 (2): 115–50.

Puckett, Anita, Elizabeth Fine, Mary Hufford, Betsy Taylor, and Ann Kingsolver. 2013. "Who Knows? Who Tells? Creating a Knowledge Commons." In *Transforming Places: Lessons from Appalachia*, edited by Stephen L. Fisher and Barbara Ellen Smith, 239–51. Urbana: University of Illinois Press.

Reid, Herbert, and Betsy Taylor. 2010. *Recovering the Commons: Democracy, Place, and Global Justice.* Urbana: University of Illinois Press.

Taylor, Betsy. 2009. "'Place' as Prepolitical Grounds of Democracy: An Appalachian Case Study in Class Conflict, Forest Politics, and Civic Networks." *American Behavioral Scientist* 52 (6): 826–45.

Titon, Jeff Todd. 2016. "Orality, Commonality, Commons, Sustainability." *Journal of American Folklore* 129:486–97.

———. 2017. "Eco-Justice and Folklife." Don Yoder Lecture on Folklore and Religion at the American Folklore Society Annual Meeting, Minneapolis, MN, October 18.

Tsing, Anna. 2015. *The Mushroom at the End of the World: On the Possibility of Life in the Capitalist Ruins.* Princeton, NJ: Princeton University Press.

West Virginia Division of Environmental Protection. 1984. Armco Steel Corporation Application to Build a Wet Refuse Impoundment on Shumate's Branch. West Virginia Department of Environmental Protection, Charleston, WV.

WCED (World Commission on Environment and Development). 1987. *Our Common Future.* Oxford: Oxford University Press.

Young, Katharine. 2011. "Gestures, Intercorporeity, and the Fate of Phenomenology Folklore." *Journal of American Folklore* 124 (492): 55–87.

CHAPTER 3

Radical Critical Empathy and Cultural Sustainability

RORY TURNER

CULTURAL SUSTAINABILITY, at its heart, is an existential project, and I suggest some methodological and pedagogical orientations to this project in this chapter. A foundation of cultural sustainability work is participation and empathy. I consider here how the experiential qualities of participation and empathy are central to this project in relationship to questions that have guided the inception of a professional master's program focused on cultural sustainability at Goucher College. Attention to culture as a field of being that opens up possibilities of harmful or helpful experiences and lives has implications for both academic and applied work interested in well-being and a sustainable pluralistic future.

Category errors haunt the ways that culture is understood, represented, and operationalized in academic, public, and commercial domains. No more merely an objective thing than hope is an objective thing, culture is subsumed to epistemological reduction: as commodity, resource, analytic tool, arena for contestation, invention, and so on. I argue here not that these approaches to culture are wrong; indeed, they have been enormously generative of a variety of cultural material, and depending on how culture is grasped, more or less effective accounts of culture (as thing, as setting, as language, etc.) from that vantage point can be produced. These accounts in turn bear fruit in institution and structure, whether conservatory, tourist site, academic program, or so many other things.

If, however, we opt to view culture in relationship to sustainability, something radically interesting happens. To sustain, at its root, means to be held from underneath (Grober 2007). If we grasp culture pragmatically as that which sustains or does not sustain us, as a means of being, then we may need to regard it differently than is commonly done. Here culture becomes a field of participation characterized perhaps by care and mutuality, or by neglect and violence, always though, something for which we have an interest and responsibility as Michelle Kisliuk's contribution to this volume poignantly shows. Human realities are never fully determined, our worlds are inscribed by power and history, but indeterminacy and presence emerge in the unfolding of time through performance and interaction. We are constantly making and remaking the field of our human possibilities through our highly reflexive and complex passages through experience. There is no solution or right answer to being human; rather, we have choice (to some degree) in how we respond to and fashion the world. Culture is not a thing but a process, and its generativity and plasticity can be shaped by how we pay attention to its existential unfolding. Cultural sustainability as I view it is an intersection of well beings: of well beings for the sustaining biosphere, human systems, and coexisting individuals. It invites us into radical, deeply rooted participation and appreciation of our own and others' existence in interrelationship. From a phenomenological vantage point, it is a mode of existence, as Bruno Latour would say (2013), that irreducibly demands our consideration of "being a part of" or apart from. This existential vantage point contrasts starkly with the distancing effects of culture's conventional and academic appropriation and use. From this existential/phenomenological mode, ways of participatory knowing through music, narrative, expressive genres of many kinds, ritual, labor, play, and such, become indispensable and foundational as the radical space where we invite one another "to be" with one another, a space that I understand as a necessity for sustainability (Titon 2008, 31–32).

All this begs the question of the consequences of our current approaches to culture. If cultural sustainability is a necessary aspiration in the Anthropocene (Steffen, Crutzen, and McNeill 2007; Latour 2017; Yates 2012), then those interested in it would be well served methodologically to ground themselves in deep observed, critical, participatory action and research, rooted in radical empathy. From this vantage point practitioners can act and work in ways that sustain culture rather than transposing or dissecting it, and act and work in authentic solidarity with those we are with, in a relationship of care. This perspective has implications for how we educate students, make policy, and work with communities. Before launching into this, some discussion of the roots of the perspective I propose—what we might call a cultural existentialism—are in order.

Though these roots are both very old and quite new, and disparate in origin, their character can perhaps be discerned in reference to the work of four scholars: Michael Jackson, Henry Glassie, Jeff Todd Titon, and my mother, Edie

Turner. Jackson, in a prolific and groundbreaking series of writings (1989, 2009, etc.), has argued for a radical empirical anthropology of the human condition characterized by a resistance to reductionisms. His work encounters and shares through vivid, humble writing the predicaments of lived reality as he and his subjects struggle with such enduring challenges of life as balancing security and freedom, the known and the unknowable, alienation and belonging. Inspired by the phenomenological tradition of Edmund Husserl, Martin Heidegger, and especially Maurice Merleau-Ponty, he shares with these thinkers in problematizing the truth claims and science of Cartesian rationality as sufficient to account for what is apparent in human experience. Elusive, ambiguous, particular, and in the end indeterminate, this experience is never fully plumbed, but it can become humanly meaningful through such means as narrative and at its best, ethnography. In the end, Jackson writes not to rise above life but to enter into it with his interlocutors and readers, inviting a deeper ethical presence in the world for all of us.

As Leonard Primiano reminded us as a discussant to Henry Glassie's keynote at the Santa Fe American Folklore Society annual meetings in 2014, Glassie's work (e.g., 1989, 1995, 2011) has been a sustained meditation on the role of creativity and craft as a response to the existential dilemmas and epiphanies of the human condition. The folk artists that Glassie celebrates are taking action in their work in relationship to agendas that are not reducible to instrumental logics of power or commerce. Their efforts flow from culturally articulated attitudes in relationship to ultimate questions of meaning, and their creations deserve to be viewed and experienced accordingly. Glassie reminds us that the symbolic acts of such creators invite us into a mode of being with just as much ontological legitimacy as the dominant planetary symbolic strategies of economic commerce. It is the field of this experience, between creator, object, community, and witness, that we might keep in mind when we speak of cultural sustainability. Almost inevitably the field of being proffered by such creation implicates researchers (Cantwell 2001) and all participants into a relationship of empathy, a sharing of what it might be like to be in a fuller and deeper relationship with the world. It puzzles me how work undertaken in relationship to culture can evade an essential reliance on accepting such an invitation, since the invitation itself is the matter at hand, not the creation itself, not the context, not the other accounts that can be drawn from the deployment of other analytic projects originating from different ontic modes.

Jeff Todd Titon, our wisest and most influential scholar of music, culture, and sustainability, carefully explores the challenges of cultural existentialism, especially in his work with the sacred sound of the Old Regular Baptist communities he participated with as a radically empathic researcher (2015). Titon helps reveal for us the problematic dimensions of applied scholarship in terms of power relationships; contexts of performance; the agendas of funders, academia, and participants in local and nonlocal fields of power; and cultural politics. Always, though, his writings flow from the great gift he received from the Regular Baptists: the invitation into a lived experience of presence that was the field of being performatively enacted in their services. For Titon, and for the rest of us, it would be presumptuous and inaccurate to speak of a definitive knowledge and revelation of a fully realized essence in these encounters. Rather, returning to Jackson, we can speak of sharing together the disclosure of being that cannot be resolved or understood, that takes us beyond ourselves. Margarita Mazo in this volume reveals the deep power of lament to partake in this field of being, even when these forms are recontextualized. This is the ground of deep empathy, and the space for genuine intersubjective recognition, from which real solidarity and care can arise. Titon's questions around the ethics and aesthetics of interventions hold this space at their heart and challenge us to not forget that the intangibility of cultural heritage—like Old Regular Baptist song—does not only lie in its ephemeral substance. This is a powerful lesson for scholars and even more powerful for culture workers to always begin from and not lose sight of.

My mother, Edie Turner, walked this same terrain and found in *communitas* a gift that served her as topic and pedagogical mode (2012), and from which she developed a simple but potent methodology. I have written of this elsewhere (R. Turner 2014) of the easing into intimacy through simple human commonalities, of conversations about the weather and family, of the eschewal of privilege in this epistemological vantage point. She was a harbinger of the current interest in perspectivism in anthropology (Vivieros de Castro 2004), and like Jackson again, saw the ground on which we exist in relationship with one another as one of mystery, beyond objective account. More bravely and perhaps foolishly than the perspectivists who have refreshed anthropology, she thought the ontological frontiers were not between people but could be both within us and without, and she joyfully invited participation for her students and her colleagues and those she studied and for herself. The task she set herself was one of conveyance, of using story to open up lines of possible sense, to provide not closure but invitation to the site of cultural alchemy, painstakingly empirical and accurate, true to what transpires, but shameless in her willingness to share the irreducibly ambiguous but no less constitutive flows of information and energy that are the ways that humans imbue reality with mind (Siegel 2007). With her, even more than with Jackson, Titon, and Glassie, methodology opens beyond text, and story blurs into enactment and genre that is of the same nature as the very things she abides with, healing, music, dance, ceremony, and the rest.

So if we follow phenomenology to consider being itself as culturally constituted—as the landscape of our existential predicament and invitation—we have to shift our practices in order to come to terms with it decently, as scholars, teachers, and partners in culture making. To do this, we must become porous to others and find in ourselves our own otherness to be able to have empathy, not as a gesture of condescending appreciation, but as a lived experience of the implications of how things can be for others. If we are to sustain, we must hold this from below.

Over the years, public folklorists and applied ethnomusicologists have been shifting from a role characterized by the collection and archiving of cultural materials and the presentation of "culture bearers" and their artistic productions for elite culturally informed audiences to the role of cultural partnership. In this role, scholars seek first to develop a deep appreciation and understanding for the cultural world of those with whom they work, then engage in dialogue with practitioners and cultural participants to consider ethical and effective projects and actions that will serve to help sustain the cultural practices, contexts, knowledge, and skills that they have determined are of value to them. This shift in emphasis responds to powerful critiques of representational strategies that reinforce hierarchical cultural orders and the imperialist/colonialist assumptions behind them (Marcus and Fischer 1999). Practitioners in these fields have continued to use expressive genres like exhibits, festivals, and publications, and interventions like archival documentation, but have reflexively repositioned themselves and those they work with (Baron 2010), considering as a priority the value of the project in inspiring or supporting cultural participation by community members in the contexts where the culture on display is practiced.

When my colleagues and I envisioned the Master of the Arts in Cultural Sustainability at Goucher College in 2008, we developed a curriculum emphasizing fieldwork, the craft and ethics of cultural partnership, and best practices in such areas as museum programs, education, and public display events. The program also offers training in such areas as management and organizational development, including communications, finances for nonprofits, and grant writing. The notion here was not only to offer marketable skills but also to empower students with the capacity to respond to the needs of the communities they work with effectively and thus to undertake a broader spectrum of possible actions with them than most culturally centered academic programs do. For example, if fieldwork and the development of a real partnership revealed that what was in fact a key factor in retaining culture through language for a group was the creation of a childcare language center, we hoped that our students would have the skills and initiative to help lead in such an effort. It is important to note here that the aim was not to blindly accept the cultural presuppositions of a managerial understanding of the world but rather to equip students to work effectively in such a world while keeping a focus on the practical dimensions of action that serve the interests of cultural participation and experience in a world dominated by instrumental objectification.

The centrality of empathy in this approach to cultural sustainability pertains especially to the ethnographic and partnership phases of the work. As many have commented, ethnographic fieldwork is a practice of empirical observation and documentation but also involves deep commitments to participation. Participation is performative, both in its inevitable social dynamics and in its exploration of identity and consciousness. The self that participates in fieldwork is not a bounded and discrete self, unaffected by the milieus it engages, nor should it be merely a self pretending to participate in a world of social practice. Instead, the fieldwork encounter becomes a subjunctive liminal zone of possibility where seeds of shared being through affinities or commonalities flower in recognition and reflection. The register of such contact emerges most often in the very form of much of the culture that cultural sustainability practitioners value—story, food, music, dance, carnivalesque foolishness, and the like. In this volume, Mary Hufford's reflections on dialogic story making are a powerful example of this phenomenon. In a slightly different register, Tom Rankin's reflections on local photographic ethnographers illustrate how embeddedness yields modes of culture making in a documentarian idiom that discloses cultural being through a genred lens. Through these genre-framed experiences, the empathy that fostered them to come to fruition can be conveyed and reenacted, though always subject to the vicissitudes of recontextualization (Bauman and Briggs 1990).

The traces of such experience are not sufficient to authorize the ethnographic account, but without them, such accounts too often become little more than stylized exercises in academic application replicating existing forms and politics of cultural understanding. Public folklore work derived from fieldwork can resist existential engagement, often substituting representational strategies and interpretive frameworks that objectify the people whose culture is on display. Rather than opening up space for alternative experiences of reality, of culture as a lived participation, we engage in an inadvertent form of cultural colonization, a reframing of consciousness into the terms and categories of our own version of the world (Comaroff and Comaroff 1989). In so doing, we reinforce hegemonic assessments of otherness and reinforce narratives that use culture as a tool for other projects of interest to agendas authorized by dominant ideologies. Thus in public work, cultural programs can uncritically adopt arguments of economic value in making the case for support. In academia, cultural analysis selectively uses cultural signifiers that are extracted from lived experience to support arguments in relationship to the theoretical issues of the moment. To be fair, most academics are painstaking in their efforts to support such accounts with attention to context and use formal and informal methodologies to ground their ideas in evidence and example. The point, though, is that these genres of cultural action/representation are inevitably transpositions, transcriptions, and inscriptions and are embedded with broad ontological assumptions. If we are interested in sustaining cultural modes of being that differed in their assumptions, we are not doing good work by surreptitiously framing them within cultural logics alien to them. It is true that in this era of global communication and hegemony, most people have already to a greater or lesser extent internalized the assumptions of capitalism and positivist science, of a semiotics that reduces value to price and segments the world into selves encountering one another through the boundaries of individual self-interest. As scholars we have been complicit in providing textual definitions and authorized accounts of culture that stand now as realities generated through the subjunctive process of culture making. Nevertheless, the genres of action and expression that cultural workers have engaged with invite us to experiences that are not reducible to these logics, and part of our job, I think, is to be active partners in the decolonization of these forms, an effort explored in both Timothy J. Cooley's and Thomas Faux's contributions to this volume. An awareness of the tensions of recontextualization and the complex interplays of ontic reification and power must complement and balance the capacity for empathy that I am advocating. Our work as cultural experts needs both flow and reflexivity, transformative participation and understanding of power and identity politics, thus a radical critical empathy.

Along with the foundational questions that arise around sustaining the cultural practices that communities identify as meaningful to them, other questions are provoked by engaging with cultural sustainability as an idea. Unpacking the juxtaposition of culture and sustainability invites consideration of the broader issue of adaptation and human survival, along with questions about the role of culture in supporting human thriving. The challenge of adaptation and human survival is stark and sufficiently documented. To use one example, the Worldwatch Institute in its *State of the World 2010* publication reminds us that for the world as a whole to live in the manner of the middle class in developed economies would require 2.7 planets worth of resources (Assadourian 2010, 6). This simple evidence confronts us with stark ethical choices. Either we turn our backs on billions of people and try to justify the acceptability of living in a way available only to the few lucky enough to be born into circumstances where this is possible, or we must engage with the larger project of critiquing and transforming the cultural systems that drive our unsustainable lifestyles.

The challenge of cultural sustainability here becomes not only safeguarding and maintaining appropriate relationships with marginalized cultural projects and the people who sustain them but also imagining and designing a human world that abides in ethically equitable balance with the biological systems and material limits within which it exists. This challenge requires a rapprochement of the humanities with empirical sciences that model ecological systems in understanding the limits of what is possible, but even more important, it requires collective symbols, myths, and rituals different from those that have shaped economic and political action in modernity. This is not a new idea, and radical environmentalists, feminists, anarchists, and artists have been issuing this call all the way back to William Blake and beyond. Thinking in these ways is often derided as utopian, but as has been pointed out, it is no less utopian than the thinking of neoliberals and technologists who believe we can engineer our ways out of the mess we have made if we only allow markets and positivist science to have their way with us. It is likely that our approach to nature (Rappaport 1999) has taken us to a point where geo-engineering endeavors of enormous scale will be necessary to address atmospheric carbon and a runaway greenhouse effect. But adapting to an increasingly extreme and unpredictable global climate is a challenge that we will all have to face. Global consumer capitalism and its underlying metaphysical assumptions are not going away anytime soon. However, there remain, to use Raymond Williams's terms, residual and emergent traditions, along with subaltern perspectives that embody alternative possibilities of human self-understanding, social relationships, and economic practices (1977, 121–27). These are by their nature wildly diverse and represent a variety of possibilities for adaptation and livelihood that hold promise. The cultural work we do with communities under threat is thus a key contribution to the emergence of sustainable cultures, and the designs and adaptations of these lifeways have lessons for all of us.

Bill McKibben (2007) reminds us that we need to break with the axiom that "more is better." Paul Hawken (2008) suggests that counter-power to a global system based on environmental and human exploitation flows as a collective and decentralized immune response. Gilles Deleuze and Félix Guattari (1987) refashion semiosis as a recursive iteration constrained by power and discipline but potentially recoverable as organic and rhizomic, a calculus of sense extruded from and connected to the biological. The world's traditions demonstrate that alternative environmentalisms and experiences of nature/culture are possible, and that the entailments of these worldviews are different ecologies and human adaptations. Drawing attention to these processes, as Jennifer C. Post does in this volume regarding Mongolian herders, can both generate solidarity and at the least track the lived experience of climate change in the Anthropocene. From such inspirations, the lineaments of sustainable culture can be discerned. Adaptations begin small and locally and are sustained by genre-generated solidarities of cultural participation grounded in the satisfactions of empathy and communitas. They are grounded in existential projects that insist on commonalities of interest and experience based on empathies of care that connect beyond humans to life in general.

For another approach to this process, the work of J. K. Gibson-Graham around hybrid research collectives (Gibson-Graham and Roelvink 2010) and alternative economies (Gibson-Graham 2008) also points a way forward. The creative dimensions of such a transition take us beyond the boundaries of authorized approaches to discourse and invite new ways of conceptualizing identity and relationship, value and nature. Moving toward such emergences is a process that is subjunctive and liminal in character; the work involves hybridity and participation in culture making and a critical reflexivity concerning the systems of metaphor that undergird such projects (see Baron and Walker in this volume) with implications here for education at all levels, with the cultivation of empathy and solidarities at the heart of the endeavor.

The promise for restorative culture making, for cultural health, is necessarily a local project, but for it to help significantly shift the status quo, such work requires scale. I think of parallels to the work of Paul Farmer (2007) and Partners in Health in its commitment to care based on ethnographic engagement but infused with the rigors of scientific inquiry into evidence-based health care and coordinated organizationally through a global and powerful response network. I'm not certain that the Archimedean clarity of their approach to the science of disease and medicine is necessary to a sustainable culture movement, but the vertical connection of local efforts multiplies and strengthens their ability to respond to the structural violence inflicted on those they serve. I would imagine a fractal structure, connected and infused with empathy and participation in relationships committed to well-being at different levels of scale that was capable of responding effectively to support cultural sustainability work at local levels through resource sharing, inspiration, and exchange. Here we need to consider how sustaining and existentially satisfying are the contexts that we live and work in, blurring the lines of what we do as professionals looking outward, asking hard questions about our own institutions and their cultural logics.

The final question that developed from the Goucher Master of Arts in Cultural Sustainability program to be posed here intersects with the two questions already considered. Cultural sustainability invites us to engage with well-being to consider the human condition from an existential vantage point and challenges us to creatively explore the possibilities of human thriving. How can culture serve to sustain human thriving and well-being? Our current approach to well-being seems to be to privatize its access through a social Darwinism of conformity to a technocratic meritocracy. If one can supply a certain kind of labor to our reward system, one is entitled to remove oneself from responsibility for others and the environmental and social consequences of one's privilege. We fantasize that this privilege can be extended to all, but this seems to be the height of self-deceit given the constraints that our ecological embeddedness entail. A politics of well-being requires us to ask questions about value and what can constitute a good life in a world mired in inequality and a system that seems to inevitably reproduce such inequalities. The good news is that to meet life's satisfactions—basic gifts of security and sustenance—we seem not to require lavish wealth; rather these gifts flow from the quality of relationships and the opportunity to participate and contribute meaningfully to shared endeavors, an insight developed usefully around the concept of cultural integrity by Burt Feintuch in this volume. We find these opportunities in the very forms that folklorists and ethnomusicologists have been interested in all along.

References

Assadourian, Erik. 2010. "The Rise and Fall of Consumer Cultures." In *State of the World 2010: Transforming Cultures from Consumerism to Sustainability*, Worldwatch Institute, 3–20. New York: W. W. Norton.

Baron, Robert. 2010. "Sins of Objectification? Agency, Mediation, and Community Cultural Self-Determination in Public Folklore and Cultural Tourism Programming." *Journal of American Folklore* 123 (487): 63–91.

Bauman, Richard, and Charles Briggs. 1990. "Poetics and Performance as Critical Perspectives on Language and Social Life." *Annual Review of Anthropology* 19:59–88.

Cantwell, Robert. 2001. "Folklore's Pathetic Fallacy." *Journal of American Folklore* 114 (451): 56–67.

Comaroff, Jean, and John L. Comaroff. 1989. "The Colonization of Consciousness in South Africa." *Economy and Society* 18 (3): 267–96.

Deleuze, Gilles, and Félix Guattari. 1987. *A Thousand Plateaus*. Minneapolis: University of Minnesota Press.

Farmer, P. 2007. "From Marvelous Momentum to Health Care for All—Success Is Possible with the Right Programs." *Foreign Affairs* 86:155–61.

Gibson-Graham, J. K. 2008. "Diverse Economies: Performative Practices for 'Other Worlds.'" *Progress in Human Geography* 32 (5): 613–32.

Gibson-Graham, J. K., and Gerda Roelvink. 2010. "An Economic Ethics for the Anthropocene." *Antipode* 41:320–46.

Glassie, Henry. 1989. *The Spirit of Folk Art: The Girard Collection at the Museum of International Folk Art*. New York: Abrams in association with the Museum of New Mexico, Santa Fe.

———. 1995. "Tradition." *Journal of American Folklore* 108 (430): 395–412.

———. 2011. "A Life of Learning." ACLS Occasional Paper 68. New York: American Council of Learned Societies.

Grober, Ulrich. 2007. "Deep Roots: A Conceptual History of 'Sustainable Development' (Nachhaltigkeit)." *WZB Discussion Paper P 2007-002* (February): 1–30.

Hawken, Paul. 2008. *Blessed Unrest: How the Largest Social Movement in History Is Restoring Grace, Justice, and Beauty to the World*. New York: Penguin Books.

Jackson, Michael. 1989. *Paths toward a Clearing: Radical Empiricism and Ethnographic Inquiry*. Bloomington: Indiana University Press.

———. 2009. *The Palm at the End of the Mind: Relatedness, Religiosity, and the Real*. Durham, NC: Duke University Press.

Latour, Bruno. 2013. *An Inquiry into Modes of Existence: An Anthropology of the Moderns*. Cambridge, MA: Harvard University Press.

———. 2017. "Anthropology at the Time of the Anthropocene: A Personal View of What Is to Be Studied." In *The Anthropology of Sustainability*, edited by Marc Brightman and Jerome Lewis, 35–50. New York: Palgrave Macmillan.

Marcus, George E., and Michael M. J. Fischer. 1999. *Anthropology as Cultural Critique: An Experimental Moment in the Human Sciences*. 2nd ed. Chicago: University of Chicago Press.

McKibben, Bill. 2007. *Deep Economy: The Wealth of Communities and the Durable Future*. New York: Henry Holt.

Rappaport, Roy A. 1999. *Ritual and Religion in the Making of Humanity*. Cambridge: Cambridge University Press.

Siegel, Daniel J. 2007. *The Mindful Brain: Reflection and Attunement in the Cultivation of Well-Being*. New York: W. W. Norton.

Steffen, W., P. J. Crutzen, and J. R. McNeill. 2007. "The Anthropocene: Are Humans Now Overwhelming the Great Forces of Nature?" *AMBIO: A Journal of the Human* 38 (8): 614–21.

Titon, Jeff Todd. 2008. "Knowing Fieldwork." In *Shadows in the Field: New Perspectives for Fieldwork in Ethnomusicology*, edited by Gregory Barz and Timothy J. Cooley, 25–41. New York: Oxford University Press.

———. 2015. "Sustainability, Resilience, and Adaptive Management for Applied Ethno-musicology." In *The Oxford Handbook of Applied Ethnomusicology*, edited by Svanibor Pettan and Jeff Todd Titon, 157–96. New York: Oxford University Press.

Turner, Edith. 2012. *Communitas: The Anthropology of Collective Joy*. New York: Palgrave Macmillan US.

Turner, Rory. 2014. "Talking about the Weather." Paper presented at AAA 2014, Washington, D.C. https://www.academia.edu/28231913/Talking_About_the_Weather.

Viveiros de Castro, Eduardo. 2004. "Perspectival Anthropology and the Method of Controlled Equivocation." *Tipití: Journal of the Society for the Anthropology of Lowland South America* 2 (1): 3–22.

Williams, Raymond. 1977. *Marxism and Literature*. Oxford: Oxford University Press.

Yates, Joshua J. 2012. "Abundance on Trial: The Cultural Significance of Sustainability." *Hedgehog Review* 14 (2): 1–8.

CHAPTER 4

Sounding Sustainable; or, The Challenge of Sustainability

AARON S. ALLEN

Sustainabilities

Sustainability is a terrible—and terribly important—term. In everyday, political, and scholarly discourse, *sustainability* reflects its etymological roots (*sus-tenere*, "up-hold") and means to endure, maintain, preserve, keep doing something. This "goal" of "dipped-in-amber stasis" is intended, as Andrew Zolli and Ann Marie Healy find in their critique of sustainability, "to achieve a broad equilibrium between humanity and our planet" (2012, 21). Yet *sustainability* also means to stop, change, do something different. How useful is a concept that is so inherently contradictory? Without being defined at every turn, the term is at constant risk of confusion and misinterpretation; if it is (re)defined continually, it may mean everything and nothing.

But perhaps never in the entire history of humanity has a keyword been so important. Through cultural practices developed over centuries—but that have come to a head particularly since the nineteenth century and have magnified especially after World War II—and through increasing global connectivity, certain humans are threatening all life-forms on planet Earth. Humanity's consumption of natural resources is out of control, our exploitation and decimation of other species are unraveling the biodiversity that knits together the planet, anthropogenic climate change will deprive subsequent generations of the gains made over centuries of human development, and our technologies (e.g., nuclear weapons, fossil fuels, and disposables) and the resulting pollution are threatening human and nonhuman life-forms in every niche of the planet. Globalized capitalism, especially of the deregulated kind known as neoliberalism, increases levels of inequity throughout the world, resulting in social strife that causes increasingly negative impacts on human cultural activities and the ecosystems that support them. These problems contribute to feedback loops with increasingly harsh consequences for people, more-than-human life, and the planet.[1]

Sustainability—when it means to change, to do something differently—has been called on to save life on the planet: to maintain human life on the planet for a long time, but also to stop limitless consumption and excessive pollution and instead adopt new and different practices that preserve the integrity of ecosystems and respect human dignity. I refer to this concept as "sustainability-change," which asks that we humans ensure that the environment is clean, healthy, and productive for all human and nonhuman life; create more socially just human relationships that diminish strife and increase fairness; formulate new ways of managing our economic and natural resources that are more responsible, very long term, and equitable; and support diverse human cultures and their practices that share meaning, fulfillment, value, and joy. Yet if we humans "sustain-maintain" our current lifestyles and dominant cultural practices without changing them radically, we will continue on a path toward the collapse of the natural systems that human societies need: defiling our own nests as we pollute and overconsume; increasing discontent and conflict between humans as our inequities become ever greater and harder to bridge; squandering long-term collective viability for short-term selfish profitability; and distancing human values from meaningful practices as we lose sight of important ethical perspectives. Sustainability-change reimagines modern human civilizations on new, potentially progressive paths; sustainability-maintain keeps us navigating our established, destructive routes. And if that were not bad enough, sometimes an appeal to sustainability-change is used as a guise for doing sustainability-maintain (otherwise known as "greenwashing," see Allen and Dawe 2016, 290).

Is an oxymoronic term such as *sustainability* up to the challenge? Ironically, given the enormity and diversity of the problems and solutions humanity faces, perhaps our only hope is such a debatable, incongruous, and complex term.

The challenges of sustainability are usually related to the physical, natural, and social sciences such as physics, chemistry, ecology, economics, and governance. But it is important to remember that humans do science, and humans are informed by culture—and human culture is in turn informed by our own science and technology (see White 1967). Neither scientific nor humanistic approaches have any claim to primacy; all must contribute to facing our self-made challenges. What roles are there for the arts and humanities in general and for music and sound studies in particular? Can we scholars in music and sound studies do more than just sound sustainable?

By "sounding sustainable" I intend a double entendre similar to the two sustainabilities described above. First, I do believe that sustainability research and activism are important in music. We can seek out sounds and music—realms that rely on cultural practices based in values—that embody and support the importance of sustainability-change, and we can advocate for musicians, sounds, communities, policies, and so on that preserve and promote such ethically informed and aesthetically valuable music, sounds, and ways of living. But, second, "sounding sustainable" is also a critique of a weak form of sustainability that uses the readily apparent meaning of *sustainability* (to preserve) without questioning the greater problems that may precipitate when we maintain cultural practices or that come as baggage with narrowly anthropocentric sustainability. Music scholars, especially ethnomusicologists and historical musicologists, often adopt a sense of conservatorship for what we study: we record, disseminate, and archive sonic traditions from people different from or similar to us, or we uncover, recreate, and promote music from the past in order to bring it into the present (see Titon 2015b). Individual scholarly goals may take other approaches, but our disciplines operate in a general sense to conserve, preserve, protect, appreciate, and maintain artistic practices from various traditions. In other words, we aim to sustain cultures.

But is that sustaining always good? Do we engage in that practice in a respectful and appropriate way that does no harm to humans or the more-than-human environment? Is what we are doing/studying/advocating ethical and just? And do we aim for sustainability-change or sustainability-maintain? Simple answers here are apparent, but I believe the situation is more complex and requires careful consideration. For surely we do not want to sustain cultural practices that waste natural resources, decimate biodiversity, contribute to climate change, create harmful pollution, and condone exploitative economic and social practices—from war and violence to slavery and colonialism—that exacerbate inequities and human strife. Yet some of the cultures we seek to sustain-maintain and some of the methods we use to sustain them can be correlated with negative outcomes we would rather not support.

This chapter is a critique of sustainability that, I hope, will encourage us to be better (not perfect) advocates of cultural sustainabilities, particularly with regard to ecomusicology, sound studies, and music. While I will problematize others' uses of sustainability, I must make it clear that I too am implicated in this critique. With an undergraduate environmental studies degree and a resume peppered with positions including the term *sustainability* (e.g., as my university's academic sustainability coordinator and as director of its Environment & Sustainability Program), I do use that weak meaning of sustainability-maintain that I critique (even in my Introduction to Sustainability course and throughout my published writings). But herein lies one particularly important role of the humanities in dealing with this problematic term: self-reflexivity that provides for a more robust, aware, and nuanced deployment of sustainability.

My aim with this chapter is to expand the idea of sustainability in music and sound studies in four connected ways. First, we must acknowledge the challenge of sustainability, get past the basic meaning "to endure," and use the term *sustainability* more robustly in its meanings of change. Second, the role of nature/environment is foundational. Third, more than a noun or verb, the word *sustainability* is better understood as a framework or lens. Finally, aesthetics is an important fourth element to add to standard three-part conceptions of sustainability.

Viewed through the lens of a change-oriented, environment-based sustainability, it is in aesthetics that music and sound studies have their most obvious importance. Music and sound scholars who engage in or with ecomusicology can make important contributions through the connection of ethics and aesthetics: we can demonstrate how listeners and music makers value sounds and therefore cultural actions, and we can show how those value actions exist in contexts that are ethically charged. When what we value is destructive to the planet and to other humans, we find ourselves faced with a fundamental challenge—a challenge, as with sustainability in general, that is potentially oxymoronic. We may not entirely meet this challenge, but we ignore it at our peril.

The Challenge of Sustainability

According to David W. Orr, the challenge of sustainability "is to avoid crossing irreversible thresholds that damage the life systems of Earth while creating long-term economic, political, and moral arrangements that secure the well-being of current and future generations" (2010, 68).[2] Orr is one of the most widely respected thinkers on sustainability: a distinguished academic with over two hundred publications (including seven books), he has consistently sought to break down barriers between theory and practice, particularly in his innovative design work and community engagement at Oberlin College. Orr advocates sustainability-change, not sustainability-maintain (see also Baron and Walker in this volume); to avoid those thresholds, humanity must change fundamental aspects of the way we operate on earth (see especially Orr 2010, 55–161). His use (and regular critique) of sustainability comes from this term's contemporary origins in regenerative agriculture as well as the social, economic, and political work connected to the United Nations' World Commission on Environment and Development (WCED). "Sustainable development" is the key concept of the seminal WCED report of 1987, known also as the "Brundtland Report" after WCED chair Gro Harlem Brundtland (former prime minister of Norway). The Brundtland Report definition is perhaps the most widespread understanding of sustainable development: "meet[ing] the needs of the present without compromising the ability of future generations to meet their own needs" (World Commission on Environment and Development 1987, 43). Orr's own formulation of the challenge of sustainability relies on this definition (and on the tripartite models described below), but his also differs from it (and them). In particular, he identifies an ambiguity in the WCED definition, which "confused sustainable growth, an oxymoron, and sustainable development, a possibility" (Orr 2010, 66; see also Titon 2015b, 170).

The contradictory sustainabilities I have outlined above are more complex than the simplistic, heuristic binary I established. Using the term *sustainable growth* is neither realistic on a finite planet nor is it a robust measure of health because continual growth is known by another term that no one likes to hear: *cancer*. A less negative way to think about growth is that it is merely quantifying accumulated activities that may be good or bad.[3] The term *sustainable development* is also contradictory but has somewhat less negative potential; it means to maintain progress, to keep improving—also an impossibility on a planet with limits, but something that is more likely when amended to mean focusing (as the WCED does) on people who have true needs to be met in particular places over a discernible timescale. (However, *development* can be interpreted differently in the real estate world, which leads to still further problems with the phrase.) Since the late 1980s, these two two-word phrases have been simplified to the single term *sustainability* (or its adjective form, *sustainable*)—and thus made even more ambiguous and subject to manipulation.

Sustainability is a complex, multivalent, and continually evolving idea.[4] As scholars, we must approach this misleadingly straightforward term with caution to avoid falling into unseemly traps—and to realize greater understanding and to achieve the goals we seek (whether those goals are to change or to maintain or to achieve something in between). When trying to do work that preserves culture, that keeps a practice alive (even allowing for it to change), we risk associating ourselves with sustainabilities that cloak themselves in ethical responsibility while undermining true benefits by providing gains for the few.

Sustainability is described regularly as a three-legged stool involving environment, equity, and economics (Herndl 2014, xxiii).[5] Said differently (and thus with different political intentions), these three realms are nature, society, and business, or differently still, planet, people, and profit. In each iteration of that trio involving humans and earth, one of the three stands out: the financial realm, which itself is but one facet of human societies on earth. That prominence gives undue equivalence to the idea that money makes the world go around for humans, or that efficiency is as important as planetary life-support systems or social and intergenerational equity. As a result of this critique of economy/business/profit in that three-part model, an upshot is a model involving hierarchical nested realms that has nature cradling society, which in turns envelopes economics. (And depending on the political position of the actor using such three-part thinking, we can infer different meanings of economics: from a more neutral idea of systems of exchange of goods and services in a place, to a more environmentally inflected idea of conservation of resources, to a Wall Street–inflected idea of business profit.) This standard three-part approach to a more robust, change-oriented sustainability—one that includes and may or may not equally balance concerns of ecological economics, social justice, and environmental conservation—is an important, if basic, step beyond the simplistic approach of sustainability-maintain.

Yet something is missing. Where do the arts and humanities fit into that tripartite model? Do those of us interested in music and sound concern ourselves primarily with questions of social justice, economic exchange, or the environment? Any field of inquiry beyond basic research should blur boundaries and not fit neatly into just one of these categories. But even if we might imagine our music and sound disciplines spread throughout all three areas, there still is no good fit here for those of us concerned with culture writ large. The tripartite model is inadequate. Alternatives have been offered: a fourth pillar of culture (see Hufford, this volume), of education, or of ethics, or even the broader interdisciplinary movement coalescing as the environmental humanities (Heise, Christensen, and Niemann 2017). Although recognizing no singular fix is possible, I propose another, alternative four-part model that adds the element of aesthetics, a concept that involves the arts, culture, education, ethics, and more—and that provides a pivot point for scholars of music and sound to leverage our contributions to confronting the challenge of sustainability. Rather than considering money as a linking or lubricating factor connecting environment (nature, planet) and humans (people, society, equity), it is instead the values (ethics) stemming from aesthetics that can link those areas of a sustainability framework.[6]

While I propose adding this fourth area of aesthetics, it is important to keep our sights on that most fundamental area, that largest realm, that most complex of ideas: nature. Widely critiqued and appropriately problematized, and even referred to as one of the most complex words in the English language (Williams 1985), *nature* at root refers to the physical environment of the planet that provides for all life, humans included. When we scholars focus solely on cultural practices, that is, when we are anthropocentric, we often overlook environmental factors that can contribute to the unraveling of human civilization and life on Earth. Ecomusicology emphasizes this problem: culture is already addressed in standard approaches to music and sound study, so incorporating environment/nature is a key additional approach that ecomusicology provides (Allen and Dawe 2016, 8–10). In essence, ecomusicology is sustainability studies of music and sound.

Jeff Todd Titon has been a central figure in ecomusicology. Titon studied the sciences in college and has long practiced organic gardening; it is no surprise, then, that he has been a pioneer in ecological approaches to the study of music (Allen, Titon, and Von Glahn 2014; Titon and Ostashewski 2014). After delivering a number of lectures and papers on the subject, he edited a groundbreaking special issue titled "Music and Sustainability" in *the world of music* (Titon 2009a). His introduction relies on sustainability to theorize a way for ethnomusicologists to understand the application of cultural management. Titon regards music as "a biocultural resource, a product of human life; further, it is a renewable resource.... In short, sustaining music means sustaining people making music" (2009b, 5–6). Titon argues that, "instead of heritage management, sustainability and stewardship appear more promising avenues for cultural policymaking, despite criticisms of those two concepts as well" (7). Ideas from conservation ecology—diversity, limits to growth, connectedness, and stewardship—are Titon's basis for an analogy between sustainability and cultural policy (2009c).[7] Besides this analogy and other examples about ecological matters, Titon here is not concerned with nature or environmental issues as they are connected to music.[8] The other five authors in the special edition all reference sustainability for their musical topics, but they do so using sustainability-maintain with no mention of environmental issues.[9] All six authors in "Music and Sustainability" make significant contributions to moving beyond corporatized heritage management and toward more ethically appropriate approaches to sustaining culture; they do so by focusing on the human realm of music making (such focus on the human is, of course, entirely normal in the *human*-ities). On the one hand, this anthropocentricism is positive because it can swing the pendulum in ecological sciences and environmental studies back to thinking about humans rather than spaces, places, and nonhuman species (something the environmental humanities are doing as well). But on the other hand, anthropocentricism can ignore environmental issues as related to music and sound and thus result in the same "unintended consequences" that Titon notes as being problematic (2009c, 121–27).

An ecomusicological example of these "unintended consequences" can be found in Western art music, in particular the materials necessary to sustain-maintain the classical tradition (Allen 2012). Fundamental to the sound of Western art music, the violin family forms the backbone of most ensembles from chamber to stage. Professional violins depend on at least two endemic natural resources: Brazilian pernambuco and Italian spruce. Bows are made from wild pernambuco that grows only in Brazil's Atlantic coastal forest. *Pau brasil* was so important that European colonial powers warred over it with one another and with indigenous peoples; eventually, the country Brazil was named after the wood. Today the tree is nearly extinct: 8 percent of the original forest is extant, and only 5 percent of pernambuco habitat remains. But Italian red spruce has fared better in the unusual alpine microclimate of the Val di Fiemme's Paneveggio Forest. The species is widely distributed, but Paneveggian spruce makes excellent resonance wood for soundboards. Stradivari used this primary material, and his creations have contributed to the renown of the Paneveggio, which is called the "forest of violins." Despite various threats during the past millennium, Fiemmesi traditions have preserved the forest; at the turn of the twenty-first century, more trees grow than loggers harvest. The values accorded to musical traditions and the instruments necessary for them can reverberate through individual tree species to particular forests. Western art music, sometimes seen as an endangered (elite) tradition in need of preservation (sustaining), contributes to both threatening and protecting the unique resources on which it depends. The unintended consequences of sustaining culture are contributions to the preservation *and* the destruction of forest environments.[10]

Since Titon's sustainability analogy of 2009, he has increasingly incorporated and advocated for a more robust understanding of sustainability in music to include nature and environment, hence acknowledging unintended environmental consequences in addition to social ones. His research blog, *Sustainable Music*, chronicles this transition, as do a number of his writings. In 2012 he observed, "It's all connected: music to sound, human to animal, culture to nature." (See also his discussion in Allen, Titon, and Von Glahn 2014.) In 2013 Titon engaged with the often polarized views of nature found in science and in critical theory to advocate that ecomusicologists face the challenges of the term *nature* and rely on "a relational epistemology of diversity, interconnectedness, and co-presence" so that "ecomusicology can work meaningfully towards sustaining music within the soundscape of life on planet Earth" (8). He has elaborated on those ideas in an illuminating study of Henry David Thoreau, finding a proto-ecomusicologist in that oft-studied environmental literary figure (Titon 2016b). In 2016–17 he was working toward a sound ecology, which he laid out in a keynote address to the Southwest Chapter of the American Musicological Society and a series of lectures at East Tennessee State University; this sound ecology is rooted in the environment, critical of neoliberal economics, dedicated to social justice, and focused on aesthetics (see also Titon 2015a and 2016a; the latter offers a brief example of his critique of ecological and environmental restoration efforts at sustainability-maintaining).

Titon's journey to and through sustainability has relied on his understanding of nature along with his increasingly focused concern about the environment and its fundamental relationship with human societies and cultural practices. This foundational relationship is made clear in the seminal document on sustainability; in the conclusion to the chapter on sustainable development, the authors of the WCED report emphasize that "in its broadest sense, the strategy for sustainable development aims to promote harmony among human beings and between humanity and nature" (World Commission on Environment and Development 1987, 65). When studying, deploying, advocating, or referencing sustainability in music studies, we too should move beyond analogy and rely on the foundational aspect of nature/environment. When advancing a sustainability-maintain argument, then, a more appropriate keyword might be *preservation* or *conservation* (although even these keywords have baggage; see Titon 2015b, 159–66, 167). And when advocating sustainability-change, the elements of our critique and the structure of our sustainability framework should make it clear that we seek to move beyond analogy and do more than simply maintain.

A Framework Including Aesthetics and Ethics

Titon's ideas of relational epistemology and sound ecology are powerful approaches to understanding and confronting the challenges of sustainability; with them, he demonstrates the foundational importance and relevance of environment/nature. Building on his and others' thinking, I propose a practical framework incorporating aesthetics to continue work toward that higher-level understanding. This framework helps address both the challenges of sustainability that Orr has articulated and the terminological quandaries I outlined above. Furthermore, it contrasts with Titon's own characterization of sustainability as a goal but not a process (2015b, 158). Rather than use *sustainability* as a noun (as something to achieve: "the sustainability of the symphonic tradition"), as an adjective (modifying something else: "sustainable lutherie"), or even as the more active verb (as in an exhortation: "we must sustain this soundscape"), I suggest using it as a framework—a prism, a lens, a filter, a theory—to analyze and solve cultural problems that impinge on and rely on nature. Rather than just saying one is concerned with or about the sustainability (preservation, continuation) of some music, sound, tradition, culture, and so on, one can use sustainability as a framework to analyze the situation (ask questions) and suggest future actions (pose answers), hence going from sustainability-maintain to sustainability-change in the same broad approach without making them mutually exclusive. Moreover, even when a life-form or cultural practice is provided with sustenance for the long term, it still may change and develop. We therefore do ourselves no favor by assuming that sustainability is something to achieve. Rather than a destination, sustainability is a journey; rather than a goal, sustainability is a process.

The sustainability framework I propose relies on the nested-realm model referenced above: environment (nature, the life support systems of the planet), equity (social justice, fairness in how others are treated), and economy (systems of exchange, responsible use), to which I add aesthetics (perceptions of beauty

and their correlated values). For each of these, a simple ethical prompt starts a
chain reaction of related questions: Is it right?

My previous example of violin woods (Allen 2012) can be used to flesh out
this framework.[11] The question to be asked in four variants is, are those elite
violins of the Western art music tradition right? With regard to the environment, the answer is yes and no: spruce forests are conserved (positive), while
forests home to pernambuco are not (negative). The destruction of one seems
to come at the expense of conserving the other: without the bow the violin is
worthless. But the choice is not a binary here, so could the violin be played with
different bows, with bows that are not so destructive? Could elite players use
alternative materials that might move the answer to the first question from "yes
and no" to "yes"? One common suggestion is to use carbon-fiber bows, but all
material choices have impacts: if the carbon comes from petroleum, we have not
come any closer to "yes" because petroleum is ultimately ancient sunlight and
therefore nonrenewable. Trees, however, are a potentially renewable resource
relying on current sunlight, so perhaps a more fully "yes" answer relies on the
model provided by spruce (i.e., find other woods to use for bows and steward
those resources responsibly). At this point the aesthetic question is most obvious. Elaborated from my starting point, the question becomes, with regard to
aesthetics, are pernambuco bows right for violins? Ask any violinist, and she
will tell you yes, of course, they are the best because they allow the player to
make the best sound. This misalignment between what is right for aesthetics and
for the environment provides the opportunity for change—and in this case, a
change in aesthetics is necessary to do what is right regarding the environment.

Are the elite violins of the Western art-music tradition right for equity, for the
economy? The answer to each of these questions is a similar "yes and no." The
Fiemmesi people benefit as a whole from their communal and democratically
controlled forest resources. But they are in a small, isolated, relatively culturally
homogenous area that contrasts with the large and diverse Atlantic coastal forest of Brazil. The Fiemmesi are not exploited to harvest, prepare, and sell their
wood products; on balance, the violin tradition and its associated mythology are
good for them. One might find similar examples for select Brazilian pernambuco
sources, but given the larger scale and more diverse cultural situation—namely,
the history of colonialism and slavery, the rapacious extraction of forest and
other natural resources in Brazil, and the ecological indicators pointing in negative directions—there are more problematic possibilities of poaching trees and
having a negative impact on pernambuco habitat. Thus, the violin (bow) is not
right for Brazilians when considering equity and economics. This conclusion
leads us back to those of environment and aesthetics: sustainability-change is
necessary even—especially—if we want to sustain-maintain the Western art
music tradition that relies on violins.

Aesthetics is not just what looks pretty or sounds nice. Rather, it is a philosophy of the senses, and it is through philosophy that aesthetics connects with culture and ultimately ethics: what is good, what is right, what we value. Aesthetics is etymologically derived from the Greek αἰσθητικός, "sentient." From sensing the world, we humans develop judgments (I like it / I don't like it) that lead to personal feelings (it's good / it's bad), which in turn lead to empathy; we connect with others who feel similarly. These connections inform communal values; we are more likely to support those things we value. So, for example, if I hear and like a violin, and if I therefore think it is good and want to connect with others who feel and think similarly, then we could come together around our shared values to support the musical cultures that make the sounds we like to hear. In essence, our scholarly communities of music and sound studies do something similar, which is why a fourth perspective of aesthetics is useful to a sustainability framework.[12] This simplistic aesthetic-ethic concatenation is complicated, however, when we learn that what we value causes economic and social injustice or that it damages the environment. Even if one casts aside ethics and rushes toward hedonism, thus disregarding injustices and environmental harms, the point remains: connections between aesthetics and ethics are relevant to sustainability, aesthetics therefore makes sense in a sustainability framework, and aesthetics are the entry point for music and sound studies.[13]

American naturalist Aldo Leopold (1887–1948), whose Wilderness Society eventually won passage of the landmark Wilderness Act in 1964, wrote of a "land ethic," which has become a central concept in environmental philosophy. "The land ethic simply enlarges the boundaries of the community to include soils, waters, plants, and animals, or collectively: the land" (Leopold [1949] 1989, 204). In this expansion of the concept of community from an anthropocentric to an ecocentric perspective (that still includes humans), Leopold exhorts us to "examine each question in terms of what is ethically and aesthetically right, as well as what is economically expedient. A thing is right when it tends to preserve the integrity, stability, and beauty of the biotic community. It is wrong when it tends otherwise" (224–25). In this influential formulation, Leopold expanded ethics from human social justice to include the entire animate and inanimate world (all the while criticizing business-as-usual economics); he also argued for including aesthetics via its connections with ethics. Leopold's approach is illustrative of the fourfold sustainability framework I advocate: an ecological environmentalism that expands equity to include humans and nonhumans, that recognizes the subordinate but nevertheless important role of appropriate economics, and that gives aesthetics a fundamental role in analyzing and addressing sustainability challenges.

The two sustainabilities—which I introduced as a simplistic binary in order to move beyond them—are, of course, fundamentally related: sustainability-

change seeks the sustainability-maintain of our species. Given we are neither a
perfect nor perfectible species, embracing the new paths of sustainability-change
will result inevitably in carrying with us habits from the old, well-trodden,
and sometimes problematic paths. Perhaps, then, we might acknowledge that
it is too much to expect the music- and sound-studies communities to engage
robustly with sustainability; we might just as well carry on as we always have,
or maybe at most we might give a tip of the hat to sustainability, as if it were a
fad. But given the stakes (human life on Earth), the passion and intellect within
our scholarly and artistic communities, and the importance of making sure that
what we seek to sustain robustly is both grounded in the laws of nature and allows for the important messiness of culture in general and of sound and music
study in particular, I believe that artists and scholars are up to the challenge.

Notes

1. This and the following paragraphs are my summaries of standard environmental
research and social development work regarding the health of the planet and human
populations on it. While most points would be elaborated in basic environmental studies textbooks, perhaps the most authoritative source is the United Nations Millennium
Ecosystem Assessment (MA), which involved contributions and peer reviews from
over 1,300 experts and culminated in a series of reports issued circa 2003–5 (one is
Alcamo, Bennet, and Millennium Ecosystem Assessment 2003). Another project of
United Nations Environment (formerly the UN Environment Programme, UNEP) is
the Intergovernmental Panel on Climate Change (IPCC), which since 1988 has been
a joint project with the World Meteorological Organization to assess climate change
and its impacts. While the MA concluded in 2005, the IPCC continues issuing regular reports. Related to both are the United Nation's Sustainable Development Goals
of 2016, which in turn replaced the Millennium Development Goals of 2000–2015.
See also the United Nations' WCED (1987) as well as Orr (2010) and Klein (2014).
Nobel Prize laureate Paul Crutzen (2002) is in part responsible for popularizing the
term Anthropocene, which identifies the Industrial Revolution as the beginning of the
human-caused planetary impacts described here. As Klein (2014) points out, however,
not all humans do the causing; some—particularly fossil-fuel producers and users—are
more culpable than others.

2. Herndl's anthology chronicles a number of other "challenges of sustainability," but
he also identifies a general one as an umbrella concept: "making the invisible visible"
(2014, xxiv). Sustainability, he says, can be invisible because of the complexities of time
(the difficulties in knowing the future) and space (the problem of consequences being
felt far from actions) and because of just how ordinary some issues are (we take for
granted air, water, food, and shelter, yet they are threatened resources).

3. A common measure of growth is "economic growth," which is representative of the
fundamental problems of using the term *growth*. The GDP (gross domestic product),
which measures economic growth, is flawed—and demonstrably destructive to the human endeavor (Philipsen 2015).

4. McCallum and his colleagues (2016) report that the concept of sustainability can be traced to the early twelfth century and that the United Nations has identified approximately one hundred different definitions of the term. They also demonstrate stable interest in sustainability circa 2004–14 (via a large data set of web searches including over three hundred related terms) while interest in environmental issues declined. Warde (2011) found a sixteenth-century basis for the concept of sustainability but nevertheless argued for a late eighteenth- and nineteenth-century basis (in agricultural sciences) for the twentieth-century concept. Caradonna (2014) traces the history of sustainability from forestry in the seventeenth century through the Industrial Revolution to the environmental movement of the twentieth century as it has moved from the margins to dominating national and international policy.

5. Sustainability may also be represented as a three-part Venn diagram, three nested baskets, or three pillars (see Hufford in this volume, who suggests that "culture" is a fourth pillar). For a sense of the diverse ways sustainability is visualized and conceptualized, consult Mann (2009). The circa 250 images and schematics collected in his article give a sense of the diversity as well as the recurrence of the themes outlined in this paragraph. See also Allen, Titon, and Von Glahn (2014).

6. For an example of a sustainability framework in action, see Reganold and Wachter (2016), who analyze organic agriculture with a four-part sustainability model that includes environmental impact, economic viability, social well-being, and productivity (the first three being the usual components, with the last an additional one that is relevant for their subject). Furthermore, Peterson outlines the standards of the three-part approach and criticizes additions by noting that "forcing complex and unprecedented socio-environmental problems into three, four, or seven distinct containers represents an outdated, unduly modernist way of problem-solving that tends to approach environmental, economic, and social issues as independent, and consequently, their solutions as separate" (2016, 3). I agree with this critique, and I agree with Peterson's proposition of a "new research practice in sustainability [that] proposes an integrated concept whereby 'social issues' are indistinguishable and inseparable from economic or environmental issues and vice versa" (3). Nevertheless, for heuristic and activist purposes, I find it necessary to incorporate a fourth category of aesthetics both because of the usual exclusion of this category and because I want to emphasize its usefulness as a platform for including the arts and humanities—and the associated aesthetics and values—in strong sustainability discourse. (I also agree with Hufford's proposal elsewhere in this volume to add culture as a fourth pillar of sustainability; I do not find our approaches mutually exclusive, nor do I find them at odds with critiques of additions to the sustainability "triumvirate.") Similar to Peterson's (2016) critique, Colocousis and his colleagues (2017) argue against using normative considerations in a sustainability framework (they find the inclusion of values to be a distraction from otherwise laudable goals). Instead, they advocate for purely functional considerations of sustainability. And my response to them is similar to my response to Peterson: while I agree that the subjective (normative, qualitative, ethical, etc.) can distract from objective (positive, quantitative, factual) matters, I find their mixing to be normal in the world. Moreover, I find that mixing necessary for heuristic purposes and for advocating the inclusion of practitioners in the arts and humanities.

A more thorough response to these issues is beyond the scope of this chapter, but such a response could involve either a critique that suggests collapsing the sustainability framework into only two realms (the human, which would include the cultural/aesthetic issues along with those of economics and equity, and the environmental, which would include everything else—along with the human) or a less articulated but potentially more intellectually robust collapsing of all binaries and divisions (which may still suffer from a narrow perspective).

7. Conservation biologists discussed and debated the shortcomings and usefulness of *sustainability* in the multiauthor "Conservation Forum" (2005).

8. It is important to note that in his essays in *the world of music*, Titon made a number of references to environmental and ecological issues. The publication of the special issue was certainly not the beginning of Titon's engagement with matters environmental. For example, his 1988 book includes a chapter on "Land and Life" that considers relationships between culture, agriculture, and ecology in the northern Blue Ridge Mountains.

9. This same approach was common at the 2010 Annual Meeting of the Society for Ethnomusicology in Los Angeles. The conference theme was "Sound Ecologies," which resulted in many (but not all) presenters using *ecology* as a mere synonym for *connections*—connections that had nothing to do with nature or the environment, which is the central subject of study in ecology. Another situation that mixed various approaches either including or excluding ecology, environment, and/or sustainability-maintain (lacking environmental concerns) is evident in Bendrups and Schippers (2015). Furthermore, Schippers and Grant (2016) used ecology and sustainability as mere metaphor to theorize and study musical traditions in the context of endangerment, preservation, and safeguarding as related, for example, to various conventions of the United Nations Educational, Scientific and Cultural Organization (see also Allen 2017).

10. Similar stories could be told for *grenadilla/mpingo* (*Dalbergia melanoxylon*) for clarinets, flutes, oboes, bagpipes, and so on, or for rosewood and ebony for guitars (which was in the US news circa 2011–12, when Gibson Guitar was raided and fined for using illegal tropical hardwoods). But sustainability challenges also come up with regard to more common woods, such as spruce from Alaska, as chronicled in the film *Musicwood* (2013).

11. The material basis for music is an obvious entree into sustainability studies of music—Allen and Libin (2014), Dawe (2016), Devine (2015), Ryan (2015), and Smith (2016) have also engaged with musical materials regarding sustainability. I propose that any cultural aspect of music or sound study, no matter how intangible, can engage with this framework: ultimately, all human activities rely on, are based on, and are part of nature. Nevertheless, most music and sound scholars are unapologetically anthropocentric and ignore foundational environmental/natural elements. For successful advocacy of cultural sustainability, we must continuously make, analyze, and articulate the fundamental connections between culture and nature.

12. A related upshot in music scholarship involves a coming together regarding concerns for human rights and cultural rights, as for example in Peddie (2011) and Weintraub and Yung (2009).

13. I am by no means the first to make the claim that aesthetics has a role in sustain-

ability. For example, the UNEP's MA addressed aesthetics with regard to the cultural services of nature (Alcamo, Bennet, and Millennium Ecosystem Assessment 2003), and its related organization in the United Nations, the UNEP, incorporated aesthetics, cultural values, religion, and tourism throughout its programs. See also Iared, Torres de Oliveira, and Payne (2016). Hosey even proclaims that productively joining aesthetics and sustainability "could save the planet" (2012, 7).

References

Alcamo, Joseph, Elena M. Bennett, and Millennium Ecosystem Assessment (Program). 2003. *Ecosystems and Human Well-Being: A Framework for Assessment*. Washington, DC: Island Press.

Allen, Aaron S. 2012. "'Fatto di Fiemme': Stradivari's Violins and the Musical Trees of the Paneveggio." In *Invaluable Trees: Cultures of Nature, 1660–1830*, edited by Laura Auricchio, Elizabeth Heckendorn Cook, and Giulia Pacini, 301–15. Oxford: Voltaire Foundation.

———. 2017. Review of *Sustainable Futures for Music Cultures: An Ecological Perspective*, edited by Huib Schippers and Catherine Grant. *Ethnomusicology Forum*, November 8. http://www.tandfonline.com/doi/full/10.1080/17411912.2017.1395288.

Allen, Aaron S., and Kevin Dawe, eds. 2016. *Current Directions in Ecomusicology: Music, Culture, Nature*. New York: Routledge.

Allen, Aaron S., and Laurence Libin. 2014. "Sustainability." In *Grove Dictionary of Musical Instruments*. New York: Oxford University Press.

Allen, Aaron S., Jeff Todd Titon, and Denise Von Glahn. 2014. "Sustainability and Sound: Ecomusicology inside and outside the University." *Music and Politics* 8 (2). http://dx.doi.org/10.3998/mp.9460447.0008.205.

Bendrups, Dan, and Huib Schippers, eds. 2015. "Sound Futures: Exploring Contexts for Music Sustainability." Special issue, *the world of music (new series)* 4 (1).

Caradonna, Jeremy L. 2014. *Sustainability: A History*. New York: Oxford University Press.

Colocousis, Chris R., Cesar J. Rebellon, Nick Smith, and Stefan Sobolowski. 2017. "How Long Can We Keep Doing This? Sustainability as a Strictly Temporal Concept." *Journal of Environmental Studies and Sciences* 7 (2): 274–87.

"Conservation Forum." 2005. *Conservation Biology* 19 (1): 23–44.

Crutzen, Paul J. 2002. "Geology of Mankind." *Nature* 415 (6867): 23–23.

Dawe, Kevin. 2016. "Materials Matter: Towards a Political Ecology of Musical Instrument Making." In Allen and Dawe 2016, 109–21.

Devine, Kyle. 2015. "Decomposed: A Political Ecology of Music." *Popular Music* 34 (3): 367–89.

Heise, Ursula K., Jon Christensen, and Michelle Niemann. 2017. *The Routledge Companion to the Environmental Humanities*. New York: Routledge.

Herndl, Carl George. 2014. *Sustainability: A Reader for Writers*. New York: Oxford University Press.

Hosey, Lance. 2012. *The Shape of Green: Aesthetics, Ecology, and Design*. Washington, DC: Island Press.

Iared, Valéria Ghisloti, Haydée Torres de Oliveira, and Phillip G. Payne. 2016. "The

Aesthetic Experience of Nature and Hermeneutic Phenomenology." *Journal of Environmental Education* 47 (3): 191–201.

Klein, Naomi. 2014. *This Changes Everything: Capitalism vs. the Climate*. New York: Simon and Schuster.

Leopold, Aldo. (1949) 1989. *A Sand County Almanac, and Sketches Here and There*. New York: Oxford University Press.

Mann, Samuel. 2009. "Visualising Sustainability." *Computing for Sustainability*, March 15. https://computingforsustainability.com/2009/03/15/visualising-sustainability/.

McCallum, Malcolm L., Lori Andrew, Daniel Arndt, Nick Beristain, Tiffany Cass, Tiffany Clow, et al. 2016. "Changes in United States' Citizens' Interest in Sustainability (2004–2014)." *Life: The Excitement of Biology* 4 (3): 138–64.

Musicwood. 2013. Documentary. Directed by Maxine Trump. http://musicwoodthefilm.com.

Orr, David W. 2010. *Hope Is an Imperative: The Essential David Orr*. Washington, DC: Island Press.

Peddie, Ian, ed. 2011. *Popular Music and Human Rights*. 2 vols. Burlington, VT: Ashgate.

Peterson, Nicole. 2016. "Introduction to the Special Issue on Social Sustainability: Integration, Context, and Governance." *Sustainability: Science, Practice & Policy* 12 (1): 3–7.

Philipsen, Dirk. 2015. "GDP's Wicked Spell," *Chronicle of Higher Education*, June 15. https://www.chronicle.com/article/GDPs-Wicked-Spell/230881.

Reganold, John, and Jonathan M. Wachter. 2016. "Organic Agriculture in the Twenty-First Century." *Nature Plants* 2 (February): 1–8.

Ryan, Robin. 2015. "'Didgeri-Doos' and 'Didgeri-Don'ts': Confronting Sustainability Issues." *Journal of Music Research Online* 6 (August). http://www.jmro.org.au/index.php.

Schippers, Huib, and Catherine Grant, eds. 2016. *Sustainable Futures for Music Cultures: An Ecological Perspective*. New York: Oxford University Press.

Smith, Alex. 2016. "New Musical Contexts for More Sustainably-Made Marimbas." *Percussive Notes Online Research Edition* 1 (December): 32–42.

Titon, Jeff Todd. 1988. *Powerhouse for God: Speech, Chant, and Song in an Appalachian Baptist Church*. Austin: University of Texas Press.

———, ed. 2009a. "Music and Sustainability." Special Issue, *the world of music* 51 (1).

———. 2009b. "Economy, Ecology, and Music: An Introduction." *the world of music* 51 (1): 5–15.

———. 2009c. "Music and Sustainability: An Ecological Viewpoint." *the world of music* 51 (1): 119–37.

———. 2012. "A Sound Commons for All Living Creatures." *Smithsonian Folkways Magazine*, Fall–Winter. https://folkways.si.edu/.

———. 2013. "The Nature of Ecomusicology." *Música e Cultura* 8 (1): 8–18.

———. 2015a. "Exhibiting Music in a Sound Community." *Ethnologies* 37 (1): 13–41.

———. 2015b. "Sustainability, Resilience, and Adaptive Management for Applied Ethnomusicology." In *The Oxford Handbook of Applied Ethnomusicology*, edited by Svanibor Pettan and Jeff Todd Titon, 157–95. New York: Oxford University Press.

———. 2016a. "The Song of the Loon—Is It Sustainable?" *Sustainable Music* (blog). July 25. https://sustainablemusic.blogspot.com.

———. 2016b. "Why Thoreau?" In Allen and Dawe 2016, 69–79.

Titon, Jeff Todd, and Marcia Ostashewski. 2014. "A Context for the Story: A Conversation with Jeff Todd Titon (with Marcia Ostashewski)." *MUSICultures* 41 (2): 170–83.

Warde, Paul. 2011. "The Invention of Sustainability." *Modern Intellectual History* 8 (1): 153–70.

Weintraub, Andrew N., and Bell Yung, eds. 2009. *Music and Cultural Rights*. Chicago: University of Illinois Press.

White, Lynn. 1967. "The Historical Roots of Our Ecologic Crisis." *Science*, n.s., 155 (3767): 1203–7.

Williams, Raymond. 1985. *Keywords: A Vocabulary of Culture and Society*. New York: Oxford University Press. First published 1976 by Fontana Press.

World Commission on Environment and Development. 1987. *Our Common Future*. Oxford: Oxford University Press.

Zolli, Andrew, and Ann Marie Healy. 2012. *Resilience: Why Things Bounce Back*. New York: Free Press.

PART 2

Responding to Anthropogenic Change

CHAPTER 5

Garbage Truck Music and Sustainability in Contemporary Taiwan

From Cockroaches to Beethoven and Beyond

NANCY GUY

A *WALL STREET JOURNAL* HEADLINE recently proclaimed the Taiwanese people to be the "World's Geniuses of Garbage Disposal" (May 17, 2016). In its description of Taipei's garbage collection routine, the *WSJ* begins: "The music arrives first: a tinny version of the Polish classic 'A Maiden's Prayer,' followed by two canary-yellow garbage trucks, then two open-bed recycling trucks. As the caravan pulls into the residential square, people scurry forward lugging bags and buckets, grocery carts and flatbed carts, all filled with trash" (Chen 2016). The sights and sounds of Taiwan's unique system for the collection of household waste has been the frequent subject of foreign writers in the popular press and in blogs. Music tends to be the focus of the greatest fascination since unsuspecting expats often imagine that the garbage truck's music announces the arrival of ice cream trucks as such "tinny" sounding melodies do in many parts of the world.

Faced with limited space for landfill, Taiwan has over the decades developed a system for waste disposal and reuse that has brought the recycling rate in the capital city of Taipei to 67 percent in 2015 and 55 percent island wide (Chen 2016).[1] This places Taiwan on par with international leaders in sustainability such as Austria, Germany, and South Korea. Music is integral to the collection of household waste throughout Taiwan. The most frequently heard tune broadcast by garbage trucks is Bądarzewska's "Maiden's Prayer" with Beethoven's "Für Elise" running a close second. The "Maiden's Prayer" is not only the most ubiquitous but also the first "garbage melody" used when prerecorded music replaced bells to announce the arrival of municipal garbage collectors. According to a report in the *Economic Daily News* (*Jingji ribao*) (January 19, 1968), the melody was introduced along with the modern, rear-loader garbage trucks (called *mifeng che*, or "sealed trucks," after the mechanism that closes to crush garbage), which first went into service in January 1968. The music came preloaded on tapes when the trucks arrived from Japan (*Economic Daily News*, November 24, 1968).

I have yet to piece together definitively when or how Beethoven's "Für Elise" came into use. Back in June 2005, I visited the Environmental Protection Division of the Taipei City government in a quest to get to the bottom of the garbage-melody conundrum. Tsung Tien Lee, a subdivision chief, told me that all the people who knew the history had retired, but he believes that "Für Elise" was added by mistake when an office worker took home an LP of piano classics to record tapes for use in the city's garbage trucks. The album included both the Beethoven and the Bądarzewska pieces, and he recorded the wrong piece. Thus Beethoven possibly became part of Taiwan's garbage collection ritual through a process no grander than worker error. Lee did not know precisely when "Für Elise" joined the garbage brigade. The earliest mention of it in the *United Daily News* database is in 2001. Ironically, this appears in an article about a Chinese-language speech contest for foreign students in which one of the contestants said that her deepest impression of Taiwan had to be of its garbage trucks and their broadcasting of "Für Elise" (Cai 2001).

In Taipei, recycling trucks, which follow behind the garbage trucks, broadcast "Are There Empty Wine Bottles to Sell?," the theme song from the 1983 award-winning Taiwanese film *Papa, Can You Hear Me Sing?*[2] Different municipalities sometimes elect to deviate from the capital city's garbage-collection playlist. Therefore, as the details of waste collection, including the music used, vary from municipality to municipality, this chapter focuses specifically on the garbage-pickup routine as it is currently executed in Taipei City.[3]

The everyday habits and practices surrounding garbage pickup, including its signature melodies, have seeped into a wide range of sensibilities in contemporary Taiwan. As Gay Hawkins argues in her book *The Ethics of Waste*, "Styles of waste disposal . . . are also styles of self; in managing waste we constitute an ethos and a sensibility. Our waste habits—all those repeated routines—leave their traces on our bodies and our environment" (2006, 15). In Taiwan traces are also left in many forms of artistic creation, including literature, theater, film, performance art, and new music. This chapter focuses on the presence of such sensibilities in the text and music of popular songs dating from the 1980s to the present.[4]

For many people living in Taiwan, garbage and the routine of its collection are a vital thread in the tapestry of daily life in a way that is simply not the case for most Americans. Taiwan is a semitropical island that is host to a human population numbering over 23.4 million, most of whom live in urban areas. The capital, Taipei, is one of the most densely populated cities in the world. Due to the tight quarters, Taipei residents generally cannot store their garbage outside their living area, unlike most Americans, who place their waste in large bins located outside in a garage, patio, or alley, where it awaits weekly pickup. In Taipei, garbage brigades spread out across the city five nights a week stopping at more than four thousand different collection points.

Taiwan's humid and warm climate, which accelerates decomposition, is especially hospitable to rats and several types of cockroaches, including those that measure over an inch in length and fly. All these factors combine to make municipal waste collection a pressing event. Missing the evening garbage pickup means risking the intrusion of cockroaches or rats into one's living space. Staying late in the office poses the risk of missing pickup. Eating a late-night snack at home presents a conundrum. What to do with the left over morsels or dirty wrappings? In my Taiwanese friend's home, where I used to stay on visits under several weeks in duration, our custom was to keep garbage generated after pickup in the refrigerator. This practice is widespread as is shifting rubbish to the home of a friend or relative who has a later garbage pickup or an alternative system for collection such as those in upscale, high-rise buildings.

The anxieties surrounding garbage and its collection resonate in a surprisingly large number of popular songs. To date, I have gathered more than eighty songs in which garbage is referenced. Textual references range from a single mention of garbage in a love song to a major theme in a dystopian ballad. References are not limited to text. Bądarzewska's or Beethoven's melodies are sometimes quoted intact while they have also provided the motivic material out of which a song's main melodic material is crafted. The title of Beethoven's "Für Elise" is referenced in the text in one song (without making a musical appearance), while it provides the title of another pop song along with a good portion of its melodic material.

Garbage in a Dystopian World

What is likely the earliest reference to garbage in Taiwan's popular music is singer/songwriter Luo Dayou's "Super Citizens," which was released in 1984 when Taiwan's environmental movement was gaining in strength. Luo takes garbage as evidence of failure on the part of both average citizens and the government to protect the environment when he sings of garbage drifting down the Tamsui River and smoke rising from a burning garbage dump. The theme of garbage as a symbol of environmental degradation continues today.

TRANSLATION OF THE FIRST STANZA OF "SUPER CITIZENS."
WORDS AND MUSIC BY LUO DAYOU.

That year when we were sitting beside the Tamsui River, in front of our
    eyes, we saw Taipei's garbage drifting past.
Thick smoke blowing from the distance; the garbage mountain has
    launched a firework celebration, and we cheer!
Dear citizens of Taipei, flourishing Taipei City, there will always be more
    garbage to burn; everyone works together with a single purpose.

An overview of songs that touch on the theme of environmental degradation shows that the severity of the pollution varies from song to song. In rocker Wu Bai's nostalgic 1992 song "Big Buildings," garbage strewn by the roadside is just one of the characteristic features of Taipei along with its tall buildings, grit in the air, chaotic traffic, and delicious food. By contrast, She Wenbin's 2000 release "Home Sweet Home" paints the picture of a landscape turned hazardscape.[5] While the lyrics at first sound positive and welcoming, "Come here to live! We welcome you to the beautiful capital city," She's melancholic singing foretells the despairing mood of the following line: "Garbage in the front, a mountain in the back, erosion turns a light drizzle into a two-foot-high flood." The rest of the first stanza describes an environment devastated by unwise development: gravel trucks roar past, a chemical plant operates just next door, overhead high-voltage wires hum loudly. The second stanza criticizes self-interested politicians. All of this is prefaced by the song's introduction, which is a celesta playing a dreamy-sounding setting of Bądarzewska's "Maiden's Prayer." The signature melody of Taipei's garbage trucks cast the entire scene as one of rubbish and decay, both social and material.

In his 2006 release "Garbage Mountain beside My House," Zhang Yuwei sings of how a garbage dump near his home has turned the area into a toxic hazardscape: neither grass nor flowers will grow. The stench-filled air traps him inside his house. The hazardscape is global in several songs, including Yuan Zhicheng's 2010 "Did You See?" Here, garbage flows down rivers and streams in a world that is out of balance, a world plagued by droughts and floods, where flowers bloom out of season and cockroaches and rats roam fearlessly.

It is not surprising to find garbage mentioned in songs with ecological themes. I have identified more than twenty such songs. Even more songs, which do not specifically mention garbage, have been produced in recent decades on the theme of environmental degradation, such as superstar Jay Chou's 2003 hit "Terraced Fields" and pop idol J. J. Lin's apocalyptic hit "Brave New World" released in 2014.[6]

In his book *Ecomusicology: Rock, Folk, and the Environment*, Mark Pedelty asks, "Where are all the environmental songs?" (2012, 45). He notes that popular musicians "have a tendency to avoid environmental themes" (46), and if they do take up activists themes, it tends to be "only after achieving star status" (47). Finally, Pedelty observes that "relatively few world-famous musicians are performing songs about environmental issues" (45). The English-language world of popular music about which Pedelty writes contrasts starkly with Taiwan's popular music scene, where songs on environmental themes are not rare. They are released by artists at all stages of their careers; some are superstars, albeit in the Chinese-speaking world, including Luo Dayou, Wu Bai, Zhang Huimei, and Jay Chou.[7]

Singing of Garbage and Love

I turn my attention away from songs with overtly ecological themes to love songs in order to illustrate some of the ways in which a garbage consciousness has permeated multiple facets of daily life in Taiwan. One might expect love songs to be garbage-free since they are so often apolitical and set in placeless zones. However, over a third of Taiwan's garbage songs involve romantic love. Love songs comprise the vast majority of pop music sung in Mandarin Chinese. Of these, more than half are about breaking up (Moskowitz 2010, 71). Wang Hsiao-fan's 2010 song "Recycling Truck" is about a breakup, yet she frames her experience entirely in terms of waste management. Though Beethoven's "Für Elise," one of the familiar refrains from Taiwan's waste-collection soundscape, isn't heard in this song, the narrator references it by name as she goes about sorting through the remnants of her failed relationship. "Für Elise" is a silent reminder that drives the perpetual sorting and separating of all manner of garbage, be it material or emotional. The song opens with the narrator playfully explaining that she wants to be fashionable when she embarks on her daily routine of chasing the garbage truck. Managing garbage and recyclable waste quickly become analogies for matters of the heart. A bad lover is unrecyclable garbage. The left over odds and ends of a broken relationship must be sorted. Photos go in the paper recycling; memories go in the general garbage; tears cannot be so easily discarded. Most importantly, she reminds herself that old lovers can't be recycled. After all, they are garbage, and she's not a recycling truck.

TRANSLATED EXCERPTS FROM "RECYCLING TRUCK."
WORDS BY WANG XIAOFAN. MUSIC BY FAN ZHEZHONG.

At the same time every day,
I keep on chasing the garbage truck,
We don't toss garbage randomly on the ground.

Old photos into the paper bin,
Old memories into the garbage,
I must remember that an old lover can't be recycled

"Für Elise" keeps on spinning,
Sigh—life is continually reorganized,
Tossing everything away with a single breath.
. . .

You are garbage and I am not the recycling truck.
. . .

There's only one earth, I also am a one and only,
I continue chasing after the garbage truck.

While Wang sings that she is not a recycling truck, the narrator in superstar boy band Mayday's 2004 song "Garbage Truck" sings that he *is* a garbage
truck. The association between garbage pickup and youthful love is first suggested when the song opens with a solo cello's upbeat rendition of Bądarzewska's
"Maiden's Prayer." The narrator's identification with garbage trucks becomes
clear in the refrain where he sings, "I'm your garbage truck. I'll be there every
day to listen to you sing. . . . If you're unhappy, I'll be your garbage truck. I'll
be there every day to hear you vent." With this simple refrain, two important
themes that are shared in much of the body of Taiwanese garbage songs present
themselves. First, the arrival of the garbage brigade is a regular and expected
event. It marks time in the evening as gongs and drums once marked the night
watch in traditional China. Second, garbage trucks carry away all manner of
waste, including emotional and material.

The regularity of garbage pickup has become a standard against which the
purging of other forms of waste is compared. In Sandee Chan's emotionally raw
song "Forgotten," from 1997, Chan equates the emotional baggage left over from
a breakup with garbage and sings that it cannot be disposed of with the ease of
a regularly scheduled trash pickup. In the music video that accompanied the
song's release, a garbage truck appears as she sings the line, "Emotional garbage
cannot be disposed of promptly at 7:45 pm." The time, of course, references the
garbage pickup schedule.

A couple sweetly bartering over who will take out the garbage is the central
theme of Waterman and Zheng Beiyi's song and video "I Love Elise." The title
is an obvious reference to Beethoven's melody, which figures prominently in
the song. After we hear the truck's ignition turning over, a solo guitar plays
Beethoven's "Für Elise" as the song's introduction. Later we hear the melody as
it is broadcast from a garbage truck. Released in 2010, like Wang Hsiao-fan's
"Recycling Truck," "I Love Elise" also mentions dressing up to take out the gar-

bage. Garbage pickup is a moment of community gathering. It is the only time in the day when neighbors come down from their multistoried apartments and meet in one location. As Zheng sings, "Neither Paris, London, New York City, nor Tokyo has anything like this." Garbage trucks supply the soundtrack for this unique community practice. The roar of their engines and the sound of their music have become "soundmarks" in the sense identified by R. Murray Schafer in that members of the community recognize them as making "the acoustic life of the community unique" (1977, 10).

This small sampling of songs that narrate themes of romantic love and break-ups illustrate some of the ways in which an awareness of garbage and its regular pickup has penetrated the everyday consciousness in Taiwan.

"Garbage People" and Social Justice

The body of Taiwanese popular music includes many more references to garbage and/or garbage truck melodies. Furthermore, there are other thematic subjects involving garbage that I do not have space to introduce in this chapter. The interrelated subjects of economic, social, and environmental justice represent one such theme. Average citizens must do the work of sorting their domestic waste into the numerous categories demanded by Taipei's current garbage collection protocol, and, of course, they must deliver it to the garbage brigade. Wealthy people, however, often live in high-rise buildings where maintenance workers not only dispose of garbage but, in some cases, even sort through it for their well-to-do patrons. Not having to trouble oneself with the waste management has, therefore, become a marker of high economic status. Rap artist MC HotDog comments on this phenomenon when he complains in his 2012 hit "Ghetto Superstar" that he is so poor that he has to take out his own garbage. He raps, "It's 7:45 and I have to take out the garbage."[8]

Released in late 2013, Chen Jianwei's song "Garbage People" and the animated video that accompanies it brilliantly combine the issue of waste collection with themes of social, economic, and environmental justice.[9] Musically, the opening five beats of Beethoven's "Für Elise" provide the material for the song's first full melody; this motif also acts as an occasional accompaniment figure. With "Garbage People," the villainous elite (i.e., those whose greed and corruption directly harm average people and the environment) are garbage personified. The story unfolds in a neat and clean village, where common folks can be seen heading out with bags to meet the garbage truck. However, a street sign using variants of both the English and the Taiwanese words for garbage ("Garbega" and "Bung so ji lo") signals trouble and is the focus for several seconds near the video's beginning. The "garbage people" about whom Chen sings are politicians and wealthy businessmen who are greedy, power hungry, and have no respect for the community or individuals. Several vignettes identify these villains. They include a businessman, who runs a factory that produces poison soy sauce and who bribes a campaigning politician; a rich and drunken sports-car driver who runs into an old woman and then kicks her repeatedly; and a backhoe that destroys the homes of protesting villagers. As the story unfolds, an average villager (whose costume bears the Chinese character *tai* for "Taiwan" as he transforms into a hero) springs into action when he witnesses multiple forms of injustice. In each vignette, he punches the villains and bags them; villagers then toss the bags onto garbage trucks, and they are dumped onto a massive garbage mountain (which, not incidentally, also includes illegally dumped nuclear waste). This piece was inspired by multiple real-life events, including a series of tragic clashes in the village of Dapu in Miaoli County related to the government's forced sale of private land. These events climaxed in 2013 with the suicide of a former homeowner.[10]

Conclusion: Music as Part of a Sustainable Assemblage

What is the significance of garbage being referenced so frequently, colorfully, and with the intimacy found in Taiwanese popular music? Based on my findings, I believe that the "garbage consciousness" exhibited in pop songs points to an assemblage, in the sense outlined by Jane Bennett in *Vibrant Matter*. For Bennett, an assemblage is an ad hoc grouping "of diverse elements, of vibrant materials of all sorts" (2010, 23). In Taiwan, humans intersect multiple times on a daily basis with co-actants in an assemblage of which material waste is central. Building on the notion of "actant" from Bruno Latour, Bennett defines an actant as a "source of action that can be either human or nonhuman" (viii). Actants have efficacy to do things, things that "make a difference, produce effects, and alter the course of events" (viii). Nonhuman actants in what I term the "garbage assemblage" might include a greasy bag that once contained lunch, a cockroach scurrying across the kitchen floor, or the garbage truck and its music as they pass by in the evening. All these actants tug at the consciousness of human dwellers, including songsters. As mentioned in this chapter's opening, Taiwan's hot and humid climate—which is also an actant—brings a keen awareness to this assemblage, the intensity of which is rarely felt by people living in most areas of the United States, for example. This awareness of the garbage assemblage makes possible "more ecological and more materially sustainable modes of production and consumption" than might otherwise be the case (ix).

Facets of this awareness are developed through educational and civic policies. Environmentally themed lessons are part of the school curriculum from kindergarten to high school. Public service announcements further drive home the message, such as in a brief televised commercial aimed at children, which was built around the "Für Elise" melody. This thirty-second-long animation was released in late 2005 by Taiwan's Environmental Protection Agency in advance of nationwide mandatory recycling of household waste to be implemented beginning in 2006. It shows three cute, biped dogs demonstrating how to sort waste into three categories (recyclable materials, unrecyclable garbage, and kitchen scraps) as they sing their message to Beethoven's tune, first in Taiwanese (i.e., Hoklo) and then in Mandarin.[11]

In this volume Mark F. DeWitt finds that songs written in response to environmental degradation in southern Louisiana seem to have failed to affect public opinion, corporate behavior, or governmental policy. In seeking an explanation for their lack of efficacy, DeWitt looks to "structural socioeconomic reasons for inaction," the possibility of defects in the messages themselves, and "the weakness of the link between cultural and environmental sustainability." Taiwan's success at reducing waste presents an opportunity for examining and comparing the efficacy of music to bring about positive change. To be clear, the tunes that accompany Taiwan's garbage collection are not protest songs (though Taiwan does have a history of activist songs forming part of efficacious movements against environmental destruction; see Guy 2009); however, this music has been integral in the creation of an awareness that has led to sustainable practices. One important element of the success of the Taiwanese case is that garbage management and the reduction of waste do not rely on abstract principles or altruistic behaviors. In Louisiana adherence to environmentally friendly practices may not bring immediate, observable, or personal benefit, while in Taipei a citizen is potentially reminded multiple times a day that his or her own living space may be invaded by pests if household waste is not delivered promptly to the musical garbage truck. Furthermore, the Taipei City government has devised a system that rewards recycling while punishing the production of unrecyclable trash: compostables and recyclables are dumped for free, but trash must be discarded in official bags that individual users must purchase. Therefore, in Taipei, there is nothing abstract about waste management. This is not to say that Taiwanese do not act altruistically. In fact, it was a social movement for environmental protection in Taiwan, ignited in the 1980s by grassroots protest, that essentially forced the government to implement environmental protection policies.[12] What we have witnessed in Taiwan over the last several decades is a combined effort of citizens who have demanded governmental action and leaders who have been bold enough to devise and implement environmentally friendly policies. By transforming garbage collection into a daily civic duty, Taiwan "has been remarkably successful at achieving something that eludes most developing nations: the richer Taiwan gets, the less trash it produces" (Spinks 2014). This is in defiance of dominant economic theories that hold that "economic growth leads to more consumption and, therefore, more waste" (Spinks 2014). Today, the average Taiwanese citizen produces less than a kilogram of trash per day.[13] By comparison, the average American produces roughly 2.58 kilograms per day.

The musicality of Taiwan's garbage trucks is no doubt partially responsible for the efficacy of waste reduction policies and practices. As the brigades pass through city streets, their melodies ring through neighborhoods, reaching into living spaces, reminding people of the great garbage assemblage. That the garbage truck melodies resound in popular music, alongside metaphors for waste management, evidences the profound degree to which the garbage consciousness and its signature melodies have permeated everyday life.

Appendix: Translated and Original Titles

"Aborigines Look Different" 長得不一樣
"Big Buildings" 樓仔厝
"Brave New World" 新地球
"Bung so ji lo" 糞埽一路
"Did You See?" 你甘有看見
"Everyone for Environmental Protection" 人人做環保
"Fly Me to the Moon" 帶我去月球
"Forgotten" 忽略
"Garbage Mountain beside My House" 垃圾倒在阮厝邊
"Garbage People" 糞埽人
"Garbage Truck" 垃圾車
"Ghetto Superstar" 貧民百萬歌星
"Home Sweet Home" 我的家
"I Love Elise" 我愛愛麗絲
"Mad Boat Captain" 船長要抓狂
Papa, Can You Hear Me Sing? 搭錯車
"Recycling Truck" 資源回收車
"Super Citizens" 超級市民
"Terraced Fields" 梯田

Notes

1. Numerous polices such as mandatory beverage container buyback and mandatory e-waste takeback have all contributed significantly to a reduction in waste. The policy whose effect on daily life is most directly witnessed bubbling up in pop songs is the "per-bag trash collection fee," whereby residents must buy official garbage bags for use in discarding unrecyclable garbage. Compostable and recyclable materials, which residents sort and separate before the garbage brigade arrives, is hauled away for free. This

program was implemented in Taipei City in the year 2000. By 2003, waste production was reduced by more than 28 percent compared with 1999, and the recycling rate had increased from under 3 percent to 23 percent (Allen 2012).

2. The film *Papa, Can You Hear Me Sing?* tells the story of a foundling raised by a man who works collecting and selling glass bottles. Ironically, one of the first lines the foundling (who as an adult narrates her story at the film's opening) speaks is: "I was only two months old. Like garbage, I was dumped alongside the road." The music to the song "Are There Empty Wine Bottles to Sell?" was written by Hou Dejian; the lyrics are by Luo Dayou.

3. For an excellent introduction to the specifics of Taipei's current routine for sorting and collecting of household waste, see the video report BBC News, "Close-Up: Taiwan's Musical Garbage Trucks," January 23, 2011, http://www.bbc.com/news/world-asia-pacific-12242914.

4. I use the moniker *popular song* as an umbrella term for a broad spectrum of music including mainstream pop, rock, hip hop, and indie. Indie, however, is the most strongly represented genre in my sampling.

5. I use the term *hazardscape* here in the sense laid out by Bimal Kanti Paul, who uses it to refer to "the landscape of hazards in a particular place or the net result of natural and artificial hazards and the risks they pose cumulatively across a given area. The concept of hazardscape includes the interaction among nature, society, and technology at a variety of spatial scales and creates a mosaic of risks that affect places and the people who live there" (2011, 44).

6. J. J. Lin is a Taiwan-based singer, songwriter, record producer, and actor who hails from Singapore.

7. "Fly Me to the Moon" was recorded by pop idol Zhang Huimei in 1998. The environmentally conscious tone of the lyrics are found in the first line: "Go, take me away from this polluted planet."

8. MC HotDog's mention of a specific time in the evening further illustrates that the arrival of the garbage collection has become a "time mark" as well as a soundmark.

9. See the video at https://www.youtube.com/watch?v=KVkCNazp81U (accessed June 17, 2016).

10. For a reference to the Dapu incident, see "Owner of Bulldozed House Found Dead," *Taipei Times*, September 19, 2013.

11. This video is available online at https://www.youtube.com/watch?v=rMGM WXN6myY and at https://www.youtube.com/watch?v=53AXT4pMqrI (both accessed June 20, 2016).

12. For an overview of this history, see Grano 2015, 42–48. According to Grano, environmental activists are credited by most scholars with challenging the long-standing authoritarian rule in Taiwan and facilitating the creation of a public sphere, which these activists ultimately employed to exert pressure for the reorganization of the country's political structure (Grano 2015, 42).

13. According to the World Wide Economic Forum, the worldwide average for waste production is 1.2kg per person per day (Muggeridge 2015).

References

Allen, Cecilia. 2012. "Taiwan: Community Action Leads Government toward Zero Waste." GAIA (June). http://www.no-burn.org/wp-content/uploads/ZW-Taiwan.pdf.

Bennett, Jane. 2010. *Vibrant Matter: A Political Ecology of Things*. Durham, NC: Duke University Press.

Cai, Huiping. 2001. "Laowai huayu yanjiang sai baoxiao sheng chuan chang" [Foreign student Mandarin/Taiwanese speech competition: Laughter fills the stage]. *Lianhe bao*, March 3.

Chen, Kathy. 2016. "Taiwan: The World's Geniuses of Garbage Disposal." *Wall Street Journal*, May 17.

Grano, Simona A. 2015. *Environmental Governance in Taiwan: A New Generation of Activists and Stakeholders*. London: Routledge.

Guy, Nancy. 2009. "Flowing down Taiwan's Tamsui River: Towards an Ecomusicology of the Environmental Imagination." *Ethnomusicology* 53 (2): 218–48.

Hawkins, Gay. 2006. *The Ethics of Waste: How We Relate to Rubbish*. Oxford: Rowman and Littlefield.

Moskowitz, Marc L. 2010. *Cries of Joy, Songs of Sorrow: Chinese Pop Music and Its Cultural Connotations*. Honolulu: University of Hawai'i Press.

Muggeridge, Paul. 2015. "Which Countries Produce the Most Waste." *World Economic Forum*. https://www.weforum.org/agenda/2015/08/which-countries-produce-the-most-waste/. Accessed June 21, 2016. (Web page no longer available.)

Paul, Bimal Kanti. 2011. *Environmental Hazards and Disasters: Contexts, Perspectives, and Management*. Chichester, UK: Wiley-Blackwell.

Pedelty, Mark. 2012. *Ecomusicolgy: Rock, Folk, and the Environment*. Philadelphia: Temple University Press.

Schafer, Murray R. 1977. *The Soundscape: Our Sonic Environment and the Tuning of the World*. Rochester, VT: Destiny Books.

Spinks, Rosie. 2014. "Yes, Richer Countries Produce More Waste. But Do They Have To?" *Good Magazine*, December 1. http://magazine.good.is/articles/taiwan-trash-program.

CHAPTER 6

Climate Change, Mobile Pastoralism, and Cultural Heritage in Western Mongolia

JENNIFER C. POST

AS WE DRIVE FROM the small city of Ölgii to Deluun in the south central part of the province of Bayan Ölgii in Mongolia, the rutted tracks we travel along span broadly across the dry desert grassland. As our old Russian jeep skids on the dirt and sand, I consider whether we are really going to arrive at our destination, and in order to take my mind off the issue of safety I scan the land around us once more: the grazing sheep and goats, the smaller flocks of camels and herds of horses. Since it is spring, there is an occasional yurt set up some distance away, and I can see the clay and wood winter homes nestled up in the nearby mountains, where they protect occupants from the wind and winter cold. I consider the beauty of the land, the stunning snow-capped mountains, and the charm of the lifestyle laid out before me. My gaze could be a tourist's and my memories—of the rough and too fast ride—might have been erased by the seemingly idyllic scenes around me were it not for the knowledge I have of the circumstances of this land, the herders' lives, and the status of their livestock along this dry expanse in far western Mongolia.

The Altai-Sayan Ecoregion, which encompasses portions of Siberia, eastern Kazakhstan, northwestern China, and western Mongolia, offers some of the most biologically diverse land and resources in the world. Four major vegetation zones are found in the westernmost provinces of Mongolia, including alpine, steppe, forest steppe, and desert steppe. The alpine zone is at the highest elevation and includes mountain meadows fed by springs and creeks; it provides a habitat for numerous animal and plant species. The forest steppe includes sparse stands of pine and fir trees that sit primarily on the northern slopes of the mountainous terrain. The steppe and desert steppe, at lower elevations, are populated with dwarf shrubs, grasses, and herbs (Murray et al. 2009). A number of climate-change events have been identified in the Altai-Sayan Ecoregion and in western Mongolia generally (see MNEM 1999; Kasparek 2011; Badenkov, Yashina, and Worboys 2012). Some scientists target this specific region to record biological changes, a few discuss the impact also on local pastoralists, and even fewer note the significance of herders' ecological knowledge and roles they might play in evaluating and developing strategies for change (Fernández-Giménez 2000). Considering the effects of changes on these steppe lands, Elena Lioubimtseva and Geoffrey Henebry (2009) note that during the last sixty years the average temperature in Mongolia has risen 1.56 degrees C (2.8 degrees Fahrenheit), and that drought years have increased. Among other impacts, these factors affect grass yields. Other scientific research references decreased precipitation amounts, increased wind velocity, noting the occurrence of extreme weather events such as long periods of bitter cold and high winds during the winter (called *zhut* in Kazakh and *dzud* in Mongolian). Climate-change events have resulted in early snowmelt; loss of—or seriously diminished—rivers, streams, and lakes; and widespread desertification affecting the availability of grasses for livestock and drying up essential sources of water (John et al. 2013; Batima, Natsagdorj, and Batnasan 2008).

Mobile pastoralists are known as caretakers of lands and holders of ecological knowledge passed from generation to generation. When studied carefully, researchers acknowledge that for centuries these pastoralists have been able to successfully eke out a living in some of the world's most unproductive and challenging lands, from North Africa to Central and North Asia. In Mongolia, as in many areas, the lands pastoralists frequent are in trouble. The vulnerable peoples and their resources struggle with drought, flooding, harsh winters, poor soil, and animal disease and infections; many of the residents and their lives and lifestyles are threatened due to privatization and the influx of mining and miners, roads and road building, tourism and tourists (Myadar 2009; Upton 2010a, 2010b; Laurie et al. 2010). Climate change may be a primary source for the devastation, but these human and nonhuman communities are caught up in complex and difficult geophysical circumstances and sociopolitical events that many struggle to manage. Together these issues have had a devastating effect on the social and cultural lives of Mongolian rural residents.

This chapter draws on my fieldwork with Mongolian Kazakh mobile pastoral herders who live in the western province of Bayan Ölgii, combined with research that contributes to current discourse on ecology and pastoralism as well as climate change and changing culture, to address the impact of climate change on cultural production in western Mongolia. This is a tale of vulnerability and adaptation that demonstrates both resilience and resignation. The changing climate combined with other biological, social, political, and economic events impact resources as well as opportunities the products of the land offer local residents. I believe that studying these changing cultural landscapes will contribute to a better understanding of some of the biological and social changes impacting herders. Connecting social, cultural, and geophysical events also reveals why herders are making radical changes in their lives and lifestyles today.

Mongolian Kazakh Pastoralists

The largest population of Mongolian Kazakh pastoralists resides in the westernmost provinces of Bayan Ölgii and Khovd, close to the Altai Mountains, near lakes and rivers, and at the far western edge of the desert. These Muslim, Kazakh-speaking peoples, who represent approximately 5 percent of the Mongolian population, are settled in the borderlands between Russia and China and also look to Kazakhstan, located west of the province (although not contiguously), where the government is assembling a culturally constructed new Kazakhstan comprising immigrants from disparate locations (including Mongolia) who have maintained specific cultural practices that Russian Kazakhs lost during the socialist era (Post 2014).

Mongolia is the country the Kazakh residents identify as their *tughan zher* (homeland). It is not only where they were born; it is also where their families have lived for generations. Eighty-year-old Minäp, who has worked the land all his life, sang about the places he and his relatives frequented in Deluun *sum* (district), saying that his *tughan zher* is "alghashqy kindik qanym tamghan terim" (Where my sweat and the first blood from my navel dropped) (Minäp Qazanbaiuly, interview, June 17, 2007, Zhalghyz aghash, Deluun sum). The region is also where several generations of their ancestors' voices and expressions are preserved in songs and recitations referencing history, nature, place, and sociality. These are repeated today by *aqyns*, respected poet-singers. For example, Suyenish opens a song he calls "The image of my cradle Qyzylqaiyng" with the lines that describe his family's homeland in Bayan Ölgii (Suyenish Zhensiqbai, interview, June 6, 2014, Ulaankhus sum):

Meken barma mynau Qyzylqaiyngdai	Is there a better place than Qyzylqaiyng?
Qobda özeni jas kelinning shaiyndai	Qobda river is like the tea served by a new daughter-in-law
Baiun Taudyng kelbetine qarasam	When I look at the appearance of Baiym mountain

Äzhelerding qaryndaghy maiyndai	It is like the butter my grandmother keeps in *qaryn* (leather bag made of goat or sheep stomach)
Tarikhtan kalghan mynau zhoramal	We know from history
Soghaq zhaqsi zher dep kepti babalar	That our ancestors came to Soghagh and declared it was good land
Aqborany shumaqtalsa beine bir	When it is windy it seems like the coiled
Arulardyng moinyndaghy oramal	Scarf around the neck of a pretty girl

The cultural forms that Kazakh mobile pastoralists create and maintain in western Mongolia offer evidence of social and cultural adjustments this group has made due to climate changes. Responses to climate events can be measured in their cultural practices and products traditionally shared from generation to generation, such as their material production of needlework and felt work, wooden tools and musical instruments, their songs and instrumental tunes. It can also be found in heritage actions, such as work patterns and ceremonial gatherings, and other forms of cultural production that engage them not only in the maintenance of knowledge systems but also provide opportunities for innovation. While these expressions of tangible and intangible heritage have been maintained in conjunction with their lives and lifestyles for generations, today many have been disrupted. A closer look at a few examples reveals herders' efforts to respect the land, resist change, and remain resilient. Their expressive forms also reveal warnings and demonstrate that some of the pastoralists have begun to recognize that they are having difficulties managing the many changes impacting their lives.

Material Responses to Climate Change

In rural Mongolian Kazakh families and communities, women and men engage in essential social and cultural practices that provide support for their work and lifestyles. Their material culture utilizes local resources, some from domestic and wild animals, ranging from goats and sheep to fox and wolf; others from plant life, including trees and shrubs. Anna Portisch, who has researched textile production in rural Bayan Ölgii, notes that animal-product use reflects household economic, social, and political circumstances (2013, 2). The wool and hair from domestic animals are sheared or combed to be used for textiles: felt made from sheep's wool is produced in large quantities for the outer wall of the yurts; wool (from sheep, camels, and yaks) is used for decorative straps in the yurts and has also traditionally been used for rugs (called *syrmaq*) adorned with Kazakh designs. Yak hair and horsehair are braided for rope. The Kazakh people are eagle hunters. They raise eagles to hunt with, and the fur of wild animals—some killed by their eagles—may be used to line their coats and hats for winter warmth. Wolf and fox pelts are also hung on the walls to demonstrate the prowess of their eagle or of the hunter(s) in the family. Among all these activities, the product with the highest economic value for textile production is goat's wool, which in fact is not used locally but is sold for income, supporting the world's seemingly insatiable desire for cashmere products.

The increasing issues in connection with climate change, along with poor economic and political systems nationally and regionally, have had a negative impact on the products of the land and the processes families use to sustain and use them. There is correlation between location and climate and the quality of wool and hair products. Bayan Ölgii has been widely known to produce some of the finest quality cashmere, as well as camel and sheep wool, due to its elevation and climate. Research indicates that the growth rate and quality (such as tensile strength) of wool fibers is associated with nutrient supply. While green forage provides the highest level of protein and energy, poor-quality grazing land and hay stored for winter use without the necessary protein value are responsible for diminishing quality in wool products and impact animal health and milk production as well (Anderson et al. 1995). There is also movement away from locally created felt rugs and other household goods once produced communally (such as embroidered wall hangings [tus qyiz]). The availability of inexpensive Chinese goods is tied to a cash economy identified especially with cashmere production. The replacement of rugs and embroidered and woven work with synthetic fiber products from China in fact provides herders larger and thicker wall and floor covering, offering better insulation during the more volatile winter weather. Many of these socially created objects used in their homes embody skills that have been passed down in families from generation to generation. The greatest loss to the pastoralists, then, may be in the opportunities for sociality and the transmission of skills during local production.

The status of trees and other woody materials during this period of climate change affect production of cultural resources using wood products. Local trees in Bayan Ölgii, primarily the forest-steppe larch (qaraghai; Larix sibirica) and Siberian pine (samarsan; Pinus sibirica), the now-rare Siberian spruce (shyrsha; Picea sibirica), along with lower-elevation willow (tal; Salix) and birch (qaiyng; Betula platyphylla) are also caught up in complex ecological and socioeconomic circumstances. Little land in the province is heavily forested, and wide expanses are nearly bare except near rivers, where low bushes and sparse stands of willow and occasionally birch, may be found. Dorjburegdaa Lkhagvadorj and others who have conducted research on plant life in Bayan Ölgii note that "since forests grow at their drought limit on the edge of the steppe, and increasingly suffer from water constraints due to rising temperatures, they are, like the grasslands, highly susceptible to land-use intensity" (Lkhagvadorj et al. 2013, 83). Similarly, Choimaa Dulamsuren and her colleagues (2010) have noted the impact of drought on the common taiga and forest-steppe Siberian larch (*Larix sibirica*) in the same region.

Most families use wood for their yurts, for tool making, for fuel, and to make musical instruments, and increasingly winter homes are being made entirely of wood, rather than the previously more common wood and mud/clay structures. The poles, lattice walls, and other key yurt parts are made of willow, a soft but strong wood that still grows relatively widely in the province. The situation for musical instruments, though, is different. An industry for making the *dombyra*, the Kazakh two-string lute, has been maintained in rural locations and towns and in the small city of Ölgii, where a few artisans have worked to establish instrument-making businesses for their communities. Only a few have been successful; many struggle with access to the quality of wood needed to make musical sound. The increasingly vulnerable trees in the forested regions of Mongolia are now officially government controlled, drought and poor soils impact wood quality, and a few makers rely on wood poaching close to the Chinese border. The acoustical effect of the poor-quality wood (and other materials) can be heard in instruments throughout the province. The makers of local Kazakh dombyras recognize that the softwood cut in the northern forests of Mongolia for construction, not for musical instruments, cannot provide the same kind of sound that an instrument made with hardwood or old-growth wood produces. Most makers tolerate the knots, poor grain, and porous texture of the local softwood as a condition they cannot change.

Musical Responses to Climate Change

In Bayan Ölgii both urban and rural Kazakh performers maintain ever-evolving vocal and instrumental music traditions linked to the Mongolian landscape and to their history in this location. In the countryside, the pastoralists are influenced by mediated and Russified repertoires and practices that have affected the entire region, but many remain deeply engaged with some of the older musical styles as well. These include vocal forms (*terme, tolghau,* and *qara öleng*) sung in family and community settings that frequently offer personal views expressed by individual performers who also represent collective values, concerns, and histories. Some musicians maintain a narrative instrumental genre (*küi* played on the dombyra or the *sybyzghy)* in which performers describe nature and the peopled landscapes, traditionally contextualized with narrated stories.

The relationships between the everyday life of herders and the workings of the natural world in the steppes play a critical role in their music. These Kazakh expressive forms not only provide evidence of their ecological actions, behaviors, and concerns; they also have a practical function in conjunction with their critical stewardship roles (Post 2017). Community-based singing by local aqyns is widely enjoyed, especially at *tois* (celebrations) that provide intergenerational opportunities for information sharing, recounting histories, and expressing and reinforcing values. Some musician-herders have openly expressed concern about changes in the land in their songs at these events. In Deluun, Zhangabyl Doldash (interview, June 19, 2007, Zhalghiz aghash) sang about the "trouble" on the slopes of a nearby mountain that the people rely on for grazing and as a source for water, singing: "Qalady au qary ketse shölirkenip" (If the snow disappears it will be thirsty). And Oktyabr sang (interview, June 28, 2007, Tövshin köl, Deluun sum):

Ulary qoysha örgen Ayu Dara	Ayu Dara, your mountain grouse graze like sheep
Köktemey zherdng keni ketip qaldy au	Yet it doesn't turn green and our resources are gone
Yapyrau ne bolasyng bara bara	Oh what will happen over time?

Ayu Dara, along the Chinese border, has been a popular place for Kazakh livestock grazing for several generations. Yet the changing herd composition and grazing patterns due to the global demand for cashmere encourage pastoralists to swell their herds with goats, and the flowers once left in enough abundance to re-pollinate the land are now gone (Dorj et al. 2013).

The increasing appearance of the zhut, the extreme bitter cold, wind, and snow that are responsible for the deaths of thousands of livestock in Bayan Ölgii during the winter months, is also the subject of songs. The nature of some of these songs reveals the singers' recognition that they cannot address such a monstrous weather event even with their years of experience in the steppes. Aqylbek Zavchan sang about the zhut in Bulghyn, referencing Mongolia's nine times nine, or eighty-one days of winter cold (interview, July 19, 2008). He sang, "The storm is growing gradually. Mongolia's nine times nine is difficult; even the bulls were frozen." Altai Tügelbai's family song about horses that died in the zhut identifies individual horses that were lost and expresses both the emotional and economic difficulties that result from these events (interview, June 3, 2014, Ulaankhus). He sings: "Oh my poor reddish brown horse. . . you made my travel seem shorter"; "My poor *qunan* [four-year-old horse] . . . you were like a fish that plays in the river"; and "My poor *baital* [three-year-old horse], I will never forget how you died before my eyes."

Descriptions of resources such as rivers and birds played in instrumental tunes (especially in conjunction with expressed values in conversation and action) demonstrate that these elements play a key role in daily and seasonal lives, and that with ecological changes, the melodies become references instead to imagined or historical landscapes. One popular *küi* played by pastoralists on the dombyra, for example, named "Tasty bulaq" (Stream with stones) mimics the sound of a healthy stream with the water running quickly over the rocks. Bodies of water are essential to herders' lives—for both animal and human consumption—and they are quickly disappearing in this region.

Vulnerability—Adaptation—Resilience—Resignation

As we study the global impact of climate change today, we need to listen to and consider the fate of some of the socially, economically, and culturally vulnerable peoples who have been caretakers of lands for generations. For pastoralists living close to the resources they use, environmental changes deeply impact every aspect of their lives. When drought and harsh winters influence resource production, the products needed for daily life and economic gain are reduced in quantity and quality. Cooperative social systems used for production and cultural support are affected as well. Mobile pastoral herders of Bayan Ölgii have demonstrated that they can adapt in conjunction with some of the changes. Faced with climate change, they have found ways to be productive while maintaining ecological values. Moderating some of their practices includes altering herd composition and size, changing production values, moving more frequently, or selecting new grazing sites, all in relation to ecological and sociopolitical changes occurring around them.

Climate events are not only embedded in mobility practices of pastoralists; they are also the cause of human migration in response to changes. In fact, scientists and social scientists working in Mongolia and other locations document migration and movement as a key result of climate change (Saad, Shariff, and Gariola 2013). In Bayan Ölgii, herders have not only moved from grazing lands used for generations by their families in search of new locations for their livestock; for some the decreasing productivity of pastures that is reflected in their diminishing social and cultural productions has been so devastating that they have moved away from the countryside altogether. Some have attempted new lives in a local residential center, including Ölgii city (population twenty-five thousand), where they seldom find work. Many have taken up offers from Kazakhstan to become *oralmandar* (immigrants or repatriates) in a new country where they have ethnic ties but little social and economic support (Diener 2009; Barcus and Werner 2015).

In postsocialist Mongolia, mobile pastoralism was a survival strategy for many. Herders carried traditional ecological skills passed down in families embedded in various forms of cultural production. These skills were maintained despite the collectivization that was imposed on the pastoralists until 1991 (Mearns 1996). Due to the impact of recent sociopolitical and geophysical events, including climate change, their subsistence living with small herds of animals does not always offer the support needed to survive. If a zhut does not devastate their herds, the drought makes it impossible to feed livestock and to provide essential water for families.

At Zhangabyl's summer grazing place near Tövshin Lake, I walked with his son on his daily round to collect water from a mountain spring. We arrived at the site, but to the boy's surprise, the spring was dry. We found water at a more distant location, but this became a subject of conversation with the family when we returned to their camp. I stood with Zhangabyl as he looked out toward the Tövshin Lake site just a hundred meters from their yurt. He spoke about the lake as a beautiful body of water surrounded by lush grazing land and active birdlife. Just six or seven years before, he said, the lake was full, then the next summer when he returned to graze his livestock, it was gone. I looked out, then, at the dry lake bed, the barren land, and marveled at the resilience of this family and others who returned again and again each spring and summer to these grazing lands. They were resilient but also resigned to the fact that they were unable to affect such grand changes to the climate.

Studying the relationships between pastoralists and the natural resources that structure their lives provides a direct link to their cultural forms: their textiles, musical instruments, foods, expressions of knowledge of wildlife and animal husbandry, and sounds, songs, and tunes. These forms express and reflect the local values shared even during times of social and political adaptation and change. The Mongolian Kazakh pastoralists I focused on in this study carry knowledge into the twenty-first century that contributes to their carefully designed social, cultural, and scientific lives, which rely first on adequate resources to support their families and livestock. This knowledge is passed along in social communities through actions that range from felt production to song construction.

Some scholars who have documented significant relationships between the natural world and human expressive forms use concepts such as cultural sustainability, adaptive management, and resilience metaphorically (see Barron and Walker, this volume). This provides a forum for discussion and action in the face of extreme climate change. Yet in the developing body of research on responses to natural resource loss, scholars studying cultural expressions who use the language of scientific environmental and ecological discourse do not always acknowledge the direct relationships that exist between adaptive social and cultural behaviors and biological and other geophysical actions that sometimes seamlessly engage humans and nonhumans who adapt together in order to conserve resources (see Allen, this volume). Furthermore, when scientific and cultural data are used together, they reinforce both cultural and scientific research. In this period of ecological change, scholars have opportunities to develop new models for understanding both cultural and biological sustainability

(Titon 2013). I urge all scholars to construct collaborative work that privileges the vulnerable, the adapting, the resilient, and even those who have resigned.

My interviews with both Oktyabr and Zhangabyl took place in Deluun sum in 2006 and 2007. When I returned to find them a few years later, they both had disappeared. Oktyabr had left the pastoral life for Ölgii, and I heard that Zhangabyl had moved first to a site in a nearby province but then finally left the country altogether for Kazakhstan.

In "Qeng dalama" (To my wide steppe), I recorded Zhangabyl singing poignantly to the land as he had done many times before. He also offered advice to his community as he was expected to do as an aqyn, and he reflected on the social behavior of his people (Zhangabyl Doldash, interview, June 19, 2007, Zhalghiz aghash, Deluun sum). His song, once intended for his local community, now speaks to a wider group of people who would also benefit from listening to this young but experienced pastoralist.

Kümilzhip qaldyng nege baytaq dalam	Why do you hesitate, my vast steppe?
Boldy ma birdengeden köngiling alang	Are you worried about something?
Arshyndap songghy kezde köktemeding	You haven't turned deep green recently
Özgerip barama älde bul bir ghalam	Or is the world changing?
Zharatqan bir allanyng tabighaty	Nature is created by Allah,
Üstinde tirlik qylghan adamzaty	Humans live on what he has made.
Alla berer nesibe yryzdyghyn	Allah gives his blessings and resources
Nysyrap qylsa bergenin zhamaghaty	Yet the people waste what he has given.

References

Anderson, N., D. W. Peter, David G. Masters, and David A. Petch, eds. 1995. *Production of Fine Wool in Northern China: Effect on Nutrition and Helminth Infections.* Canberra: Australian Centre for International Agricultural Research.

Badenkov, Yuri, Tatyana Yashina, and Graeme Worboys. 2012. "Altai-Sayan, Eurasia." In *Climate and Conservation Landscape and Seascape Science, Planning and Action*, edited by Jodi A. Hilty, Charles C. Chester, and Molly S. Cross, 187–201. Washington, DC: Island Press.

Barcus, Holly, and Cynthia Werner. 2015. "Immobility and the Re-imaginings of Ethnic Identity among Mongolian Kazakhs in the 21st Century." *Geoforum* 29:119–28.

Batima, Punsalmaa, Luvsan Natsagdorj, and Nyamsurengyn Batnasan. 2008. "Vulnerability of Mongolia's Pastoralists to Climate Extremes and Change." In *Climate Change and Vulnerability*, edited by Neil Leary, Cecilia Conde, Jyoti Kulkarni, Anthony Nyong, and Juan Pulhin, 67–87. London: Earthscan.

Diener, Alexander. 2009. *One Homeland or Two? The Nationalization and Transnationalization of Mongolia's Kazakhs.* Stanford, CA: Stanford University Press.

Dorj, O., M. Enkhbold, S. Lkhamyanjin, Kh. Mijiddorj, A. Nosmoo, M. Puntsagnamil, and U. Sainjargal. 2013. "Mongolia: Country Features, the Main Cause of Desertification and Remediation Efforts." In *Combating Desertification in Asia, Africa and the Middle East: Proven Practices*, edited by G. Ali Heshmati and Victor Squires, 217–29. New York: Springer.

Dulamsuren, Choimaa, Markus Hauck, Mookhor Khishigjargal, and Hanns Hubert Leuschner. 2010. "Diverging Climate Trends in Mongolian Taiga Forests Influence Growth and Regeneration of Larix sibirica." *Oecologia* 163:1091–1102.

Fernández-Giménez, Maria E. 2000. "The Role of Mongolian Nomadic Pastoralists' Ecological Knowledge in Rangeland Management." *Ecological Applications* 10 (5): 1318–26.

John, Ranjeet, Jiquan Chen, Zu-Tao Ou-Yang, Jingfeng Xiao, Richard Becker, Arindam Samanta, Sangram Ganguly, Wenping Yuan, and Ochirbat Batkhishig. 2013. "Vegetation Response to Extreme Climate Events on the Mongolian Plateau from 2000 to 2010." *Environmental Research Letters* 8 (3): 1–12.

Kasparek, Max. 2011. Biodiversity Conservation in the Russian Portion of the Altai-Sayan Ecoregion ("Altai-Sayan Project"). PIMS 1685. United Nations Development Program/ Global Environment Facility Government of the Russian Federation. https://www. thegef.org/project/biodiversity-conservation-russian-portion-altai-sayan-ecoregion.

Laurie, Andrew, Jargal Jamsranjav, Onno van den Heuvel, and Erdensaikhan Nyamjav. 2010. "Biodiversity Conservation and the Ecological Limits to Development Options in the Mongolian Altai: Formulation of a Strategy and Discussion of Priorities." *Central Asian Survey* 29 (3): 321–43.

Lioubimtseva, Elena, and Geoffrey M. Henebry. 2009. "Climate and Environmental Change in Arid Central Asia: Impacts, Vulnerability, and Adaptations." *Journal of Arid Environments* 73:963–77.

Lkhagvadorj, Dorjburegdaa, Markus Hauck, Choimaa Dulamsuren, and Jamsran Tsogtbaatar. 2013. "Pastoral Nomadism in the Forest-Steppe of the Mongolian Altai under a Changing Economy and a Warming Climate." *Journal of Arid Environments* 88:82–89.

Mearns, Robin. 1996. "Community, Collective Action and Common Grazing: The Case of Post-Socialist Mongolia." *Journal of Development Studies* 32 (3): 297–339.

Murray, Martyn, Peter Hunnam, Badam-Ochir Damjin, Ganbat Munkhtuvshin, and Kirk Olson. 2009. *Community-Based Conservation of Biological Diversity in the Mountain Landscapes of Mongolia's Altai Sayan Eco-Region—Mid-term Evaluation: Findings of the Evaluation Team, 14th February 2009*. [Ulaanbaatar]: UNDP Mongolia. https:// erc.undp.org/evaluation/evaluations/detail/4074.

Myadar, Orhon. 2009. "Nomads in a Fenced Land: Land Reform in Post-Socialist Mongolia." *Asian-Pacific Law & Policy Journal* 11 (1): 161–203.

MNEM (Ministry of Nature and Environment, Mongolia). 1999. "Country Report on Natural Disasters in Mongolia." Ulaanbaatar: Ministry of Nature and Environment, Mongolia.

Portisch, Anna. 2013. "Social and Economic Aspects of the Uses of Animal Wool and Hair in Western Mongolia." *Études mongoles et sibériennes, centrasiatiques et tibétaines* 43–44:2–20.

Post, Jennifer C. 2014. "Performing Transition in Mongolia: Repatriation and Loss in the Music of Kazakh Mobile Pastoralists." *Yearbook for Traditional Music* 46:43–61.

———. 2017. "Ecological Knowledge: Collaborative Management and Musical Production in Western Mongolia." In *Ethnomusicology: A Contemporary Reader. Volume II*, edited by Jennifer C. Post, 161–79. New York: Routledge Press.

Saad, Ali Mansour, Noresah Mohd Shariff, and Sanjay Gariola. 2013. "Libya: Reversal of Land Degradation and Desertification through Better Land Management." In *Combating Desertification in Asia, Africa and the Middle East*, edited by G. Ali Heshmati and Victor R. Squires, 75–90. New York: Springer.

Titon, Jeff Todd. 2013. "The Nature of Ecomusicology." *Música e Cultura: Revista da ABET* 8 (1): 8–18.

Upton, Caroline. 2010a. "Living off the Land: Nature and Nomadism in Mongolia." *Geoforum* 41:865–74.

———. 2010b. "Nomadism, Identity, and the Politics of Conservation." *Central Asian Survey* 29 (3): 305–19.

CHAPTER 7

Singing for *la Mêche Perdue*

Reconciling Economic, Environmental, and Cultural Imperatives in Louisiana

MARK F. DEWITT

THE MISSISSIPPI RIVER watershed brings a fecund mixture of water, life, and culture to Louisiana from a great swath of the United States, and people have also flowed in by way of the Gulf of Mexico from Europe, Africa, and the Caribbean. By the nineteenth century, diverse and vibrant cultures had come to life in this rich, nourishing environment. The discovery of oil on- and off-shore stimulated the twentieth-century capitalist economy of the region. While the oil industry's presence has radically changed the lifestyles of working people in south Louisiana and thus the context for folkways, as a spinoff it has also provided the capital necessary to prop up what traditional culture remains as heritage. Long-term environmental problems caused by oil development and public works projects further erode the natural and economic worlds in which traditional Louisiana cultures formed.[1]

Songs written in protest of environmental degradation, along with the artists who write them and the public response to them, raise questions taken up in this volume and elsewhere in relation to sustainability and to protest music. What is the relationship between cultural sustainability and environmental sustainability? How is the music's ability to move people to action affected by the politico-economic context in which it is heard?

In this volume folklorist Mary Hufford writes of speech genres that "function at the local level to integrate times, spaces, practices, and social identities not only of humans but of a wide range of species and land forms." I argue that songs written in and about Louisiana's environment and its fate have similarly represented a range of human and "more-than-human" (Hufford, this volume) points of view, including other species and disappearing land forms. As Nancy Guy does with songs about garbage in Taiwan (this volume), I use songs from the local popular music industry as a window into popular sentiments about environmental issues. The rest of south Louisiana shares with New Orleans a cultural integrity (Feintuch, this volume) identified with the foodways and the music of rural Cajuns and Creoles, as well as with economic resourcefulness in an environment that is both challenging and bountiful. One songwriter adopts the perspective of a fisherman, another that of an oil worker, each embodying what Burt Feintuch describes as the "moral and ethical standards in community life." The dialogue that Hufford so prizes is present but muted by the oil and gas industry's enormous role in the economic life of the region.

Two Environmental Issues facing Louisiana

This chapter covers musical responses to two environmental issues currently facing Louisiana: coastal wetlands loss and the aftermath of the 2010 British Petroleum (BP) oil spill in the Gulf of Mexico. I chose these two instances because they have each engendered music that has registered little effect thus far on public opinion, corporate behavior (save for public relations efforts), or governmental policy.[2]

Until the twentieth century, the Mississippi River flowed unimpeded to the Gulf of Mexico. As the Mississippi met the Gulf, the river slowed, and sediments were deposited at the coast. Once sediments built up sufficiently, the river changed course to find other paths of least resistance. Louisiana's land mass increased as the river deposited sediment in coastal wetlands faster than the combined rate of natural subsidence and erosion from normal wave action and violent storms. Two twentieth-century developments changed this balance of causes and effects on Louisiana's coastline. Starting in the 1930s, sediment deposition decreased due to federal dam building upriver and levee building in Louisiana that controlled flooding and the accompanying distribution of sediments. Meanwhile, drilling for oil in the wetlands has increased the rate of subsidence by pumping material out of the ground.[3] Navigation and pipeline canals that the oil companies cleared in the coastal marshes allowed salt water into previously freshwater and brackish marshes, killing the vegetation there and weakening the soil's resistance to erosion. According to a study by the United States Geological Survey, the land area represented by Louisiana's wetlands decreased by 25 percent between 1932 and 2010 (Couvillion et al. 2011). Observers frequently note that the land lost so far is equivalent in size to the American state of Delaware. As with the Alaskan situation that Susan Hurley-Glowa describes in this volume, anthropogenic climate change also looms in the form of increasingly intense storms that accelerate coastal erosion and rising sea levels (Holland and Bruyere 2014; Balaguru, Judi, and Leung 2016). A 2016 revelation that an indigenous community on Isle de Jean Charles had been awarded a $48 million resettlement plan from the federal government created a controversy, in that coastal communities in Alaska similarly affected by climate change were not yet receiving such assistance (Spanne 2016).

On April 20, 2010, BP's Deepwater Horizon drilling rig was destroyed in a well explosion in the Gulf of Mexico in which eleven offshore workers died. The ruptured well continued to gush oil for almost three months, until July 15 (Biello 2011). During the spill, the official estimate of the oil flow rate was five thousand barrels a day. Canals dredged in the wetlands for onshore oil development allowed oil from the spill to penetrate farther inland. By the time the leak was finally plugged, the government had raised the estimate of the oil-spill flow rate to approximately 60,000 barrels a day and a total spill volume of 4.9 million barrels (Freudenberg and Gramling 2011, 13).

Environmental sociologists have previously found that accidents on the scale of the Exxon Valdez oil spill in Alaska "often produce long-term (6 to 14 years) social disruption and psychological stress" and that, "in contrast to natural disasters, massive human-caused toxic disasters appear to engender a social context of uncertainty, anger, and isolation" (Picou 2000, 79). Congruent with this finding, the U.S. government's response to the BP oil spill pleased no one. The Obama administration imposed a moratorium on deep-sea oil drilling in the Gulf for several months after the spill. BP itself was in charge of the cleanup operation because, according to a Coast Guard official, the federal government had neither the equipment nor the money to do it. BP spent massive sums of money on public relations, cleanup operations using the controversial chemical dispersant Corexit, grants for research on the effects of the spill (referred to by some as hush money), and compensation to spill victims, the process for which has not been well received. Local anger at President Obama's drilling moratorium, which was perceived as forcing layoffs of oil industry workers, seemed at times more intense than anger at BP itself. Songwriter Mike Dean wrote and recorded a song, "Lift the Ban," which was uploaded to YouTube shortly after the well was finally capped (2010). In the second verse, he sings, "When you talk about bannin' drillin' / you're talkin' 'bout bannin' jobs / You might as well starve us all / You might as well drop the bomb."

Creative Musical Responses

In her book on antinuclear protest music following the earthquake- and tsunami-triggered Fukushima Daiichi nuclear plant disaster in 2011, Noriko Manabe analyzes the role of protest music according to four types of socially constructed space: demonstrations, festivals/concerts, recordings, and cyberspace (2015, 15–27). Most of my data collection for this project has been in the form of recordings, along with some attendance at festivals and concerts, and Internet research. I have gathered and studied many, but by no means all, professionally produced music recordings of songs and sound collages that address coastal wetlands loss and/or the BP oil spill. Space does not permit here a comprehensive discussion of all that I have found.

While coastal wetlands loss began decades before the 2010 BP oil spill and scientific consensus about what has been causing it had been reached by the early 1980s (Theriot 2014, 131–62), the earliest musical compositions I have found in response to this crisis date from 2003 to 2005. Tommy Michot, research biologist and accordionist in the Cajun family band Les Frères Michot, diagnoses the coastal erosion problem with scientific accuracy in his 2003 song, "La valse de la mèche perdue" (The lost marsh waltz) (Les Frères Michot 2003). The song offers eyewitness testimony of wetlands remembered in youth that have disappeared along with an explanation of how the levees have deprived the marshes of fresh river water. It concludes with a question: "Sans les sédiments et le nourriture du fleuve / Les mèches ont commencé à s'abbaisser et à mourir /Combien des années avant [que] notre culture suivra les mèches?" (Without the sediments and the nutrients from the river / The marsh began to subside and die / How many years before our culture will follow the marsh?) (Les Frères Michot 2003). The songwriter's view of the connection between environmental and cultural sustainability could not be expressed more clearly.

Tommy Michot's sons Louis and Andre meanwhile had started their own band, the Lost Bayou Ramblers, after apprenticing with Les Frères Michot as youths. They did not become scientists like their father, but they have incorporated an ecological sensibility into their own endeavors. In 2007, Louis Michot founded the Cultural Research Institute of Acadiana, a nonprofit organization that established a seed bank for "heirloom and heritage plants" of the region along with an archive of interviews with practitioners of traditional horticulture and agriculture (Cultural Research Institute of Acadiana 2016). The Lost Bayou Ramblers covered (and slightly retitled) "Valse de mèche perdu" on their 2008 *Vermilionaire* album, a tribute to the richness of the environment surrounding the Vermilion River, which runs south through Lafayette, Louisiana, and on to the Gulf. They felt this richness violated two years later when they went into the studio to make their next album in the summer of 2010, while the oil spill was still going on. This album became *Mammoth Waltz*, named after an extinct species, with two songs commenting on the spill ("Bastille" and "Marée noire") (Lost Bayou Ramblers 2012) and an opening song that concludes, "Louisiane réveille-toi!" (Louisiana, wake up!) (Cry You One 2013). Even the name of the band, which was suggested some ten years earlier by a friend on a whim, took on new significance for Louis after the oil spill: "You can say that we're lost, but really it's the bayou that's lost" (Spitzer 2015). Louis Michot's conviction about the connection between traditional culture and Louisiana's natural environment was given another outlet for expression when filmmaker Benh Zeitlin invited him to contribute to the soundtrack of *Beasts of the Southern Wild* (2012), an Oscar-nominated feature film set in a dystopian future coastal wetland community (inspired by Isle de Jean Charles) whose inhabitants are economically poor, culturally rich, and resolute to remain there in the face of rising ocean levels caused by global warming and efforts by authorities on "the dry side" of the ocean wall to evacuate them (Arons 2012).

Another artist who became concerned with coastal wetlands loss before the intensifying events of Hurricane Katrina and the BP oil spill was blues guitarist Tab Benoit, whose 2002 album *Wetlands* signaled early his intention to bring public awareness to the issue. In 2003, he founded Voice of the Wetlands, a nonprofit "focused on driving awareness and developing educational outlets/ programs about the loss of the wetlands in southern Louisiana" (http://www. voiceofthewetlands.org/), and began work on an IMAX film with the Audubon Nature Institute, narrated by actress Meryl Streep, that became *Hurricane on the Bayou* (2007). Over the following two years, Voice of the Wetlands held its first music festival in south Louisiana, and the Voice of the Wetlands All-Stars— consisting of New Orleans musical celebrities such as Dr. John, Cyril Neville, and Big Chief Monk Boudreaux—released their eponymous first album in 2005. The release of *Hurricane on the Bayou*, conceived as a film portrayal of what might happen *if* a hurricane hit New Orleans, was delayed to 2006 after Katrina made the scenario real. Targeting a youth audience ages nine to fourteen, the film gives explicit visual evidence of how wetlands loss has made New Orleans and other areas along the Louisiana coast more vulnerable to hurricane damage, reinforcing the message with voiceovers and music from Benoit and a diverse group of Louisiana musicians including zydeco accordionist Chubby Carrier, young Cajun fiddler Amanda Shaw, and well-known New Orleans producer Allen Toussaint. Benoit and his organization have continued this public awareness campaign, producing the Voice of the Wetlands festival annually in Louisiana's Terrebonne Parish. The Voice of the Wetlands All-Stars, who perform live occasionally, recorded a second album, *Box of Pictures*, in 2011.

Musical commentary on Louisiana's environmental issues has not been limited to folk and popular music. In 1998, Earl Robicheaux returned from completing a doctorate in music composition at the University of Texas to live with and care for his mother in Berwick, Louisiana. By 2002, he had bought a Nagra tape recorder and was using his electronic composition training to make sound collages from field recordings he made in nature, getting some contract work from radio, the Louisiana State Museum, and Cornell University's Ornithology Lab. He self-produced *Atchafalaya Soundscapes*, his first CD-length work, in 2004. In his "soundscape compositions" he sought to create an ideal aural trace of the natural world, free from human intrusion, which a listener can compare to what those environments actually sound like today, thereby inspiring reflection on the human impact to those environments (McCutchan 2011, 129). Robicheaux went on to complete another sound collage project, *Grand Isle Diaries*, for the Louisiana Sea Grant Program in 2009 (McCutchan 2011, 171–75). This project involved recording not only nature sounds but also oral histories and other sounds of human habitation on one coastal barrier island. The work was published on the Sea Grant's website, which states: "In many respects, Grand Isle serves as the ultimate metaphor for Louisiana's vanishing coast. It is steeped in rich history involving nationalities from across the world that created a distinct coastal culture. Yet, it is a place where environmental vulnerability makes the future uncertain, and where the residents are unsure about their long-term survival on the coast" (Louisiana Sea Grant 2016).

At the close of 2010, Steve Riley and the Mamou Playboys released their *Grand Isle* album with a depiction of an oil-covered waterfowl on the cover (see figure 7.1); in contrast to the cover's direct visual statement, three songs on the album, make artistically indirect comment on Louisiana's environmental problems. On the title track, David Greely sings nostalgically about the pleasure resort that was the Grand Isle of his childhood, with only one line hinting at current troubles: "Ouais, la table était pleine / Mais le check s'en vient" (Yes, the table was full / But here comes the check).

Hurricane Katrina in 2005 provided both a distraction from and an intensification of environmentalist sentiment about south Louisiana's long-term problems. Canal dredging and anthropogenic wetlands loss were identified as environmental factors that exposed New Orleans to a greater magnitude of storm surge, thereby exacerbating the flooding (Freudenberg et al. 2009, 111–34; Theriot 2014, 196–97). However, public debate in the wake of Katrina largely focused on other matters: faulty engineering of the levees and other public works that led to the flooding of the city; media sensationalism and misinformation in the first days after the hurricane; and government bureaucratic incompetence and malfeasance in the months and years of recovery that followed. As evidenced by a dearth of topical songs written between 2005 and 2010, it was not until the BP oil spill that passionate protest returned to environmental issues.

The spill's impact on the region's wildlife, fishing, and tourism was immediately visible, and volunteers quickly organized fund-raising events to benefit wildlife rescue and families who were economically impacted by the spill. Following the celebrity concert precedent of Live Aid (Davis 2010), Gulf Aid concerts were held in New Orleans and Lafayette. I attended the Gulf Aid Aca-

steve riley & the mamou playboys grand isle

FIG. 7.1. Album cover art, Steve Riley and the Mamou Playboys, *Grand Isle*, 2010

diana concert in Lafayette in October 2010, where Marianne Faithful and Ani DiFranco performed along with Zachary Richard, a singer-songwriter from the area with an international reputation. Adopting the more-than-human point of view, Richard had already written and recorded two songs written from the points of view of birds, "Le grand gosier" and "Le pélican," and had them pressed and available for sale at the event (Richard 2010).[4] Other songs about the spill that were recorded and sold with proceeds to benefit oil-spill relief included Drew Landry's "BP Blues" and a cover of Smokey Johnson's 1960s New Orleans instrumental hit "It Ain't My Fault" by members of the Preservation Hall Jazz Band and guests, calling themselves the Gulf Aid All Stars, with rapped and sung commentary added by Mos Def (Gulf Aid All Stars 2010). A music video of the latter was also produced and available for sale on iTunes, showing the song being recorded at Preservation Hall with additional cachet lent by New Orleans bandleader Trombone Shorty, rock musician Lenny Kravitz, and Hollywood actor Tim Robbins, all of whom were in town in May 2010 to appear at the New Orleans Gulf Aid concert a few days later (Rawls 2010).

New Orleans trumpeter Shamarr Allen, who played at the same Gulf Aid concert, also created a song and accompanying music video using elements of hip hop and New Orleans brass band music, similar to "It Ain't My Fault" but using an all–New Orleans cast and outdoor shot locations, including Grand Isle (in front of a Grand Isle welcome sign, making it obvious) and the banks of the Mississippi. Allen, rapper Dee-1, singer-songwriter Paul Sanchez, and sousaphonist Bennie Pete from the Hot 8 Brass Band wrote and produced "Sorry Ain't Enough No More," posted it on YouTube in July 2010, and made it available for a time as a free download. Environmental justice is a major theme of the song. Shamarr Allen raps, "The only quality time I had coming from my dad was fishin' and you took that from me," while the video shows him fishing in the river with his father and a younger black man (0:54) and later pulling up a fish on the line that has been fouled by oil. Dee-1 adds, "We mad and we don't know how to act / This ain't 'bout white or black, 's 'bout green and I'm statin' the facts" (1:58).

Based near Lafayette, singer-songwriter Drew Landry took his guitar in July 2010 to a New Orleans meeting of a presidential commission on the oil spill and sang his "BP Blues" as a public comment, a performance that was captured on the C-SPAN cable television channel and gained further exposure online via YouTube (National Commission on the BP Deepwater Horizon Oil Spill and Offshore Drilling 2010). Not politically active previously, Landry brought a dual concern for the environment and for the hunter-gatherers in the wetlands that make their living from it. The lyrics of "BP Blues" stress the importance of hunting, fishing, and livelihood, not the environment for its own sake (Landry 2010). His activism for the people of the wetlands extends to the health of those fisherman who, unable to fish because of the spill, took jobs on oil-cleanup crews and soon thereafter developed illnesses related to toxic substance exposure. Attributing these health woes in part to the dispersant chemical Corexit, which BP used during the cleanup, and in part to BP's instructions to the cleanup crews, he subsequently wrote the song "3rd World Country Blues" ("They killed all the turtles, they killed all the turtles, and now they tryin' to kill the humans too") (Landry 2011) and making a feature-length documentary film using his own music as soundtrack, *The Restoration* (2014), which he has screened locally but has not released as of this writing.

Street protests, which figure so prominently in Manabe's account of music after the Fukushima disaster in Japan, were a notable but relatively brief phenom-enon after the oil spill.[5] Combining New Orleans jazz funeral and Mardi Gras traditions, costume designer Ro Mayer organized the Krewe of Dead Pelicans and staged a funeral on June 5, 2010, for all who lost their lives—humans and animals—in the BP incident. A brass band was hired to lead the procession, with clever costumes in the political parody tradition of some New Orleans Mardi Gras krewes, commenting on the disaster (Krewe of Dead Pelicans 2010).

> As petrochemicals flooded into the Gulf unabated, Mayer continued to orga-nize funeral processions for wildlife, leading people behind the slogan "Stop the Oil, Save the Gulf." However with weeks turning into months, the force of the Krewe of Dead Pelicans' street pageantry began to fade. As news of the oil disappeared from the front pages of newspapers, as people scrambled to get their share of the $20 billion payout, protestors stopped showing up to the Krewe of Dead Pelicans marches. Street theater no longer seemed capable of remedying the long term ecological consequences of the disaster. (Kirksey, Shapiro, and Brodine 2016)

Interpretations and Conclusions

Given the variety of musically creative responses in protest of environmen-tal degradation, why have these messages had a minimal impact thus far on the body politic in Louisiana? I shall reflect here on structural socioeconomic reasons for inaction and on the weakness of the link between cultural and environmental sustainability.

I spoke with a couple of songwriters who felt dwarfed by the scale of the economic forces aligned against any changes in the corporate and government behavior that have led to the current environmental situation. Drew Landry said, "I don't know how successful I was as an organizer. Because we made some differences but as long as they can pay for more commercials than you can pay for, you're not going to make too much noise" (interview, July 23, 2012, Scott, LA). Zachary Richard was similarly gloomy: "Politics is about money. And as long as a barrel of oil is going to be worth a hundred dollars, there's no real reason to change. There's no economic incentive for us to change our habits because so much of this economy is fueled by oil" (interview, March 27, 2013, Lafayette, LA).

The oil industry not only has financial capital; it also has high social capital across a wide range of income levels in Louisiana, what environmental sociolo-gists William R. Freudenberg and Robert Gramling have termed "the social multiplier effect." The social network of people tied to the oil industry and related services is thick, and the economic resources represented by that net-work are considerable. "It's one thing to decide whether to support or oppose a new industry, in the abstract, but it's another matter entirely to make such a decision about an industry that employs your next-door neighbor, or even your neighbor's second cousin" (Freudenberg and Gramling 2011, 137).

In the Japanese case of protest against the nuclear industry, Manabe outlines several legal and economic reasons why "Japanese record companies, producers, and artists censor their own work. . . . This internalized self-restraint can be more insidious than actual censorship as producers err on the side of caution, closing off avenues for thought" (2015, 10). In Louisiana, while some musicians may feel free to speak their minds due to a lack of music industry pressure (almost none have contracts with major labels), outside the musical context others in the community may feel more constrained due to social ties and political alliances. In *Creole Belle*, an installment (written after the BP oil spill) of his Dave Robicheaux detective series, novelist James Lee Burke's main character asks a law enforcement colleague about the underlying cause of a spate of violence: "What is the one subject around here that nobody brings up in a negative way, that no local journalist goes near? A subject so sensitive that people will walk away from you if they sense the wrong words are about to come out of your mouth?" The answer that comes back is one frequently espoused in the region of south Louisiana where the novel is set: "The country wants cheap gasoline. They don't care how they get it" (Burke 2012, 201–2). Defenders of the oil industry are quick to paint those who raise concerns about environmental damage as naive and hypocritical, pointing out that those critics also depend on the energy provided by oil and gas in their daily lives. This simplistic argument carries the day in an area where so many depend economically on the fossil-fuel industry. Musicians who adopt oppositional viewpoints may be dismissed as marginal members of society, working to raise the awareness of a population that remains unmoved.

Finally, while the various music scenes in south Louisiana have produced many songs in environmental protest and some would argue that traditional culture is disappearing at a rate commensurate with the receding of the state's coastline, it is worth remembering the point echoed in several other chapters in this volume, namely, that there is not necessarily any positive correlation between cultural sustainability and environmental sustainability. In fact, the correlation can be negative. The 1901 discovery of oil in Louisiana (Theriot 2014, 17) predates the earliest recording we have of Cajun music, made in 1928, by almost three decades; one of those early commercial recordings was Amédé Ardoin's 1934 "La valse des chantiers petroliperes" (Waltz of the oilfields). In the entire phonographic history of traditional music in south Louisiana, then, the oil and gas industry has always been part of the economic reality for everyone living there. This early twentieth-century state of tradition has been the subject of a successful revival since the 1960s (Baron and Walker, this volume). How closely musical and economic development were intertwined in the twentieth century is seldom discussed and bears further examination. In contemporary Louisiana, we have not only the Voice of the Wetlands festival in Houma but also the Shrimp and Petroleum Festival in Morgan City, which features live music and "recognizes the working men and women of both the seafood and petroleum industries . . . the economic lifeblood of the area" (Louisiana Shrimp and Petroleum Festival 2016). We have heard not only songs written in protest against the environmental degradation caused by the BP oil spill but also Mike Dean's song calling on President Obama to "lift the ban" on further offshore drilling immediately after BP's leaking well was capped. Traditional and popular culture are not aligned solely with one side or the other in the political debate over oil-field jobs and the "way of life" (Dean's words) they represent versus the environment and the pre-oil, hunter/gatherer economy it once sustained (*la mêche perdue*). Thus far, music has not tipped the balance in this debate one way or the other.

Notes

1. I acknowledge here my professional and intellectual debt to Jeff Todd Titon, dating back to a postcard he wrote me from his sabbatical leave at Berea College when I applied to graduate school at Brown University. Although I did not attend Brown, it was my privilege to work with Jeff on two SEM conference panels that led to special issues of *the world of music*, on tourism (41 [3]) and sustainability (51 [1]). His vision and example of doing applied ethnomusicology from an academic position have provided sturdy support for the work I do now at the University of Louisiana at Lafayette.

2. Measuring impact on popular opinion scientifically requires resources far beyond the scope of this project. I can only characterize it based on anecdotal evidence, which indicates that in Louisiana we are far away from a tipping point whereby environmental concerns would take political precedence over the economic status quo.

3. A spectacular example of subsidence in recent years has been Bayou Corne, the subject of a documentary film, *Forgotten Bayou* (2016), and a song by Christine Lavin, "Sinkholes!" (Lavin 2016).

4. Richard wrote a third song with an avian perspective on the oil spill, which became the title track of his 2012 album, *Le Fou*.

5. A later production (2013) by two New Orleans theater companies combined the processional aspect of the jazz funeral with more avant-garde music and theater (Artspot Productions and Mondo Bizarro 2013). From this came a compact disc of music written for the show (ArtSpot Productions and Mondo Bizarro 2015).

References

Arons, Rachel. 2012. "A Mythical Bayou's All-Too-Real Peril: The Making of 'Beasts of the Southern Wild.'" *New York Times*, June 10, 2012. http://www.nytimes.com.

Artspot Productions and Mondo Bizarro. 2013. "What Is CRY YOU ONE?" September 24. http://www.cryyouone.com/stories/detail/1/What-is-CRY-YOU-ONE.

Balaguru, Karthik, David R. Judi, and L. Ruby Leung. 2016. "Future Hurricane Storm Surge Risk for the US Gulf and Florida Coasts Based on Projections of Thermodynamic Potential Intensity." *Climatic Change* 138 (1–2): 99–110.

Biello, David. 2011. "How Science Stopped BP's Gulf of Mexico Oil Spill." *Sustainability* (blog), *Scientific American*, April 19. http://www.scientificamerican.com/article/how-science-stopped-bp-gulf-of-mexico-oil-spill/.

Burke, James Lee. 2012. *Creole Belle*. New York: Simon and Schuster.

Couvillion, Brady R., John A. Barras, Gregory D. Steyer, William Sleavin, Michelle Fischer, Holly Beck, Nadine Trahan, Brad Griffin, and David Heckman. 2011. *Land Area Change in Coastal Louisiana from 1932 to 2010*. Reston, VA: US Geological Survey.

Cry You One. 2013. "Louis Michot." October 3. http://cryyouone.com/stories/detail/26/Louis-Michot.

Cultural Research Institute of Acadiana. 2016. "What We Do." http://www.criacadiana.org/what-we-do.html. Accessed June 16.

Davis, H. Louise. 2010. "Feeding the World a Line? Celebrity Activism and Ethical Consumer Practices from Live Aid to Product Red." *Nordic Journal of English Studies* 9 (3): 89–118

Freudenberg, William R., and Robert Gramling. 2011. *Blowout in the Gulf*. Cambridge, MA: MIT Press.

Freudenberg, William R., Robert Gramling, Shirley Laska, and Kai T. Erikson. 2009. *Catastrophe in the Making: The Engineering of Katrina and the Disasters of Tomorrow*. Washington, DC: Island Press.

Holland, Greg, and Cindy L. Bruyere. 2014. "Recent Intense Hurricane Response to Global Climate Change." *Climate Dynamics* 42 (3–4): 617–27.

Kirksey, Eben, Nicholas Shapiro, and Maria Brodine. 2016. "Krewe of Dead Pelicans." http://www.multispecies-salon.org/dead-pelicans/. Accessed June 30.

Louisiana Sea Grant. 2016. "Grand Isle Diaries." http://www.laseagrant.org/communications/voices/grand-isle-diaries/. Accessed August 16.

Louisiana Shrimp and Petroleum Festival. 2016. "History." http://www.shrimpandpetroleum.org/history. Accessed August 10.

Manabe, Noriko. 2015. *The Revolution Will Not Be Televised: Protest Music after Fukushima*. New York: Oxford University Press.

McCutchan, Ann. 2011. *River Music: An Atchafalaya Story*. College Station, TX: Texas A&M University Press.

National Commission on the BP Deepwater Horizon Oil Spill and Offshore Drilling. 2010. "Drew Landry—BP Blues (CPSAN [*sic*] committee meeting)." Excerpt from C-SPAN broadcast of commission meetings held July 12–13, 2010, in New Orleans, LA. YouTube video, 5:16, uploaded by "dirtycajuns," July 13, 2010. https://www.youtube.com/watch?v=EApX41i1tio.

Picou, J. Steven. 2000. "The 'Talking Circle' as Sociological Practice: Cultural Transformation of Chronic Disaster Impacts." *Sociological Practice: A Journal of Clinical and Applied Sociology* 2 (2): 77–97.

Rawls, Alex. 2010. "Kravitz, Legend, Mos Def Headline Gulf Aid Concert." *Spin*, May 17. http://www.spin.com/2010/05/kravitz-legend-mos-def-headline-gulf-aid-concert/.

Spanne, Autumn. 2016. "The Lucky Ones: Native American Tribe Receives $48m to Flee Climate Change." *Guardian*, March 23, 2016. https://www.theguardian.com.

Theriot, Jason P. 2014. *American Energy, Imperiled Coast: Oil and Gas Development in Louisiana's Wetlands*. Baton Rouge: Louisiana State University Press.

Discography

Allen, Shamarr, Dee-1, Paul Sanchez, and Bennie Pete. 2010. "Sorry Ain't Enough No More (bp oil spill song)." YouTube video, 5 min., uploaded by shamarrallenmusic, July 12. https://www.youtube.com/watch?v=ZCTn9tqU-mE.

Ardoin, Amédé. 1934. "La valse des chantiers petroliperes." Decca 17002, 78 rpm disc. Reissued in 1995 on Amédé Ardoin, *I'm Never Comin' Back*, Arhoolie/Folklyric 7007, compact disc.

Artspot Productions and Mondo Bizarro. 2015. *Cry You One*. Self-produced, compact disc.

Benoit, Tab. 2002. *Wetlands*. Telarc CD-83530, compact disc.

Dean, Mike. 2010. "Mike Dean: BP Song 'LIFT THE BAN.'" YouTube video, 2:36, uploaded by Eric Breaux, July 31. https://www.youtube.com/watch?v=zq9sTqVPSnI.

Gulf Aid All Stars. 2010. "It Ain't My Fault." Preservation Hall Records, digital download.

Landry, Drew. 2010. "BP Blues." Warner Bros. Records, digital download.

———. 2011. "3rd World Country Blues." *Share Cropper's Whine*. Self-produced, compact disc.

Lavin, Christine. 2016. "'Sinkholes!' by Christine Lavin—Be Careful Where You Step!" YouTube video, 4:05, published by Christine Lavin, April 11. https://www.youtube.com/watch?v=Waps2-TBorA.

Les Frères Michot. 2003. "La valse de la mèche perdue." *La roue qui pend*. Swallow Records 6174, compact disc.

Lost Bayou Ramblers. 2008. "Valse de mèche perdu." On *Vermilionaire*, Bayou Perdu Records, compact disc.

———. 2012. "Bastille" and "Marée noire." On *Mammoth Waltz*, Bayou Perdu Records BPR003, compact disc.

Richard, Zachary. 2010. "Le grand gosier" and "Le pélican." On *Le grand gosier*, RZ Records, digital download.

———. 2012. *Le Fou*. Avalanche AVA2-0002, compact disc.

Robicheaux, Earl. 2004. *Atchafalaya Soundscapes*. Self-produced, compact disc. Reissued as the CD included with the book *River Music* (McCutchan 2011).

Steve Riley and the Mamou Playboys. 2010. *Grand Isle*. Self-produced, compact disc.

Voice of the Wetlands All-Stars. 2005. *VOW: Voice of the Wetlands*. Rykodisc RCD 10829, compact disc.

———. 2011. *Box of Pictures*. Self-produced, compact disc.

Filmography

Beasts of the Southern Wild. 2012. Directed by Benh Zeitlin. Feature, 93 min.

Forgotten Bayou: Life on the Sinkhole. 2016. Directed by Victoria Greene. Documentary. http://www.forgottenbayou.com/videos, 70 min.

Hurricane on the Bayou. 2007. Directed by Greg MacGillivray. Codirected by Glen Pitre. IMAX documentary, 42 min.

Krewe of Dead Pelicans. 2010. "Krewe of Dead Pelicans: A Protest against the BP Oil Spill." YouTube video, 9:42, uploaded by John Menszer, June 6. 2010. https://www.youtube.com/watch?v=zcLJqWDx3lo.

The Restoration. 2014. Directed by Drew Landry. Unreleased documentary. Vimeo video trailer, 12:48, published by Drew Landry, April 14. https://vimeo.com/92307568.

Spitzer, Nick, interviewer. 2015. "Benh Zeitlin and Louis Michot with Nick Spitzer." Public event in "The Katrina Disaster Now" series sponsored by the Tulane Environmental Studies Program. Held Wednesday, October 7, 5:30 p.m., in Stone Auditorium, Tulane University, New Orleans, LA. YouTube video, 1:25:53, published by Andy Horowitz, October 29. https://www.youtube.com/watch?v=B4R1M45x4YI.

CHAPTER 8

Alaska Native Ways of Knowing and the Sustenance of Musical Communities in an Ailing Petrostate

SUSAN HURLEY-GLOWA

ALASKANS ARE IN THE midst of an economic, cultural, and ecological maelstrom as a result of a major decline in oil production and profits in combination with the effects of anthropogenic climate change. Examining two very different case studies that take place in the very same concert hall, this chapter illuminates ways that some musical communities are responding to Alaska's new conditions. More specifically, I compare the relative resilience of the Fairbanks Festival of Native Arts (FNA) and the Fairbanks Symphony Orchestra (FSO). The Festival of Native Arts has thrived since the 1970s by reviving and sustaining Indigenous traditions while embracing new performance ideas. These practices resonate with Indigenous values, beliefs, and worldviews that have helped to make Alaska Native traditions resilient in the past (Kawagley 1993; Williams 1993, 1996; Barnhardt 2001, 5; Barnhardt and Kawagley 2005; John 2010; Perea 2011; Hogan and Topkok 2015). Both organizations are affected by Alaska's deepening recession, but the Indigenous community's dynamic, adaptive nature contributes to its resilience, while the orchestra's high level of specialization, cost, thinning audience, and colonial legacy call its future into question when placed in Aaron S. Allen's proposed sustainability framework and subjected to the "Is it right?" prompt (Allen, this volume; see also Cooley).

This study references theoretical models of sustainability developed within applied ethnomusicology by Jeff Titon and others in recent decades (Titon 2009a,

2015; Allen, this volume). The models suggest that music cultures behave like ecosystems in nature and that the keys to maintaining healthy systems mirror those found in sound ecological practices. Environmental resource management seeks sustainability through continuity, equity, and diversity within ecosystems. Titon's model transfers those aims to music cultures and situates the development of resilience as a strategy leading to sustainability. Shared features of resilient music cultures include the ability to manage change without sacrificing future identity, continuity, integrity, or resources, along with the assertion that music cultures can become more resilient through adaptive management (2015, 158). Titon suggests that the best resilience strategies often come from within the community rather than from above, in informal networks rooted in deep trust (Titon 2009b, 120, 130).

I had the opportunity to observe some of these ideas in practice when my family began a new life in Fairbanks, Alaska, in 2007. Before the move, both my husband and I had tenure-track positions at East Coast liberal arts colleges located some ninety miles apart. We also had two young boys. After six stressful years of urban commuting, my husband accepted a teaching position at the University of Alaska Fairbanks (UAF). We sold the house, bought a camper, and took the long road to Alaska in hopes of a lifestyle that was closer to our ideals: one where we could garden, hike, forage, ski, and fish—to live altogether closer to nature.

Many wishes were realized in Fairbanks over time, but a full-time teaching job for me failed to materialize. Instead, I taught Western art music as an adjunct in UAF's largely Eurocentric music program. My small salary was in rude contrast to the high Alaskan costs of living, and money was tight. Although it wasn't paid work, I began playing horn in the Fairbanks Symphony Orchestra.

We performed and rehearsed in the beautiful new concert hall on the UAF campus, built with public and private funding. From a postcolonial perspective, this orchestra and hall can be seen as a symbol upholding the ideals of Western culture in this isolated college town (Sercombe 2016, 149–52). If you leave the greater Fairbanks area (population about ninety-nine thousand), you are surrounded by literally hundreds of miles of taiga and wild country dotted with only a few small Indigenous villages. Anchorage is 360 miles south of Fairbanks with the massive Alaskan mountain range in between. In this sense, Fairbanks feels like an island in an ocean of wilderness, especially to newcomers, and the FSO has served as an anchor binding some to Western cultural ideas.

From the performers' perspectives, the orchestra creates an expatriate community of sorts where instrumentalists skilled in Western classical music find satisfaction making music together during cold, dark winter evenings, motivations that resonate with the ideas of shared company and cooperative music-making described elsewhere in this volume (see Hutchinson, this volume). To their Alaska Native neighbors, whose cultural traditions nearly disappeared when outsiders' ways were forced on them in the twentieth century, the orchestra may have other meanings.

In 2008, my second year in Fairbanks, I began to learn about Alaska Native cultures through work with Theresa Arevgaq John, a respected professor, scholar, performer, and Yup'ik traditional culture bearer. Theresa was writing her dissertation on Yup'ik music and dance traditions, and she sought a graduate-level independent study to learn more about theoretical frameworks used in ethnomusicology. Although I was officially the instructor, Theresa introduced me to her culture and to the concept of Indigenous ways of knowing. A wonderful translator of culture, Theresa captivated me with stories of prophecies and events that crossed into the world of the unexplainable and magical, and she introduced me to Yup'ik songs, motion dances, rituals, and regalia. She thanked me for my help with the gift of a large frozen salmon, which I accepted with surprise and gratitude. Theresa John, who went on to earn her doctorate at the University of Alaska Fairbanks, has devoted her life to the statewide revitalization of Alaska Native arts, helping to establish several major festivals, including the one in Fairbanks and the annual Cama-i celebration in Bethel, Alaska. Our interactions opened my eyes to Alaska Native music cultures and Indigenous ways of knowing and prompted me to cautiously learn more.

Despite the trauma of colonialism and missionary schools, Alaska Native music cultures have demonstrated deep resilience in recent decades (Kingston 1999; Williams 1993, 149). The revitalization of festivals, rituals, and dance groups based on traditional knowledge shared by culture bearers like Theresa John has helped communities survive profound changes. One deep-rooted resilience strategy embedded in many Alaska Native cultures is respect for tradition but tolerance for new ideas (Williams 1993, 149–51). Embracing change is compatible with Alaska Native ways of knowing, an epistemology based on the balance of the environment, family, community, and spirituality (Barnhardt 2001, 5; Barnhardt and Kawagley 2005; Hogan and Topkok 2015; John 2010; Kawagley 1993; Perea 2011). Traditional knowledge "offers lessons that can benefit everyone, from educator to scientist, as we search for a more satisfying and sustainable way to live on this planet" (Barnhardt and Kawagley 2005, 2). Alaska Native ways encourage all of us to (1) look to the environment for both practical and spiritual insights; (2) honor community relationships, families, and friends; (3) respect diversity; (4) leave enough resources to sustain the future; and (5) remain flexible in the face of change. In effect, there is much overlap between the resilience strategies suggested by my respected mentor, Jeff Titon, and those derived from Alaska Native traditional knowledge. Alaska's precontact bounty reflects the efficacy of its Indigenous people as stewards of the land, and their actions resonate with the ideals of climate scientists today.

Alaska in Context

In a pattern established by eighteenth-century Russian trappers, people have eagerly extracted Alaska's bountiful marine life, furs, lumber, minerals, and especially oil for profit with little regard for the environmental or cultural consequences. When the state opened Prudhoe Bay for development and the Trans-Alaska Pipeline System was constructed in the 1970s, Alaskans of all backgrounds felt the strong flow of money into new state education, infrastructure, and healthcare programs, thus improving life in the emerging petrostate in some ways for most citizens. Conditions changed when both oil prices and production began to drop in 2010, pushing Alaska's undiversified oil-based economy into rapid decline, creating today's multibillion-dollar state budget deficit crisis (Associated Press 2016; Johnson 2016; Younger 2016).

During the same time frame, problems caused by Alaska's anthropogenic climate change began to intensify as the result of worldwide fossil-fuel dependency. Melting sea ice, unstable permafrost, and coastal erosion began to displace Indigenous coastal communities, and vast summer forest fires and changing flora and fauna patterns put all Alaskans on notice. Indigenous Alaskans have been disproportionately affected by climate change as it has disrupted traditional subsistence lifestyles and destroyed villages (Mooney 2015; Struzik 2016).

It is worthwhile to take a quick look at a map of Alaska and its demographics to put the region in context. Alaska is vast, but its population is just 740,000: it has the United States' lowest population density. About 19 percent of the population is Indigenous, representing the five major Alaska Native groupings. Alaska has only three small urban areas: Anchorage, Fairbanks, and Juneau, and it may come as a surprise to learn that some of their neighborhoods are considered the most diverse in the entire United States (Swann 2016). More than 40 percent of Alaskans live close to Anchorage; for the rest, the isolation of rural life is the norm. Alaska Natives have traditionally lived in small communities where they practiced a subsistence lifestyle, but there is now a migration flow to larger Alaskan cities because of climate change consequences as well as greater economic and educational opportunities. Village friends and family continue to cultivate their ties in urban settings, however. Throughout Alaska, community interactions take on almost life-and-death importance because winters are so long, dark, and isolating: music, arts, and sports help folks maintain their health, identities, and sanity.

The University of Alaska has a series of satellite campuses spread throughout the state supporting educational programs, as well as cultural and athletic events. Because of the $4 billion state budget deficit, UA is undergoing draconian cuts, slashing whole programs and losing faculty to other jobs (Hanlon 2016). Alaska state education funding for public schools has also suffered deep cuts, and programs deemed nonessential by legislators like music, arts, and languages are often the first to be eliminated. As both the Fairbanks Symphony Orchestra and the Festival of Native Arts use the UAF concert hall and receive financial support from the university, their futures are all intertwined. Altogether, Alaskans today must cope with an ailing state government, high living costs, austerity budgets, and rapid climate change.

Two Alaskan Case Studies

The Fairbanks Festival of Native Arts

The unlikely comparison between an orchestra (with its legacy of cultural imperialism) and an Indigenous arts celebration (with its legacy of colonial repression) came to me back in 2008 while rehearsing on the concert stage that houses them both. I looked out at the rows of seats and recalled festival nights when the hall was filled with cheering Alaska Native students and families who joined the ensembles from their villages on stage during invitational dances. On those evenings, I liked to stay until closing ceremonies, exhilarated to experience a major expression of traditional culture right on campus.

I quickly learned that my point of view was not shared by some of my colleagues from the music department. In contrast, they viewed the Festival of Native Arts as an annual nuisance and siege to be endured. Barricades were erected to keep participants out of the department corridors, and one colleague told me that the "sacred" symphony space had been as good as defiled by the festival, citing a dirty diaper left among the seats as damning evidence.

I found these attitudes and the all-too-obvious inequities in support for diversity at UAF as well as the music program's single-minded focus on Western art music to be deeply disturbing. I began to see the annual occupation of the concert hall by Alaska Natives as a symbol of the long-overdue decolonization of Alaska by its ousted owners, viewing it as one little step in righting deep social wrongs (Hogan and Topkok 2015; Smith 1999). To be fair, overall support of Alaska Native students, languages, and Indigenous studies has been strong at UA for some years, but the UAF music department curriculum has only recently become a little more inclusive. The inequities put me in a dilemma: although I enjoy the craft and conversation of good orchestral horn playing (Hutchinson, this volume), like Christopher Small, I am uncomfortable with the hierarchical social relationships and the vast sums of money required to train, outfit, and maintain an orchestra (Small 1998, 15–16), especially in Alaska, where the costs to maintain such manifestations of Western culture are high and may even work against the sustenance of Alaska Native cultural traditions. As I weighed the equity differences in institutional support for the symphony (and the Eurocentric music degree that feeds it) in comparison to support for Alaska Native music cultures, the imbalances were all too evident. Still, the FSO and the FNA have both had the resilience to survive for decades, so I decided to continue to explore the topic.

The Festival of Native Arts was first held on the UAF campus in late winter of 1974. Musicians, dancers, and artisans representing the primary Alaskan Indigenous groups have gathered each year since to share their cultural heritage in a public multiday event. Following good adaptive management and stewardship principles, this student-run event expresses rejuvenated interest in Alaska Native music cultures and includes group participation in songs and dances, some of which were nearly lost as a result of the disruption of traditional culture in Alaskan Indigenous communities during the past century. During the festival, performances are held each evening featuring community groups from across Alaska who have raised money to attend the event. The audience is primarily Alaska Natives, but outsiders are welcomed and do attend. Craftspeople display and sell their work nearby. To conclude the event, university students organize a potlatch featuring social dancing and Native foods. Altogether, the festival is an annual time of community pride signifying the resilience of Alaska Native music cultures.

In 1971 the Alaska Native Claims Settlement Act (ANCSA) settled the long-standing land claims of Alaska Natives, and they received forty million acres, divided among twelve regional administrating corporations. These regional corporations have provided funding for schools, medical facilities, and housing, along with dividend payout to individuals based on investments selected by the corporations' tribal members. The Fairbanks Festival of Native Arts was established soon after the settlement, and it marks the beginning of recovery for Indigenous communities (Williams 1993, 1996). Other regional festivals have followed since then.

Alaskan ethnomusicologist Paul Krejci and I began new fieldwork in 2008 documenting ways that Alaska Native music cultures incorporated new musical sounds and ideas as they expressed their identities at the Festival of Native Arts. Following a period of cultural dormancy and repression, we found that local songs, dances, languages, crafts, and regalia were reviving and returning to active use. Remaining firmly rooted in their Indigenous identity, traditional practitioners were also adopting new ideas and new contexts, including public festivals and concert halls. Artistic experimentation included the mixing of forms and styles from neighboring Indigenous groups, southern powwow culture, and cosmopolitan popular music, including rock, hip hop, and fiddling (Hurley-Glowa and Krejci 2008). The student-run Iñu-Yupiaq drum and dance ensemble (the FNA's host drum) demonstrates some of these changes. The ensemble's name reflects the unusual mixture of Inupiat and Yup'ik motion-dance repertoire, and students can now learn Alaska Native traditions across ethnic boundaries and in new contexts (see http://inuyupiaqdancers.tripod.com/ and https://en.wikipedia.org/wiki/Inu-Yupiaq). Many Alaska Native educational, health, and cultural programs have been developed since ANCSA, and a robust 20 percent of the total UAF student enrollment has Indigenous heritage. The number of Alaska Natives with doctoral degrees is also growing rapidly (Perea 2013). All these developments are signs of further cultural recovery.

Social media, computers, cell phones, and digital video have become powerful aids in developing resilience for Alaska Natives. Byron Nicholai, a young Yup'ik singer, drum leader, and basketball player from Toksook Bay, provides an interesting example of the effective use of social media in reinforcing Indigenous identity. Nicholai began posting his songs, which playfully combine traditional Yup'ik and US popular styles, on his Facebook site around 2012. His site went viral, and his drum-dance song "I Am Yup'ik" has become an anthem for his generation, expressing pride in Yup'ik heritage (Luger 2014). Nicholai is now an ambassador of Alaska Native culture, he has performed throughout the United States including for President Obama in Washington, DC, and his story is featured in a film screened at the 2016 Sundance Film Festival (Anastasion and Golon 2016). Altogether, new media usage demonstrates how Alaska Natives have been adapting to the contemporary world since the time of their first contact with outsiders (Barnhardt and Kawagley 2005; Williams 1993, 151). As Alaska Natives relocate as the result of climate and economic change, new technologies, new drum and dance groups, festivals, and social events in new urban locations help people deal with displacement and lifestyle changes (http://www.frontierofchange.org/). Resilience, close connections to the environment, and close-knit communities are helping people through the process.

The Fairbanks Symphony Orchestra

The Fairbanks Symphony Orchestra was established in 1959. Over time, it became affiliated with the UAF music program, and faculty member Eduard Zilberkant has been the music director since 2000, conducting an eight-concert season. UAF music faculty and professional military-band musicians cover key chairs, but only the conductor and the orchestra administrators receive pay. To date, the value of the FSO to a segment of Fairbanks society is demonstrated through ongoing corporate and university funding and community support. However, several factors threaten the orchestra's future stability: (1) the loss of UAF music faculty and student performers as programs are cut; (2) the dispersing of army-band personnel; (3) aging performers and audiences; (4) diminished state and corporate funding sources; (5) a dearth of new skilled players on some instruments; and (6) changing musical tastes.

Recent problems with American orchestras are well documented as ensembles deal with high maintenance costs, declining sponsorship, new audience demographics, union demands, a glutted market for performers, and perceptions of irrelevance (Botstein 2012; Flanagan 2012). The Fairbanks Symphony Orchestra shares these issues. Western art music is clearly not the music of the mainstream United States. Small has persuasively argued that a symphony by nature is not egalitarian or diverse; its inflexible form and structure have made the orchestra a costly symbol of "the power holding class" in Western society (Small 1987, 7). Like an intricate machine that is only as strong as its weakest link, if one part of the system fails—for example, a lack of double reed players—the whole organization can quickly grind to a halt. The reality is that a complex entity like an orchestra can't change or adapt much without losing its identity and function, and keeping it in equilibrium means that its beautiful music comes at a high cost at every level of production. Small might ask if such an ensemble is worth keeping, especially since it reflects and ritually enacts relationships that are inequitable (1998), and I would encourage Alaskans to weigh the same questions.

That said, an experimental model for a more sustainable orchestra may be found within the FSO's own history. Older musicians suggest that under conductor and composer Gordon Wright from 1969 to 1989, the orchestra was more tuned into Alaska's social and natural environment than it is today. They mention its emphasis on regular tours to remote villages, its cultural exchanges, and its new repertoire by Alaskan and other composers (personal communications with Jane and John Aspnes; Jim Kowalsky; Ted and Kay DeCorso; Richard Tremarello; Ray Funk, summer 2016). In those days, the orchestra board prioritized Alaskan village outreach concerts and worked hard to secure the orchestra's financial future, which included a National Endowment for the Arts grant to support village tours and other grants to commission new works. Narrated works like *Peter and the Wolf* were also translated into Alaska Native languages for rural audience performances. In a literal cultural exchange, Indigenous musicians and dancers often performed for the orchestra members before or after the formal concert.

This older FSO community produced remarkably resilient lifelong musicians, and many were dedicated environmentalists like Gordon Wright himself (1934–2007). Reflecting the 1960s' environmental movement and pioneer spirit, they embraced the Alaskan lifestyle, and under Wright's dogged leadership, they traveled to remote villages on bush planes, boats, buses, and even dogsleds, with concert dress that included parkas and bunny boots (Wakin 2007). Rather than edifying new audiences with Western art music, the main tour objective for Wright and many orchestra members was the human exchange of culture. Observations of villagers' responses to the concerts can be found in Thomas

Johnston's 1976 article and Sarah Elder's documentary film *Overture on Ice* (1983). In contrast, today's FSO follows a traditional Enlightenment model based on Western art music canons and conservatory ideals. Wright's great experiment, this small touring orchestra that played in numerous hard-to-reach Indigenous Alaskan villages, was admittedly expensive to maintain, but it did break down barriers, and perhaps most importantly, it opened space for some musical dialogue between cultures (Sercombe 2016).

Several Fairbanksans attracted international acclaim for their uniquely environmental-oriented aesthetic lens. Wright was part of a trio of creative Alaskan thinkers who lived in neighboring cabins, alongside composer John Luther Adams and Alaskan poet laureate John Haines (Adams 2015a, 2015b). These three—Adams, Haines, and Wright—represent a sensibility in their works that is grounded in their experiences in the Alaskan environment (Poetry Foundation 2016). Not inconsequentially, Adams was the director of the Northern Alaska Environmental Center and a percussionist in the FSO. Adams's compositions have tapped into a rich new musical vein by creating music that is closely tied to the environment. For example, Adams's work *The Place Where You Go to Listen*, located in the Museum of the North on the UAF campus, uses sound waves generated by Alaska's ecosystem as trigger sources in this sound and light installation. Most of Adams's works dialogue with the natural world in one way or another—some compositions are written to be performed in specific wilderness locations. Like Alaska Native cultures, the resilience of his music is derived in part from observations of the natural world, creatively blending Indigenous songs, words, names, places, and rhythmic figures in his works. Successfully grounding his music in natural soundscapes, Adams is a now highly respected international composer; he won a Pulitzer Prize in 2014 and a Grammy in 2015 for his orchestra composition *Become Ocean* (Adams 2015b; Ross 2008; see also http://johnlutheradams.net/).

In the case of the FSO, a measure of resilience may come by learning from its past when the orchestra was interested in the diversity gained through cultural exchanges, in innovative new compositions, and in prioritizing regional tours. These measures resonate with steadfast Alaska Native values and practices. Deep-rooted knowledge of the environment provides practical guides for living responsibly, and for John Luther Adams and many Alaska Native artists this knowledge serves as the basis for meaningful musical creations. John Luther Adams captured this ethos in his "Credo" for Gordon Wright:

> I believe in the mystery of being, in the wholeness of life, and the spirit in all things. I believe in the tundra, in the forests, in the rivers, and the nameless mountains stretching to the sea. I believe in the music of the rising wind, the

rushing water, and the bell-tones of the hermit thrush ringing in the twilight.
I believe we are relatives of the moose, and the swans, of the birch, the cran-
berry, and the wild rose. I believe that our destiny is to know our place, to live
in peace, and to listen to the earth. (Adams 2015a)

This chapter's case studies of the FNA and the FSO illustrate reactions to
economic and environmental stresses caused by an undiversified economy based
on problematic fossil fuels. The comparison also exposes inequalities that can't
easily be righted. To begin with, Western epistemologies and intellectual ideals
have dominated Alaskan public educational policy ever since outsiders settled
the region at the expense of Indigenous cultures and their ways of knowing.
Second, the stakes in struggles for cultural sustainability are not equal. If Western traditions like the FSO prove to be unsustainable in Alaska, many people,
including me, will be sad, but Western classical music will persist elsewhere. In
comparison, if festivals like the FNA disappear, Alaska Native cultures will lose
important footholds in their recovery from the effects of colonialism as well as
the potential loss of irreplaceable cultural heritage. Third, the power balances in
the rare exchanges of culture in recent years have been lopsided, with Western art
music ensembles often serving as cultural missionaries or ambassadors with the
goal of converting subjects (Alaska Native and/or any of "the great unwashed"
who will listen) to their aesthetic values. These exchanges have rarely happened
the other way around. The last on a long list of problems is the fact that Alaska
Native communities are disproportionately suffering from man-made climate
change even though the problems are not of their making.

While solutions are hard to come by, Titon has suggested that a sustainable
musical ecosystem can be achieved through diversity, equity, and continuity
(2015). Alaskan cultures are truly diverse, and there is theoretically enough
room for everyone if resources are distributed equitably. Indigenous people are
the original citizens of the land, and their voices should be strongly represented
in the mix. Progress has been made toward this goal. Alaska Native educators,
linguists, artists, and social activists are now organizing from the grassroots up
to create new opportunities and artifacts to foster their cultures, all activities
that represent best practices in developing resilience and continuity (Titon 2015).
Working together united by deep community trust, Alaska Natives themselves
are finding optimal ways to teach and share their heritage. Western art music
traditions like the FSO have the right to thrive as well, but they must also be
held accountable for their costs by asking, "Is this right?" If they are allocated
cultural capital at the expense of diversity, it is not right. In the best of all possible scenarios, all Alaskan musical communities will function with flexibility
informed by the natural world and adopt principles of cultural stewardship that
resonate with Alaska Native traditional worldviews.

References

Adams, John Luther. 2015a. "Gordon B. Wright." March 17. http://www.gordonbwright.com/?q=john-luther-adams-memories.

———. 2015b. "Leaving Alaska." *New Yorker*, June 17. http://www.newyorker.com.

Anastasion, Daniele, and Nathan Golon, dirs. 2016. *I am Yup'ik*. Documentary film. https://www.youtube.com/watch?v=pfCQqCkIdBs.

Associated Press. 2016. "Alaska Faces a Clear Budget Deficit without an Evident Solution." *New York Times*, April 9. http://nyti.ms/20qsouF.

Barnhardt, Carol. 2001. "A History of Schooling for Alaska Native People." *Journal of American Indian Education* 4 (1): 1–20. https://tinyurl.com/y7hmgfsa.

Barnhardt, Ray, and Angayuqaq Oscar Kawagley. 2005. "Indigenous Knowledge Systems and Alaska Native Ways of Knowing." *Anthropology and Education Quarterly* 36 (1): 823. https://www.fws.gov/nativeamerican/pdf/tek-barnhardt-kawagley.pdf.

Botstein, Leon. 2012. "The Symphony Orchestra: What Is to be Done?" *Peabody Magazine*, Spring 2012. http://www.peabody.jhu.edu/past_issues/spring12/botstein.html.

Elder, Sarah. 1983. *Overture on Ice*. Documentary film produced the Fairbanks Symphony Association.

Flanagan, Robert J. 2012. *The Perilous Life of Symphony Orchestra: Artistic Triumphs and Economic Challenges*. New Haven, CT: Yale University Press.

Hanlon, Tegan. 2016. "Looming Budget Cuts Leave Some UAA Professors Concerned, Others Packing Their Bags. *Alaska Dispatch News*, May 28. Updated August 25, 2016. http://www.adn.com.

Hogan, Maureen P., and Sean A. Topkok. 2015. "Teaching Indigenous Methodology and An Iñupiaq Example." *Decolonization: Indigeneity, Education & Society* 4 (2): 50–75. http://decolonization.org/index.php/des/article/view/22152.

Hurley-Glowa, Susan, and Paul Krejci. 2008. "Alaska's Festival of Native Arts: A Balance between Musical Innovation and Tradition." Poster Session at Society for Ethnomusicology Annual Meeting, Wesleyan University, October 25, Middletown, CT.

John, Theresa Arevgaq. 2010. "Yuraryararput Kangiit-Llu: Our Ways of Dance and Their Meanings." PhD diss., University of Alaska Fairbanks. http://ankn.uaf.edu/curriculum/phd_projects/arevgaq/yuraryaraput_kangiit-llu.pdf.

Johnson, Kirk. 2016. "Alaskans Brace for Spending Cuts as Oil Prices Tumble. *New York Times*, July 15. http://www.nytimes.com.

Johnston, Thomas. 1976. "The Social Background of Eskimo Music in Northwest Alaska." *Journal of American Folklore* 89 (354): 438–48.

Kawagley, Angayuqaq Oscar. 1993. "A Yupiaq Worldview: Implications for Cultural, Educational and Technological Adaptation in a Contemporary World." PhD diss., University of British Columbia, Vancouver.

Kingston, Deanna. 1999. "Returning: Twentieth Century Performances of the King Island Wolf Dance." PhD diss., University of Alaska Fairbanks.

Luger, Chelsey. 2014. "Must See: This 16-Year-Old Singer from Alaska Is Amazing." *Indian Country Today*, December 19. https://tinyurl.com/y9f3hqdw.

Mooney, Chris. 2016. "The Remote Alaskan Village That Needs to Be Relocated Due to Climate Change." *Washington Post*, February 25. https://www.washingtonpost.com.

Perea, Jessica Bissett. 2011. "The Politics of Inuit Musical Modernities in Alaska." PhD diss., University of California, Los Angeles.

———. 2013. "A Tribalography of Alaska Native Presence in Academia." *American Indian Culture and Research Journal* 37 (3): 3–27. Special issue, "Reducing Barriers to Native American Student Success in Higher Education: Challenges and Best Practices," ed. Robert Keith Collins.

Poetry Foundation. 2016. "John Haines." https://www.poetryfoundation.org/poems-and-poets/poets/detail/john-haines.

Ross, Alex. 2008. "Song of the Earth. A Composer Takes Inspiration from the Arctic." *New Yorker*, May 12. http://www.newyorker.com.

Sercombe, Laurel. 2016. "Native Seattle in the Concert Hall: An Ethnography of Two Symphonies." *Ethnomusicology* 60 (1): 148–69.

Small, Christopher. 1987. "Performance as Ritual: Sketch for an Enquiry into the True Nature of a Symphony Concert." In *Lost in Music: Culture, Style and the Musical Event*, edited by Avron Levine White, 6–32. New York: Routledge and Kegan Paul.

———. 1998. *Musicking: The Meanings of Performance and Listening.* Middletown, CT: Wesleyan University Press.

Smith, Linda Tuhuwai. 1999. *Decolonizing Methodologies: Research and Indigenous Peoples.* London: Zed Books.

Struzik, Ed. 2016. "Food Insecurity: Arctic Heat Is Threatening Indigenous Life." *Yale Environment 360*, March 16. https://tinyurl.com/h3f2sqx.

Swann, Kirsten. 2016. "The Most Diverse Neighborhood in the U.S. May Surprise You." *Smithsonian Journeys Quarterly*, July 7. http://www.smithsonianmag.com.

Titon, Jeff Todd, ed. 2009a. "Music and Sustainability." Special issue, *the world of music* 51 (1).

———. 2009b. "Music and Sustainability: An Ecological Viewpoint." In Titon 2009a, 119–37.

———. 2015. "Sustainability, Resilience, and Adaptive Management for Applied Ethnomusicology." In *The Oxford Handbook of Applied Ethnomusicology*, edited Svanibor Pettan and Jeff Todd Titon. Oxford: Oxford University Press. Published online February 2016. http://dx.doi.org/10.1093/oxfordhb/9780199351701.013.8.

Wakin, Daniel J. 2007. "Gordon Wright, Founder of Arctic Chamber Orchestra, Dies at 72." *New York Times*, Feb. 17. http://www.nytimes.com.

Williams, Maria. 1993. "Contemporary Alaska Native Music and Dance: The Spirit of Tradition." In *Native American Dance: Ceremonies and Social Traditions*, edited by Charlotte Heth, 149–68. Washington, DC: National Museum of the American Indian with Starwood Publishing.

———. 1996. "Alaska Native Music and Dance: The Spirit of Survival." PhD diss., University of California Los Angeles.

Younger, Levi. 2016. "For Brighter Future, Alaska Must Pursue Diverse Sources of Energy and Economy." *Alaska Dispatch*, October 17. https://tinyurl.com/yb63ddys.

CHAPTER 9

The New River Updated

Charles Ives and the Disappearing River Gods

DENISE VON GLAHN

IN 1911 THE American composer Charles Ives wrote a song he named "The New River." A pencil sketch for the piece included a note identifying the precise river he had in mind and, more than that, where along the 139 miles of waterway he had experienced it that day: "back from Zoar Bridge—June [?] 9th [recte 11?] 1911—Gas Machine kills Housatonic!" Ives's original text reveals his thoughts about a river he had just three years earlier described as "contented."[1]

> Down the river comes a noise!
> It is not the voice of rolling waters;
> It's only the sounds of man:
> Phonographs and gasoline,
> dancing halls and tambourine,
> [Human beings gone machine.]
> Killed is the blare of the hunting horn;
> The River Gods are gone.[2]

This essay contextualizes "The New River," a work that is unique among Ives's nature-inspired compositions for its unrestrained musical and textual criticism of environmental degradation. When Ives arranged it in 1913 to be part of a chamber orchestra set, he called it "The Ruined River." Given events that occurred on the national scene and in Ives's more local environment at the time having to do with rivers, the name change is not inconsequential. Beyond offering a statement on riparian conditions or rights, however, Ives's song makes a larger statement on what many understood to be the increasing mechanization of daily life. In 1904 American economist and sociologist Thorstein Veblen had observed that "the ubiquitous presence of the machine . . . is the unequivocal mark of the western culture of today as contrasted with the culture of other times and places." Ives captures Veblen's conclusion that "the machine throws out anthropomorphic habits of thought" in his cogent one-liner: "human beings gone machine" (Veblen 1904, 5–19). Ives's "New River," a song written over a century ago that lasts just under a minute, reminds us to consider the costs of an increasingly technology-driven world and what it does to our environment and perhaps our souls.

* * *

The natural world is omnipresent in the music of Charles Ives (1874–1954). Whether this reality reflects his early exposure to transcendentalist thought, which as a philosophy regularly invokes nature and preaches its numinous qualities, or is the outcome of some less lofty impulse is immaterial for the purposes of this chapter. Ives scholars agree that the composer was familiar with Ralph Waldo Emerson's essays, "Nature" included, as he was with *Walden* by Henry David Thoreau, and many works by Whitman and Hawthorne. He had written an essay on Emerson in his senior year at Yale for an American literature course taught by a beloved professor, William Lyon Phelps. Ives used it as the starting point for the first section of his extended program notes *Essays before a Sonata*, which would accompany his second piano sonata, *The Concord*, whose first movement Ives titled "Emerson."[3] Although transcendentalism informs a part of Ives's worldview, so too do more quotidian realities, as this study demonstrates.

I situate "The New River" within the larger social and political events of its time and demonstrate Ives's engagement with early twentieth-century proto-environmental initiatives. I argue that the song is Ives's response to the controversy swirling around increasing encroachment on the natural environment and specifically to the threat posed by redirecting and repurposing waterways and building dams. Such topics were of significant contemporary concern. The pros and cons of diverting a large volume of California's Tuolumne River through the Hetch Hetchy Valley to create a reservoir were argued by interested parties on both sides in the press and before Congress. Starting in 1900 and for more than a decade thereafter, newspapers and magazines ran stories about this controversial claim on public lands: "Hetch Hetchy" became a rallying cry. Articles, essays, and letters by those others labeled as "unreasonable" and "misinformed nature lovers" and "nature fakers" decried the "theft" and the damage inflicted on the natural world, while corporate and political allies in favor of development

enumerated the serious impediments to human progress such shortsighted opposition to a planned reservoir and dam presented.[4]

Many stories appeared across the nation in local papers and specialized
journals, but two publications focused considerable attention on the debate:
the *New York Times* and *Century Magazine*. In each of these publications, the
charge was led by writer, editor, and later diplomat Robert Underwood Johnson,
whose poetry Ives set four times between 1908 and 1921. It seems likely that the
composer followed Johnson's more politically motivated writings of the time
as well and agreed with his positions.[5] Based on Ives's clippings files, we know
that he read the *New York Times*, and given the presence of Johnson and William Lyon Phelps in *Century Magazine* and the influence of both men on Ives's
life and work, it also seems reasonable to assume that he was familiar with the
monthly magazine as well. The topics of their stories became source material
for his music.

On December 21, 1908, Johnson's challenge to the then secretary of the interior James Rudolph Garfield to "dispose at will of the nation's property" was
referenced in a "Special to the *New York Times*" (*New York Times* 1908, 4).
Yosemite had been declared a national park by an act of Congress on October
1, 1890. In 1906 the larger Yosemite Valley and Mariposa Grove were added. As
soon as the park's 1,500 square miles of land had been identified as belonging to
the nation's citizens, however, efforts to exempt some of the land and resources
began.[6] By "disposing of the nation's property," Underwood referenced the attempts by San Franciscan political heavyweights to claim the picturesque and
ecologically diverse Hetch Hetchy Valley as the logical site for a new reservoir
to supply water to the city's residents. The 1906 earthquake and resulting fires
that had leveled so much of that city raised awareness of the inadequate water
supply for the growing population and provided an emotional argument to
move with all haste to secure more.

Studies by the Army Corps of Engineers had identified at least six sites along
the Sierras that could provide needed water, a number of them closer to the
city, but all were eliminated except the one going through the park. Underwood
extrapolated that conceding the Tuolumne and Hetch Hetchy to San Francisco
would in effect turn over half of Yosemite National Park to the City by the
Bay. And while the reservoir might create a new, beautiful, scenic site (as was
argued), it would eliminate the valley's use by visitors forever after and change
their understanding of the place.

The valley had been a seasonal home to Miwok and Paiute peoples for at
least six thousand years before European settlers drove them out in the 1850s.
Although that action seemed not to trouble most Americans in the latter part
of the century, the fact that the valley provided unmatched opportunities for

naturalists studying a unique environment and also a direct link between the western and eastern sides of the valley did. Flooding the valley floor would eliminate that passageway and bury human and natural history. Even if parts of the reservoir area were left accessible to the public, Johnson argued, the water supply couldn't be safeguarded; it would be in immediate and constant danger of contamination. He wondered what the land grab portended for access to the Tuolumne's tributary waters? Would they be snatched by private interests and the public cut off from their use as well?[7]

But Johnson's arguments were met by Secretary Garfield's response that "the greatest good to the greatest number justifies alienating the park for the benefit of the citizens of San Francisco" (*New York Times* 1908).[8] Despite vocal opposition, "a conditional and revocable grant for its use was obtained from the Secretary of the Interior . . . on May 11, 1908" (*New York Times* 1910, 10).

In a January 1910 letter to the editor of the *New York Times*, preservationist Frederick G. Schwartz enumerated the negative implications of the proposed reservoir in the Hetch Hetchy Valley. He reviewed ten years of arguments in favor of flooding the valley by well-placed individuals on behalf of San Francisco. He reminded readers that in the beginning all parties had agreed that there *were* other sites that would work just as well without encroaching on the national park, and he quoted former mayor of San Francisco James D. Phelan himself as acknowledging this. Phelan did not deny it was true, but he owned rights to much of the land and water acreage, including the Tuolumne River flow through the Hetch Hetchy. In retrospect, it seems hardly coincidental that none of the other sites was pursued.

As the battle neared its end in 1912–13, Sierra Club founder John Muir wrote to his close friend Robert Underwood Johnson telling him about a recent club meeting. Muir had urged "everybody to write to Senators and the president keeping letters flying all next month thick as storm snow flakes, loaded with park pictures, short circulars, etc. Stir up all other park and playground clubs, women's clubs, etc." (Sierra Club 2017). Muir's Hetch Hetchy campaign became a national movement that Sierra Club historians take pride in characterizing as "perhaps the first effort at what is now known as 'grassroots lobbying'" (Sierra Club 2017).

Using his clout as editor of the *Century Magazine*, Johnson did what Muir requested. Muir had written about Yosemite for *Century* earlier. Photographs and stories about and by Muir and fellow naturalist and conservationist John Burroughs were regular features in the magazine. Burroughs's article "The Spell of Yosemite" spoke not only of Muir but also about Emerson's May 1871 visit with Muir at Yosemite, when the philosopher was sixty-eight years old. Burroughs concluded that "Emerson was greatly taken with Muir—a new kind of Thoreau, a Thoreau browsing upon the cedars and sequoias of the Sierra, instead of upon the scrub-oaks of Concord; not greater, as that remark might seem to imply, but different, schooled in nature, and not stamped with the Emersonian stamp as Thoreau was" (Burroughs 1910–11, 48). Connections with transcendentalist thought would have been concomitant with the evocation of Emerson's name in most readers' minds. If Ives had been drawn to the Hetch Hetchy issue because of its transcendentalist associations, Burroughs's reference to the Concord Bard could have provided the link. But there were other events happening closer to Ives's New York and Connecticut homes that likely brought him to Zoar Bridge in 1911; to understand the connection more background is useful.

* * *

In 1911 Muir wrote "Three Adventures in Yosemite" for the *Century Magazine* (Muir 1911–12, 656), and in 1912 Burroughs shared his thoughts in the essay "The Gospel of Nature," concluding that nature "teaches more than she preaches. There are no sermons in stones" (Burroughs 1912, 247). He rejected any "religious enthusiasm" (263) (Christian or otherwise) as a prerequisite for appreciating Yosemite or nature.

In late 1912 Johnson used his pulpit at *Century* to write an editorial in the column "Topics of the Time." "Giving Away the Nation's Property" captures the thrust and tone of Johnson's position and deserves quoting at length:

> The mainspring of the assault upon the people's National Park—and, if it shall succeed, it will be but the first of many similar assaults on other parks—is the desire to get something for nothing. The public interest in resisting the attempt is to save from destruction one of the most wonderful of the Sierra gorges, which a good wagon road would make an integral part of the Yosemite trip. It remains to be seen whether any amount of speciousness, any elaborate and misleading volume of argument will be able to obscure the main issue—the wanton invasion of the people's greatest park.
>
> We believe that the Roosevelt administration had no more legal or moral right to divert a part of this National Park from the purposes for which it was created, as was done by the Garfield grant, than it would have had to give away the nation's coal-fields in Alaska. The Sierra Club, contending with the unlimited financial resources of San Francisco, has yet presented a "brief" which riddles the arguments of the city's case.
>
> That fable teaches that the time to save the rest of our great scenery is before it is largely visited, for then it will become to the advantage of some "interest" to divert it from the use of posterity. (Johnson 1912–13)

In May 1913 Johnson wrote another editorial in which he compared the precarious position of Niagara Falls to that of Hetch Hetchy. In "Niagara Again in Danger: The Commercializing of Great Scenery," Johnson connected the common threat to two iconic natural wonders, thus reminding people on both coasts that this was not a regional issue: "The willingness to destroy or impair great scenery by commercializing it, whether at Niagara or in the Yosemite National Park makes it necessary that the fight for our natural treasures should be kept up with vigilance. . . . Should its advocates go to Congress, it must be remembered that the same principle underlies the defense of Niagara and of Hetch Hetchy—the conservation of great scenery for the ultimate benefit of mankind" (Johnson 1913a, 150)

The battle continued through 1913 and so did articles by Muir and Johnson in the *New York Times*. On August 1, 1913, Johnson wrote and distributed a broadside, "An Open Letter to the American People": "The Hetch Hetchy Scheme: Why It Should Not Be Rushed through the Extra Session." He addressed it to "Fellow-Owners of the Yosemite National Park." Unlike Burroughs, who rejected a religious explanation for the value of the valley, Johnson saw the Hetch Hetchy as "a veritable temple of the Living God." Evoking the biblical story in Matthew 21 of Jesus upturning the tables of the money changers, Johnson observed, "Again the money-changers are in the temple!" (Johnson 1913c).

Despite Burroughs's, Muir's, and Johnson's passionate arguments to preserve the park intact and the involvement of thousands of other "fellow owners" expressing their distress with the situation, Hetch Hetchy Valley was doomed. Their protest was dismissed largely on the grounds that it was "aesthetic." The Raker Act, named for its sponsor, John E. Raker, a representative from California, unanimously passed in both House and Senate committees, was voted on December 6, and signed into law on December 19. Rights to the valley were ceded to the City of San Francisco for its public water-supply system. Although former San Francisco mayor James D. Phelan was no longer in office by the time the vote took place, his interests won over the "aesthetic cranks" (Phelan quoted in Johnson 1913b). Over the next six years Hetch Hetchy Valley became a much-enlarged riverbed and the Tuolumne its flooding waters. It would take ten years to complete the dam, hardly soon enough to meet the water emergency that had originally been used to argue for its creation. Robert Underwood Johnson resigned the *Century Magazine* editorship in 1913 and focused his energies elsewhere.

* * *

While events at Yosemite and the Hetch Hetchy Valley commanded center stage in national headlines for the first three decades of the twentieth century, a similar situation was playing out closer to Ives's home during the same period of time, and it provided him with an even more personally resonant experience of environmental degradation. This is what he referenced in his note at the top of the song sketch: at Zoar Bridge Ives would have recognized the similarities between the fates of the Tuolumne and the Housatonic rivers. Both of them were victims of industry; both were killed by "the machine."

Both situations involved fears of land grabs, disputed water rights, engineers' reports, diverting rivers, building dams, concerns for contamination, worries about the degradation of the natural environment, the occurrence of large fires, evocations of real and possible emergencies as causes for immediate action, and ultimately the triumph of industry and industry-induced needs. The Housatonic River, the waterway Ives memorialized in his 1908 song commemorating a honeymoon walk and for which he set lines from a poem by Robert Underwood Johnson, was the river at the center of this debate. If the 1906 earthquake and fires had been used, initially at least, as a rationale for diverting waters from the Tuolumne River to San Francisco, then a record-breaking drought and heat wave that gripped the Northeast in 1910–11 and numerous reports of an impending "water famine" in New York City served a similar purpose in redirecting waters from Connecticut's Housatonic.[9]

Just three weeks before Ives's visit to Zoar Bridge, an article in the *New York Times* predicted "a calamity well-nigh past imagination" if waters weren't diverted "from Ten Mile River with Connecticut's Consent." The Ten Mile (Tenmile) River in eastern New York flows into the larger Housatonic in western Connecticut. It was impossible to capture enough water from the smaller river without impacting and using flow from the Housatonic. The anonymous author speculated that the drought would "annihilate industry" and become "a peril to household health"; ramping up his emotional argument, he imagined that there was the possibility of a "conflagration" and "wholesale riots in the wake." For Ives, an insurance man with his own agency in New York, the author's prediction that "insurance companies would cancel their policies covering property all over the city" likely caught his eye (*New York Times* 1911b, 8). The city needed to look beyond its borders to supply its water needs, and the Housatonic River was the target in its sights. Although the *New York Times* hosted this debate as it did the Hetch Hetchy one, stories in the *Danbury Evening News* (Ives's hometown newspaper), *Engineering News*, the *Farmer* (a newspaper reporting on Connecticut news), and various other local papers in both states also kept the issue in the forefront of stakeholders' minds.

Throughout May and June 1911, the *Danbury Evening News* regularly ran stories on the dry weather conditions and the implications for water supplies and general safety. Farmers were concerned about damage to their crops and livestock as a result of possible forest fires, and this was not mere fantasizing. On May 6 the *Danbury Evening News* (1911) ran an article titled "Big Fire Rages at Sandy Hook: Woods Blaze Is Sweeping along Bank of Housatonic River and Farms and Mill in Danger." Having started near a train station "soon after the Poughkeepsie Express passe[d]," the fire was "raging along a portion of the bank of the Housatonic river" and had grown to be a mile wide. It was "sweeping onward in spectacular fashion, threatening the farm buildings of Mr. Curtis, Mr. Beresford, Mr. Bradley, and Mr. Meeker, and causing worry to Representative Scoville, who has a mill in the path of the fire" (*Danbury Evening News* 1911). The story closed with a plea for help from local residents in fighting the blaze. Less than two months earlier the infamous Triangle Shirtwaist Factory fire in New York City had claimed the lives of 125 young immigrant women trapped in a building. People were keenly aware of their vulnerability to fire, especially in an unusually parched season. Others were anxious about increasing pollution of rivers and streams. Local officials forbade the unnecessary use of water for lawns or yard work. Earthquakes, droughts, and fires turned everyone's attention to water.

By the time Ives visited Zoar Bridge in June 1911, it was the fifth iteration of the span; each of the preceding bridges had been damaged or destroyed in whole or part by storms and spring thaws. This bridge, built in 1876, two years after Ives's birth, was the one he saw in 1911 when increasing claims on the Housatonic and plans for a new dam were well under way. The bridge and the waterway had a lot of history behind them, and Ives, like all locals, would have known it. The Zoar Bridge he visited remained in use until 1918, "when the Stevenson Dam was built and a roadway placed atop the dam" (Debisschop 2011). But the River Gods and the Housatonic of old were already gone before this newest building project or the call to divert waters were topics of conversation. Hunting horns had been drowned out when the first mills and factories were built on the river's shores in the nineteenth century. By 1911, the River Gods were long resigned to their eviction even if Ives had only recently acknowledged that reality in his music.

Whether intended as such or not, Ives's song responds to all that was happening around him at the time. Ives *heard* the problem that Muir saw and Johnson wrote about. The text and music reflect his position as a musician grappling with environmental issues: a person who understood his world first through sound; a person who processed the world by listening. Ives spoke of the new river's sounds, the audible and the silent ones. The "contented river" that Johnson set to poetry and Ives musicalized had been overwhelmed by mechanized man.

The text positions man's machine sounds against nature's water sounds; the "noise" of the former has drowned out the "voice" of the latter. It is clearly not the loudness of the sound, however, that most upsets Ives: he doesn't object to the "*blare* of the hunting horn." It's more the source of the sound and what it blocks out that troubles him. On the surface, Ives appears to hear the world in a binary relationship: man's machines (and perhaps man himself) separate from nature. But the machines that Ives hears are only the sounds of "human beings *gone* machine." He suggests that humans are not born noisy but become that way when their technology overwhelms their human-ness, when in Veblen's words, "the machine throws out anthropomorphic habits of thought" (quoted in Rhodes 1999, 42).

Given the uniqueness of this song within Ives's oeuvre, it is worth considering more deeply what provoked this musical jeremiad.[10] More than an argument that the composer sees the world in dichotomies—old versus new, tradition versus progress—"The New River" is Ives's argument that the world operates as a single entity that has gotten out of balance with itself. It is the proxy-like quality of phonographs and gasoline-operated engines that Ives objects to. Phonographs replace live music and music making, and automobiles substitute speedy movement *through* a place for deliberate contemplation *of* a place.[11] Both inventions challenge direct engagement with sound, time, and place. Both remove personal experience. The hunting horn, long associated with bucolic landscapes, is killed, silenced. The River Gods, the one hundred-plus deities who oversaw ancient civilizations and were once considered the first kings of the land, have left and taken with them the inexplicable. Amid the din, Ives hears and feels their absence (Theoi Project 2016). Ives's water-focused pieces are especially numerous and noteworthy in his nature-related works, and all speak to his awareness of a position *within* a living, breathing, sounding community where humans sing one part in a larger chorus. In "The New River," however, Ives is unable to hear beyond that one part.

Unlike the near-mystical waterway pieces found in Ives's oeuvre, which often paint their subject with soft, slow cyclic motions outlining triadic harmonies or orchestral tuning gestures of the fifth, the proto-environmentalist critique of "The New River" tacks a different sonic course. There is nothing transcending or otherworldly about this music; listeners aren't transported to another realm. On the contrary they are swept up, "fast and rough," in a loud, discordant, cascading rush of popular musics. From the crunching opening chords, filled with minor ninths and major sevenths, the music, like the text, rails against humankind's deafening, acoustic onslaught. Besides the insistent dissonant language, an initially unsettling series of meter changes prevents the music from finding a firm footing. It is only when the music "settles" into a ragtime that it achieves any kind of rhythmic stability, but then this is a pyrrhic victory, as ragged rhythms depend on instability for their effect. The first six measures set the noisy scene.

As Ives struggles to hear "the voice of rolling waters" buried beneath "the sounds of man," he notices the missing River Gods. The acoustic niche they once inhabited is overwhelmed.[12] Although R. Murray Schafer popularized the idea of soundscapes and soundwalks in his 1977 book *The Soundscape and the Tuning of the World*, Ives had regularly spent time listening to his acoustic environment decades earlier as he did at Zoar Bridge (Schafer 1977). Today bioacousticians,

FIG. 9.1. Charles Ives, "The New River," mm. 1–6

acoustical engineers, sound ecologists, and ecomusicologists have taken up Ives's concern regarding the impact that a louder, more mechanized world has on our environment.[13]

The idea of Ives as a composer so rooted in the nineteenth-century New England countryside that he was out of step with his twentieth-century city life is a popular one; it has become the essential Ives myth. The long shadows of Emerson, Thoreau, and transcendentalist thinking eclipse all other influences, but there is more to Ives than this backward-glancing figure. Not even the abundance of nature references in his music or his fond recollections of youth and an earlier time can erase evidence of his full presence, awareness, and participation in debates, issues, and concerns affecting large numbers of people in the first half of the twentieth century. And these debates included social, political, cultural, aesthetic, and environmental ones.

Danbury, Connecticut, Ives's birthplace, often pointed to as the site of his *bucolic* childhood, was no idyllic, rural retreat when he was growing up. Danbury experienced the wide array of challenges that attend a diverse population with large numbers of immigrant workers laboring in its many factories. In 1902, the "Danbury Hatters' Case" brought the town national attention when Dietrich Loewe, a local hat manufacturer, refused to recognize the hatter's union. His workers struck, and he replaced them with scabs. After six years of litigation, the US Supreme Court decided in his favor, and the union members had to pay the fines ("Danbury Hatters Case" 2016). By the first decade of the twentieth century, Danbury was the center of the American hatting industry, producing 25 percent of all hats in the country. It was no sylvan setting.

Dams and reservoirs had been built early in the nineteenth century to provide burgeoning industries with needed water supplies. But polluted streams and rivers became a concern early on in Danbury as the mills and factories that supported the hat industry pumped their waste into the surrounding waterways. Danbury had experienced a reservoir-related tragedy in January 1869, when the Kohanza Reservoir dam broke, and a flood of icy water killed eleven people in thirty minutes; it destroyed nearby homes and farms. The water reached Main Street, where the Ives family home stood (*Harper's Weekly* 1869). Starting in the 1880s the Still River, a tributary to the Housatonic, was regularly contaminated with mercury nitrate, an essential chemical for fur removal and felt making. The P. Robinson Fur Cutting Company was located in Danbury on the banks of the Still. Concerns for environmental degradation were part of Ives's cultural heritage; they were not just a twentieth-century issue.

Ives's "New River" it turns out, was not a response to a new situation, or a sentimental plea for a return to an earlier time, or a prescient statement on an issue that would one day dominate the media, but a comment on a continuing issue that he lived with. Where the environment was concerned, he understood the indivisibility of past, present, and future. Today Danbury is considered part of the greater New York metropolitan area. It is one in a ring of cities and towns in Connecticut, New Jersey, and upstate New York where those Manhattanites who can afford a home in the country own a house, enabling them to hop on a train and escape. Once Ives was a professional insurance man with a summer place in West Redding, the commuter rail system allowed him to travel easily between his Connecticut and Manhattan homes. Waterways and railroad lines made manifest the connections that existed between all aspects of Ives's life and the environment in which he lived.

We don't need to speculate whether Ives understood the inviolable network of relationships that exists at the root of all healthy systems and governs their continuation; he talked of such interdependency on multiple occasions and in multiple contexts. In his 1929 essay "Music and Its Future," Ives refers to Emerson and Thoreau, but he also talks about acoustics and overtones and the limitations of radio technology and advocates for funding musical experimentation. The past and the future were one. Waxing philosophical, he observes that "all things in their variety are of one essence and are limited only by themselves." The future of music, he concludes, lies "in the way it encourages and extends, rather than limits" (Ives 1998, 68–69). His concerns with the future and moving beyond comfortable truisms challenge the monochromatic myth of Ives as fixed on the past.

A final observation by the composer also bears repeating, especially in a collection of essays held together by their loose bonds of indebtedness to the lifework of Jeff Todd Titon and devoted to the idea of cultural sustainability. In an interview with Ives in 1933, the composer Henry Bellamann asked him how he balanced his work as an insurance executive with his life as a composer. Ives's response reveals his recognition of the balance that is required in all facets of the human endeavor: "The fabric of existence weaves itself whole. You can not set an art off in the corner and hope for it to have vitality, reality and substance. There can be nothing 'exclusive' about a substantial art. It comes directly out of the heart of experience of life and thinking about life and living life. My work in music helped my business and my work in business helped my music" (Bellamann 1933). It is easy to imagine Titon nodding his head in agreement. Ives understood the intrinsic connections at work in all aspects of his life, what Titon might think of as Ives's "dynamic ecological system."

There was more at stake than increased noise levels or the intrusion of gasoline-powered engines at Zoar Bridge, although as a composer Ives would have thought in terms of sound and heard the crises more acutely than others visiting the same site. For Ives, a delicate balance had been upset, and he heard it. People needed to listen and think of the implications for the future; and over a hundred years later, they still do.

Notes

1. The phrase "contented river" comes from Robert Underwood Johnson's poem "To the Housatonic at Stockbridge," first published in Johnson's poem (1897). Ives set fourteen of Johnson's sixty-six lines to song in 1908. For the note on the pencil sketch to "The New River," see Sinclair (1999, 447).

2. See Charles Ives's self-published collection of songs, *114 Songs* (1922). The text in brackets comes from a smaller collection of songs, *Thirty-Four Songs*, published in 1933. As H. Wiley Hitchcock explains in his critical edition of *129 Songs, Thirty-Four Songs* includes thirty-one that are reproduced from *114 Songs*, twenty-six with revisions, and three new songs. Hitchcock reads the revised text as *ossias* (see Ives 2004, xxi and 197).

3. Ralph Waldo Emerson's essay "Nature," written in 1836, is a seminal text of American transcendentalism (1983). (See Ives 1972, 82–83.) When Ives sent *Essays before a Sonata* (1962) to Phelps, the former professor was effusive in his praise. See Burkholder (1985) for the most thorough study of the wealth of ideas and forces influencing Ives.

4. See Hays (1999) for a discussion of how sides lined up. Hays summarized California congressman William Kent's fear of "a conspiracy engineered by misinformed nature lovers and power interests who are working through the women's clubs" (194). For a discussion of the role women's clubs played in turn-of-the-century environmental initiatives, see Musil (2015, 229–31).

5. The four songs are "The Housatonic at Stockbridge" (1908), "Luck and Work" (1920), "At Sea" (1921), and "Premonitions" (1921).

6. The 1,500 square mile figure comes from www.history.com/this-day-in-history/ yosemite-national-park-established/print (accessed June 6, 2016). The size refers to the amount of land set aside in 1890. Today the figure is put closer to 1,200 square miles.

7. The Weeks Act approved on March 1, 1911, was designed to prevent just such private profiteering from happening. It "authorized the federal government to purchase private lands for stream-flow protection and to maintain the acquired lands as national forests." See www.WeeksAct.org (accessed June 13, 2016).

8. Given the population of San Francisco as compared with the number of visitors to Yosemite National Park each year, Garfield's reference to "greatest number" is debatable. In 2016 San Francisco had a total population of 805,235, and the number of visitors to Yosemite National Park was 5,217,114. See https://suburbanstats.org/population/ california/how-many-people-live-in-san-francisco and https://www.nps.gov/yose/learn/ management/statistics.htm (accessed December 20, 2017).

9. See two *New York Times* articles (1911a, 1911c). In the May 23, 1911, piece (1911c), the unnamed author implores "every resident of Manhattan and the Bronx [to] do his share toward averting a water famine by using water economically."

10. Ives was perfectly capable of associating deafeningly loud sounds with water while evoking the divine. "The Housatonic at Stockbridge," song and chamber orchestra versions, climax at *fff* and *ffff* respectively.

11. Ives's 1908 song was inspired by a honeymoon *walk* that he and his bride took along the banks of the Housatonic River.

12. The Acoustic Niche Hypothesis was first articulated by sound ecologist Bernie Krause. See Krause's 2013 article for a discussion of acoustic niches in the context of the larger sound environment.

13. It is no surprise that Ives grouped this song with three others as musical statements in the set *The Other Side [The Downside?] of Pioneering*, or *Sidelights on American Enterprise*. See also my discussion of two other pieces that Ives included in this commentary on American enterprise, his songs "Charlie Rutlage" and "The Indians" (Von Glahn 2001).

The final song was "Ann Street," a study of a narrow street in the Wall Street district of Manhattan with which Ives was familiar from his work downtown.

References

Bellamann, Henry. 1933. "Charles Ives: The Man and His Music." *Musical Quarterly* 19 (January): 47.

Burkholder, J. Peter. 1985. *Charles Ives: The Ideas behind the Music*. New Haven, CT: Yale University Press.

Burroughs, John. 1910–11. "The Spell of Yosemite." *Century Magazine* 81, n.s., 59 (November 1910–April 1911): 47–53. Accessed December 21, 2016, via Google Books.

———. 1912. "The Gospel of Nature." In *The Complete Nature Writings of John Burroughs: Time and Change*, 243–773. New York: Wm. H. Wise. Accessed December 21, 2016, via Google Books.

Danbury Evening News. 1911. "Big Fire." May 6.

"The Danbury Hatters Case." 2016. *State of Connecticut Judicial Branch, Law Library Services*. http://www.jud.ct.gov/lawlib/history/Hatters.htm. Accessed June 15, 2016.

Debisschop, Dorothy. 2011. "Lake Zoar Bridge and the Lost Village around Pleasant Vale." *Oxford Patch*. https://tinyurl.com/y7pgvkks.

Emerson, Ralph Waldo. 1983. "Nature." In *Emerson: Essays and Lectures*, 5–49. New York: Library of America.

Harper's Weekly. 1869. "The Danbury Disaster." February 20.

Hays, Samuel P. 1999. *Conservation and the Gospel of Efficiency: The Progressive Conservation Movement, 1890–1920*. Pittsburgh: University of Pittsburgh Press.

Ives, Charles. 1922. *114 Songs*. Redding, CT: C. E. Ives.

———. 1933. *Thirty-Four Songs*. San Francisco: New Music Society.

———. 1962. *Essays before a Sonata, and Other Writings*. Edited by Howard Boatwright. New York: W. W. Norton.

———. 1972. *Memos*. New York: W. W. Norton.

———. 1998. "Music and Its Future." In *Source Readings in Music History: The Twentieth Century*, edited by Robert P. Morgan, 68–69. New York: W. W. Norton.

———. 2004. *129 Songs*. Edited by H. Wiley Hitchcock. Middleton, WI: A-R Editions.

Johnson, Robert Underwood. 1897. "To the Housatonic at Stockbridge." In *Songs of Liberty and Other Poems*, 13–15. New York: Century.

———. 1912–13. "Giving Away the Nation's Property: The Needless Invasion of the Yosemite National Park." *Century Magazine* 85, n.s., 63 (November 1912–April 1913): 315.

———. 1913a. "Niagara Again in Danger." *Century Magazine* 86, n.s., 64 (May): 150.

———. 1913b. "The Hetch Hetchy Plan: Robert Underwood Johnson Gives Advice on How to Defeat It." *New York Times*, July 27.

———. 1913c. "The Hetch Hetchy Scheme: Why It Should Not Be Rushed through the Extra Session; An Open Letter to the American People." http://www.intimeandplace.org/HetchHetchy/image2.html.

Krause, Bernie. 2013. "The Voice of the Natural World." TEDGlobal. https://www.ted.com/talks/bernie_krause_the_voice_of_the_natural_world?language.

Muir, John. 1911–12. "Three Adventures in the Yosemite." *Century Magazine* 83, n.s., 61 (November 1911–April 1912): 656.

Musil, Robert K. 2015. *Rachel Carson and Her Sisters*. New Brunswick, NJ: Rutgers University Press.

New York Times. 1908. "Oppose Reservoir in Yosemite Park." December 21.

———. 1910. "Hetch Hetchy Transfer." January 5.

———. 1911a. "City Water Supply near Danger Point." March 29.

———. 1911b. "Water Supply Down to Half Normal Size." May 20.

———. 1911c. "Short Supply of Water." May 23.

Rhodes, Richard. 1999. *Visions of Technology: A Century of Vital Debate about Machines, Systems and the Human World*. New York: Simon and Schuster.

Schafer, R. Murray. 1977. *The Soundscape: Our Sonic Environment and the Tuning of the World*. Rochester, VT: Destiny Books.

Sierra Club. 2017. "Hetch Hetchy: History." http://vault.sierraclub.org/ca/hetchhetchy/history.asp. Accessed December 21, 2017.

Sinclair, James B. 1999. *A Descriptive Catalogue of the Music of Charles Ives*. New Haven, CT: Yale University Press.

Theoi Project. 2016. "Potamoi." http://www.theoi.com/. Accessed June 2, 2016.

Veblen, Thorstein. 1904. "The Machine Process." In *The Theory of Business Enterprise*, 5–19. New York: Charles Scribner's Sons, A-R Editions.

Von Glahn, Denise. 2001. "Charles Ives, Cowboys, and Indians: Aspects of 'the Other Side of Pioneering.'" *American Music* 19 (3): 291–314.

PART 3

Musics, Sustainability, and Media

CHAPTER 10

Fandom's Remix

Popular Music, Participation, and Sustainability

DANIEL CAVICCHI

SUSTAINABILITY IS A BIG TENT. Many books and essays have been written on its long history and changing definitions across different cultures and contexts (Kidd 1992; Beatley 1995; DuPisani, 2006; Goggin 2009, 2013; Caradonna 2014; Portney 2015), and it has been applied to issues in fields as diverse as product design, tourism, library management, fashion, and college composition (e.g., Owens 2001; Chapman 2005; Bradley 2007; Newcomb 2012; Hethorm and Ulasewicz 2015; Hughes, Weaver, and Pforr 2015). In fact, its contested and ambiguous meanings have led ecologist Ian Scoones to argue that sustainability is best understood as doing "boundary work" to connect diverse social groups and interests. He explains, "While academics continue to endeavour to refine its meaning, locating it in ever more precise terms within particular disciplinary debates, it is the more over-arching, symbolic role—of aspiration, vision, and normative commitment—that remains so politically potent" (2007, 594).

Despite this potential for "boundary work," there is still one area that sustainability rarely touches: popular culture. Commercial entertainment, especially, built on a nineteenth-century industrial profit model that depended on the steady production and consumption of ephemeral leisure goods, seems more associated with the excesses of "throwaway living" than with sustainability's custodial sensibilities. This view is certainly prevalent among published environmentalists, who, like other cultural critics before them, have emphasized the ways that buying cultural experience, especially mediated amusements, is bad for individual health and inimical to community. The Worldwatch Institute's 2010 *State of the World* report most notably put this stake in the ground by forcefully condemning the "cultural pattern that leads people to find meaning, content-ment, and acceptance primarily through the consumption of goods and services" and calling for the establishment of "a sustainability paradigm" instead of a "consumerism paradigm" (Assadourian 2010, 16). Media scholar John Parkham has summed it up: "Derived variously from the Romantic reaction to modernity, doctrines of wilderness passed down from American Transcendentalism . . . and, in a more qualified sense, European critical theory, all too often, all too easily, environmentalist critics loathe media and popular culture" (2015, xiv).

Wariness abounds, even among the sympathetic. Scholars writing about popular media and environmentalism, for example, tend to engage with popu-lar television shows or songs only as texts that might communicate ecological meanings. As Mark Meister and Phyllis Japp explain: "For most citizens, popular culture is a primary site of meaning construction, probably the major area in which most understand, reinforce, and/or modify the circumstances of their lives" (2002, 1–2). Sean Cubitt rather grudgingly makes the case that "in the absence of citizens' media, we have no better place to look than the popular media for representations of popular knowledge and the long-term concerns so little addressed in dominant political and economic discourse" (2005, 2). Even John Parkham, interested in taking a more positive approach to the ecological potential of global media, still focuses his discussion in *Green Media and Popular Culture* (2015) on the affective dynamics of "green rhetoric."

Ethnomusicologists, too, have not found much merit in pop for sustainability. Mark Pedelty, for example, in *Ecomusicology: Rock, Folk, and the Environment*, is hopeful about the ways ecomusicological scholarship might foster an under-standing of rock and folk's material support for environmental sustainability but admits, in the end, that global music industries and markets significantly diminish the benefits of even the most local musicking and that "there is much greater evidence for popular music's utility as a sales tool than for its capacity to foster sustainable lives and equitable societies" (2012, 202). Ethnomusicolo-gist Thomas Turino, exploring "the potential of musical practice as a model for broader patterns of habit change" to foster sustainability (2009, 95), favors participatory forms of music based on collective dancing, singing, clapping, and playing musical instruments, which are defined by synchronous connection and the erasure of social distinctions, qualities that he sees as a "powerful resource for building and sustaining communities" (110–11). He recognizes in the kinds of concert performance common to pop that "the members of [an] ensemble may experience . . . powerful unspoken social connection during a successful rehearsal or concert," but he asserts that audiences perceive such social con-nection "second hand" (111).

I share colleagues' skepticism about aspects of commercial popular music. It is unlikely to save the planet. However, that doesn't mean that popular music can never be a source of participatory values, mutual dependency, and long-term awareness that can contribute to more-sustainable living. After all, popular music encompasses a diverse and varied category of human musical activity, and various scenes and modes of participation can have rather complicated relationships to pop's capitalist staging. This is clear in cultural studies scholarship, which has sought to redefine popular music's progressive potential (Rodman 2015), and in the more specific research on music and politics, which shows how popular music can generate political community (Mattern 1998; Pratt 1990; Love 2006) or serve as a catalyst in a variety of social movements (Lieberman 1995; Eyerman and Jamison 1998; Ward 1998; Fischlin and Heble 2003; Peddie 2006; Pieslak 2015). In fact, John Street has argued that Western political philosophy has consistently identified how music "plays a part in our constitution as moral beings and in our constitution as political ones" (2012, 159). But what does that mean, exactly, for thinking about sustainability and commercial popular music? How can we connect Thoreau and Muir with the Beatles and Billboard?

For the rest of this chapter, I want to explore fan culture as a possible answer. On the surface, popular music fans appear emblematic of the consumerist desire—for new music, stars, and spectacle—that powers the gears of the music industry. However, fans are always also working to resituate that desire, using it to sustain other kinds of meaningful connection and attachment. That is, while remaining ideal customers, lining up as soon as possible to acquire new releases or paying to see shows by favorite performers, fans foster, simultaneously, an unexpected collective sensibility about music that is less about pleasurable entertainment than about ritual efficacy (Schechner 2008, 112–69), less about responding to "hits" than about using a love for music to deepen understanding, shape daily life, and create community.

Extending Musical Encounter

There are several specific ways in which we might examine fandom through the lens of sustainability. One of the hallmarks of sustainability, for example, is the cultivation of a broader sense of scale, based on holistic and proactive awareness of "dynamic processes over the long-term" (Portney 2015, 5). This approach is vital to fans' engagement with music. The popular recording industry is focused on the moment of a work's release; tours, marketing, reviews, and distribution all support this principle. Listeners, in response, focus their energies on encounter and reaction, following the latest hits, deriving pleasure from the thrill of discovery. Fans, since the beginnings of the music business in the mid-nineteenth century, however, have challenged this system by introducing a number of activities that extend the frame of musical encounter. Fans hold on to the heightened sense of feeling and excitement they may feel during a performance or while listening to a song, after those occasions have ended, purposefully reconstituting the immediacy of musical encounter into more-enduring habits of daily life.

Thus in the nineteenth century, avid concertgoers often purchased sheet music to remember concerts they had attended and to remake, themselves, the music they heard at home. Concertgoers also notably recorded their musical experiences in diaries, writing in extraordinary detail about what they saw and heard at concerts, or annotated concert programs, noting how they felt during moments of listening, which they would then reread and savor. As Lucy Lowell, a young woman in Boston, wrote in her diary after the last concert of the season by the Boston Symphony in 1886: "I feel so desolate at thinking that this is the last, that I shall dwell on each detail, to lengthen out the enjoyment" (quoted in Cavicchi 2011, 135). Since the beginning of the twentieth century, the phonograph and subsequent recording technologies have amplified fans' ability to repeat, or "play back," music. Still, fans have continued to extend musical feeling beyond their experiences of both concerts and recordings through a variety of activities that on the surface appear nonmusical: gathering and discussing; sharing stories, visual art, and music; collecting recordings and ephemera; and making pilgrimages to music sites.

When I first started investigating Springsteen fandom in the early 1990s (Cavicchi 1998), fan discussion was moving from fanzines such as *Backstreets* or *Thunder Road* to newer online platforms, like the bulletin board "Backstreets Digest," where fans from across the world, on a daily basis, debated the meanings of songs and albums; sorted through changes in set lists during past and present concert tours; posted homemade guitar or piano scores; shared stories of "becoming a fan" or about concert experiences; and mentored one another about how to behave in the fan community. Today, of course, much of this activity has spread to websites and blogs (Kibby 2000; Echard 2005; Scodari 2007; Bennett 2012a).

Fan collecting, or curating items associated with selected music or musicians (e.g., images, news stories, bootleg recordings, ticket stubs, T-shirts, autographs, license plates, clothing, grass or rocks from sites of musical significance), is based on several older traditions, from nineteenth-century scrapbooking to record collecting in the early days of phonography. Collecting can represent a number of simultaneous motivations, including nostalgia for musical experiences, representing one's self, or the preservation of community artifacts, but it always involves some form of ongoing display. Nineteenth-century music lovers showed off their sheet music in leather binders or parlor furniture; contemporary fans show their collections in home shrines (Doss 1999) or personal websites (Mazzarella 2008). Display, especially, creates material spaces in fans' daily lives that represent their ongoing engagement with music, with which they can connect with others and to which they can easily return (Geraghty 2014, 4).

Pilgrimages and tourism are other ways that fans lengthen the enjoyment of music outside the performance. In the nineteenth century, travel to sites associated with composers or performers, including the birthplaces of Liszt, Mozart, and Wagner, was often associated with the European "grand tour," a well-planned and often expensive coming-of-age event for wealthy Americans. Contemporary fans often make similarly elaborate trips, but to significant musical places such as Elvis Presley's Graceland Mansion in Tennessee; Jim Morrison's grave in Paris; Beatles' sites in Liverpool, England; former Grateful Dead concert tour sites; or juke joints in Mississippi (Cohen et al. 2015). In many ways, just as playback, discussion, and writing extend musical experience in time, collecting and pilgrimage extend it in space. In the words of Angelina Karpovich, certain geographic sites, as the object of fan pilgrimage, can take on a metonymic role, in which the site becomes "practically interchangeable with the particular fandom" (2008, 200).

Interchangeability, on the whole, is a good way to explain how fans' musical encounters can eventually blur into a more continuous and expanded musicality. As I have suggested elsewhere (Cavicchi 1998, 126), for long-time fans, the act of listening is not necessarily limited to the sensory experience of a recording or performance but rather is an ongoing inter-animation of sound and meaning, involving memory, contextualization, and affect. Fans exemplify what Jeff Titon (1988, 7–14) has suggested is the performative connection between any folk and their lore: fans affirm their commitment to Springsteen, his work, and one another by performing that commitment, by participating in a variety of activities that imbue their lives with musical feeling.

Creating Community

Another important aspect of sustainability is a sense of personal mutual connection and cooperation, found in both ecosystems and human community, which is opposed to the competitive and often impersonal relationships engendered by global capitalism. At one level, fandom is intensely personal and self-interested in ways that do not necessarily imply strong potential for community. However, at the same time, fan self-making is possible and has meaning only in the wider communal context of fellow fans. In fact, for many "fandom" doesn't begin until it is shared—this is the very point of the "becoming-a-fan" stories that fans, across popular culture forms, often tell one another (Hills 2016). As Mark Duffett explains, "Many fans characterize their entry into fandom as a move from social and cultural isolation—whether as rogue readers, women in patriarchy, or gay men in heteronormative culture—into more active communality with kindred spirits" (2013, 244).

Fandom's gathering of diverse individuals in a community of interest requires effort, something that for many fans is jump-started by concertgoing. For fans, the concert functions not as a single theatrical event but as one in a lifelong series of communal ritual moments that primes fans to experience the music together in very specific ways, controlled by knowledge and etiquette that differs from that of the rest of the audience. Springsteen fans, for instance, continually educate one another about when to arrive to hear the sound check, where to sit to hear the music best, how to dress, how to respond to the performers' cues, and where to greet musicians backstage. They usually also have been study-ing previous set lists and listening to recordings for hours before the concert, building a shared anticipation for the performance. Some fan groups, such as Deadheads, Parrotheads, and heavy metal fans, socially reinforce the value of shared concert participation through regular "tailgating" before shows, com-plete with decorated spaces, food, drinking, costumes (ranging from T-shirts to tropical beach wear), and often enthusiastic playback of recordings, informal "air guitar" and sing-along sessions, and even amateur performances (Weeks 2012, 80–122; *Heavy Metal Parking Lot* 1986).

Of course, sharing an interest in music that is globally marketed often means that fans must build community in ways not always based on geographic prox-imity. Ever since Bruce Springsteen became a world megastar in the late 1980s, for example, his fans have created a shared sense of belonging together through the telling and sharing of stories. In line for concert tickets, before and after con-certs, at gatherings, in fanzines, and online, Springsteen fans share personal nar-ratives about becoming a fan, making pilgrimages, or "meeting Bruce." Through gentle prodding and questions, new fans to the community learn quickly that "everybody tells Bruce stories." Such stories, while about personal experience, are also deeply communal; the fans' best storytellers shape their experiences into narratives that fit the community's social conventions of form (such as how to underplay the drama of meeting Springsteen backstage) and that exhibit recognized fan values (such as the down-to-earth qualities of Springsteen).

Through such sharing and melding of experiences, Springsteen fans, in fact, nurture an *expectation* of belonging, the belief that all Springsteen fans can depend on "true" fellow fans to exhibit certain characteristics of goodwill, ex-perience, and knowledge. The use of narrative to shape and affirm ideals of community is not unlike the ways in which, as Jeff Titon reports, members of the Fellowship Independent Baptist Church use testimony and prayer to move from the "ordinary social structure of their daily lives" to realization of an "extraordinary social utopian community" (1988, 407). In fact, I found that the expectation of connection and belonging among fans was a powerful force in fans' lives in general. In addition to starting new friendships with one another, fans reported using the activities of fandom—going on pilgrimages, for example, or locating collectible items—to bond with parents, siblings, and children with whom they had not had a close relationship previously. Critical views of fandom may emphasize the lone fan, with a monomaniacal and unrequited desire for a star, but the fans I have met over the past twenty years have been more interested in befriending fellow fans or using fandom to deepen existing relationships than in actually knowing a star.

Cultivating Alternatives

One final key aspect of popular music fandom to mention is how its values of participation and community are often paired with skepticism about or resistance to usual frameworks of commercial relationship. Not all music fans fit the Birmingham School vision of youth subcultures in the 1970s, whose members consciously reused products and symbols of the dominant order to resist its hegemony, but fandom as a collective practice nevertheless offers a number of alternative approaches to the usual limited frameworks of capitalist exchange and, in fact, has been at the forefront of developing more open practices of media distribution and reception, especially in the digital age.

During the furor over Napster and file sharing in the early twenty-first century, the Recording Industry Association of America portrayed downloaders as pirates and criminals, emboldened by the capabilities of the internet, but peer-to-peer sharing of media had long been taking place among music fans. Taping trees, for example, in which concert bootleg cassette recordings were reproduced for distribution to fellow fans, was a practice institutionalized by the Grateful Dead in the late 1960s. Various forms of gifting and recirculation of already-purchased products had thrived for decades among fan collectors (Scott 2009). Among Springsteen fans, there were strict rules against profiting from sharing music with fellow fans; these rules were meant to uphold trading as an internal practice explicitly based on fans' love of Springsteen's music and to support the community's collective desire to understand and appreciate the fullness of his creativity.

Streaming services like Pandora, Spotify, and YouTube have changed the tone of much of this debate, but the manipulation and redistribution of content provided initially by the record industry still exists in the form of remixes, mash-ups, and homemade music videos, all of which are created quite easily on home laptops and can be circulated quickly across the world on the internet. Fans are not only recording and filming concerts now but also live tweeting and texting, another means of "allowing non-attendees around the world to feel part of the event" (Bennett 2012b). Indeed, Paul Booth has called for a new "philosophy of playfulness" that addresses, "more so than at any other time," the fact that "the media we use in our everyday lives has been personalized, individualized, and made pleasurable to use" (2010, 2). Whatever one's politics about these practices, they do indicate the ways in which music fans newly see themselves not as recipients of broadcast or performed music but rather as participants in a shared sound commons.

Media scholar Henry Jenkins has coined a variety of terms to get at new models of fan-creator interaction in the digital age, including "convergence culture" (2006) and "spreadable media" (Jenkins, Ford, and Green 2013). They point to ways in which entertainment corporations actually do now share processes of media production, circulation, and interpretation with fans and audiences. In music, the involvement of fans in production is exemplified in the extreme by performers like Amanda Palmer, who, abandoning her label, instead used online crowdsourcing and calls for participation to support albums and performances, which she promotes as part of a punk communal aesthetic (Potts 2012). Even artists unwilling to go to such extremes have become necessarily invested in direct communication with their fan bases, via Twitter, Instagram, or Facebook (Baym 2012). None of this escapes the dynamics of power and inequity that have historically been a part of industry-fan relations, especially the growth of companies that specialize in "monetizing" fan engagement (Booth 2015; Pearson 2010), but this is nevertheless new ground on which to negotiate meaning. As Melissa M. Brough and Sangita Shresthova explain, "Fan participation in and through commercial entertainment spaces is not predetermined to be resistant or complicit—in fact, it is often both—but its political significance lies in part in the changes in relations of power that may occur through such participation" (2012, 4.9).

Popular music fandom's connection to sustainability is not without problems. Crucial to sustainability, for example, is an understanding of resource and capacity limits to foster more-thoughtful and lasting efforts at renewal and reuse. Fans may be more interested in preserving and maintaining musical culture than ordinary audience members are, but thinking about limits on their passion (as reformers tried with music lovers in the 1870s) would be difficult. Fans, by definition, want *more*. Along similar lines, fans' intense focus on "self-making" has deep roots in models of class-privileged economic autonomy promoted in the industrial West, which have supported capitalist accumulation and competition. How can that be reconciled with notions of fan community? Indeed, scholarly emphasis on fan "agency" vis-à-vis the music industry can veer toward the utopian, failing to recognize that at fandom's heart is a contradiction: as scholar Matt Hills has explained, "Fans are both commodity-completists and they express anti-commercial beliefs" (2002, 19).

These caveats could reasonably lead one to worry about fandom as sustainable in the ecological sense, but I don't think they obviate a sustainable interpretation of fandom. As Hills suggests, such contradictions are actually the crux for thinking about how, exactly, fans apply a different sort of ethics to music consumption. Fans participate in profit-focused industries, which often work against mutuality and connection, but they expressly do so in order to revive and sustain those values. Sisyphean, perhaps, but fandom helps to make visible the potential for reclaiming human agency, community, and mutuality, through music, even in circumstances where such qualities may seem contradictory or remote. Other chapters in this volume (Dornfeld, Summit) show how thinking about sustainable ideals in a mediated world requires recognition of human beings' capability for using the technologies that surround them to foster the resilience of tradition and community. I would contend that, in a climate-changed world in urgent need of recalibration, such a pragmatic understanding of the lives of millions of consumers—who may be otherwise easily dismissed as uninformed or "part of the problem"—is a vital act.

David Graeber has advocated a reexamination of anthropologists' indiscriminate application of "consumption" to all activities affected by capitalism, "a vision that in fact sidelines most things that real people actually do and insofar as it is translated into actual economic behavior is obviously unsustainable" (2011, 501). Instead he calls for a more-reflective—and selective—use of consumption, one that is "suspicious about importing the political economy habit of seeing society as divided into two spheres, one of production and one of consumption, into cultural analysis" (501). In a different context, Grant McCracken (2013) has echoed Graeber's argument about the limited applicability of twentieth-century notions of consumption. In an age in which digital goods are neither scarce nor diminished by the act of consumption, he finds the "anti-ecological" notions that come with the term *consumer* odd and recommends using the term *multiplier* instead, pointing to the ways that consumption is not the end of "meaning manufacture" but "merely the beginning of a larger cultural process."

Multiplier strikes me as too technologically utopic to be of much use, but still, more-specific and nuanced approaches to understanding what people do with commercial popular music—and how they are variously "musical"—will allow all of us to move away from what Jonathan Chapman has provocatively described as environmental activists' "warped notions of ascetic lifestyles abounding with non-enjoyment . . . rendering the prospect of a greener existence an undesirable alternative" (2005, 34). Understanding popular music as involving not just the production of stars and hits but also a wider ecology of listeners, amateur activities, and makeshift institutions nurturing the stewardship of a shared musical life, reframes pop culture's potential. By refusing to leave the concert hall or take off their headphones, fans invest popular music with lasting existential power and, whether warranted or not, make it anew in their lives. As Jeff Todd Titon (2015) has suggested, "Music and sustainability . . . is not only about how people may sustain music, but also about how music may sustain people."

References

Assadourian, Erik. 2010. "The Rise and Fall of Consumer Cultures." In *State of the World 2010: Transforming Cultures: From Consumerism to Sustainability*, edited by the Worldwatch Institute, 3–20. New York: W. W. Norton.

Baym, Nancy K. 2012. "Fans or Friends? Seeing Social Media Audiences as Musicians Do." *Participations* 9:286–316.

Beatley, Timothy. 1995. "The Many Meanings of Sustainability." *Journal of Planning Literature* 9:339–42.

Bennett, Lucy. 2012a. "Music Fandom Online: R.E.M. Fans in Pursuit of the Ultimate First Listen." *New Media & Society* 14:748–63.

———. 2012b. "Patterns of Listening through Social Media: Online Fan Engagement with the Live Music Experience." *Social Semiotics* 22:545–57.

Booth, Paul. 2010. *Digital Fandom: New Media Studies*. New York: Peter Lang.

———. 2015. *Playing Fans: Negotiating Fandom and Media in the Digital Age*. Iowa City: University of Iowa Press.

Bradley, Kevin. 2007. "Defining Digital Sustainability." *Library Trends* 56:148–63.

Brough, Melissa M., and Sangita Shresthova. 2012. "Fandom Meets Activism: Rethinking Civic and Political Participation." *Transformative Works and Cultures* 10. https://doi.org/10.3983/twc.2012.0303.

Caradonna, Jeremy. 2014. *Sustainability: A History*. New York: Oxford University Press.

Cavicchi, Daniel. 1998. *Tramps like Us: Music and Meaning among Springsteen Fans*. New York: Oxford University Press.

———. 2011. *Listening and Longing: Music Lovers in the Age of Barnum*. Middletown, CT: Wesleyan University Press.

Chapman, Jonathan. 2005. *Emotionally Durable Design: Objects, Experiences, and Empathy*. New York: Routledge.

Cohen, Sara, Robert Knifton, Marion Leonard, and Les Roberts, eds. 2015. *Sites of Popular Music Heritage: Memories, Histories, Places*. New York: Routledge.

Cubitt, Sean. 2005. *Eco Media*. Amsterdam: Editions Rodopi.

Doss, Erika. 1999. *Elvis Culture: Fans, Faith, and Image*. Lawrence: University Press of Kansas.

Duffett, Mark. 2013. *Understanding Fandom: An Introduction to the Study of Media Fan Culture*. London: Bloomsbury.

DuPisani, Jacobus. 2006. "Sustainable Development: Historical Roots of the Concept." *Environmental Sciences* 3 (2): 83–96.

Echard, William. 2005. *Neil Young and the Politics of Energy*. Bloomington: Indiana University Press.

Eyerman, Ron, and Andrew Jamison. 1998. *Music and Social Movements*. New York: Cambridge University Press.

Fischlin, Daniel, and Ajay Heble, eds. 2003. *Rebel Musics: Human Rights, Resistant Sounds, and the Politics of Music Making.* Montreal: Black Rose Books.

Geraghty, Lincoln. 2014. *Cult Collectors: Nostalgia, Fandom, and Collecting Popular Culture.* New York: Routledge.

Goggin, Peter N. 2009. *Rhetorics, Literacies, and Narratives of Sustainability.* New York: Routledge.

———. 2013. *Environmental Rhetoric and Ecologies of Place.* New York: Routledge.

Graeber, David. 2011. "Consumption." *Current Anthropology* 52 (4): 489–511.

Heavy Metal Parking Lot. 1986. Documentary film. Directed by John Heyn and Jeff Krulik. http://www.heavymetalparkinglot.com/hmpl-home.html#watch.

Hethorm, Janet, and Connie Ulasewicz, eds. 2015. *Sustainable Fashion: What's Next?* London: Bloomsbury.

Hills, Matt. 2002. *Fan Cultures.* New York: Routledge.

———. 2016. "Returning to Becoming-a-Fan Stories: Theorising Transformational Objects and the Emergence/Extension of Fandom." In *The Ashgate Research Companion to Fan Cultures*, edited by Linda Duits, Koos Zwaan, and Stijn Reijnders, 9–22. New York: Routledge.

Hughes, Michael, David Weaver, and Christof Pforr, eds. 2015. *The Practice of Sustainable Tourism: Solving the Paradox.* New York: Routledge.

Jenkins, Henry. 2006. *Convergence Culture: Where Old and New Media Collide.* New York: New York University Press.

Jenkins, Henry, Sam Ford, and Joshua Green. 2013. *Spreadable Media: Creating Value and Meaning in a Networked Culture.* New York: New York University Press.

Karpovich, Angelina I. 2008. "Locating the '*Star Trek* Experience.'" In *The Influence of Star Trek on Television, Film, and Culture*, edited by Lincoln Geraghty, 199–217. Jefferson, NC: McFarland.

Kibby, Marjorie D. 2000. "Home on the Page: A Virtual Place of Music Community." *Popular Music* 19 (1): 91–100.

Kidd, Charles. 1992. "The Evolution of Sustainability." *Journal of Agricultural and Environmental Ethics* 5 (1): 1–26.

Lieberman, Robbie. 1995. *My Song Is My Weapon: People's Songs, American Communism, and the Politics of Culture, 1930–50.* Urbana: University of Illinois Press.

Love, Nancy S. 2006. *Musical Democracy.* Albany: State University of New York Press.

Mattern, Mark. 1998. *Acting in Concert: Music, Community, and Political Action.* New Brunswick, NJ: Rutgers University Press.

Mazzarella, Sharon R. 2008. "Claiming a Space: The Cultural Economy of Teen Girl Fandom on the Web." In *Girl Wide Web: Girls, the Internet, and the Negotiation of Identity*, edited by Sharon R. Mazzarella, 141–60. New York: Peter Lang.

McCracken, Grant. 2013. "'Consumers' or 'Multipliers'?" *Spreadable Media.* http://spreadablemedia.org/essays/mccracken/#.V6ZJJZMrJos.

Meister, Mark, and Phyllis M. Japp. 2002. *Enviropop: Studies in Environmental Rhetoric and Popular Culture.* Westport, CT: Praeger.

Newcomb, Matthew. 2012. "Sustainability as a Design Principle for Composition: Situational Creativity as a Habit of Mind." *College Composition and Communication* 63 (4): 593–615.

Owens, Derek. 2001. *Composition and Sustainability: Teaching for a Threatened Generation*. Urbana, IL: National Council of Teachers of English.

Parkham, John. 2015. *Green Media and Popular Culture: An Introduction*. London: Palgrave Macmillan.

Pearson, Roberta. 2010. "Fandom in the Digital Era." *Popular Communication* 8 (1): 84–95.

Peddie, Ian. Ed. 2006. *The Resisting Muse: Popular Music and Social Protest*. Farnham, UK: Ashgate.

Pedelty, Mark. 2012. *Ecomusicology: Rock, Folk, and the Environment*. Philadelphia: Temple University Press.

Pieslak, Jonathan. 2015. *Radicalism and Music: An Introduction to the Music Cultures of al-Qa'ida, Racist Skinheads, Christian-Affiliated Radicals, and Eco-Animal Rights Militants*. Middletown, CT: Wesleyan University Press.

Portney, Kent E. 2015. *Sustainability*. Cambridge, MA: MIT Press.

Potts, Liza. 2012. "Amanda Palmer and the #LOFNOTC: How Online Fan Participation Is Rewriting Music Labels." *Participations* 9 (2): 360–82.

Pratt, Ray. 1990. *Rhythm and Resistance: The Political Uses of American Popular Music*. Washington, DC: Smithsonian Institution Press.

Rodman, Gil. 2015. "Waiting for the Great Leap Forwards: Mixing Pop, Politics, and Cultural Studies." In *The Sage Handbook of Popular Music*, edited by Andrew Bennett and Steve Waksman, 48–63. Los Angeles: Sage.

Schechner, Richard. 2008. *Performance Theory*. New York: Routledge.

Scodari, Christine. 2007. "Yoko in Cyberspace with Beatles Fans: Gender and the Recreation of Popular Mythology." In Jonathan Gray, Cornel Sandvoss, and C. Lee Harrington, eds., *Fandom: Identities and Communities in a Mediated World, 48–59*. New York: New York University Press.

Scoones, Ian. 2007. "Sustainability." *Development in Practice* 17 (4–5): 589–96.

Scott, Suzanne. 2009. "Repackaging Fan Culture: The Regifting Economy of Ancillary Content Models." *Transformative Works and Cultures*, 3. https://doi.org/10.3983/twc.2009.0150.

Street, John. 2012. *Music and Politics*. Cambridge: Polity Press.

Titon, Jeff Todd. 1988. *Powerhouse for God: Speech, Chant, and Song in an Appalachian Baptist Church*. Austin: University of Texas Press.

———. 2015. "Music Sustains People." *Sustainable Music* (blog). April 29. http://sustainablemusic.blogspot.com/2015/04/music-sustains-people.html.

Turino, Thomas. 2009. "Four Fields of Music Making and Sustainable Living." *the world of music* 51: 95–117.

Ward, Brian. 1998. *Just My Soul Responding: Rhythm and Blues, Black Consciousness, and Race Relations*. Berkeley: University of California Press.

Weeks, Kelly C. MacDonald. 2012. "Parrotheads, Cheeseburgers, and Paradise: Adult Music Fandom and Fan Practices." PhD diss., Bowling Green State University.

CHAPTER 11

Music, Media, and Mediation

BARRY DORNFELD

IN AN ICONIC AND often referenced scene from Robert Flaherty's legendary silent documentary film *Nanook of the North* (1922), a work that cast a direction for documentary and ethnographic film for many years to come, his reality "star," Allakariallak, playing the role of Nanook, arrives at a trading post with his family. After bartering for some of Nanook's pelts of recently hunted fox and polar bear, the presumed owner of the trading post plays an early gramophone record for Nanook, who feigns surprise and bemusement at this contraption and the sound it emits. The owner then hands Nanook the shellac disc, and an intertitle comes on screen narrating the action: "In deference to Nanook, the great hunter, the trader entertains and attempts to explain the principle of the gramophone—how the white man 'cans' his voice." In an attempt to understand this mediated sound object, Nanook takes a bite of the disc and laughs—chewing on the scenery indeed—making material this ephemeral sound. What music was the owner playing for Nanook as he listened? We can only guess, as it could have been music of any of a number of genres and cultural traditions, though we can assume it was music of the West and not indigenous music. Of course, the film itself was silent in its production, though accompanied in its theatrical run by an orchestra playing a score by the well-known film composer Rudolph Schramm. The phonograph on screen is not heard but seen, a symbol simultaneously of emerging sound technology, modernity, and colonial imposition.

The phonograph also bears the symbolic burden of cultural intervention in Werner Herzog's 1982 feature film, *Fitzcarraldo*, centered on the main character, played by Klaus Kinski, commissioning and propelling a steamship down

FIG. 11.1. *Nanook of the North* (1922, dir. Robert Flaherty)

FIG. 11.2. Klaus Kinski as Fitzcarraldo

FIG. 11.3. Werner Herzog directing *Fitzcarraldo* (1982)

the Amazon River in an endeavor to bring opera to the Peruvian jungle in the early 1900s (see Hurley-Glowa in this volume for more recent efforts to bring Western art music to remote populations). Most memorable are scenes of this bizarre colonial character floating down the Amazon while operatic strains of Caruso's arias blast from the gramophone. Fitzcarraldo and his crew encounter indigenous Amazonian tribal people along the way and essentially enslave them in the effort to drag his ship across a mountain pass. Many die in this epic struggle (as do several people in the making of the film), whose ultimate aim is to build an opera house in this small city east of the Andes Mountains, the center of the booming rubber trade.

In the same year, documentary filmmaker Les Blank released *Burden of Dreams* (1982), his unforgettable portrait of the making of Herzog's *Fitzcarraldo*. Blank, a prolific documentary filmmaker, directed many memorable films about traditional music in the United States—blues, Cajun, old timey, and many others. This project was a bit of detour for Blank, depicting the intensity of Herzog's epic production and the exploitative nature of the film's use of the native Aguaruna people (Brown 1982) in its making. In these interconnected narratives of cultural encounters at the edge of exploration and exploitation, the recorded musical object stands in for the complexity of the encounter, media as the symbol of a more violent mediation.

Media Embedded in Ethnomusicological Practice

The social-scientific encounter with music of the world's people has become increasingly and perhaps permanently intertwined with media in their multiple forms (see Milner 2009, for instance, for a music-industry-centered view of this history). And although recording technologies were used by ethnomusicologists from the discipline's earliest days, it took some time for the field of ethnomusicology to embrace media as a fundamental tool for expression. In the early years, ethnomusicologists and other ethnographically oriented scholars understood that the documentary capabilities of audio-recording technology and eventually film had a critical role to play in capturing and analyzing—and at times distributing—the cultural forms they were studying. And, of course, there is a long history of work looking at media from an ethnographic perspective in the traditions of visual anthropology, communication studies, and media studies more generally. Yet it took time for social scientists to embrace media as a fundamental form of expression, in part because of the shared belief that indigenous cultural expression was "often eroded by . . . the industrialized culture purveyed by the mass media" (1989 UNESCO Recommendation cited in Titon 2015, 167). By the 1960s and 1970s, a small group of ethnomusicologists began to experiment with and then embrace media distribution technologies—film, television, radio, recordings—as they quickly evolved in access and verisimilitude. Those interested in these forms, however, remained a small group.

A nascent literature developed considering the use of media for documenting, analyzing, and presenting musical expression (see Feld 1976; Zemp 1990; Dornfeld 1992; Titon 1992; Lange 2001; Baily 2009; Hutchinson this volume). Others looked at how media technologies spread music (Manuel 1993) or how they are integrating it into musical expression (Novak 2011, 2013). And, of course, Alan Lomax's evolution from cantometrics to "global jukebox" exemplifies the centrality of recording for ethnomusicological analysis (see Wood 2018 for a candid recounting of her father's work with mediated music). Over the last decade or two, more have embraced the power of the vastly more accessible (in terms of cost, training, and distribution) formats for audio recording, photography, film, video, and digital media to document, analyze, and share musical experience, offering great richness in understanding, representing, and perhaps sustaining musical experience across culture and time (Krüger 2009, 189–208).

We might characterize these people as mediators in a double sense: those who use media technologies in their work on understanding world music and those who mediate between the worlds of academic scholarship and more-popular knowledge, a productive tension in this domain.

So how has this shift to a more intensively mediated practice changed the work of those who take the cultural study of world music seriously? I consider this shift from the perspective of a filmmaker trained in ethnographic film/visual anthropology and, to a lesser extent, in ethnomusicology, focusing on the material, experiential dimensions of working with film/video in the representation of musical culture.

From this point of view, I see an inherent duality built into musical expression, a tension around its materiality. On the one hand, music is primarily of the moment, demanding presence, face-to-face experience, and engagement as it plays out in real time—ephemeral, invisible, complex, and transient. On the other, there have long been efforts to capture and freeze this experience in more enduring and accessible forms: musical notation, transcription, and recordings in various media. This situation might present a contradiction or dilemma to manage: "Do your best to capture this experience though we know that your attempts will be marginal, thin rather than thick, incomplete and less than satisfying." Notes on the page represent only so much musical texture and nuance and impose a Western cultural framework on other cultures' musical forms. Audio recording is limited, too, to this one sensual modality. Even multimedia forms of documentation—film, video, digital interactive, and now "immersive"—only provide so much verisimilitude.[1] The map is not the territory, the sign not the referent.

But more recently media have become embedded in the social-scientific encounter with music just as it has in daily life more generally, and therefore mediation has become more pervasive. Of course, this penetration of media exists in the way people in diverse societies experience music and in how music is produced and consumed and documented globally. We have to be careful, though, not to gloss over extreme differences in material access and resources across regional, national, and local boundaries; access to media, even in their more accessible forms, still plays out across great inequalities. In this media-saturated age, at least in the privileged West, technology is a part of many expressive experiences, and by extension our own experiences as mediators. As Debra S. Vidali writes in a consideration of multisensorial anthropology, "What better way to be more fully human than to richly examine, express, and document our various ways of knowing and being through multisensorial enunciation?" (2016, 399). And "polymedia" is one avenue into this multisensorial world. She goes on to write that this recasts traditional distinctions between media modes by "recognizing that people—including anthropological practitioners—live embodied, multisensorial, polymedia (Miller and Madianou 2012), polymodal (Loveless and Griffith 2014), multimedia, and multimodal lives within mediated multimodal genre systems" (398).

Ethnomusicology's "Mediators"

Media technology has always been part of the sociotechnical system of musical analysis. Metronomes, tape recorders, digital audio workstations, YouTube, and streaming media all represent assistive technologies through which ethnomusicological mediators understand their objects of study and media making. Now, as these technologies spread and become much more accessible, we should ask whether the practices by which these media makers mediate these musical experiences change. Can we helpfully think of these scholars/makers as mediators, as actors in the mediation practices working with musical cultures? The technologies put to work are evidence of an integrated way to think about media, musical scholarship, and musical experience and to enhance the depth and lasting power of these specific musical encounters. As we live in an increasingly mediated world, these examples help us focus on how media can shape our study of music as they clearly shape our consumption of it and can be a vehicle for sustaining that music.

We can see this spectrum of possibilities in Steven Feld's recent work in Accra, Ghana. Feld is an anthropologist and ethnomusicologist who has worked in multiple media throughout his career and a pioneer in the discipline of visual anthropology. He muses in the introduction to his latest book on jazz in Ghana about how he focused initially on publishing this research in media form rather than through academic writing:

> I didn't write a word about the Accra jazz world. Why? Well, first, it felt more natural to let photographs, recordings, video, and performances express the sensuous substance and spirit of my inquiry as an artist among artists. Both as a matter of credibility and engagement, I wanted to make everything immediately accessible in Ghana, to make sound and image the centerpiece of our collective musical exchanges. Besides, I didn't set out to gather material to write another scholarly book. And as it all got going, I bluntly asked Nii Noi, and then the others, "What do you want out of working with me?" Their priorities were unanimous and pointed: first, to have their creative work well-documented and to get paid for it, and second, through the prestige of the documentation, to get more gigs, income, and resources useful for the continuation of their work. (Feld 2012, 5–6)

Feld's recent work exists in a historical narrative of media makers like Jean Rouch, Hugo Zemp, John Bailey, Les Blank, Tom Davenport, and Jeff Titon—

anthropologists, folklorists, and ethnomusicologists who work with media as an integral part of their practice, extending their reach outside academics. In a fascinating interview about his early focus on sound, Feld describes his entry into the study of the anthropology of sound through deep listening to several of Colin Turnbull's early albums of Mbuti music from Central Africa and the power they had to invoke music in its cultural and physical environment (Feld and Brenneis 2004). I did not realize until I read this description that I shared this experience with Steve, my mentor through my early graduate studies and beyond, as I too was pulled into ethnomusicology by wearing out my copy of the Ethnic Folkways Library recording of *The Pygmies of the Ituri Forest* (1958). I wonder how many other mediators have had this same experience (I know that Michelle Kisliuk, an old friend and contributor to this volume, had an analogous transformative experience). And this narrative connects forward as well to the notion of a multisensory anthropology that writers such as Vidali have argued for in considering the future of media anthropology, and to which some ethnographic filmmakers have connected their work (see, for example, Harvard's Sensory Ethnography Lab, https://sel.fas.harvard.edu/index.html).

Reflecting on Media Practice

As I reflect on my own journey of being drawn into ethnomusicology and film, some formative instances where the intersection of media and music demonstrated for me their combinatorial power come to mind:

- *1976. Tufts University, Medford, Massachusetts.* An early morning university class on world music and ritual, where students in an undergraduate haze listen to reel-to-reel field recordings of traditional Navajo chants. The professor, Jeff Titon, encourages us to chant or at least hum along with the recording as a way to understand it and engage with it. Some watch from a mental distance, some participate passively and compliantly, others, like me, plunge into the rhythm and the chants, singing and drumming along with the recording on wooden desktops, moving past sophomoric shyness into engaged immersion. Jeff introduces this process to help us experience the concept of bi-musicality—that we can best understand the music of others by trying to perform that music, even through this elementary mediated means. Throughout the semester, other media examples invite our learning and bring to life the musical experience of a range of world cultures, and engage us in understanding these other musical worlds.
- *1996. Philadelphia.* Engrossed in film production with folklorist Debora Kodish for *Plenty of Good Women Dancers* (2004), a documentary about accomplished African American performers in Philadelphia, produced by the

FIG. 11.4. Cover of the influential *Worlds of Music: An Introduction to the Music of the World's Peoples* (1984, ed. Jeff Todd Titon)

Philadelphia Folklore Project. This project documented the song, dance, and narratives of a group of successful Philadelphia-based tap and stage dancers who performed from the 1920s through the 1950s, gathered back together by this organization to document and reconstruct their performative histories. A key figure in the project, Hortense Allen Jordan, had led dance groups

FIG. 11.5. Hortense Allen Jordan watches herself on screen for the first time in *Plenty of Good Women Dancers* (2004)

that traveled throughout the United States, performing for many thousands of people over her career mostly in black community venues. We were able to capture a remarkable moment with Hortense when she viewed archival footage of herself dancing with Billy Eckstine's big band. This moment was the first time Hortense had viewed film or video of herself performing, here in footage shot many years earlier for a Hollywood production, and the result was both a revelatory personal moment and one that said a great deal about the issues of power and visibility of black women performers, issues central to this film. In a real sense, the medium became the message in this encounter, with the documentary moment spooling out layers of cultural meaning.

- *2015. Philadelphia.* Preparing for a concert by the Liberian Women's Chorus for Change at World Café Live, a popular music venue in West Philadelphia.[2] The chorus is a performing group made up of resettled Liberian refugee singers and dancers who have reunited in Philadelphia through the help of the Philadelphia Folklore Project. Our documentary work with this powerful group of performers and political refugees included this concert in Philadelphia for a mixed audience of Liberian American immigrants, Af-

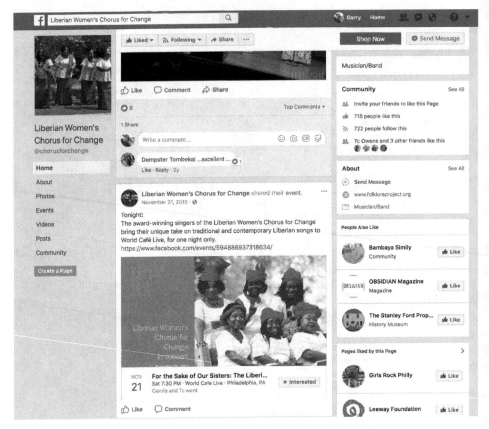

FIG. 11.6. Screenshot of Facebook page for the Philadelphia Folklore Project's Liberian Women's Chorus for Change Project, 2015

rican American and white cultural patrons, and a mix of others, including an audience of a few hundred viewers gathered in homes and internet cafés in Liberia, where the concert was streamed through Facebook. This distant social media audience kept up a digital dialogue of comments back to the women in the chorus and to others.

World Café Live provided a digital broadcast and recording package with multiple cameras positioned throughout the hall recording six angles simultaneously, with high-quality digital audio and live streamed the feed to the web. I shot additional footage from front and back stage, though I felt almost superfluous to this high-production-value and semirobotic documentary crew. The footage looked impressive, if produced in more of a music television style than we might have chosen ourselves. The performative experience was heightened in its mediated form.

These anecdotes indicate ways that media forms become integrated into work on music and in doing so enhance both the understanding of and the representations of those musical expressions.

The Benefits of Mediated Music

In each of the vignettes above, media are critical to the musical experience and to documentary practice, and meaning thickens when these two come together. More personally, my experience with mediated music has taught me a few things:

- *Mediated experience is multisensorial experience.* While we tend to privilege direct, face-to-face experience, in fact mediated experience is experience nonetheless—flattened in some ways, made deeper and more lasting in others. We are able to learn from our encounters with world music through media—recordings, film, and video—through multiple senses, visual, aural, even tactile. Working with music as a media maker offers a depth of encounter and sustainable learning.
- *Repetition matters, and media enable and empower repetition.* The ability to watch an edited sequence of musical behavior—performance, rehearsal, teaching, instrument making—over and over again gives you an intimate knowledge of the behavior you are documenting and analyzing. Through repetition, the mediated musical action and makers reveal themselves more and more over time.
- *Media enable intersubjective participation in the ethnomusicological encounter.* Social scientists have argued for collaborative models of work and for work that matters to the communities represented. Media projects offer opportunities for substantive collaboration in planning, decision making, editing, and distribution. They enable the kind of "speaking with" rather than "speaking for" that many have advocated and some have practiced.[3]
- *Media objects have value for the communities with whom we collaborate.* The scholarly text, even in collaborative production, offers limited value for our ethnographic partners. The book or article conveys significance and credibility but less joy in its consumption or potential spread in its distribution. The CD, DVD, YouTube clip, or website offer more to the communities in which we work, as Feld's collaborator Nii Noi told him, and for a musician or dancer more social and economic capital.
- *Media projects raise the stakes of social-scientific and documentary encounters.* The addition of the camera and/or recorder has the potential to heighten musical events and give them greater cultural import, value, and perhaps lasting impact. Of course, this heightening is not always welcome and can shape the nature of the musical event being documented in unpredictable ways,

FIG. 11.7. "Kunuk Uncovered" (2015)

as the previous vignettes suggest, though these tradeoffs can be navigated in positive ways.

Almost one hundred years after Nanook chomped on a shellac recording in the northern Arctic, presumably with encouragement of a white American filmmaker, two referential mediations bring our focus back to this film historical moment:

- In an episode of the recent television mockumentary series *Documentary Now*, "Kunuk Uncovered," the television actor and comedian Fred Armisen reenacts this originally acted encounter as part of a remarkably spot-on parody of *Nanook of the North*. The irony of an American actor playing an Inuit documentary subject parodying an Inuit man playing a fictional Inuit character biting a piece of Western technology in a documentary re-creation includes too many cultural refractions to track. The meta-references pull us both back into the documentary past and forward into the mediated future.
- In 2016, the Inuk performance artist Tanya Tagaq turned another loop in the referential mediation process. Tagaq performed Inuit throat singing in front of scenes from Flaherty's original documentary *Nanook* in what one reviewer described as "a reclaiming of experience, identity, and history" and Tagaq herself calls "some hardcore punk to challenge Flaherty's vision" (Barker 2016).

FIG. 11.8. Tanya Tagaq performing at the 2018 Dark Mofo Festival, Hobart, Australia, before scenes from Nanook of the North (http://www.backseatmafia.com/live-dark -mofo-festival-2018-tanya-tagiq-soundtrack-to-nanook-of-the-north/

The power of this performance and the power of the original mediated experience of Nanook resonate across time and space. The reviewer Jeremy Barker writes:

> As much as the film may represent the racist perspectives of its maker, it's also a document—one of the few—that sought to capture the experience of Tagaq's own ancestors and their way of life, which Flaherty (an engineer and operative of European and American corporate concerns, who in fact funded his film) was guilty of helping transform and end. The world Tagaq grew up in, in a small modern town in Northern Canada, is the creation of Flaherty and his associates. And the only way she and her kin can see (literally see, through the film) back to where they came from, is through a mechanism of his own devising. (Barker 2016)

What matters most here is to appreciate the ways that media make musical experience more vital, long-lasting, and amenable to interpretive work. Media allow us to interact with musical expression in rich ways that deepen our understanding of the music, its making, and its cultural power. And we are well past the time that media can be seen simply as an eroding force on traditional cultures, since so much of our cultural experience is embedded in and shaped by media forms. In fact, the mediations considered here suggest that the impact swings toward sustaining the cultural life of these musical moments and experiences, and even deepening them at times, in the spirit that Robert Baron and Thomas Walker suggest in this volume. Both the pasts and the presents of diverse musical worlds are made more accessible through these forms. Are the futures made more durable as well? As we extend our understandings of how our practices and relationships with the communities we work in shift when we use media as a primary modality, we will be able to use these technologies of mediation more thoughtfully and better understand their complicated impact.

Notes

1. The literature on virtual reality and immersive media is emerging as the forms are spreading. See Perlmutter 2014 for an early consideration; for ongoing insights, see *Immerse: Creative Discussion of Emerging Nonfiction Storytelling*, edited by Jessica Clark, https://immerse.news.

2. Fatu Gayflor, Marie Nyenabo, Zaye Tete, and Tokay Tomah are principal performers for the Liberian Women's Chorus for Change. Toni Shapiro-Phim directs the project for the Philadelphia Folklore Project.

3. See Ruby 1991; Asch et al. 1991; and Ginsburg 1991 for early arguments for a shift toward collaborative modes of media making.

References

Asch, Timothy, with Jesus Ignacio Cardoza, Hortensia Cabellero, and Jose Bortoli. 1991. "The Story We Now Want to hear Is Not Ours to Tell." *Visual Anthropology Review* 7 (2): 102–6.

Baily, John. 2009. "The Art of the 'Fieldwork Movie': 35 Years of Making Ethnomusicological Films." *Ethnomusicology Forum* 18 (1): 55–64.

Barker, Jeremy. 2016. "Tanya Tagaq's 'Nanook of the North' at Under the Radar 2016." Deeply Fascinating, March 17. https://tinyurl.com/y7756jp.

Brown, Michael F. 1982. "Art of Darkness." *Progressive* 46 (8) (August): 20–21.

Burden of Dreams. 1982. Documentary film. Directed by Les Blank. Les Blank Films.

Dornfeld, Barry. 1992. "Representation and Authority in Ethnographic Film/Video: Reception." *Ethnomusicology* 36 (1): 95–98

Feld, Steven. 1976. "Ethnomusicology and Visual Communication." *Ethnomusicology* 20 (2): 293–325.

———. 2012. *Jazz Cosmopolitanism in Accra: Five Musical Years in Ghana*. Durham, NC: Duke University Press.

Feld, Steven, and Donald Brenneis. 2004. "Doing Anthropology in Sound." *American Ethnologist* 31 (4): 461–74.

Fitzcarraldo. 1982. Feature film. Directed by Werner Herzog. Werner Herzog Filmproduktion.

Ginsburg, Faye. 1991. "Indigenous Media: Faustian Contract or Global Village?" *Cultural Anthropology* 6 (1): 92–112.

Krüger, Simone. 2009. *Experiencing Ethnomusicology: Teaching and Learning in European Universities*. Burlington, VT: Ashgate.

"Kunuk Uncovered." 2015. Directed by Alexander Buono and Rhys Thomas. Season 1, episode 2, of *Documentary Now!* Originally aired August 27, 2015, on the Independent Film Channel.

Lange, Barbara Rose. 2001. "Hypermedia and Ethnomusicology." *Ethnomusicology* 45 (1): 132–49.

Loveless, Douglas, and Bryant Griffith. 2014. *Critical Pedagogy for a Polymodal World.* Rotterdam: Sense.

Manuel, Peter. 1993. *Cassette Culture: Popular Music and Technology in North India.* Chicago: University of Chicago Press.

Miller, Daniel, and Mirca Madianou. 2012. "Polymedia: Towards a New Theory of Digital Media in Interpersonal Communication." *International Journal of Cultural Studies* 16 (2): 169–87.

Milner, Greg. 2009. *Perfecting Sound Forever: An Aural History of Recorded Music.* New York: Faber and Faber.

Nanook of the North. 1922. Documentary film. Directed by Robert Flaherty. Financed by Revillion Freres.

Novak, David. 2011. "The Sublime Frequencies of New Old Media." *Public Culture* 23 (3): 601–34.

———. 2013. *Japanoise: Music at the Edge of Circulation.* Durham, NC: Duke University Press.

Perlmutter, Tom. 2014. "The Interactive Documentary: A Transformative Art Form." *Policy Options / Options Politiques,* November–December 2014, 10–15.

Plenty of Good Women Dancers. 2004. Documentary film. Film by Barry Dornfeld, Debora Kodish, and Germaine Ingram. Philadelphia Folklore Project. http://www.folkstreams.net/film,293.

The Pygmies of the Ituri Forest. 1958. Recorded by Colin Turnbull and Francis S. Chapman. Folkways LP FW04457/FE 4457. Reissued in 1992 as *Mbuti Pygmies of the Ituri Rainforest,* Smithsonian Folkways CD SFW40401, compact disc.

Ruby, Jay. 1991. "Speaking for, Speaking about, Speaking with, or Speaking alongside—an Anthropological and Documentary Dilemma." *Visual Anthropology Review* 7 (2): 50–67.

Titon, Jeff Todd, ed. 1984. *Worlds of Music: An Introduction to the Music of the World's Peoples.* New York: Schirmer.

———. 1992. "Representation and Authority in Ethnographic Film/Video: Production." *Ethnomusicology* 36 (1): 89–94.

———. 2015. "Sustainability, Resilience, and Adaptive Management for Applied Ethnomusicology." In *The Oxford Handbook of Applied Ethnomusicology,* edited by Svanibor Pettan and Jeff Todd Titon, 158–96. New York: Oxford University Press.

Vidali, Debra S. 2016. "Multisensorial Anthropology: A Retrofit Cracking Open of the Field." *American Anthropologist* 118 (2): 395–400.

Wood, Anna L. C. 2018. "'Like a Cry from the Heart': An Insider's View of the Genesis of Alan Lomax's Ideas and the Legacy of His Research; Part I." *Ethnomusicology* 62 (2): 230–64.

Zemp, Hugo. 1990. "Ethical Issues in Ethnomusicological Filmmaking." *Visual Anthropology* 3 (1): 49–64.

CHAPTER 12

Photography, Memory, and the Frail Instant

TOM RANKIN

I THINK OFTEN OF Kentucky poet, novelist, and essayist Wendell Berry's character Jayber Crow (in Berry's 2000 novel by the same name) who, while sitting on his porch one day, reflects on life and the passing of time: "Back at the beginning, as I see now, my life was all time and almost no memory. . . . And now, nearing the end, I see that my life is almost entirely memory and very little time" (2000, 24). That time and the passing of time, and memory and memory's eternal companions—imagination and creativity—are natural ingredients in the photographic process is no surprise. Central to any interaction with a photograph, whether as maker or viewer, is the relationship of recording to time, of creativity to memory, of history to fertility of imagination. How do some photographs hold and sustain our place in the world, how do they locate our position in time, in work, in culture, in ourselves? Photographs are often "made" in order to stop time, to bear witness to something quickly passing. Eudora Welty recognized her snapshots as a "record," as a way to arrest time, whether those moments were subtle gestures, a fleeting relationship, or an entire way of life. A snapshot is "now or never," she has said (1989, xiii). She saw her images, she has said, as "a record of a kind—a record of fact, putting together some of the elements of one time and one place" (1978, 350–51). Fellow Mississippian William Faulkner talked about how the role of the artist was not only to arrest time but to "strive with all the means and all the talents he possesses—his imagination, his experience, his powers of observation—to put into more lasting form than his own frail, ephemeral instant of life . . . what he has known first hand" (1974, 165).

Welty's idea of "the elements of one time and one place" and Faulkner's contention that we attempt to "arrest time" in order to register "into more lasting form" human creativity connect nicely with Jeff Titon's idea of music as a "renewable resource." The photograph, born of an ephemeral instant, never preserves a moment but instead fertilizes and urges memory. At the root of responsible sustainability is the remembered place, time, and people, the reverence necessary for the common good. As with Titon's idea of connections and communities made and sustained through sound, there's an analogous ecology born of image and memory, of place and time.

Two photographers from distinctly different geographic places and with contrasting backgrounds—Maggie Lee Sayre and Paul Kwilecki—both saw their work as a way to mark and sustain memory, to engage in the moment, and to make a body of work that might in some very personal sense represent home. Faulkner's idea of creating images that render what the maker "has known first hand" is central to the discussion of both of these photographers, the firsthand account so often the implicit power of the photograph, knowing that in most cases it was made by someone physically present at the moment of creation.

* * *

"I shot the fish," photographer Maggie Lee Sayre told me when I asked her to explain why she made a particular image of a large catfish. "And I really enjoyed when we had those big fish. So I shot the fish." "Shooting" those fish were essential to Maggie Lee Sayre's photographic vision, with her desire to document her experiences—those moments that would reinforce and help define her memory. "When we caught a large fish I'd take a picture before it was sold," she carefully explained through a sign interpreter. "Then I could remember the big fish hanging on the scale" (Sayre in Rankin 1995, 21).

I first met Sayre while trying to take my own photographs of traditional river life, meeting commercial fishermen, net makers, trappers, boat builders, and others who made their living along the lower Tennessee River. Working for and in collaboration with Bob Fulcher of the Tennessee State Parks, I had asked far and wide about any families still living in boats on the river, embracing that river lifestyle that many chose to avoid the financial realities of land ownership and more-regular day jobs. The Sayre family was mentioned often by people we met. They were said to be one of the few families who had continued to live on their houseboat into the 1970s. Finally one person told us where we might find the Sayre boat.

Fulcher and I found the boat one Sunday afternoon on land very near the Tennessee River in Decatur County—a sixty-foot, three-room cypress artifact of an earlier, river-based lifestyle. A nearby neighbor, an old Sayre family friend, encouraged us to visit the nursing home several miles away in Parsons and meet

FIG. 12.1. Archie Sayre with fish buyer Robert Haynes. Photograph
by Maggie Lee Sayre. Courtesy Tom Rankin and the Maggie Lee
Collection, Southern Media Archive, University of Mississippi.

Maggie Lee Sayre, the only surviving member of family at that time. Maggie,
the neighbor said, might have some old pictures.

On that late Sunday afternoon in 1982, we went straight to Decatur County
Manor, the small nursing home in Parsons. With the other residents overtly
curious about who we were, pulling up their wheelchairs and walkers to compete
for our attention, we explained to Sayre our purpose and our particular interest
in photographs. After motioning for us to sit on a nearby couch, she disappeared

FIG. 12.2. Maggie Lee Sayre with her camera, Decatur County, Tennessee, 1987.
Photograph by Tom Rankin.

down a hallway and then returned with two large photographic albums, one
dating from the 1930s. Maggie pointed to an early photograph dated 1937 of her
father cleaning a hoop net and used handwritten notes and gestures to explain
Archie Sayre's work in the picture, revealing her role as both a participant in the
river economy and as the consummate observer with a camera. As she turned
page after page of her carefully edited and sequenced photo albums, it became
powerfully clear that she was sharing her pictorial life story, a visual narrative
seasoned with a nuance of description and the mystery of meaning inherent
in the best of stories.

Sometime later, again through sign language, Maggie Sayre explained more
about her ideas around her photographs and the memories of her family's life.
"I used the pictures to show people so they would enjoy it," she recalled. "My
snapshots. But other pictures that I could have, that I could keep for myself
and remember. . . . For several years I took pictures all the time, all the time. Of
different things around." When I asked why she took so many pictures—some

FIG. 12.3. Series of photographs documenting the process of tarring hoop nets, 1939. Photographs by Maggie Lee Sayre. Courtesy Tom Rankin and the Maggie Lee Collection, Southern Media Archive, University of Mississippi.

250 negatives were in the "archive" shoebox in her nursing-home room, which she shared with another resident—she would respond by simply saying, "I want to remember" (in Rankin 1995, 19).

Her desire to execute simple, clear documentation of her father's work is obvious in her four-part series of the tarring of nets. Before the advent of nylon line, commercial fishermen had to tar their nets regularly to prevent rotting of the cotton twine. This tarring process is something Maggie Sayre saw countless times and occasionally helped with. Her documenting of such a routine task affirms her persistent focus on the ordinary, the everyday. "This is a series of pictures," she told me. And she continued, with the picture series calling forth from her mind the details of the day: "The second one you see there is a helper helping my father. And the helper's name is Charles East. Charles is hoisting the net up out of the tar. And then on the third picture down here [pointing] you see how long the net is when it's strung out. And the fourth picture over there is dragging the nets along and setting them to the side" (Sayre in Rankin 1995, 21). Could any series suggest more conscious documentation of work or process? An outside ethnographer could hardly have timed a four-part series

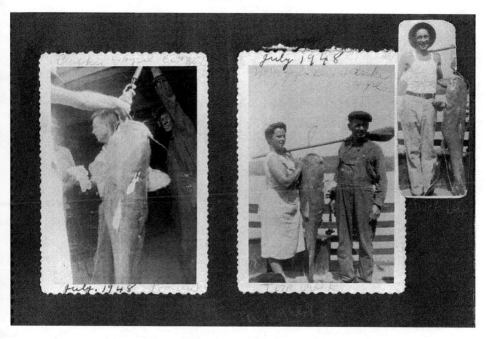

FIG. 12.4. Page from Sayre scrapbook, 1948. Courtesy Tom Rankin and the Maggie Lee Collection, Southern Media Archive, University of Mississippi.

of still images any better. Yet for Maggie Sayre the fundamental goal was to sustain her memory, to allow her to share what she knows, to be able to recall for others, like me, a river life that by the time I met her was dimly seen, a kind of vague communal recollection from the past.

Photography served multiple purposes for Maggie Lee Sayre. First, she could engage in the immediate dialogue that occurs in the taking of a picture—with family, visitors, and the inanimate landscape around her. Second, she was able to define and represent the world as she saw it, as she wanted to remember it, thus affirming her own particular place within it. And finally, by editing and organizing her prints in well-conceived, sequenced photo albums, with names and dates sparsely added, she created a pictorial narrative analogous to an autobiography. Thus her pictures exist simultaneously as autobiography, regional and occupational reflection, cultural document, and personal story. For a woman unable to hear or speak, the photographic medium offered a fundamental and poignant way to communicate, and in that perhaps an escape from isolation. Her photographs are the result of a rare confluence of factors: her deafness, her fifty-one years on the river, her intimate knowledge of the work and life of commercial fishing families like her own, and her abiding desire to create a record of her days, a way to recollect and revisit.

* * *

For all his thinking and articulate writing about the virtues of staying home and photographing the familiar, photographer Paul Kwilecki was the consummate outsider, even in his own local or familial space. He felt true empathy for the overlooked in his South Georgia community, those who were ignored and invisible. Sometimes he saw his southern Jewish family history as a story of outsiders, of newcomers who had to work their way into the culture. But his self-image as an observer on the fringes, an artist trying to say something vital and authentic, seems to have been an even deeper identity. It's no coincidence that he often felt alone in his pursuit, making his way as an artist in a family of successful merchants and businessmen. What his family's hardware business didn't offer in the way of direct opportunities in the arts, it did in a deep familiarity with the diversity of Decatur County. The Kwilecki and Sons store was a virtual crossroads of the whole demographic of the town and county. Whether consciously or not, Paul Kwilecki received a full education as people of all ages, backgrounds, and occupations moved through the store and traded with the Kwilecki family.

Staying put in Decatur County was a kind of artistic dictum, an aesthetic ethos at the foundation of all his work. But this attitude was more complicated than a pure artistic position, reflects his daughter Susan, who believes he was "stuck" in Bainbridge. "I think the heart is usually torn in most big decisions that we make, and there was a part of Daddy that wanted to leave, but I don't believe that he could do it. I don't think he was capable of that" (in Rankin 2013, 7).

If it ever crossed his mind to leave, he never admitted it in any direct way. "My father is buried less than a mile as the crow flies from the spot where he was born, married, and worked for sixty years, and died," he began a talk in 2001. "I was born just down the street at Riverside Hospital, have lived in Bainbridge all my life, and will be buried in Oak City Cemetery beside my wife, a mother and father, brother, uncles and aunts, my grandparents, great-grandparents, and a cousin who survived five Nazi concentration camps." His love for Decatur County, he went on to say, was as "old and deep" as he was (Kwilecki 2001).

From his earliest efforts as a photographer, Kwilecki identified with and was attracted to photographing the rural, humble, working-class residents of his county. That interest may well have been informed by his understanding of the documentary tradition in which countless photographers, filmmakers, and ethnographers have sought to portray the power and poetry embedded within the everyday life of common people. But something greater was happening with Kwilecki, I believe, as he recognized in both shade-tobacco and town factory workers a certain misunderstood invisibility, a quality that he identified in himself, however comfortably situated in a merchant-class lifestyle. He often

FIG. 12.5. Water tower through cemetery gate, Bainbridge, Georgia, 1982. Paul Kwilecki Photographs and Papers, David M. Rubenstein Rare Book and Manuscript Library, Duke University.

expressed dismay, even disdain, for what he perceived as the blindness of the Bainbridge elite. One of the ways he found to coexist and stay settled was to search for the quiet and contemplative human element in what others seemed to exploit, take for granted, or simply ignore. Of his interest in agricultural labor he once said, "The land, the crop, and the workers caught my eye immediately. All were beautiful" (undated lecture notes, Kwilecki Collection, Duke University).

In 1968 he wrote a letter to Oriole Farb at the Riverside Museum in New York. "I am a photographer, an amateur. Is there a chance of having my work shown at your museum?" he began and continued by explaining that all his work came from the Georgia county where he lived. "I dislike New York. . . . It is too far away and too big, but I understand there are people there that like good photography" (Kwilecki 1968). An outsider at home, he also defined himself as an outsider in the world of photography.

His sense of isolation as a photographer made him long for encouragement and conversation about his chosen medium. Paul Kwilecki was a voluminous letter writer, attempting to reach out to anyone in photography who he thought could help him in his quest to be the best self-taught photographer he could be.

FIG. 12.6. Flint River, Bainbridge, Georgia, 1979. Paul Kwilecki Photographs and Papers, David M. Rubenstein Rare Book and Manuscript Library, Duke University.

He wrote to Ansel Adams in the fall of 1963, asking for advice on developers, printing paper, and film. Adams rushed off a quick response to his first letter, typed on a card: "I am up to my ears in the preparation of my large retrospective exhibit which opens in San Francisco October 4th. I cannot give you a decent reply to your question until the pressure of work here is over. But you will hear from me——cordially" (in Rankin 2013, 9). As promised, Adams responded in mid-December 1963, making specific recommendations for printing that would lead to more saturated black tones in Kwilecki's prints. If it seems surprising that Kwilecki would write to someone like Adams out of the blue, it shouldn't; he wrote to magazine editors, curators, museum directors, anyone he thought could help him. And most wrote back. With each piece of correspondence, he asked for advice and attempted to explain his own work, his personal photographic ideas and process. In a 1966 letter to Ansel Adams, he talked of his desire to someday make a book of photographs: "Maybe one good book in a lifetime. No text; just pictures" (9) He went on to describe in detail how he was going about teaching himself, how he went about making his photographic work:

> I am taking my 35 mm camera into places around here no cameras have ever gone: into shanties, into tawdry, small-town cafes (not the Robert Frank kind,

FIG. 12.7. Preacher, Decatur County, Georgia, 1965. Paul Kwilecki Photographs and Papers, David M. Rubenstein Rare Book and Manuscript Library, Duke University.

the south-Georgia, bible-belt kind), into the kitchens and hallways of farm houses and there, in the middle of things these people live with, I make their pictures. I use the 35 mm partly like a view camera and partly like a 35. I use it on a tripod and I pose the subjects. The pose is my effort to get them to look into the lens and react naturally. The tripod is because the light is usually so bad, the exposures, even on Tri-X, are around a second duration. Anyway, I'm getting a good look at these people, and sometimes the look yields up a strong but tender image that speaks the truth. (Kwilecki in Rankin 2013, 10)

He was working hard to locate his subject matter, point of view, and technique. He had great respect for writers and writing, specifically the power that comes from the accretion of daily writing, words piling up over time. His own daily journal entries recorded parts of his artistic evolution, many of his feelings about photography. "Day to day most people experience a good many important feelings and if one had the power to put them down in a literary way," he observed, "so that the gut feelings came through and the anxieties were recalled with some real candor and vividness, something really strong and worthwhile might be compiled over the years. . . . In a way this is what I *am* doing photographically" (in Rankin 2013, 12).

FIG. 12.8. Putting up the shades, tobacco field, Decatur County, Georgia, 1962. Paul Kwilecki Photographs and Papers, David M. Rubenstein Rare Book and Manuscript Library, Duke University.

When he wrote this entry, he had been working on the Decatur County project for over ten years and was beginning to see the virtue of the long view, his steady gaze on home. However, as much as he often questioned the merits of his photographic work, he could also see—and truly believe in—what it might all add up to if pursued over time. "Until recently," he muses in the same 1971 diary entry, "I have been more or less unsure just what it was I really wanted from photography. About four years ago I began to sense an interest in documentary work, but it was weak and non-specific and little more than an idea." His taste, he said, was "moving toward documentary work."

He often found inspiration and encouragement in southern writers who had stayed close to home, in literature that clearly revealed the universal poetry in the particular patterns of mundane life. Looking at his copy of Eudora Welty's *One Writer's Beginning*, I find passages that he underlined, sometimes twice, with comments in the margins. "My work, in the terms in which I see it, is as dearly matched to the world as its secret sharer," writes Welty (1984, 84). Welty's interest in the local but even more importantly in the "outer and inner" drew Kwilecki's interest. When she writes of her own picture making and what she learned from it, he affirms her words with more underlining: "With the accretion of years, the hundreds of photographs—life as I found it, all unposed—constitute a record of that desolate period; but most of what I learned for myself came right at the time and directly out of the *taking* of pictures. The camera was a hand-held auxiliary of wanting-to-know" (84). As unwavering as Kwilecki was in his intent to create his monumental and lasting "record" of Decatur County—and to complete it by producing nearly five hundred archival prints—it was the process of photographing the place where he lived that provided him a way of living there, a method of knowing, a means of using the full power of his singular vision.

At different times throughout the four decades Paul Kwilecki worked on his opus about his home terrain, he used different words to describe it. He called it a "project," a "photographic journal," something "more than a catalogue," and perhaps most often, a "document." But none of these rather simple words and descriptions communicates the depth and nuance with which he approached his work. There were times when he talked about his decision in the late fifties to limit his photographic content to his home county that made it sound like a kind of epiphany, inspired by Eugène Atget's pictures of Paris, by William Faulkner's mythic landscape and stories from his "own little postage stamp of native soil" (Gourevitch 2007, 57). To be sure, these and other lessons from art and literature contributed, but even he admitted that he came to create his document of Decatur County gradually. In 1975, in what was the first of two Guggenheim Fellowship applications, he explained that "the idea of a long, sustained project, depicting life in one county, took shape slowly and from its own momentum; certainly not by conscious design or in a flash of recognition" (Kwilecki 1975).

He closed his Guggenheim application narrative, "I believe in its ultimate value as a document, provided the promise that is now in evidence can be fulfilled. Hopefully, it will be distinctive, not for its uniqueness of concept, nor for its tacit premise that Decatur County is the world in microcosm, but for its consistently personal and therefore human point of view." When he submitted his second Guggenheim application in 1980, he was successful. When he received the good news in the mail, he drove straight to Oak City Cemetery, parked near the Jewish section, and walked to his mother's grave. Standing there alone, he read her the award letter from the Guggenheim Foundation.

"I am one man, one mind, one pair of eyes trying to distinguish what is significant in an entire community," he said in one 2001 lecture. As much as he lauded the tradition of documentary photography, he strove to see it on his own terms, to understand it through his own particular way of working. "Good documentary photography," he stated, "is simultaneously a record of reality and an editorial on that reality. . . . I am making a factual record out of bits and pieces of experience and they are stubborn about bonding to aesthetic standards. Much is lost in translation from reality to photographs of reality,

FIG. 12.9. Trailways bus station, Bainbridge, Georgia, 1977. Paul Kwilecki
Photographs and Papers, David M. Rubenstein Rare Book and Manuscript Library,
Duke University.

most of it bringing order to something that is by nature random." And maybe
his most poignant perception, an idea so honest and reflexive as to leave no
room for further comment: "I rearrange sacred furniture. Because my brain,
not my camera, is my instrument, beauty isn't enough. I'm looking at subject,
not at the surface of the print, though I'm grateful when the surface turns out
to be beautiful" (Kwilecki 2001).

Paul Kwilecki ruminated regularly about his legacy and the lasting quality of
his work—and, as he more than once said to me, the futility—of his obsession.
He had an outward demeanor and capacity for genuine patience and believed in
the long view that his work would stand on its own and gradually find increasing
relevance and attention. But no one is ever certain, to be sure, and expressions
of doubt were never far from his lips when we talked. "If photographs are strong
they will find their audience sooner or later," he wrote to one gallery owner about
a possible exhibition. "Later is not altogether a bad thing: it leaves more time
for making the photographs, which, after all, is everything" (in Rankin 2013,
18). As belief doesn't exist without doubt, his faith in his own vision and work

is best witnessed by how often he turned his attention to making new pictures, stacking up prints, further refining how he felt about his home place, regardless of outside opportunities to exhibit or publish.

Kwilecki's attempt over four decades to make this one place felt in his pictures was just as mysterious an act and was met by others with a similar silence and ambiguity. "Feeling is one of the highest forms of knowing," he once observed (email to the author, November 2005), and yet he was adamant that local Decatur County people—friends as well as strangers—didn't understand his emotional commitment to his enduring pursuit. His dark mythology of the lone artist laboring, unrecognized, in the vineyard day after day, year after year, may well have sustained him, may have emboldened the quiet doggedness that allowed him to repel any neglect he felt. However it worked, his confidence in the merits of his project never waned. When he said he "rearranged the sacred furniture" of his home, he could have honestly added that he did so by trying to show it as true to how he found and felt it as possible. "Mine is an egocentric document," he said in 2001, making no claim to "comprehensiveness or objectivity. . . . I photograph subjects who are, to me, vivid and substantial. I leave everything else alone" (Kwilecki 2001).

* * *

When I was a child, I would take forced naps at my grandmother's house on a daybed in a room on her second floor. For a handful of years my grandmother had seriously pursued photography. The over fifty rolls of her black-and-white 35 mm negatives that I have in my possession are evidence of a careful picture maker. Photographs covered the entire wall at her house above me while I slept. I well remember waking to first sight of unknown relatives, some in casual attire and others in more formal studio poses, parading across the wall in assorted sizes and frames. Most of the faces were unknown to me, appearing as wayfaring strangers in a family collection, unfamiliar in any way except that I'd seen the wall many times before. I knew the photographs but nothing of what they meant. My grandparents could point at the wall and talk endlessly about this person and that: the day the picture of my mother was taken, what happened to that tree my uncle was standing next to, which Sunday on which farm that picture comes from, the day the lightning struck *that* house, who this is and what that person died from. My family found sustenance in the tones and tenors of those images, a wall that not only marked an earlier time but one that worked to regularly renew elements of story and memory. That wall was my first regular exposure to photographs, to what they mean to the people who made and have them, and to how the meanings shift over time and place, how different sets of eyes find diverse meanings, and how they prompt the stories

FIG. 12.10. Bird feeder, Louisville, Kentucky, 1966. Photograph by Tom Rankin.

of different people. Even the most anonymous of images, the most mysterious and unknown, seemed to possess the power to call forth meaning and story, something analogous with Titon's notion of music as an ever renewable resource.

I took my own first pictures, like many, when I was a child. Growing up in Louisville, Kentucky, I had a small Kodak camera that used 127 film. I started organizing the world through the viewfinder of my camera when I was seven or eight, photographing what was closest to me day by day: family, home, and scenes of the everyday. One of my early pictures is of a bird feeder hanging from a maple tree out the back door of our house. My grandfather's cousin, whom we called Uncle Charlie, worked for the *Louisville Courier-Journal* and made bird feeders as a hobby. He was known for these wooden feeders the way people become known for what they make and share. I remember him bringing us the feeder, shaped like a house, the roof covered with a few red asphalt shingles. My picture is nothing if not the innocent and naive work of a child, an upward gaze that can't quite reach or frame the entire object. With the feeder way beyond my reach, the camera allowed me to get a little closer or at least offered an *illusion* of more immediate connection and closeness. For years the picture was in a box I carried around for no apparent reason, only, I suppose, because it belonged to me. And now, many years later, the photograph has grown to provide a way into remembered time and place. We didn't see Uncle Charlie very often, and I was prompted to take the picture after overhearing that he had either fallen very ill or had died; I can't remember which. Whatever the case, the news of his failing sent me looking to photograph the bird feeder he had made.

Paradoxically, my memory of that tree, the feeder, and Charlie Johanboeke are now dominated—even maybe controlled (limited?)—by a small snapshot photograph. Not that I couldn't recall it all without the photograph—I can, for instance, still see him in my mind's eye getting out of his car in his long, dark overcoat and hat, carrying the bird feeder on the day he brought it to our house—but I know that memory and those times mostly through the portal of this one flawed photograph, a photograph made through innocent impulse, saved, carried forward, a part of my memory ecology, and now held tightly as a slight representation of an ephemeral instant.

References

Berry, Wendell. 2000. *Jayber Crow: A Novel*. Washington, DC: Counterpoint.

Faulkner, William. 1974. "Speech of Acceptance for the Andres Bello Award, Caracas, 1961." In *A Faulkner Miscellany*, edited by James B. Meriwether, 164–66. Jackson: University Press of Mississippi.

Gourevitch, Philip. 2007. *The "Paris Review" Interviews*. Vol. 2. New York: Picador.

Kwilecki, Paul. 1968. Letter to Oriole Farb. Paul Kwilecki Photographs and Papers, Rubenstein Library, Duke University, Durham, NC.

———. 1975. Guggenheim Fellowship application. Paul Kwilecki Photographs and Papers, Rubenstein Library, Duke University, Durham, NC.

———. 2001. Manuscript of public talk, in conjunction with exhibition *Paul Kwilecki: Photographs from Decatur County, Georgia* at Duke University. Paul Kwilecki Photographs and Papers, Rubenstein Library, Duke University, Durham, NC.

Rankin, Tom. 1995. *Deaf Maggie Lee Sayre: Photographs of a River Life*. Jackson: University Press of Mississippi.

———. 2013. *One Place: Paul Kwilecki and Four Decades of Photographs from Decatur County, Georgia*. Chapel Hill: University of North Carolina Press.

Welty, Eudora. 1978. "One Time, One Place." In *The Eye of the Story: Selected Essays and Reviews*, 349–55. New York: Random House.

———. 1984. *One Writer's Beginnings*. Cambridge, MA: Harvard University Press.

———. 1989. *Eudora Welty Photographs*. Jackson: University Press of Mississippi.

CHAPTER 13

'Tis the Company

Irish Traditional Music as Social Medium in the Age of Social Media

PATRICK HUTCHINSON

AS A PIPER, a *budoka*, and an academic, I have been very lucky with my teachers, for in each of these disparate fields I have been blessed to fall under the influence of men and women who valued neighborliness, and who taught that it should inform and guide the way the things they taught were practiced.

From the get-go, Jeff Titon and I shared an appreciation of the idea of music as gift and of the importance of visiting, of the writing of Wendell Berry, and of the obvious superiority of small-scale, handmade cider and small-scale, handmade music—of "local, participatory music in small groups, based on commons, social networks and gifts exchanges" (Titon 2013).

Under his guidance I wrote about the man who taught me everything I know about piping and the uilleann pipes, Chris Langan (Hutchinson 1997). From Chris I learned that Irish traditional music, and uilleann piping in particular, could be a way of enacting the value of neighborliness, in the way that playing together offered the opportunity to achieve a musical and social groove. Every aspect of piping tradition—from tune titles, to ways of explaining piping movements through reference to players past and present, to the preservation of stylistic nuance in both playing and instrument design—seemed almost designed to encourage chat, to bring those personalities into the conversation in the present, and, I thought, worked to enable the social virtues of neighborliness, local connectedness, participation, and humility.

This chapter asks whether that inseparability of the musical and the social still holds in 2018. In what ways has the digital age enabled and constrained and reconfigured the possibility of creating community that Chris Langan saw as being at the heart of the tradition? How does conversation survive being stuffed down a wire? How do players of Irish traditional music in New England and elsewhere create the local out of myriad strands of repertoire and style, living and dead, past and present?

I tackle this by telling stories that bristle with connection (I kind of wish this chapter bristled with clickable hot links, which would more closely mimic the web of connections): to the social nature of tune transmission; to the persistence of personal style, and to tradition as conversation; and to a long history of subversive generosity in a story about finding an instrument. These are necessarily brief, impressionistic, and subjective postcards from one outpost, the view from where I stand: the community of players, singers, and dancers involved in Irish traditional music in New England, especially in Boston and Providence, and from my own experience with Irish musicians both in Ireland and abroad.

At the Behan

At the Brendan Behan pub in Jamaica Plain in Boston, two uilleann pipers discuss the next set of tunes. I'm one of the pipers. The other is Joey Abarta, a piper from California. Joey says: "I was in Detroit with So-and-So and we played this one, do you remember it?"

He plays, I join in, and we play eight bars or so, as we remind ourselves of how it goes.

He continues: "Yeah that's 'An Ceannaí Sugach,' 'The Jolly Merchant.' I had that from *you*, remember. Where did that come from?"

"Ah, I dug it out of the Miscellaneous section in O'Neill's."[1]

"I played that at the Oireachtas you know," he says.[2]

One by one, five or six other players in the session join in with the tune. I realize that I do not even know some of these players, yet a tune I put back into circulation a few years ago has spread beyond my immediate geographical, social, and musical circles and is enabling people to play together, and to talk about playing together, and to talk together.

Tunes are like that; they come with a freight of social memory. Players play and pass on the tunes, and they remember where, when, and from whom they learned them, and they talk about those connections with the past, and so remake connection in the present.

Another Saturday, another session, a similar interaction. To finish a set of reels I go into "Eddie Moloney's" (Harker 2005, 31, no. 99.), a reel I learned from Mike Rafferty, a flute player who lived in New Jersey but who was born in the same parish in East Galway as Eddie Moloney. It a simple and repetitive tune, with similarities to other, better-known tunes. It sows a little melodic confusion, and the groove falters until the other players pick it up.

"Was that not 'Hand Me Down the Tackle'?"

"I thought it was 'The Dublin Reel' at first."

"It sounded like a setting of some other tune."

"No, that was 'Eddie Moloney's.'"

"Was he not the flute player in the Ballinakill?"[3]

"Not the original band but the next generation, I think."

Danny Noveck puts down his guitar and picks up his fiddle: "He had some interesting settings," he says, and plays an unusual setting of the reel "Toss the Feathers."

"Where did you get that, Danny?" I ask.

"Oh, from that tape of him that made the rounds."

A musician dead in 1980 whom none of us here in this Boston session ever met (and all but a few of whom are too young to even remember 1980), yet we all have a piece of his story, an almost casual acquaintance with the man's music and style and his place in the web of connections.

Many non-Irish musicians playing this music outside Ireland create local community through a paradoxical turn to intensely local styles and repertoire at a great geographical and temporal remove, such as the way Lucy Farr played "The Maids of Mitchellstown" or Patrick Kelly's setting of "The Foxhunter's," to the repertoire of Padraig O'Keefe, tunes from County Fermanagh hitherto obscure (except in County Fermanagh), tunes reanimated from manuscript collections.

In the Kitchen

I spend some time in my kitchen with a battered old B♭ whistle and an equally battered copy of volume 2 of Goodman's collection *Tunes of the Munster Pipers* (Shields and Shields 2013). I love this book. I keep it in the kitchen bookshelf next to the *Book of Miso* (I keep the whistle in the utensils canister). I dip into it the way I raid the fridge. Being an ocean away from any locally based repertoire of Irish music, I am forced to be a musical magpie, and this collection is full of especially shiny things.

I could go on at length about how this book is a snapshot of piping repertoire from the 1850s in Kerry, about the insights it gives us into piping technique and the kinds of tunes in the repertoire at that time, and so on, but that does not convey anything about how contemporary musicians use such a resource. Instead here I offer a brief example of how I use it.

Tune collections are sources of repertoire, not style. I have no qualms about running the tunes notated here through the filters of my own aesthetic and technique; this is inevitable and commonplace. By way of example, consider the simple jig called "The Angler" (http://port.itma.ie/score/ITMA_5645).

Sight-reading this in the kitchen I heard a fine modal piping tune emerging from behind the dots and immediately changed it to a key more suitable to the pipes. And then I played it the way I play everything, applying contemporary (early twenty-first-century) piping technique, and ended up with a neat little jig that is great for the beginners I teach (only one octave) yet equally useful for challenging advanced players to incorporate the Ennis "instant cran" and a fair amount of tight playing.[4]

I travel soon after to a *tionól* (gathering) in Prince Edward Island to teach, and I swap it with Mickey Dunne for "Miss Hamilton's," a piece by Cornelius Lyons, an eighteenth-century harp player. Mickey reckons he will get some mileage out of the new tune later in the summer when he teaches at the Willie Clancy Summer School. And perhaps it will be played in Kerry again soon.

I am doing precisely what my own teacher and friend, Chris Langan, did thirty-odd years earlier when he made a setting of a tune from the Francis Roche collection (1982), then shared it with me (Hutchinson 1997, 48). Keegan Loesel, a young piper in Philadelphia is now my student and friend, and I have shared the tune with him—over Skype.

One of the many wonderful results of the digital revolution is the ready availability of such tune collections, and Taisce Cheol Dúchais Éireann, or the Irish Traditional Music Archive (in Merrion Square in Dublin; available online at https://www.itma.ie), has many such collections, mostly in the form of interactive scores (think follow the bouncing ball with easy transposition added). So I point Keegan to its web address, where both of those collections, among many others, are online. And I make a video of myself playing the tune and put it up on my Facebook page. And the conversation, the tradition of musical and social connection, of making and sharing tunes, continues.

Failing memory. As my little gray cells make their protracted farewells, I resort to this most comical of scenarios: holding my iPhone up to my iPad, feeding Tunepal with Voice Recorder, playing a recording made on the fly at the session. Tunepal is not yet connected to Siri; if it was, I suppose I should have to buy it a pint in return for the capaciously memoried program's swiftly disgorged hairball of information: it is "John Doherty's reel" (90 percent certainty), and here are the dots.

Since the Kerry fiddle master Padraig O'Keefe first put pen to paper to record a tune in his own fiddle tablature for a student, since the first person put a finger on the turning 78 rpm record in order to slow it down, since we all wore out the rewind buttons on our Sony Walkman Pros, people have been using technology to externalize memory in order to facilitate learning.

We have instant access to obscure repertoire, as described above; instant access to the minutiae of style via Audio Stretch or the Amazing Slowdowner; instant access to tune names and biographies via Tunepal and the Traditional Tune Archive. What is the downside of the digital revolution? What has been lost? What happens when it is too easy? Is it simply that a certain kind of hard-won listening skill becomes atrophied, or is it that acquiring a tune no longer requires the interrogation of an encounter with a human being? And what might it mean that geographically and temporally separated tunes become transformed into mere "repertoire"? Are we perhaps hastening a separation between the process of making music and its objects, between people and tunes? Questions for a larger study, perhaps.

Despite the appurtenances of convenience and externalized memory, that which remains constant is playing together. At the leading edge of the tune where we enact togetherness, none of that matters. Groove is everything. Good work and love is the only way that can succeed. And that has ever been so.[5]

A Chanter's Life

After a few years of weekly visits to my teacher Chris Langan, one time he sat me down in the kitchen and said, mysteriously, "I *have* something for you." He had sawdust on his slippers. He disappeared down the stairs to the basement, where he had his workshop, and after a few minutes emerged with a set of drones. "You *need* these," he said. He would take no payment. A year later the same thing happened, except this time he emerged from the basement with two regulators, and the same shake of the head when I attempted to negotiate a price. I still play that set of pipes today.

Now, was Chris just an exceptionally and uniquely generous individual? I would maintain that while he certainly was, he was also enacting a tradition of generosity and neighborliness that stretches forward and backward in time.

For alongside the more conventional economic transactions between pipe maker and customer is a more informal network that aims to get decent instruments into the hands of deserving pipers, either through the recycling and redistribution of older instruments or by the occasional jumping of the queue: the less-than-strict adherence to a chronological waiting list of clients according to the druthers of the pipe maker.

To explain further, I'll make a brief foray, then, into anecdotal organography, the life story of a chanter—a story bristling with personalities, populated by generous men and women, that unfolds (like the music I prefer) at old-guy pace, over some eighteen years.

In 1999 I organized a pipers' gathering, or *tionól*, in Providence, and as is usual at such gatherings, I invited a piper from Ireland to teach, in this case, Joe McKenna. Joe's friend Dublin pipe maker Steve Vickers decided to accompany him to the Providence tionól. Steve is not a big name, but he does good work. Steve brought with him a blackwood chanter pitched in C and let me have it for a ridiculous price, I think no more than one hundred dollars. The reed that Steve had included with the chanter suffered the usual fate of the immigrant in that it could not adapt to the extremes of New England weather and was eventually adjusted to death.

In 2006 at another tionól in Atlanta, Pat Sky was trying his hand at making a reed for the chanter (gratis) and dropped it on the floor. The imitation ivory turnings shattered, so I had Bill Thomas (a lovely man, a brilliant furniture maker, and a decent pipe maker) replace them with boxwood, and while he had it, install a chanter stop valve I had designed—all this in exchange for some lessons. I never got a decent reed going in it, so when my sometime student Torrin Ryan expressed interest in an extended loan of it, I sent it back to Steve in Dublin, who informed me that somewhere along the way the throat of the chanter had been "interfered with" by a well-meaning or perhaps merely frustrated reed maker. Anyway, I guess Steve readjusted it somehow and got a good reed going in it, and I had good reports from Torrin that he was getting good usage out of it. I then heard that pipe maker and reed maker extraordinaire Benedict Koehler had reeded up a Johnny Bourke C chanter, which would be going to Torrin. Which would free my chanter up for an extended loan to another deserving piper. I will email Torrin and see if he has the Bourke yet. Johnny Bourke is one of the Dublin pipe-making gods, dead since the late 1980s, I think. My teacher Chris Langan knew him well, and I myself started on a chanter he made, which later I gave to Ian Goodfellow in Toronto.

I ring Benedict to check whether there is any degree of hush-hush about the chanter that would be going to Torrin (i.e., would I be spoiling the surprise of a piece of stealth pipe gifting generosity if I mentioned it to him).

He corrects me that it is not a Johnny Bourke chanter, rather it was made by Al Purcell's father, Leo. Al Purcell now, he was a lovely man, lived and taught in Detroit and was Tyler Duncan's teacher. I first met him with Chris, and some years later played "An Feochán," Tommy Peoples's lovely slow air, at his memorial. Tyler played "Blue Rondo à la Turque." Leo, Al's father, was a great friend of Chris when he was in Ireland, as he taught the Highland pipes in Dublin and led a rival pipe band. (In Lusk, up the coast from Dublin near Chris's hometown of Rush, Chris led the Black Raven Pipe Band, founded by

Thomas Ashe, one of the leaders of the Easter Rising of 1916.) And Benedict thinks that Leo probably made the chanter in someone else's workshop, quite possibly Johnny Bourke's, or Dan O'Dowd's, or Matt Kiernan's—the Holy Trinity of Dublin pipe makers from the 1960s to the 1980s. In 2015 I handed the Vickers chanter on to my own student Keegan Loesel, and he has been given to understand that he is its steward until his own student needs it.

Friendships sealed and community sustained by generosity sidelining actuarial sense in purchase price; free reed making; bartering repairs for lessons; the gift to young players of the tools they need to improve; a tradition of sharing the tools of pipecraft—these are some of the interconnected stories of generous and neighborly individuals recalled and shared that make up the history of any single instrument (such as my Vickers chanter). It is not simply a monetary transaction: there are stories, acts of generosity, values enacted that are not "necessary" in a simple commodity transaction but are essential parts of an economy of neighborliness.

'Tis the Company

The news came (via the internet, unsurprisingly) that Connemara piper Tommy Canavan had died. I met him on a hot day in 1989. He was too busy bringing in the hay to play music, he said, but then he brought me down the boreen to a rusty old pickup truck, popped a cassette in the player, and turned it up full blast. As the wild strains of the pipes took flight with the meadow birds, he said, as if to reassure me: "That's *me* you know!"

But he *did* show up that evening to the house of Micheál Ó Cuaig, where we were staying, and he played a rake of big reels and big hornpipes in a big style. We played for hours. I remember the reed in his Moss Kennedy chanter was shaped like a thistle, the widest reed I have ever seen. And he suffered patiently the callow and amateur questions from the nascent ethnomusicologist: "Why," I asked, "do you think we play, and continue to play this music? What is it about it, do you think, that makes it so special?" "Sure," he replied unhesitatingly, "'tis the *company*. 'Tis the *company*."

I was talking about Tommy not too long ago with Seán McKiernan, another fine piper, whom I had visited in Carna on that same trip. This time Seán was visiting me. He was in Boston with relatives and dropped by the piping class I teach for Comhaltas Ceoltóirí Éireann. After a few tunes we were reminiscing about Tommy, and I told him the story I just told you.

"He had a lovely setting of 'Casaidh an tSugáin.' Do you remember?"

"He *did*," said Seán. "Do you *have* that one?"

"I *do*," I said, and I played it for him on the pipes, the lovely song air that

I had learned from the same recording that Tommy had stuck in the cassette player in the truck in the boreen some twenty-eight years earlier.

"That's *right*," said Seán, "you have it now; that was how he played it."

Seán wrote Tommy's obituary for the uilleann pipers' journal *An Píobaire*: "Tommy . . . never became a big 'star,' as it were, but I don't think he wanted that—*'Níl ann ach pastime,' déarfadh sé* . . . ['it's naught but a pastime,' he would say]" (Mac Chiarnáin 2016, 11, translated by the author).

Modesty incarnate, for he was a fine player. But we would do well to remember Henry Glassie's disquisition on the crucial importance of passing the time: "Passing the time in entertainment is more than momentary distraction, it is heartsome, not lonesome, an epitome of connectivity" (1982, 472).

Our memories of Tommy are incised in the sound, in his way with the tune, that I have adopted. Seán quoted his words; I quoted his music. I can bring him to mind, bring him into the conversation, as close as an embrace, by playing his setting of an air, by playing his music his way. Remembering, re-membering, inviting back those who are passed, the remaking of community, all this is possible because of the way individual variation in Irish traditional music is baked into performance practice—the musical and the social, inseparable.

Any fool knows that is what the music is about.

'Tis the company, *cinnte*, certainly.

Envoi

Despite the internet, despite Riverdance, despite the short-lived musical fusions resulting from the arguments that a tradition that did not change was moribund, Irish traditional music, it seems to me, counterpoised the idea of change as inevitable and desirable, not with stagnation but with *constancy*: the music is still about the company; it still offers the potential for neighborly exchange and interchange. I put this to Jeff:

"Good thought," he wrote. "Constancy connotes devotion along with, ah, sustainability :-)" (email, October 20, 2013).

I maintain that constancy to this core notion—that community can be created and maintained through cooperative music making—continues to hold.

Notes

1. O'Neill's *Dance Music of Ireland* (1965) is the "bible" of Irish traditional music, although certain of the "Apocrypha" (Goodman, Breathnach, among others) have become almost as important as sources of repertoire.

2. Joey is the only American ever to win the coveted Oireachtas piping title.

3. The Ballinakill Ceili Band made some of the first ensemble recordings of Irish

traditional music in the 1930s. Stephen Moloney, the flute player in the original band, was Eddie's father.

4. Even something apparently as mundane and asocial as the terminology that describes how to move your fingers is an encyclopedia of personalities and memories associated with those finger movements, thus an Ennis C, an Ennis instant cran, a Clancy roll, Patsy Tuohey backstitching, Chris Langan's "half-closed roll," and so on. A simplified transcription of the resulting pipes setting can be found at http://web.mit.edu/~santucci/www/ph/sheetmusic/angler.pdf, courtesy of my friend and student Rosanne Santucci.

5. Groove, musical and social intimacy, and community are, of course, a contingent outcome (Hutchinson 1997, 109). Nothing is guaranteed. I am well aware of the dangers of projecting communitarian ideals onto musical performance, as Helen O'Shea (2007) notes.

References

Glassie, Henry. 1982. *Passing the Time in Ballymenone: Culture and History of an Ulster Community.* Philadelphia: University of Pennsylvania Press.

Harker, Lesl. 2005. *300 Tunes from Mike Rafferty.* Self-published.

Hutchinson, Patrick. 1997. "A Life in the Making: Chris Langan, Uilleann Piper." PhD diss., Brown University, Providence, RI.

Mac Chiarnáin, Seán. 2016. "Obituary: Tomás Ó Ceannabháin." *An Píobaire* 12 (2) (Aibreán/April). http://162.13.136.126/data/PIOBAIRE/PIOB1202.PDF.

O'Neill, Francis, ed. 1965. *The Dance Music of Ireland: 1001 Gems.* Dublin: Walton's Musical Instruments Galleries.

O'Shea, Helen. 2007. "Getting to the Heart of the Music: Idealizing Musical Community and Irish Traditional Music Sessions." *Journal of the Society for Musicology in Ireland* 2:1–18. http://openmusiclibrary.org/article/5425/.

Roche, Francis. 1982. *The Roche Collection of Traditional Irish Music.* Cork: Ossian.

Shields, Hugh, and Lisa Shields, eds. 2013. *Tunes of the Munster Pipers: Irish Traditional Music from the James Goodman Manuscripts.* Vol. 2. Dublin: Irish Traditional Music Archive / Taisce Cheol Dúchais Éireann.

Titon, Jeff Todd. 2013. "Music Is Not a Cultural Asset (2)." *Sustainable Music: A Research Blog on the Subject of Sustainability and Music.* http://sustainablemusic.blogspot.com/2013_03_01_archive.html.

CHAPTER 14

Sustaining Indigenous Sounds

Music Broadcasting and Cultural Vitalization in Highland Peru

JOSHUA TUCKER

ON OCTOBER 12, 2013, I sat near the DJ booth of Radio Quispillaccta, a Quechua-language AM station in the south Andean city of Ayacucho, Peru, capital of the Department (State) of Ayacucho, listening as manager Graciano Machaca wrapped up his morning show. Typically, his program featured a mix of news from the rural-indigenous towns surrounding Ayacucho, leavened with music from the station's namesake community of Quispillaccta. Sometimes it was spiced with commentary about things that were on his mind, often the need to preserve Quispillaccta's *chimaycha* music, a local variant of the *huayno* song style that dominates the entire highland region. On this day his concern was the politics of indigeneity, and his comments followed the announcement of a festival marking a nearby town's designation as an Indigenous community. International treaties offer key protections to such settlements, but the Peruvian government routinely violates them, and Machaca spoke of the listening public's duty to claim the identity and the rights entailed. Speaking in Quechua, he used the first-person inclusive pronoun that marks speaker and addressees as members of a shared community: "We," he said—meaning "I who speak and you who listen"—need to "recognize and remember that we are members of *Indigenous* communities," with all the entitlements enumerated in international law.[1]

Such a statement is striking in the broader context of Andean Peru. Communities of the kind that Machaca addressed have not been widely described as "indigenous" since the late 1960s, when a Marxist government officially abolished the social category of "Indian" in favor of "peasant." And Peru's highlands have long been treated as an enigma by scholars and activists: a place of indigenous majority and deep inequality that has not yielded a political movement aimed at ethnic redress.[2] However, Radio Quispillaccta is not a typical organization. Staffed by Quechua speakers from its eponymous town, it was the only local entity that broadcast entirely in the Indigenous language. It maintained a program of service to and advocacy for the region's indigenous majority, and by 2013 its promotion had made chimaycha music into Ayacucho's most dynamic sound. Its twin missions of providing a public Quechua-language voice for silenced citizens and of vitalizing indigenous practices raise questions about the relation between governance, activism, and cultural practice.[3] In a country dismissive of indigenous claims for rights and recognition, could the station's efforts be viewed as a tactical redeployment of political work through other channels? Should we perhaps look for indigenous activism outside the narrow realm of party politics—in, say, the realm of cultural sustainability?

Such were the questions that had brought me to Radio Quispillaccta in the first place—that, and my love for the chimaycha music that dominated the station's musical programming. However, Machaca's on-air affirmation raised a slightly different question: did the station's staff even understand their mission in terms of a distinction between "political" and "cultural" activism? A partial answer came in a later interview with Marcela Machaca, cofounder and codirector of the parent NGO that had established Radio Quispillaccta in the late 1990s. For her, becoming legible as rights-bearing Indigenous people meant more than simply adopting a political term of art. It meant claiming and vitalizing distinctive cultural practices, and in service to that project, the station supported the maintenance of indigenous language and music. "Many of our cultural lifeways are expressed in music," she told me. "It's a sign of our cultural strength. . . . Without music, without singing about nature, feelings—we wouldn't be alive." Wrapping up moments later, she was even more explicit: "When we speak of strengthening our culture . . . you know, the music is in Quechua, and we Quechuas have a unique vision, of a world of beings, people. This is expressed in a particular language, and it's everywhere in the music. See?" (interview, March 24, 2014, Ayacucho).

Machaca's words testify to the self-consciously central role that chimaycha plays in the work of cultural vitalization the she and her organizations perform. However, there is another way to tell the story of chimaycha's centrality in the contemporary work of indigenous activists, one that passes through the offices of the local university, and the work of a previous generation of scholars who worked there. It is, in short, a story about the ways that engaged researchers can foster sustainable music communities—and perhaps about the ways that their efforts take unexpected effect once the community involved seizes full control over its resources.

Peruvian Precedents for Applied Ethnomusicology and Cultural Sustainability

Many recent writings in the field of applied ethnomusicology engage in the foundational work that attends the birth of any scholarly subdiscipline. One facet of this work involves recruiting ancestors and allies who might stand as inspiration for future practice. Far from being merely anecdotal or exhortatory in nature, such exercises clarify what has worked and is liable to work again. Although applied ethnomusicologists have drawn their disciplinary history in laudably catholic fashion (see, for example, Harrison 2013; Pettan 2015; Titon 2015a), most move within a frame of reference that is delimited by Euro-American concerns. Benchmark forums like the 2009 special issue of *the world of music* on "Music and Sustainability" (Titon 2009a), or *The Oxford Handbook of Applied Ethnomusicology* (Pettan and Titon 2015) mainly describe projects that are situated within the Global North or designed by scholars trained there. Given the field's self-identified openness to diverse perspectives, it is urgent to describe how projects of cultural sustainability develop in contexts marked by different histories.

In that spirit, this chapter moves outward from the scene described above and presents the prehistory of chimaycha's entanglement with Andean cultural politics. This, I argue, is underpinned by interventions carried out in the 1980s by scholars tied to Ayacucho's Universidad Nacional San Cristóbal de Huamanga (UNSCH), who worked through university offices and allied development agencies to foster a flourishing Quechua-language music scene throughout the 1980s.[4] Though the term is anachronistic in this context, such people can be described as *advocates* for cultural sustainability, insofar as their concerns involved "a music culture's capacity to maintain and develop its music now and in the foreseeable future" (Titon 2015b, 157). From the vantage point of the present, it certainly suits them better than the more usual label of *folklorist*. In highland Peru "folklorists" have been associated mainly with the arrangements of Andean music and dance that trained professionals began to create in the early twentieth century—in the words of a leading American scholar, folklore remains "a Peruvian term for portions of culture immobilized and separated for display as fetishes of localism" (Salomon 2002, 490). That work was more heavily informed by elite nationalism than the needs of Indigenous peoples, who watched as familiar practices were alienated, stylized, and staged largely for the education and pleasure of nonindigenous elites (see Mendoza 2000 and Turino 1993). However, as Mendoza has argued (2008), such activity could empower Indigenous musicians in significant ways, and sometimes it involved consultation and partnership.

The people involved in UNSCH-sponsored projects took the latter approach. They viewed themselves more properly as sponsors than arrangers of indigenous practices and aimed to serve the communities of origin. Through broadcasts and concert promotion, they helped Indigenous musicians boost their artistic prestige, personal autonomy, and self-esteem. In making a space for community members to continue their labors, they stand as a corrective to the taint that has often accrued to Andean folkloric endeavor. Elsewhere in this volume Aaron S. Allen argues that far from representing a thing, "*sustainability* is better understood as a lens," while Robert Baron and Thomas Walker note that the term's deployment has the power to alter our perceptions of existing arrangements and practices. If the people I discuss below departed from within an older framework, something more closely resembling preservation discourse, then their working methods ended up building the infrastructure to sustain a musical culture in a context of social transformation. Treating them as advocates for cultural sustainability avant la lettre is not, then, out of place: it can only expand our understanding of the term.

By telling this story I wish to emphasize the extent to which scholars are well served when they learn from the work of knowledge producers located in different institutional systems and on different kinds of career paths (see also Ochoa 2003). This is particularly true in a place like Peru, where the distinction between pure and applied research is typically weaker than it is in the North American academy. Certainly all that is signaled in the dismissive phrase "ivory tower," with its connotations of esoteric analysis and unconcern for community engagement, does not guide university life there as thoroughly as it is purported to do in the Global North. Service to the local citizenry was an explicit part of the UNSCH's mission upon its 1959 refounding after seven decades without any institution of higher learning in Ayacucho (the original university was closed in 1886). It was meant to be an engine of development for the impoverished region, and its scholars assumed the role in earnest. Bringing the record of their achievements into the burgeoning conversation about applied work can perhaps provide models for similarly invested scholars located elsewhere.

Acquiring and Applying Scholarly Expertise: Uriel Salcedo and the CCC

Over the last forty years Uriel Salcedo, an anthropologist and broadcaster from the nearby city of Andahuaylas, has had an outsized influence on Ayacucho's indigenous performance scene. Again and again, musicians like Marco Tucno and Óscar Conde—influential artists who more than anyone else taught me about chimaycha—urged me to consult him. When I met Salcedo at the UNSCH in 2014, he evaluated his own reputation with modest confidence, but he was glad to acknowledge his role in facilitating indigenous musical careers and to tell me his story.

Upon his graduation from the UNSCH in 1979, Salcedo began working for an agronomic program, and he quickly developed a keen interest in the music of its target communities. There he found something different from the era's dominant pop styles: music that was topical and continually fresh, a far cry from the unchanging themes of romance and heartbreak that guided pop-cultural production. "They're well informed," he told me. "For instance, if there's a new president in your country—Clinton, Obama—a song will appear about it right away" (personal communication, March 20, 2014, Ayacucho). Intrigued, he began to make field recordings and quickly gained a reputation as an expert on local forms of music.

His growing interest in rural-indigenous music intersected felicitously with a project housed and run by the UNSCH's Centro de Capacitación Campesina (Center for Peasant Training, or CCC). The UNSCH had partnered with foreign NGOs to execute development projects in the poorest communities of Ayacucho's hinterland, and the CCC became a key office for channeling those activities. During the 1970s it worked with the Dutch agency COTESU to improve irrigation, crop yields, and livestock management in places like Quispillaccta. Despite the CCC's agronomic focus, Ayacucho's Indigenous musicians remember it most fondly for *Allpanchik* (Our soil), the AM radio program that it broadcast to the indigenous countryside in the early 1980s.

Broadcast in Quechua, *Allpanchik* operated along collaborative lines. The CCC made community-based associates into citizen reporters by lending them tape recorders and encouraging them to capture sounds and stories from home. At the CCC offices, *Allpanchik's* producers stitched together a mix of current events, advice, didactic drama, and music for daily broadcast. This model quickly became imperative due to the eruption of Peru's devastating internal conflict, which hit the Department of Ayacucho earliest and hardest. The university that sponsored the CCC had also nourished the Shining Path guerrilla organization, a Maoist group that grew from within its professorial ranks. Aiming to overthrow the capitalist order, the group viewed rural indigenous towns as the most efficient base from which to strangle urban strongholds, building networks there before plunging the countryside into bloody violence on May 17, 1980. The conflict made citizen-reporters more crucial than ever, since it was difficult for CCC workers to travel within the affected zone, and the institution scaled back efforts to focus on places relatively close to the city—places like Quispillaccta's high neighborhood of Unión Potrero, a focus that would have later consequences, as people from that barrio leveraged the association into social and economic capital.

While the violence certainly affected the stories that *Allpanchik* ran, it did not have a significant impact on the featured music. Songs of political protest or support for Shining Path became central to some of the Department of Aya-cucho's musical communities (Ritter 2002), but they received little airplay; it was unwise to broadcast them, given the state's interest in brutally repressing all signs of support for the guerrillas. For musicians, more important was the mere fact that *Allpanchik*'s broadcasts featured indigenous sounds otherwise inaudible in Peru's media landscape. Inspired by the unexpected possibility of an outlet for their talents, Indigenous musicians soon made the CCC's offices into something of a clubhouse.

One of them was Marco Tucno, who in the early 1980s had moved to Aya-cucho from Chuschi, a town contiguous with Quispillaccta. An avid chimaycha performer, he listened diligently to *Allpanchik* in its early days, impressed by its connection to community events. Upon enrolling at the UNSCH, he became a regular at the CCC, along with fellows who had been playing in household chimaycha sessions around the city. This paid off handsomely, since the staff regularly called on them to record for the program. However, Marco remem-bered the CCC as an engine of indigenous musical performance more gener-ally. "They sponsored recordings for the radio, publicized artists. . . . They also held competitions. They had a meeting of Indigenous communities almost every year. And there were other events, too, for example other university de-partments had symposiums, and the CCC coordinated with them [to provide music]" (interview, January 12, 2012, Ayacucho). Singling out Carlos Condori, who coordinated *Allpanchik* and related competitions, Marco described how instrumental he was in encouraging young musicians:

> He helped arrange opportunities for us, but more than that, he encouraged us. He'd say, "Why don't you record this song for us, or that one," and he had this habit of picking songs from all over, unknown songs, that came from new groups. I don't know how he got them. He probably had contacts. It was a university office so professors, sociologists who traveled, probably brought things back to the CCC. Anyway, he had them there, and would say, "Hey, listen to this song; it's a nice one." He made us listen, and we'd laugh and talk about it. (interview, January 12, 2012, Ayacucho)

Hanging around the office and connecting with the show's staff, learning from correspondents' cassettes, making themselves available to produce quick recordings for broadcast, forming stable groups that might generate the reliably high-quality performances that come with regular rehearsal, all these activities that amount to the infrastructure of musical professionalization, were channeled through the CCC. Rural dwellers, too, began to form groups in their hometowns, sending in tapes to promote their skills. In this way the CCC became a launching pad for something unprecedented: formal chimaycha bands, including such Ayacucho-based groups as Marco Tucno's Los Chikitukus de Chuschi, as well as countless groups based in Quispillaccta and neighboring towns.

Allpanchik's importance for Ayacucho's nascent indigenous music scene only grew after the departure of host Félix Gavilán (who later gained tragic renown as a victim in the Uchuraccay Massacre, a turning point in Peru's era of violence). This provided a space for Salcedo, who brought his expertise, his impressive collection of field recordings, and the boldness required to visit embattled communities, pursuing endangered music and unheard stories. Homemade recordings poured in from rural areas, and as he expanded his broadcast hours, *Allpanchik* became an even more dynamic space for publicizing indigenous sounds. However, the program soon yielded influence for two reasons. First, the CCC had lost the support of its international partners by the mid-1980s, forcing the program to wander unstably among other agencies and eventually peter out in the late 1990s. Second, Salcedo decided to establish a new program, one entirely under his own charismatic guidance. In 1983 he created *Takiyninchik* (Our songs), the music program with which his name is indelibly associated.

Takiyninchik grew steadily in influence, not least because it was tied to competitions and festival performances that Salcedo began to sponsor in Ayacucho. This was not his innovation, as folkloric competitions had long been popular in Andean Peru. The CCC, too, had earlier run music contests in the towns where it operated, awarding communal prizes and inviting participants to process in the UNSCH's annual anniversary parade in Ayacucho. Nevertheless his competition-cum-concerts, advertised via his highly successful radio program, fostered a live music scene that complemented the performances that enlivened kitchens, bedrooms, and courtyards in migrant households. While other institutions copied the model, years later musicians still singled out Salcedo's events and the CCC-sponsored parades as early, rare instances of legitimation in an urban context that remained hostile to indigenous culture.

Óscar Conde insisted on this latter point. He remained in Quispillaccta during the 1980s, but in describing how chimaycha performance grew during that time, he credited the same series of urban institutions, invoking the same qualities of solidarity and support that animated Marco's memories. After detailing how *Allpanchik* aired chimaycha recordings made by community members at Quispillaccta's festivals and showing me pictures of him and his wife at CCC-sponsored events in town and in Ayacucho's plaza, he went on to characterize the work of the CCC in terms of cultural confidence: "They worked directly with the communities; for the university's anniversary they brought the best groups to compete in [Ayacucho's] main plaza. You went there to show off your customs, your music, your attire, so little by little we were losing that fear. Or let's say, little by little, we conquered the city, something like that. Yes, the 1980s, that was the boom era" (Óscar Conde, interview, January 14, 2012, Ayacucho).

Conde estimated that the number of groups that formed to play in town during the festival season increased by half. Furthermore, as he put it, "the music developed more," since publicity and competition drove changes in vocal technique, instrumental dexterity, and lyrical composition that his generation found compelling. He suggested that today's chimaycha musicians are only repeating and modifying the songs and innovations that animated a "golden age," one that resulted from a confluence of talented Indigenous musicians and new institutional channels of support.

Allpanchik, Takiyninchik, and their scholar-activist staff ushered in an era that Tucno, Conde, and their peers describe as a high-water mark for indigenous performance. Such memories are perhaps filtered through generational nostalgia, but in their emphasis on feeling they point to a key, often underspecified aspect of the efforts made by such institutions. Indeed, Marco's remarks on the *communitas* and the emotional infrastructure that the CCC offered young musicians are perhaps the most noteworthy of his comments cited above. In evaluating this era many performers emphasize support, appreciation, and solidarity over the infrequent opportunities for public or paid performance. Here, especially, Salcedo was instrumental, regularly inviting musicians to perform at parties in his apartment in the respectable neighborhood of Pío Max. Marco insisted that this patronage inspired confidence in young students like himself, leading them to challenge the marginalization of indigenous music and Indigenous people generally. Critically, they transmitted that feeling to their followers, via acts of comfort that were especially welcomed amid the violence afflicting their hometowns:

> For me that was what it was about; by recording these things we were giving support. Listening, or dancing, enjoying yourself for a while and forgetting your pains—that's how I took things in those days. We would play a contest or an event, and our *paisanos* would follow us around afterward. Hearing us play they would cheer up, shake our hands, invite us to a pop or a little liquor in the neighborhood. . . . As students, it was the only thing we could do. We were poor; we couldn't really do anything else, support people [financially] or say, "Know what? You don't have to suffer," but through music we could do *something*, a little something. (Marco Tucno, interview, January 12, 2012, Ayacucho)

Programs like *Allpanchik* and *Takiyninchik* were hardly unprecedented in Andean Peru. Neither were indigenous music competitions or intellectual support for indigenous performance. However, their legacy is unlike that left by earlier hobbyists and ideologues, whose work is often treasured as "heritage" by

Peru's nonindigenous elites, while remaining marginal to Indigenous communities themselves. Without exception, prominent chimaycha musicians confirm the outlines of Marco and Óscar's experiences—at least, those belonging to the same generation. Ninay Urucha, who enjoyed success in the second decade of this century, owed that opportunity to recordings aired by *Allpanchik* in the late 1980s, recordings that were remembered two decades later by fans who encouraged her to record again, after Radio Quispillaccta opened new spaces for chimaycha's vitalization. José Tomaylla, dean of chimaycha instrumentalists, launched his group Waylla Ichu de Llacctahurán by recording the first of seven cassettes at the CCC. There was, in short, a dynamic scene that would hardly have existed if not for the mediation of dedicated scholar-activists like Gavilán, Salcedo, and Condori. Moreover, this scene was not organized along narrowly nationalist lines or primarily for commercial profit, and it was insulated from the representational challenges that attend those kinds of efforts. Rather than speaking for Indigenous artists, these institutions let Indigenous artists speak through them.

This is not to say, of course, that their interventions were free from unexpected consequences. Conde argued that the CCC erred by focusing on Quispillaccta's high-altitude settlements, creating a bank of recordings that emphasized the neighborhood of Unión Potrero at the expense of lower, musically distinct barrios, including his own Huertahuasi. This is true, and contemporary broadcasts at Radio Quispillaccta, which are filled with songs taken from 1980s-era CCC recordings, lean on that neighborhood as a matter of course. Of course, the main legacies of the CCC's investment in Unión Potrero are Radio Quispillaccta and ABA, since each is staffed mainly by people from that neighborhood. And in this sense, chimaycha's centrality to Ayacucho's emergent indigenous politics depends on overlapping musical, material, and affective investments made a generation before.

The story that I have told here engages one more set of concerns that animate contemporary scholarship on cultural sustainability: "If one grants that sustaining music is a legitimate public policy pursuit, a number of further questions arise: what are the wisest policies, how may they be achieved, and what role might ethnomusicologists play in defining them?" (Titon, 2009b, 6). Such questions are best answered, as Titon and Pettan have both maintained, by amassing examples of interventions and considering their effects. The cultural conservationist work of *Allpanchik* and *Takiyninchik* and the forums of dissemination that became associated with them issued from scholarly contexts not unlike those occupied by most contemporary applied ethnomusicologists. However, the legacy of the encouragement and material support that they gave to highly peripheralized music was a self-sustaining scene, one that is a central motor of popular culture for all residents of Ayacucho and its surrounding region. It seems possible that something comparable might have developed without such support, but this is far from certain: what is certain is that indigenous musical culture in Ayacucho, if left to market forces alone, would have taken a very different form—one possibly controlled by nonindigenous elites, one surely less just, and probably one that was less musically interesting.

Notes

1. In Quechua, the first-person inclusive plural pronoun, *ñuqanchik*, indicates that a statement's subject includes "I the speaker, you the listener(s), and perhaps others of the same group." By contrast, the first-person exclusive plural pronoun, *ñuqayku*, indicates that the statement's subject includes "I the speaker, perhaps others of the same group, but *not* you the listener."

2. The situation is more complicated than I have stated here, since nonindigenous Peruvians have often claimed a sort of pride in Indigenous heritage and cultural manifestations. However, personal identification as Indigenous remains contentious, and stands as a political act. See Thorp and Paredes's study (2010) for a recent summary of work on Peruvian categories of racial and ethnic identification.

3. I borrow the notion of *vitalization* from ethnomusicologist Beverley Diamond, who has advocated the term over *revitalization* in describing contemporary indigenous cultural production. The term *revitalization* suggests a cultural etiolation that is not necessarily viewed as such by the communities in question. See Diamond 2011.

4. In previous research I have explored the relationships between media work, social transformation, and the UNSCH in greater detail, albeit in relation to the music of a different community. See Tucker 2013.

References

Diamond, Beverley. 2011. "'Re' Thinking: Revitalization, Return, and Reconciliation in Contemporary Indigenous Expressive Culture." Lecture in Big Thinking Lecture Series, St. Thomas University/ University of New Brunswick, St. John, NB, July 6.

Harrison, Klisala. 2013. "Epistemologies of Applied Ethnomusicology." *Ethnomusicology* 56 (3): 505–29.

Mendoza, Zoila S. 2000. *Shaping Society through Dance: Mestizo Ritual Performance in the Peruvian Andes*. Chicago: University of Chicago Press.

———. 2008. *Creating Our Own: Folklore, Performance, and Identity in Cuzco, Peru*. Durham, NC: Duke University Press.

Ochoa, Ana María. 2003. *Entre los deseos y los derechos: Un ensayo crítico sobre políticas culturales*. Bogotá: ICANH.

Pettan, Svanibor. 2015. "Applied Ethnomusicology in the Global Arena." In Pettan and Titon, 29–52.

Pettan, Svanibor, and Jeff Todd Titon, eds. 2015. *The Oxford Handbook of Applied Ethnomusicology*. New York: Oxford University Press.

Ritter, Jonathan. 2002. "Siren Songs: Ritual and Revolution in the Peruvian Andes." *British Journal of Ethnomusicology* 11 (1): 9–42.

Salomon, Frank. 2002. "Unethnic Ethnohistory: On Peruvian Peasant Historiography and Ideas of Autochthony." *Ethnohistory* 49 (3): 475–506.

Thorp, Rosemary, and Maritza Paredes. 2010. *Ethnicity and the Persistence of Inequality: The Case of Peru.* New York: Palgrave Macmillan.

Titon, Jeff Todd, ed. 2009a. "Music and Sustainability." Special Issue, *the world of music* 51 (1).

———. 2009b. "Economy, Ecology, and Music: An Introduction." *the world of music* 51 (1): 5–16.

———. 2015a. "Applied Ethnomusicology: A Descriptive and Historical Account." In Svanibor Pettan and Titon, 4–28.

———. 2015b. "Sustainability, Resilience, and Adaptive Management for Applied Ethnomusicology." In Pettan and Titon, 157–98.

Tucker, Joshua. 2013. *Gentleman Troubadours and Andean Pop Stars: Huayno Music, Media Work, and Ethnic Imaginaries in Urban Peru.* Chicago: University of Chicago Press.

Turino, Thomas. 1993. *Moving Away from Silence: Music of the Peruvian Altiplano and the Experiment of Urban Migration.* Chicago: University of Chicago Press.

PART 4

Voice, Language, Trauma, and Resilience

CHAPTER 15

Digital Technology, Chanting Torah, and the Sustainability of Tradition

JEFFREY A. SUMMIT

IN THE EARLY 1950S, the American Jewish philosopher Simon Rawido-wicz delivered a lecture in which he called the Jews "the ever-dying people." He asserted that while the world makes many images of the Jewish people, the Jews have only one image of themselves, "that of a being constantly on the verge of ceasing to be, of disappearing" (1986, 53). Yet Jewish life in America in the twenty-first century has sustained a communal and institutional vibrancy even as the rate of intermarriage is now more than 50 percent. How do we understand this cultural resilience when faced with such powerful forces of assimilation?

A number of chapters in this volume address how human beings sustain cultures of music making within social and ecological conditions that increasingly threaten to destroy them. Jeff Todd Titon understands cultural sustainability as "a music culture's capacity to maintain and develop its music now and in the foreseeable future" (2015, 157). In this chapter, I examine strategies in which individual Jews employ digital technology to sustain and transmit musical traditions of the performance of biblical chant, a core ritual in contemporary Jewish worship.[1] While these examples focus more on personal agency than institutional sustainability, they underscore new approaches to integrating meaningful ritual into the lives of these liberal Jews. An analysis of these empowered approaches used by individuals, families, and teachers evidences great resilience as secular culture pulls them away from religious practice, exclusionary association, and institutional affiliation. Titon defines resilience as referring "to a system's capacity to recover and maintain its integrity, identity and continuity when subjected to forces of disturbance and change." In this way, "resilience implies a way to manage disruptance . . . and guide the outcome toward a desirable end" (158). As I examine in this chapter, even as certain contemporary Jews have moved away from traditional structures of learning and authority—synagogues, religious schools, rabbis, and cantors—they have developed and supported innovative means to transmit traditional music performance in a way that sustains traditional rituals while empowering their personal style of Jewish expression and identity.

Technology and Teaching Torah

Chanting Torah is a mark of core cultural and religious competence initially learned by many Jews in preparation for bar or bat mitzvah, a ritual that remains a rite of passage in the contemporary Jewish community. With this ritual, a young man or woman is seen as responsible for his or her religious observance and assumes a new status in the community, able to lead prayers and chant from the Torah.

In the past sixty years, it has been common for Jews to learn these skills in the context of congregationally run religious and Hebrew schools, with the congregation's cantor, rabbi, educator, and bar/bat mitzvah tutors preparing a student for this ritual celebration. The highly detailed and musically nuanced performance of Torah requires that the reader memorize both the pronunciation of unvocalized Hebrew text and the *te'amim* (cantillation signs, also *ta'amey ha-mikra*) that indicate the musical motif applied to each word of scripture. More than half the Jews in America have had a bar or bat mitzvah and have learned and performed biblical chant (Pew Research Center 2013, 66). This is occurring at a time of widespread cultural assimilation, when only about 30 percent of American Jews belong to synagogues. Many readers understand chanting Torah as the most powerful, personal, and authentic way that a layperson can publically perform his or her commitment to Judaism. When choosing to chant Torah, the reader enters a rich field of Jewish expression. This act requires esoteric, specialized knowledge, and the details of performance are complex and exacting. Many readers correctly understand chanted text to be one of the oldest Jewish musics that Jews perform today. Its melodies resonate with history both imagined and experienced.

New strategies are being developed to sustain this ritual at a time when congregational affiliation is declining, the traditional loci of religious authority are being challenged, and the individual, rather than the community, is becoming a primary focus in religious expression. This chapter considers three case studies where contemporary Jews look to alternative sources of authority and employ digital technology to learn, preserve, and perform these musical/liturgical traditions. These strategies sustain cultural and religious performance while altering and challenging traditional models of musical transmission, congregational affiliation, and participation.

Learning Online: New Structures for the Transmission of Tradition

For millennia, Jews assumed the importance and necessity of community. This is simply how Jews thought, born out of need, religious requirement, tradition, and history. Whether it was the quorum of ten Jews required for a full communal prayer service, the organization needed to collect and distribute charity, or enough dancers at a wedding, Jews require other Jews to fully express, celebrate, and realize Jewish culture. Generations of forced isolation and separation from Christian society in Europe made it imperative that Jews organize their economic, cultural, and religious lives.

In America, freedom from government regulation and religious direction from a centralized Jewish authority has allowed Jews to develop many different ways to be Jewish. This autonomy, combined with the Protestant ethos of an America that supported local control and a broad spectrum of individual choice in worship, led to the development of an American Jewish community rich in diverse religious and cultural expression. Still, in the twentieth century, the American synagogue became the communal hub for worship, religious education, and life-cycle celebrations. Yet today, liberal Jews increasingly challenge the assumption that Jewish celebration, practice, and education should be based in a synagogue community.

Personal agency is not new in the Jewish tradition, but it is playing out in new ways at the beginning of the twenty-first century. Steven M. Cohen and Arnold Eisen describe the centrality of the individual as driving contemporary Jewish involvement (2001). In their research, they found that personal meaning is increasingly "the arbiter of . . . Jewish involvement" and "voluntarist in the extreme." These women and men do not assume a given trajectory for their religious lives, and Jewish meaning is "constructed one experience at a time." While these Jews value tradition, they feel "free to borrow selectively from traditional religious and cultural sources." As Cohen and Eisen observe, while increased numbers of Jews express a concern for spirituality, they exhibit a "severely diminished interest in the organizational life of the Jewish community." Applying these observations to the issues I consider in this chapter, this social context sets the stage for men and women in the liberal movements to occasionally participate in core religious acts, such as bar and bat mitzvah, while not feeling the need or obligation to be regular members of religious communities.

When Rabbi Dani Eskow was a rabbinic student at the Conservative Movement's Jewish Theological Seminary, she tutored students preparing for bar and bat mitzvah in New York City. As students learn how to read Hebrew and the system of biblical cantillation to chant from the Torah and the Prophets (haftarah), it is common to work with tutors, often recommended or provided by their synagogues to supplement their Hebrew school and religious school curriculum. When Eskow began to tutor her students over Skype, demand grew quickly, and she soon recognized a clear need to provide educational services and support to students and families who, for a variety of reasons, were not members of synagogues. Together with her sister Marisa Gobuty, a fluent Hebrew speaker and medical student, Eskow founded MyBarMitzvahTutors. com, which then developed into OnlineJewishLearning.com. She said, "The goal was to provide flexible, meaningful Jewish education as outreach for Jews who didn't feel connected to the Jewish community and wanted to reconnect to Jewish tradition, to make a bar or bat mitzvah a deeper experience, more than the party. I started with thirty students and two teachers. By my fifth year, I had three hundred students and thirty teachers." All lessons are conducted though video conferencing and screen sharing with a personalized program informed by the student's and the family's goals. Eskow said, "Technology is the language our students speak today and this can break down barriers. If you make it fun, if kids see that you are using a cool app, they stay connected" (interview, August 26, 2016, Boston).

As described on its website, the organization's mission is "to make Jewish learning an easy and enjoyable experience for every student, regardless of background or prior knowledge. [The organization's] experienced teachers use interactive and innovative online teaching methods to bring Jewish education into the home, providing a convenient option for families far from synagogues or overbooked with hectic schedules." This approach to bar/bat mitzvah education is in marked contrast to the experience of Hebrew school and religious school in which families are required to join a congregation, often three years before the date of a bar or bat mitzvah, and attend afternoon Hebrew school once or twice a week as well as religious school on Sunday morning. A vibrant synagogue provides families with rich communal, educational, and spiritual experiences, regular access to rabbis, cantors, and educators, as well as youth programming and social justice opportunities. Still, the time commitment is substantial. Education by video conferencing addresses the problem many families experience with overcommitted student and parent schedules, after-school activities, and hours of commuting long distances in the suburbs or through heavy traffic in the city.

OnlineJewishLearning.com augments its program with free educational podcasts on Jewish values, rituals, holidays, and prayers. While most of its business comes from families who have chosen not to affiliate with congregations because of the time constraints of attending weekly Hebrew and religious school, the substantial expense of congregational dues, or simply a lack of interest in participating in services and congregational life, other Jewish families access the organization's services because they live in remote locations, such as a military family stationed in Japan or the student in a remote town in Alaska. In addition to bar and bat mitzvah preparation, OnlineJewishLearning.com will help families plan a personalized bar or bat mitzvah and find a rabbi, cantor, or educator to officiate at the ceremony.

Yoni Heilman, who worked as the company's chief operating officer, said that one of the company's biggest strengths is the ability to assess a student's individual needs and tailor a program to ensure that the student can master the skills of reading Hebrew, chanting text, and preparing a bar/bat mitzvah speech in order to feel successful and accomplished in this process (interview, August 16, 2016, Boston). In fact, the actual methodology that OnLineJewishLearning.com uses to teach Torah and haftarah cantillation is not that different from how tutors teach these musical traditions face-to-face. Tutors work on Hebrew reading skills; demonstrate, teach, and record the melodies associated with the trope signs; and use PDFs of Torah and haftarah text in which recurring musical phrases of the trope are color highlighted. The difference is that this process is all done through video conferencing with the focus on the individual student and teacher. Eskow explained that it is common for students to develop important relationships with their online tutors, and parents often fly teachers out to attend the student's bar or bar mitzvah. Eskow continued, "When I speak to families, I encourage affiliation and explain that you can't be Jewish without being a part of a community. But it's better to get a high quality Jewish education and make the kid feel good rather than not do it at all." She stressed that this model was also an important option for interfaith families who had trouble finding a synagogue where they felt welcome and comfortable. These families often continue to use OnLineJewishLearning.com as a Jewish resource for learning and life-cycle events after the bar and bat mitzvah.

Over time, OnLineJewishLearning.com has also grown into a resource to help synagogues expand their educational offerings. Eskow explained that online learning was a more effective way to teach skills that necessitated repetitive drills such as Hebrew language acquisition, memorizing prayers, and practicing the melodies of the trope. Then congregations were able to make full use of religious school time for interactive activities, community service, holiday experiences, and discussions on Jewish values and ethics.

While such online platforms for Jewish learning do allow greater flexibility in Jewish education, Heilman observed that it is more challenging for this experience to become a gateway to deeper involvement in the Jewish community. In an American culture where experience in increasingly commodified, there is the fear that a bar or bat mitzvah becomes an isolated Jewish experience, not shared with classmates or marking the beginning of a deeper connection to a congregation where one might use and reinforce these liturgical skills again during high school and university.[2] Students can develop meaningful relationships with their tutors as they learn how to chant Torah and haftarah for their bar or bat mitzvah. But after that celebration, they have few opportunities to develop deeper associations with these musical traditions as they are performed regularly in communal worship. There is the tendency for online learning to facilitate a "one-off" individual performance of tradition disassociated from the sounds and memories of a congregational worship experience. While Jewish religious schools do not have stellar track records in retaining students after bar and bat mitzvah, they do provide a physical location, with resident educators, rabbis, cantors, youth group programming, and cultural resources to sustain the ongoing performance of identity and tradition.

Sustaining Tradition without Traditional Structures

My student Alexa Horwitz described the experiences of her family when her brother approached his bar mitzvah. Committed to sustaining Jewish tradition yet alienated from organizational Jewish life, her family brought together a group of families who engaged an independent teacher who used digital technology to teach their children how to chant Torah and haftarah. At the same time, they supplemented this bar/bat mitzvah tutoring by creating a microcommunity where each family was responsible for preparing and presenting Jewish educational programming for the group.

Alexa explained that both she and her parents learned to chant Torah following a traditional approach. Her parents had grown up affiliated with congregations where they attended Hebrew school and worked with their respective cantors to prepare for their bar and bat mitzvahs. Alexa followed this model. Each of them sat face to face with their cantor as he taught the melodic motifs associated with each trope sign. After learning the trope by repetition, they applied these melodies to the Hebrew words of the Torah and haftarah reading. Alexa's father is a musician, and he even became a trope tutor at his synagogue after his bar mitzvah. But this approach did not work when her brother Zack approached the age for bar mitzvah. His mother explained that Zack excelled at baseball, traveled for games on the weekend, and practiced every day after school. Hebrew school was not an option. A friend introduced the family to Sandra Freedman, a tutor who over the years has tutored more than five hundred children for their bar and bat mitzvahs and specializes in families who are not affiliated with synagogues. Many unaffiliated children were drawn to celebrate this rite of passage as they attended the celebrations of Jewish friends, watched them speak and chant in front of their synagogue communities, and enjoyed the often impressive parties that followed. Others were encouraged to have bar and bat mitzvahs by more traditional grandparents.

Freedman, whose son is a congregational rabbi and who belongs to a congregation herself, recognized that many factors drove families to nontraditional models for celebration: "Some parents had terrible experiences in religious school—almost posttraumatic stress disorder," she joked (interview, August 16, 2016, Boston). She also explained that private schools have sports practice until 5:30, and many families ski and go away every weekend. Congregations were not flexible in providing other time slots for Hebrew and religious school. While most congregational bar and bat mitzvahs are held in the context of regular Shabbat worship on Saturday mornings, many families wanted a shorter, late-afternoon Saturday bar or bat mitzvah that would lead into the evening party. Still, she was conflicted about providing a "work around" for families who did not want to join synagogues and sought the advice of her rabbi as she considered expanding her online tutoring. "Do it," he counseled. "If you don't provide this Jewish experience for them, no one will" (Freedman interview).

Freedman meets weekly with her students and does all her tutoring through video conferencing. While she sometimes uses Skype, she prefers whatever technology is most familiar to her students, now primarily using the FaceTime app on her iPhone or iPad. While admitting that it is somewhat counterintuitive, she maintains that video conferencing is a *more* personal connection than meeting face-to-face with students. In their homes, there are constant distractions, and students are very self-conscious that parents will listen in as they are learning how to chant. Freedman also stressed that kids are on their phones and computers hours each day, and this forum is natural and easy for them. As she teaches the melodies of the trope to her students, she records them on the app Voice Memos and texts her recording to her students. Freedman explained that twelve-year-olds simply do not use email. She prints out hard copies of the Hebrew text and translation from the computer program Navigating the Bible (http://bible.ort.org), which allowed her to color-code recurring combinations of the trope, but she does not have her students listen to the recorded chant on that program. She explained that the voice of this male cantor from England is "too formal," and his version of the trope is somewhat different than the trope she teaches. But more importantly, she wanted her students to associate the trope melodies with her voice, and with her as a person, so the connection to the tradition felt strongly personal. Freedman officiates at her students' ceremonies, and she wants them to have had the experience of chanting together: "Kids are often nervous when it comes to this performance and I want them to know that I have their back." She asserted, "Technology is very helpful for learning the skills. If I couldn't send them voice memos and they had to remember it from one week to the next, nothing would be learned. But it's a combination: you need the technology but you also need hugs" (Freedman interview).

Freedman also uses technology to help students with the visual aspects of learning to chant Hebrew text from the scroll of the Torah. The handwritten Hebrew script on each parchment scroll is unique, and it can be very disorienting for a student to prepare from a printed sheet and then see the scroll with different word placement and somewhat different script. To put her students at ease, she texts them an actual picture of their reading from the Torah scroll they will be using in their ceremony.

Zack's mother, Kasey Kaufman, stressed that she wanted his bar mitzvah experience to be more than "one-off tutoring" and described the group they created to deepen their families' experience, explaining that the group learned by preparing to teach one another. "Taking ownership made it amazing. We all had to take a topic—Jewish entertainment, humor, demographics, holidays, food—and we were responsible to do presentations and lead discussions with the group" (interview, August 6, 2016, Boston). Many of the families called this group their "Jewish journey"; others referred to it as "the Jew Crew." For the bar mitzvah itself, Zack's family reached out to a friend who was a composer and musician to lead the music in the service. Kasey laughed as she remarked, "It was the longest service that no one complained about" (interview, August 6, 2016, Boston).

American Judaism is American, and while I am describing the impact of "the sovereign self" on contemporary Judaism, in certain ways the experience of Alexa's family reflects broader trends in our culture. In the late twentieth and early twenty-first century, American culture has supported many ways for empowered individuals to use their personal agency to create affinity groups and institutions that fulfill individual needs and values. American religious expression is increasingly centered in the empowered individual. In a lecture in 1986, Robert Bellah referenced a Gallup poll indicating that 80 percent of Americans agreed with the statement that "an individual should arrive at his or her own religious beliefs independent of any churches or synagogues." He commented, "The notion that religious belief ought to be a purely internal thing, and then you go to the church or synagogue of your choice, shows how deeply ingrained a kind of religious privatism is, which turns the church into something like the Kiwanis Club or some other kind of voluntary association that you go to or not if you feel comfortable with it—but which has no organic claim upon you" (Bellah 1986; see also Pew Research Center 2013). In the example Alexa provided, we see this group of families constructing a microcommunity where they celebrate Jewish tradition and perform identity in ways they understand to be authentic and historically grounded even as they disassociate from synagogues and traditional models of religious authority.

Expanding Opportunities for Inclusion through Technology

My third example of using technology to sustain the musical/liturgical traditions of chanting Torah briefly examines the work of Cantor Linda Sue Sohn, a Jewish educator who has pioneered the use of technology to teach neurodivergent learners, particularly students with dyslexia (2011). Here I expand the concept of sustainability to embrace a broader inclusivity in the Jewish community, one that has often left out students who found it especially challenging to learn the Hebrew alphabet, language, trope signs, and traditions of biblical chant. As recently as twenty years ago, it was common for cantors and rabbis to tell families that neurodivergent learners simply could not handle the difficulties of learning to chant Torah and haftarah, effectively excluding them from celebrating bar and bat mitzvah. Teachers such as Cantor Sohn are challenging this assumption. I am influenced here by Michael B. Bakan's work on music and autism in which he proposes "an ethnographic model of disability as a potential alternative and complement to the existing social and medical models, arguing that the ethnographic and relativistic tenets of applied ethnomusicology hold the potential to effectively promote neurodiversity and autism acceptance by helping to transform customary tropes of deficit, disorder, despair, and hopelessness into alternate visions of wholeness, ability, diversity , and possibility" (2015, 278). Cantor Sohn has used digital technology in her work with hundreds of students over the past sixteen years, providing strategies for these dyslexic students to learn and perform Jewish biblical chant. On both a personal and an institutional level, her work confronts the disruption of exclusion for neurodivergent children in the Jewish community.

Cantor Sohn entered this work well prepared to address these issues. She worked as a software engineer for twenty-five years before being ordained as a cantor and earning her MA in Jewish education with a specialization in Jewish special education. She states, "Dyslexia presents itself in different ways so I don't have only one way to teach. Each student is an individual" (interview, August 16, 2016, Boston). She explains that she developed various technological resources to solve individual problems for particular students. This led her to develop the approach of setting up a personalized webpage for each of her students with customized options for learning the systems of cantillation and the Hebrew text that the student will chant.

Students first must learn how to read Hebrew before they can proceed to learn the system of biblical cantillation. Sohn discovered the importance of Hebrew text formatting and being able to manipulate fonts, line spacing, and word spacing, factors that had a tremendous impact on her students' ability to learn Hebrew. She observed that when most students learn to read English, the words are huge, and there are only a few words on a page. Yet in Hebrew school, once students learns the alphabet, they are given pages with small words and close line spacing. On her personalized webpages, Sohn has the ability to "explode" the syllables in each word, creating what she calls a "syllabified" text, making it much easier for students to learn the Hebrew. She also found that larger line spacing made a significant difference in how easily students could read. Sohn took advantage of larger spaces between lines to include innovative "dot diagrams" indicating the melodic shape of more difficult trope motifs, with higher and lower placement of dots indicating higher and lower pitches.

Like many teachers, Sohn makes recordings of the trope for her students, but she has found it crucial to slow the recordings down as beginners began to learn these musical traditions. She said, "On my website, listening to these recordings is like listening to grass grow." As students become more competent, they have the option to speed up the recordings. Sohn spoke about how the process of learning these musical traditions is a repetitive task, foreign to the educational approach that many students now experience in school, where memorizing multiplication tables or poetry is no longer part of the current curriculum. She gives students a recording of several chanted verses to memorize, and once the student has learned these verses, she works with the student to identify recurring grouping of trope. Only at that point does she teach the names of the individual trope and apply them to other passages with the same groupings. In this way, she builds up knowledge of the trope signs like a musical alphabet, each associated with a particular melody. On her individual websites, she also uses the popular electronic flashcard program Quizlet to drill the names and signs of the trope. The melodies are taught in the context of commonly recurring phrases that students can apply to their own Torah and haftarah readings. While Cantor Sohn uses a similar educational approach with neurotypical students, she says that the flexibility of the technology allows her to develop effective and successful outcomes with neurodivergent learners. Sohn is proud that in the past sixteen years, every one of her students has been able to have a bar or bat mitzvah and chant from the scroll of the Torah before the congregation.

In my previous work examining the use of digital technology to teach biblical cantillation, I was especially interested in the impact of digital learning on the primacy of the student-teacher relationship in the Jewish tradition. Increasingly students are accessing digital resources on their own and learning these musical traditions without the guidance and benefit of a teacher. In fact, it is now possible to learn how to chant Torah online and become a "technician of the sacred" (Rothenberg 1985) with very little involvement in the cultural and religious life of a worship community.

While many bar and bat mitzvah tutors use a broad range of digital resources, they believe that technology should supplement, not replace, the teacher's role in the transmission of oral tradition. Teachers understand that more is taught in this transmission of trope than the musical motifs of the accents: a reverence for the tradition, ethical values, the liturgical context of the Torah service, the physical gestures that one uses to show respect for the scroll, and more. But once the technology is available, there are few controls on how it is used.

This is clearly not the case with the examples examined above, where committed teachers develop personal relationships with their students online and are often present to lead their students' bar or bat mitzvah services. In the work of OnlineJewishLearning.com, Sandra Freedman, and Cantor Linda Sue Sohn, technology supplements, rather than replaces, the teacher's role in the transmission of oral tradition. Many families who would have never affiliated with a synagogue construct bar and bat mitzvah celebrations that they later describe as essential expressions of their Jewish identity and as seminal moments in their spiritual lives. Still, when we examine the processes that sustain music culture, it is important to critically consider what is maintained, what is changed, and what is lost. In his writing on sustainability, resilience, and adaptive management, Titon states that "resilience recognizes that perturbation, disturbance, and flux are constant characteristics of any complex system" (2015, 193). Traditionally, the obligation to chant Torah is understood as a religious commandment to publically present the text of scripture in the context of weekly worship, a cyclical recitation that performs the entire five books of the Torah over the course of the year. Even as these contemporary Jews evidence a creative resilience in developing new educational methodologies, they untether their lives from the institutions that maintain and support communal worship—the weekly venue for this ritual performance.

As these teachers use technology to transmit and sustain the performance of these musical/liturgical traditions, they provide these skills without an ongoing immersion in active Jewish communities. Sandra Freedman spoke about a student she was tutoring over FaceTime in an isolated community that had no Jewish congregation: "He is doing this for his grandparents, and that is meaningful, but where he lives, he has no Jewish friends. How will he connect to tradition and community the day after his bar mitzvah?" Additionally, many students learn how to perform biblical cantillation but do not develop cultural familiarity or competency in the worship service that provides a context for the Torah service. Some of these tutors do teach their students certain central prayers in the service as part of their bar and bat mitzvah preparation. While this does provide familiarity with the Shabbat service, it does not replace the sense of ease or familiarity that organically develops from regular exposure to Jewish worship. While this rite of passage can be experienced as a peak event for the individual, a personally constructed celebration does little to introduce and acculturate the student should he or she choose to become involved in

Jewish religious life in America. In these examples, while certain aspects of musical performance are sustained, other aspects of tradition undergo significant disruption.

This is hardly a new phenomenon in Jewish culture. In an article examining sustainability in minority culture, the historian David N. Myers discusses how "tradition" is never the "passive receipt of a set of unchanging ancient norms" (2014, 397). He quotes the scholar of Jewish mysticism Gershom Scholem, who states, "Tradition is not simply the totality of that which the community possesses as its cultural patrimony and which it bequeaths to its posterity; it is a specific selection from this patrimony, which is elevated and garbed with religious authority" (1971, 285–86). So, too, the processes of sustainability in the transmission of a music culture are selective. Teaching outside the structure of a synagogue with digital technology still allows much to be sustained: the musical traditions of chant, the ability to perform ritual in the Hebrew language, and a deep exposure to the text of the Hebrew bible. This approach evidences a resilience that enables Jews separated or alienated from organizational life to perform their cultural and religious identity in the context of family and friends. But as these liberal Jews use technology and independent teachers to create individually tailored bar and bat mitzvah celebrations, some aspects of culture are not sustained: a connection to the full cycle of the Jewish liturgical year through Shabbat and holiday worship; relationships with rabbis, cantors, and educators as spiritual and educational resources; a web of community connection that enriches life cycle events; and the opportunities for deeper cultural and educational immersion.

At the conclusion of the Torah service, it is traditional for congregants to sing a verse from the book of Proverbs as the Torah is returned to the Ark: "It is a tree of life to them that hold it fast" (3:18). As empowered contemporary Jews teach and perform their relationship with Jewish practice and tradition, they sustain certain aspects of music culture even as they embrace new models of transmission and celebration. In the face of disruption and cultural change, they send down new roots and hope they are strong and deep enough to sustain the "living tree of Torah."

Notes

1. For three semesters, I taught an ethnomusicology course at Tuft University titled "Technology and Jewish Oral Tradition." The field research of my students was invaluable to my study of this subject. In this chapter, I draw from the work of two students, Alexa Horwitz (in 2012) and Austin Bendetson (in 2014). I am indebted to their ethnographic research for this project. After reading their fieldwork projects, I conducted my own interviews with a number of the cantors, tutors, and students they interviewed, and I quote from my own interviews in this chapter. For a fuller examination of the impact

of digital technology on the transmission of the traditions of biblical chant, see Summit 2016a, 215–39; also Summit 2016b.

2. Martin Jay discusses how sociologists negatively characterize our society as an *Erlebnisgesellschaft* (experience society), where "the commodification of experience [is] one of the most prevalent tendencies of our age, ranging from extreme sports to packaged tourism" (2005, 407; see also Schulze 1992 on this terminology).

References

Bakan, Michael B. 2015. "Being Applied in the Ethnomusicology of Autism." In *The Oxford Handbook of Applied Ethnomusicology*, edited by Svanibor Pettan and Jeff Todd Titon, 278–316. New York: Oxford University Press.

Bellah, Robert. 1986. "Habits of the Heart: Implications for Religion." Lecture delivered at St. Mark's Catholic Church, Isla Vista, CA, February 21. http://www.robertbellah.com/lectures_5.htm.

Cohen, Steven M., and Arnold Eisen. 2001. *The Sovereign Self: Jewish Identity in Post-Modern America. Jerusalem Letter / Viewpoints*, Jerusalem Center for Public Affairs (JCPA), May 1. http://www.bjpa.org/Publications/details.cfm?PublicationID=2193.

Jay, Martin. 2005. *Songs of Experience: Modern American and European Variations on a Universal Theme*. Berkeley: University of California Press.

Myers, David N. 2014. "Six Theses on the Sustainability of a Minority Culture in a Majority Society: The Jewish and Muslim Cases." *Muslim World* 104 (October): 397–400.

Pew Research Center. 2013. *A Portrait of Jewish Americans: Findings from a Pew Research Center Survey of U.S. Jews*. http://www.pewforum.org/files/2013/10/jewish-american-full-report-for-web.pdf.

Rawidowicz, Simon. 1986. "Israel: The Ever-Dying People." In *Israel: The Ever-Dying People and Other Essays*, edited by Benjamin C. I. Ravid, 53–63. Rutherford, NJ: Fairleigh Dickinson University Press.

Rothenberg, Jerome. 1985. *Technicians of the Sacred: A Range of Poetries from Africa, America, Asia and Oceania*. Berkeley: University of California Press.

Scholem, Gershom. 1971. "Revelation and Tradition as Religious Categories in Judaism." In *The Messianic Idea in Judaism*, 282–303. New York: Schocken Books.

Schulze, Gerhard. 1992. *Die Erlebnisgesellschaft: Kultursoziologie der Gegenwart*. Frankfurt am Main: Campus.

Sohn, Linda. 2011. "New Orthographic Methods for Teaching Novice Hebrew Readers." MA thesis, Hebrew College, Newton Centre, MA.

Summit, Jeffrey A. 2016a. *Singing God's Words: The Performance of Biblical Chant in Contemporary Judaism*. New York: Oxford University Press.

———. 2016b. "Technology and the Transmission of Oral Tradition in the Contemporary Jewish Community." In *Resounding Transcendence: Transitions in Music, Ritual, and Religion*, edited by Philip Bohlman and Jeffers Engelhardt, 147–62. New York: Oxford University Press.

Titon, Jeff Todd. 2015. "Sustainability, Resilience, and Adaptive Management for Applied Ethnomusicology." In *The Oxford Handbook of Applied Ethnomusicology, edited by Svanibor Pettan and Jeff Todd Titon*, 157–95. New York: Oxford University Press.

CHAPTER 16

Cultural Integrity and Local Music in Cape Breton and New Orleans

BURT FEINTUCH

I BASE THIS CHAPTER primarily on my ethnographic work in Cape Breton, in Canada, adding some thoughts on a very different place—New Orleans, in the United States. My photographer colleague, Gary Samson, and I have recently published a book of conversations with, and photographs of, New Orleans musicians, following our earlier book, which focused on musicians and other culture workers in Cape Breton (Feintuch 2015; Feintuch and Samson 2010). Here I write about how local music in those places connects to what I have lately been calling *cultural integrity.*

Culture is in the air in Cape Breton and New Orleans; in each, there's a public conversation about the value and significance of culture and about music's importance for the integrity of local life. Many residents consider local music integral to a good life and emblematic of a kind of wholeness—or *integrity*—in life. While those conversations can be heated, both places are creative hotspots, celebrated for their distinctive music.

An island in the Canadian province of Nova Scotia, Cape Breton comprises about four thousand square miles. Its population is about 136,000 and steadily declining. Between the late eighteenth and the mid-nineteenth century, thousands of Scots from the Highlands and western islands moved to Cape Breton. They joined Native people and a scattering of Francophone and Anglophone settlers. Today, the island is populated largely by three groups: descendants of the Scots settlers, Francophones, and Native people. Local music is thriving, especially the fiddle tradition (Doherty 2015; Feintuch 2004; Graham 2006).

That music is locked into community life and memory, especially in those places that identify primarily as Scottish in descent.

Life isn't easy in Cape Breton's communities; for decades the economy has been sour. But especially on the western side of the island—Inverness County—life has a social ease, a grace, a kind of mutual support and community orientation, as well as an ongoing reference to local ideas of tradition, especially regarding music, that, at least for me, sets the place apart. Of course, I recognize that, viewed from other vantage points, the island may not seem musically distinctive. There are many other spots in the world where place, local identity, and musical vitality are prominent and entangled. In my experience, though, Cape Breton is noteworthy because of the vigor of its community-based music, music that is at the center of important conversations about culture. How to think about that is the issue.

In the past, I've found writer Robert D. Kaplan's idea of "community-mindedness" useful for describing Cape Breton's small communities and their music. Community-mindedness characterizes sites where a shared identity is grounded in a particular place and conditioned by respect for what local people view as tradition (1996, 278). That's one way of summing up what I see in Cape Breton communities. The idea of social capital is also helpful. Sociologist Robert Putnam (2001), who popularized the idea, largely ignores artistic realms. But it is inconceivable that Cape Bretoners would ever be found bowling alone, and local music is part of what brings them together in community. As I encounter what I consider the Cape Breton anxiety about culture—often expressed as a worry that the music is in decline—I've been thinking about cultural sustainability. My thought is that all of this—the music, the distinctiveness of the communities, the anxiety about culture, what we might learn from Cape Breton examples—can come together under the rubric of *cultural integrity*.

I like the sound and implications of the term *cultural integrity*. In fact, for a moment I thought I had made it up. But my euphoria passed when I found that the term isn't new. Unfortunately, while it does appear in print, useful definitions are harder to find. *Cultural integrity* sometimes appears in discussions of human rights, typically undefined. And in other contexts, from anthropology to business to education to development, the term is undefined, generally used with the implication that to be secure in one's culture is a good thing (Hughes and Hudson 2001).

Some environmental scholars use the word *integrity* in a way that's analogous to what I'm thinking. Jeff Titon has occasionally sent me a reference to other instances of *integrity* appearing in sustainability literatures, as in *ecosystem integrity*. So, as Jeff said to me in an email, in some sustainability discourses, the term *integrity* is "out there." I think we should stake a claim to it for the realm of culture.

Henry A. Regier, former director of the Institute for Environmental Studies at the University of Toronto, is helpful. Writing about what he calls "ecological integrity," Regier says, "A living system exhibits integrity if, when subjected to disturbance, it sustains an organizing, self-correcting capability to recover toward an end-state that is normal and 'good' for that system" (1993, 3). Substitute "cultural" for "living," reflect on "normal and good," and I think we have some organizing principles for beginning to consider cultural integrity. Regier also links environmental and cultural integrity, writing about "human capability, both individually and through institutions, to complement the integrity of a modified natural ecosystem in an overall context that is inevitably turbulent socially and ecologically" (3). See also Aldo Leopold's statement: "A thing is right when it tends to preserve the integrity, stability, and beauty of the biotic community. It is wrong when it tends otherwise" (quoted by Aaron Allen, this volume).

Mindful of Regier's formulation of normal and good and thinking about communities, I mean several things by *cultural integrity*. For me, it's about a community's ability to articulate and maintain what it values about living a good life in the company of others who share one's place in the world. The term implies wholeness, interconnectedness, and the soundness of those connections. And, fundamentally, it involves what can only be subjective—the "goodness" or adherence to moral and ethical standards in community life. Call that last point an ethic of community life. I recognize that the claims I've made are based on terminologies and concepts that some have found problematic. At the same time, I note that for others they resonate in regard to community life. That said, I want to talk about how the idea of cultural integrity might apply in Cape Breton, a place where, to use Leopold's formation, many people have a very strong sense of when "things are right," along with a strong desire to right those things that are not.

Maintaining What the Community Values

It hasn't always been easy, but informally and formally, Inverness County communities have maintained and valued a strong sense of tradition. Those settlements represent the three largest historically established identities on the island, and there people connect music to identity. Many are of Scots-Gaelic descent, especially where the fiddle music thrives, and some are among the island's most active supporters of the cause of language revitalization—the project to reinvigorate Gaelic, originally the primary language in some communities. The island's largest Francophone area is in the county, where activists have made it possible to go to school in French and established museums and a community radio station to broadcast in French. Some are Mi'kmaq—Indigenous people—and here you see identity represented by their community cultural centers. *Tradition*, that challenging term for scholars, isn't so problematic in these communities. It stands for history and for identity and for artistic expression. The local music is one way of expressing, affirming, and celebrating tradition. And especially in the warm weather, that music seems to be everywhere: at dances, festivals, house parties, in the local paper. It's one of the main reasons why people come together. Music, language, and identity are of a piece, integrated; they are key ingredients of many Cape Bretoners' sense of—and palpable desire for—cultural integrity.

Not only have these communities maintained a strong sense of tradition; they've taken an activist stance in its maintenance. Although in the 1990s people resisted the government's closing small local schools, they ensured that the new, consolidated school in Mabou has a performance space that, for the first time, meets professional standards as a facility for indoor concerts. That hall has a strong commitment to presenting local music. It joins what seems to be an almost endless set of festivals and concerts, emphasizing the significance of local music. And, using golf tournaments and political connections, residents created the Celtic Music Interpretive Centre in Judique. Like a number of other Cape Breton facilities, it serves tourists, to some degree, but local people use it as if it were their own. They stop by for a beer or a meal, to hear local musicians in a room staged to look like a kitchen, representing the house parties where, historically and sometimes today, the music has thrived.

Sometimes, institutionalizing seems to be a way of distancing. That's plainly not the case in Cape Breton. This local creation of new infrastructure is, in Regier's words, clearly a response to a perception of disturbance in the culture, a concern about losing what matters. So culture is in the air, but residents have managed to keep it firmly on the ground, supporting the old contexts, while creating new ones. One reason I think these communities would rank high on a cultural integrity index, were there such a thing, is that many residents have made clear some of what matters for community life, and they've made it happen. They wouldn't speak of *cultural integrity*, but what they seek and support is a way of life in which music, identity, and a sense of community are well integrated.

Wholeness, Interconnectedness

A Cape Breton radio announcer said to me:

> That idea of community is the thing that really . . . defines the Cape Breton experience right now. There's a glue that ties people together—people who have been here for five or six generations and people who have come in very

recently—and it has to do with declaring to one another what's unique and what's important. That seems to be defined very clearly here. It might be because this has been a have-not region for so long that people really know the value of gathering in a fire hall; they really know the value of being pleasant to the person across the counter at the post office. It manifests itself in a thousand different ways. But at the end of the day it's that people matter.[1]

This is an articulation of the connection between the valuing of tradition and the social ease and grace that I see in Cape Breton. People gather for music. What they are doing, along with being entertained and sometimes transported by that music, is building connection. Those connections are an antidote to the alienation one might expect in small, remote communities in a cold climate.

There's a complex reciprocity involved here. Go to the weekly West Mabou dance, in the community recreation hall. Pay for admission, and along with helping musicians make ends meet, you're maintaining the hall for the community and supporting a softball team whose members live down the road. You dance, and there's a physical connection to your neighbors that goes beyond most other kinds of community interaction. Musicians, who are well paid by local standards, can continue their art. The hall gets fixed up. The ball players travel to tournaments. The music helps integrate the culture, bringing together disparate elements—music and athletics, identity and history, among them—and the community benefits.

The late Cape Breton writer Alistair MacLeod believed that the stability of community life there is one reason for that ease and grace. In Dunvegan, where his house was, nearly everyone knows nearly everyone else. He said to me,

> People here have a relationship to the landscape. People have been here a long time. Some would say, "Home is where the graves are." The area was settled basically by a homogenous people. This does not mean that they're any better than anybody else, but this is just what happens to you, historically. Here are all these people, and they've been here for six generations, eating the same food, with the same religion, and in the same weather. And their music comes out of their weather, and their music comes out of their worries, and their imagery comes from what they see around them, and this is the way all of these things have always worked. (quoted in Feintuch and Samson 2010, 62)

Once at the longest-running of all the outdoor concerts on the island, I heard Alistair, who had just won the world's most valuable literary award, talk about the singularity, in today's world, of his having volunteered to take tickets at that festival with the same friends for more than forty years.

The Goodness of Community Life:
An Ethic of Community

Regier's idea of normal and good for particular systems is complicated when we think about culture, especially in a time when some scholars see culture as contestation. Regardless, in Cape Breton many people believe that culture matters. At the same time, as I said earlier, many share an anxiety about their culture; they worry about losing what many people see as the normal and good. This is exacerbated by some forms of change, such as language loss. Until the mid-twentieth century, some Inverness County communities were primarily Gaelic speaking. Since then, the loss of first-language Gaelic speakers has been precipitous, spawning both a province-wide concern and a number of community-based initiatives. Some focus entirely on language revitalization, but in many cases the underlying concept is a cultural one. In those, Gaelic stands for both a language and a way of life. Many people say that traditional music is the heart of that way of life.

Féis Mhabu, in the small community of Mabou, an organization dedicated to strengthening the language and the culture, sponsors house parties, inviting young players to sit with master musicians and requiring the parents to stay and watch. This project serves to reinforce a way of life, not only to teach the music but also to use the music to join generations. Thus it is about art and life and, in any number of ways, about a Cape Breton ethic of community. And it is about a cultural system responding to perceived disturbance by organizing to restore local ideas of what's normal and good. More recently, Féis Cheap Breatuinn (Féis Cape Breton) has extended that model to two other sites on the island. To my mind, these efforts differ from many other heritage-related musical organizations (Faux, this volume) in that the Cape Breton projects are about more than teaching music; their goal is to teach culture, with music as the focus. They are about cultural integrity.

Cape Breton journalist, poet, playwright, and novelist Frank Macdonald has written about how, in the eyes of an increasingly urban nation, Cape Breton and the Maritime provinces as a whole are sometimes seen as a "culture of despair" (Feintuch and Samson 2010, 21–27). He's referring to the long-standing economic problems that plague the island, especially the seemingly intractable problem of unemployment. But economic problems notwithstanding, it is striking that Cape Bretoners generally rate their quality of life comparatively high on whatever scales surveys use. While employment and infrastructure are deficient, what emerges is that many residents believe that they have an unusually high quality of life.

I suggested earlier that cultural integrity is ultimately about the "goodness" or adherence to moral and ethical standards in community life. I don't have the means to quantify this, and what studies exist tend to be framed differently. But I think it's not farfetched to maintain that despite the serious challenges Cape Bretoners face, it's the cultural integrity of community life that bolsters the shared idea that life is better there. And if you've been there, you know that music is right at the heart of the good life in some of those communities. Also, if you talk to tourists, they'll often tell you that they've come both because it's a visually spectacular place and because there's something very enticing about the way people live their lives. Tourists may go to a dance for the music, but they often leave talking about the culture.

New Orleans

Although some call New Orleans the Big Easy, life there is far from easy for many of its residents. This famously creative place has fomented musical forms known around the world. Although it's best known for jazz, the city's role in rhythm and blues, funk, contemporary brass-band music, and its own more local and less widely known traditions, such as the music of the Mardi Gras Indians, is spectacular. But it's a hard place, with high rates of violent crime, poverty, a troubled public education system, much tension between some communities and the police, and a whole litany of related difficulties. And, of course, it's a city traumatized by the huge disasters of the levees breaking in 2005 in Hurricane Katrina's aftermath (see DeWitt in this volume for the impact on New Orleans of contamination of nearby coastal areas by the BP Deepwater Horizon oil spill in 2010).

Over the past few years, I've been interviewing New Orleans musicians, and with photographer Gary Samson, I've recently published a book of those conversations. *Talking New Orleans Music* presents about a dozen musicians. When I began those conversations, I thought I was in a place nearly diametrically opposed to Cape Breton: a black-majority city recovering from a huge environmental disaster. But the more I talked to musicians there, the more I started hearing parallels, and the more my idea of cultural integrity seemed applicable.

The following short interview excerpts give a sense of this:

Dr. Michael White, a leading performer of traditional jazz and an academic, who says that even in its diversity, the city's music is part of a whole, integrated, observed:

> If you look at New Orleans culture, it's branches of the same tree. We're doing the same things for the same reasons. It's just that they come out different ways, which is beautiful. I mean, it's hard to believe that an urban area in America, even today, can have unique traditions like we have. Social parades,

jazz funerals, brass bands, Mardi Gras Indians still have meaning and vitality in the community, although that meaning may have changed and outside influences have altered the course or direction of some of them somewhat. But they still are very important parts of New Orleans culture today. It's incredible. (in Feintuch 2015, 35)

Guitarist, vocalist, and bandleader Deacon John (John Moore), spoke about how culture becomes instilled in the person in an environment rich with music in public: "Being from New Orleans, you're exposed to the culture. You come up in the culture, with the second-line parades, the Mardi Gras, all that. You're exposed to that ever since you were a little kid. Your parents bring you to Mardi Gras in your costume, and you see the Mardi Gras Indians, the brass bands, the jazz funerals, and it becomes part of you" (in Feintuch 2015, 3).

Finally, Cajun accordionist, singer, and bandleader Bruce Daigrepont, who came up in the community of Cajuns who moved to New Orleans from southwest Louisiana, remarked on culture—in this case expressed as *heritage*, in the air: "I grew up knowing my heritage" (in Feintuch 2015, 3).

The more time I spent in New Orleans, the more I went to musical events, and the more I listened to what musicians had to say, the more Cape Breton kept coming to mind. For instance, it became very clear that even in a sea of people, smaller social configurations, in this case neighborhoods, mattered most for cultural creativity and continuity—for the integrity of local culture. In New Orleans, those places tend to be the neighborhoods where people have been left out of economic development, much like communities in Cape Breton. These are places, as in Cape Breton, where music is part of the public realm, accessible. And they are places where everyone seems to know everyone else. As in Cape Breton, people tend to talk about music running in families. In fact, nearly everyone I interviewed in New Orleans talked about music and family—immediate family members as musicians, growing up aware of being ensnared in a web of family musical ties stretching over generations. In Cape Breton, people say that music is in the blood, and they point out how it seems to travel along family lines. In both places, family support and encouragement are important factors in maintaining traditional music.

So, music is in the public realm in New Orleans, especially in neighborhoods that are mostly poor and black. As in Cape Breton, music is prominent in public conversations about culture, in the context of threats to those neighborhoods' cultural integrity such as gentrification, displacement for development, bad policing, and other disruptive forces.

And as anxiety about the Crescent City's music has mounted over time, an institutional infrastructure has developed to teach, promulgate, and present it—that is, to try to maintain cultural integrity. As in Cape Breton, apprehension about music is often expressed as anxiety about culture, and one kind of response is to try to create educational, archival, and presenting organizations—infrastructure to rebalance, to restore the normal and good. The city's efforts to recover from the devastation of the levees giving way have amplified those efforts, but many of those programs and projects predate Katrina. From the Tipitina's Foundation to the Ellis Marsalis Center for Music to the New Orleans Jazz and Heritage Festival and Foundation, among many others, citizens have endeavored to bolster what has been normal and good in the city, at least historically and at the neighborhood level, often with a focus on youth. The city's distinctive social aid and pleasure clubs, benevolent societies created by African Americans, play a particularly strong role in supporting music as part of their programs, especially their annual second-line parades and other public social events. A 2010 study claims that the social aid and pleasure club members "score the highest on civic engagement" of any of the constituencies (among them groups described as "high income," "high education," "white," and "church member") the authors studied (Weil 2011, 205). It's not a stretch to think of the social aid and pleasure clubs, which were originally formed to help create and sustain cultural integrity in the face of earlier kinds of devastation, as having more recently stepped up following the environmental wreckage of 2005.

In recent years, New Orleans has been the site of heated conversations about music, with official attempts to regulate music on the streets—where it's arguably most at home in the city—to control parades, and to limit "noise" in some neighborhoods. This is especially so in areas that are gentrifying, producing the irony that outsiders who claim to come to the area in part for the culture are uncomfortable with that culture being too close. The counterargument to these regulatory and limiting moves on the part of officialdom and gentrifiers is that "this is our culture, and it's too important to restrict it." That is, when what is normal and good in some New Orleans contexts is under fire, typically because of socioeconomic change, the argument from those who would be most affected by new rules and regulations is that change will damage cultural integrity.

I do not mean to imply that cultural integrity is measurable, finite, or objective. But in our work, what is?[2] We know from sustainability studies that change is part of natural systems. We also know that environmentalists believe that some states of being in the natural world are more successful, which, to return to Regier, is to say more integrated, than other, more disrupted, states. Some environmentalists use terms such as *stewardship* to describe their work to help places recover from disruption. As I think about Cape Breton and New Orleans, I wonder if, when culture is in the air, and especially when people worry about disruption, we might say that what's at stake is a desire to hold on to, or even restore, local ideas of cultural integrity. And I'd like to think that scholars can play a role in the stewardship of that integrity.[3]

Notes

1. Following the 2003 interview from which I've taken this quotation, the interviewee asked for anonymity.

2. I must cite an important voice countering this assertion. Catherine Grant (2014) is doing a remarkable job of trying to create ways of measuring music's vitality in specific milieus.

3. An earlier version of this chapter was my keynote address for the 2015 Society of Musicology in Ireland conference. Thanks to Liz Doherty for her invitation to address the conference. Thanks, too, to the many interviewees on whose words I base this work; to my partner, Jeannie Thomas, who was with me during many of the interviews; to Gary Samson for his friendship and beautiful images; and to Jeff Titon for decades of good conversation and inspiration. Those decades add up. My friendship with Jeff now goes back nearly forty years, dating to even before Jeff owned a Compaq and I was a Kaypro guy. Like many others, I've been learning from, and inspired by, Jeff and his work since we first met.

References

Doherty, Liz 2015. *The Cape Breton Fiddle Companion*. Sydney: Cape Breton University Press.

Feintuch, Burt. 2004. "The Conditions for Cape Breton Music: The Social and Economic Setting of a Regional Soundscape." *Ethnomusicology* 48 (1): 73–104.

———. 2015. *Talking New Orleans Music: Crescent City Musicians Talk about Their Music, Their Lives, and Their City*. Photographs by Gary Samson. Jackson: University Press of Mississippi.

Feintuch, Burt, and Gary Samson. 2010. *In the Blood: Cape Breton Conversations on Culture*. Logan: Utah State University Press.

Graham, Glenn. 2006. *The Cape Breton Fiddle: Making and Maintaining Tradition*. Sydney: Cape Breton University Press.

Grant, Catherine. 2014. *Music Endangerment: How Language Maintenance Can Help*. New York: Oxford University Press.

Hughes, Cheryl, and Yeager Hudson, eds. 2001. *Cultural Integrity and World Community*. Lewiston, NY: Edwin Mellen Press.

Kaplan, Robert D. 1996. *The Ends of the Earth: A Journey at the Dawn of the 21st Century*. New York: Random House.

Putnam, Robert D. 2001. *Bowling Alone: The Collapse and Revival of American Community*. New York: Simon and Schuster.

Regier, Henry A. 1993. "The Notion of Natural and Cultural Integrity." In *Ecological Integrity and the Management of Ecosystems*, edited by Stephen Woodley, James Kay, and George Francis, 3–18. Boca Raton, FL: CRC Press.

Weil, Frederick. 2011. "The Rise of Community Organizations, Citizen Engagement, and New Institutions." In *Resilience and Opportunity: Lessons from the Gulf Coast after Katrina and Rita*, edited by Amy Liu, Roland V. Anglin, Richard M. Mizelle, Jr., and Allison Plyer, 201–19. Washington, DC: Brookings Institution Press.

CHAPTER 17

BaAka Singing in a State of Emergency

Storytelling and Listening as Medium and Message

MICHELLE KISLIUK

"ONCE UPON A TIME, when animals and people were equal." That is how BaAka from the Central African forest begin their *gano* stories, their folktales. They set these tales in a mythical time when animals could speak like humans (Kisliuk [1998] 2000, 25).[1] Consider this for a moment: animals and people with equally powerful voices—voices that rise from earth and require us to listen. BaAka know this kind of listening. Their powerful singing elaborates and merges with earth's lifesounds in a process that, I think, leads people and earth to a mutual understanding, to a sympathetic vibration. The rest of us can ask, belatedly, how our world might have been had we paid better attention to nonhuman voices. As we blink and wake up to an emergency, our best chance might be a jump into a *sur*realism that takes seriously this mythical time.[2]

Where was I? Oh yes, telling a story. A life story.[3] Mine, yours, another's. Within a greater collective narrative looming in minds and hearts and set on an ailing earth. This looming story, or even a small part of it, is hard to jump into because we may never jump out—because this could be the last story we tell. We don't want to hear the ending in our lifetime, in our children's or great grandchildren's, or the next seven generations under our watch. But by diving in to tell it we may find the permission we need, during this state of emergency, to imagine a future, to bring into earshot, into the subjunctive, a hum, a rumble, a purr of what could still be. A speculative nonfiction.[4]

I grapple with this question: What does expressive culture teach that we intuitively know connects directly to survival, and which now especially needs urgent articulation? I ask myself—and you—to try to tell the stories that matter, both professional and personal—in versions and revisions, with bits that fit together in a map of living insight contained within expressive enactment; ways of singing, dancing, telling stories. With a language that listens as it speaks (Le Guin 2004, 195–98). The stories told by climate scientists and environmentalists, finally heard more widely in the second decade of this century, are still swirling in idioms too limited to effectively narrate our survival—not yet infiltrating mainstream babble or cutting through intentional obstruction to compel the required action (e.g., Kuruvilla 2016). As Rob Nixon has asked, "In an age where the media venerate the spectacular, when public policy is shaped primarily around perceived immediate need, a central question is strategic and representational: how can we convert into image and narrative the disasters that are slow moving and long in the making, disasters that are anonymous and that star nobody, disasters that are attritional and of indifferent interest to the sensation-driven technologies of our image-world? How can we turn the long emergencies of slow violence into stories dramatic enough to rouse public sentiment and warrant political intervention?" (2011, 3).[5]

What I learned from BaAka forest people about singing with one another and with our surroundings is also about surviving and thriving. I ask how this kind of collective listening-sounding-interactive practice can be adopted more widely. Where are the communitarian settings woven into our everyday lives and robust enough to channel connections between collective practices and our environmental emergency? Communitarian initiatives are routinely squelched by the same interests that created this fossil-fuel-dependent existential crisis—the forces embedded within market fundamentalism (see Harraway 2016). Stretching to clutch the ring, powerful counterforces bump us away from reaching it. We need to grasp the performative circumstances (Schechner 1977) to teach and reteach one another how to listen and to hear how we might salvage life at the mercy of industrial humanity.

Ursula K. Le Guin elucidates how speaking is listening, is relationship, and she gets to the crux of the challenge of listening: "In most cases of people actually talking to one another [or singing with one another], human communication cannot be reduced to information. The message not only involves, it *is*, a *relationship* between speaker and hearer. The medium in which the message is embedded is immensely complex, infinitely more than a code: it is a language, a function of a society, a culture, in which the language, the speaker, and the hearer are all embedded" (2004, 187). This is the task: how to migrate the multileveled, multivocal, overwhelmingly intricate messages that expressive culture offers us as practices and as tools, into a thing we can amplify and accelerate, like an airbag deploying as the car crashes.

Little Stories: Echoing from Self and Back

Starting with smaller stories that live nearby is easier emotionally and conceptually, but those stories can be harder to effectively link to that big looming story. While these small stories may distract us into inaction if we allow them to, they also contain the potential to lead us where we need to go if we pay sufficient attention and get up to follow their lead. That is the point of this pint-sized chapter and of my other endeavors: to link some smallish stories that meld working and personal life—to retell, teach and reteach, send them out to be retold in new versions beyond my control—hoping, insisting, to bring them to a speculative reality that is still only partially visible, akin to what Stephen Tyler (1986) once imagined might be a nonfictional "ethnographic surrealism."

So now a little story, close by, comfortable: Starting from the middle, where I find myself, and maybe where you find yourself—not sure in the moment where to step next. Then pulled along, you and me, by our lives, we might find each other where stories intersect. That's the best thing about stories . . . and music . . . and listening. We can meet each other there, by surprise, along a stretch of yellow brick road. Stopping to dance and sing as we go, always forgetting, then reminded that the journey *is* the story, even when snared in a cliché from which we need to twist free before passing. Our redemptive journeys might prevail if we bushwhack toward paths aimed effectively lifeward, continuing around a bend.

The only way to understand what I mean right now is to yodel. I'm not joking. Are you somewhere that echoes? Is it a generous space and place that will share its voice with you when you call out to it? Somewhere you won't put others into a panic if you sound out loudly to hear your own voice, a place where the world can call back to you? Then try it please, now. Try it a few times until you like what comes back. Can we like what comes back even now after we have tarnished our world? Can we shape what comes back into a dialogue? Will people nearby join in? If they are American teenagers this is unlikely, at least at first. The effort required to move forward is unnerving.

The other day I walked through a pedestrian tunnel with my hound, Rocco. It had been a sweaty hike on a humid day in Virginia. For a few steps in the tunnel, I could delight in slightly cooler air where an echo amplifies a footstep or even an exhaled breath, the clink of collar tags or paw nails on pavement, and beckons me to call out. When I do, I remember my time discovering my voice in Central Africa—the echo from earth and body to trees and surroundings and back—a relationship through sound, a co-presence (Titon 2015) that BaAka know intimately. Although my own thinking about the voice and its echo began decades ago, I still strive to grasp and articulate links that this micro-immediacy has with urgent matters of our time. The links *feel* evident, but making them plain to others is not always at hand. I am late trying to do this explicitly. What took me so long? Can I, should I, amplify BaAka voices reinterpreted through teaching, where those voices combine with others? Can I connect this cry into the atmosphere with this moment, with the big story. It's urgent, but real progress is slow (Kapchan 2016). The distress of not acting fast enough is ejected with a yodel into a world that sings back reassuringly that she—Gaia?—is still there and, astonishingly, resiliently forgiving, still answering, still embellishing our call with a richly elaborated echo of herself. In a sentiment that resonates here, Donna Harraway recently has made clear: "Gaia puts into question our very existence, we who have provoked its brutal mutation that threatens both human and nonhuman livable presents and futures. Gaia is not about a list of questions waiting for rational policies; Gaia is an intrusive event that undoes thinking as usual" (2016, 33).

In undoing thinking-as-usual (and by extension the conventions of scholarship that limit how we think), I want to listen to and to tell stories, to sing with you about what BaAka know of dynamic, multi-lectic, rhyzomatic interaction, grounded among people within a community and manifested in song. How does one teach those survival skills to others in person, while simultaneously sending a plea for urgent attention by local and global powers? Attention to, and active reverence for, people who have kept their expressivities and transformed them brilliantly under war, deforestation, cultural annihilation, lack of access to medical, educational, or legal support. These people suffer most from environmental collapse but are least responsible for it; their excellent practices, if those principles were understood and adapted profoundly, could still help avert collapse. Cultural survival meets literal survival at this spot along the path.

Into the Past: Learning to Listen

Some of the most memorable recordings of BaAka music include forest sounds melded with singing (for example, a recording of the BaBenzele Pygmies produced and published by Bernie Krause; see Sarno 1995). Though sometimes highly curated in the studio, this combination contrasts with an earlier preference for technologically cleansed sound. Humanly organized sound is now better understood as it melds in sympathetic vibration with sonic (and ecologically as well as socially fragile) surroundings, either recorded or live in the moment (see Eidsheim 2015). That melding is the place to focus. I remember as a student hearing saturated Ewe polyrhythms and the mixed timbres of shakers, bells, and drums, united by distance outside, and I was impelled to run toward the sound. Like sounds in campgrounds, at night, at a bluegrass festival—sounds we hear at middle distance (see Daughtry 2015) infused in the porous, especially humid, air—in woods, leaves, and ground—with vibration that is human and social. It synchs us with the immediate nonhuman vibrations of the life that surrounds us, tiny and immense.

When I first went to the Central African Republic (CAR), I was in my mid-twenties. My goal was to learn to sing like and sing with BaAka forest people—determined to understand how they bring their yodeling, polyphonic sounds into the world. I thought if I could accomplish that alone I would have done enough for one life. Looking back, my youthful ambitions seem meager considering what our earth is confronted with, among them climate emergency. Plus I had no idea what it might actually mean to have succeeded in learning something of what they know, even if the goal were limited to learning how to sing particular songs maybe well enough to teach them to others. But the question for me now, thirty years later is, once having learned some basics of BaAka practice and having devised ways to teach them in new contexts, what are the implications and responsibilities that come with this knowledge? I can teach my students to sing, but can I also in the process teach them to fight for a healthy earth—and to generate the skills they need to cultivate relationships with one another necessary for that global health? These are things that BaAka know well how to do but are not in a safe position to widely share. So it seems, at least right now, sharing further is up to people like me.

After fall 2017, in Charlottesville and at the University of Virginia, emotionally ragged people still formed musical community in the wake of a neofascist invasion, and then we reeled from an impossible massacre of country-music listeners in Las Vegas, a string of devastating hurricanes in the southern United States and in the Caribbean, and people left without adequate rescue. Then came Parkland, Florida—while the US government pitched off the rails, sending the world backward, and children rose from pools of blood to push forward. Surely once this volume has been published, and as it ages, more disasters will have already unfolded. It is a lot to ask, to sing together right now. And it is also what we most need to be doing. Is that an ironically bold assertion in the face of existential emergency? Remembering to listen, honing our sensibility, cultivating vulnerability are especially urgent right now—to keep singing through the swirling changes around us. BaAka are still singing in the midst of treacherous environmental and political changes, cradled within the dwindling "lungs" of the earth. And if BaAka can do it under the duress they face, the rest of us could too. And if we did, maybe it would signal a change in course, a new path through the woods guiding us toward what lives and thrives.

What I did not expect when I set out to learn to sing from BaAka was that doing so would require learning deeply how to listen—not only to other people, which is crucial, but also to myself within the space around me—to the life, to the presence (and the co-presence) wherever I might be in any moment. I also did not expect that I would only fully learn this by trying to teach others to do it. To cite Jean-Luc Nancy (2002, 12), to be listening is to enter into a tension and to be on the lookout for a *"relationship in self"* that is in perpetual exchange with the world. Jeff Todd Titon, whom I first met when I was his student at Tufts as a freshman in college and with whom I have since exchanged ideas over many years, has recently written about Thoreau's ear. In an article that compounds the resonance of what I have tried to say here, Titon offers a fresh hearing of that iconic figure's sensitivity to sound. Thoreau learned about our world, especially our ecological home, through listening—and in so doing learned about himself. Titon writes that for Thoreau, "music was chiefly a human echoing of environmental sounds" (2015, 144), about an attention to sound that invites a co-presence with the environment and by extension a co-presence with one another. This is what we need to understand better and make accessible within everyday practice.

Here's a story: Justin was first my friend, later my husband, who worked with me and made it possible to delve into the sociomusical world of BaAka by guiding me to meet forest people (alongside whom he had grown up and, in contrast with many in his own ethnic group, whom he deeply admired). Justin kept me safe from potential dangers ranging from poisonous snakes to falling trees and introduced me to BaAka who knew and trusted him, which led me to trust him too. Special heightened moments of listening together stand out in my memory. Moments that felt like love in all its forms: For instance on our way to a faraway forest camp, hitching a partial ride in the back of a pickup truck full of BaAka men. Something about the flow of motion, the tires over gravel, and the fresh tropical wind in our faces in the crowded truck bed gave rise immediately to singing, to fiercely interactive and joyous yodeling that I did not know yet how to join with. We two held hands—holding to this moment. The sounds of these simultaneously exuberant and gentle voices made clear why we were in this place and why we were together right now. Life feels concentrated, distilled, in moments like this (Kisliuk 2017). Then the truck stopped as did the singing, and we had to figure out where we were going in the humid, sticky heat and needing a bath.

Listening in a State of Emergency: Into an Imagined Future

I teach my students that they need to render in writing their most potent, personal, sometimes painful concerns. I firmly believe this leads to a necessarily positioned writing and thinking that enables emotional, experiential, and metaphorical connections that link profoundly to the intellectual and creative work at hand.[6] As difficult as it is at this juncture for me, I try to follow my own advice right now: addressing fear, love, mourning, missing, still aching for a different outcome in my personal life and in the global present. This is not for the sake of confession but for the sake of looking straight at reality in order to act from that place. It's what we need to do, in microcosm, individually and together.

So I face my own family story that has recently turned a traumatic corner (see Kisliuk and Mongosso 2003). I thought I could overcome, but could not as of this writing, my Central African husband's scars from early trauma and subsequent addiction that kept surfacing to contradict the story we had thought our lives would tell: I had to admit just a few weeks before writing a draft of this chapter that I could not control the narrative or heal my husband's ailments, try as I might, and no matter what I might feel. These ailments were old ones. When I first arrived in CAR as a researcher I had a parallel realization that, unwittingly, I had "walked onto a stage set to play to a Colonial audience" (Wilmsen in Kisliuk [1998] 2000, 23). And now, again, I had to acknowledge how the history of pillage large and small has shaped the stage I live on now and could threaten to extinguish it altogether, personally, globally. What the two of us had wanted at first was a life between two places, an intersection of homes, here and there, at once separated and integrated. Merciless sectarian violence in CAR and attendant desperation, seeded by escalating global plunder, made it impossible to forge that life we had imagined. Instead, now, it became clear after years of struggling for footing, that for now I must protect the rest of the family from descending with him into grief that had its seeds long before we met. Nothing gold can stay. It gets scuffed, dented. This is the challenge we face with our distressed planet. We need to entirely rethink how we live in order to survive, even when the mess is not our fault. Our world is drastically scuffed, almost beyond recognition. We all face trauma at points in our lives. Trembling under threat from a loved one who is sick, whether our spouse or our Gaia earth, what is key is how we emerge from the crisis—as individuals and as a collective in concert with the life cradled here.

Might the home (or the nation, or the planet) where we dwell and that we love—like a spouse—which has sustained us and which we thought we could sustain, which we had expected to endure, show up transformed, and instead threaten to hurt us, maybe even kill us, or our dog, or our child, or incinerate our home. Those destructive forces are alarmingly self-unaware. One cannot negotiate with rage or amnesia. Fire or flood or poison water must be answered by the fierce assertion of life. Either we and our fellow humans reject mindfulness-stealing addictions (alcohol? opioids? social media? fossil fuels? celebrity? unfettered greed? white supremacy and patriarchy?), or they will consume us too. Gaia and humanity will perish in our time if we don't act. We can, in fact, choose to steer away from the elaborately designed habits and allures that take us pitching toward disaster, along with the blameless life that falls victim to our actions. Though the window is closing fast, it's a choice we might still have time to make collectively and personally.

Whose guilt, whose responsibility, whose aspirations, whose redemption? In gratitude, we pull the good from the past and insist as best we can that what we cherish will endure beyond linear time and into the surreal real. What do we owe the world while under the immediate threat of inebriated violence or environmental catastrophe? I had to change my life's trajectory in order to protect myself and my child—at that juncture a longed-for harmony forged from difference was not an option within my nuclear family. Is such harmony still an option for our nation, for our world? I open my mouth to sing, but my throat denies the yodel as my ear listens in suspended fragility for an echoing back from the earth. Lives meshed in profound diversity produce beauty and can produce something else, something terrifying. Coming to terms with profound difference engenders pain that can, in the end, lead to another, better reality. To make it so, the trajectory itself has to change, to lead to a future we need but haven't yet envisioned. I want to sketch out a speculative nonfiction for my own life and extend it to the life we might imagine for the earth. A story that will find a way to reassemble the pieces that, in new formation, might still lead toward flourishing survival, in a new shape, a new sound that we were previously unable to perceive. That story is about to be told: Upon a future time, animals and people might sound aloud their co-presence, rippling from the drop of a voice—adding to the sustaining polyphony of a world that sings back.

Notes

1. The idea that once upon a time humans did not dominate and animals had agency is a widespread idea in human mythology, addressed, for example, by Eduardo Viveiros de Castro (2014, 42, 72) as a concept that we might return to within a broader "Anti-Narcissus" age that removes the Western gaze from the center of conceptualizations of experience.

2. After Barad's "agential realism" (2007, 150–52).

3. "My intention is to define and develop an approach to the life story as a self-contained fiction, and thus to distinguish it sharply from its historical kin: biography, oral history, and the personal history" (Titon 1980, 276). In this sense, life story joins the genre of creative nonfiction.

4. I developed these ideas over several years in talks at Johns Hopkins University, Hampshire College, University of Kentucky, University of Tennessee, Pomona College, New York University, and Iceland Academy of the Arts. See also Deborah Kapchan (2016, 2017, respectively) on slow activism and on the realm of the speculative in generating theory.

5. Since I first drafted this chapter and significantly after Nixon published the text quoted above, the world has changed to an even more dire state, and some answers to his questions have emerged. Climate disasters are fast becoming obvious. And there have been brave and widespread direct actions like the No DAPL (Dakota Access Pipe Line) protest that took place around Standing Rock, North Dakota, in 2016–17. The spiritual and moral center of that protest had, in consonance with the themes here, a music and dance core initiated by the Sioux of the Standing Rock region.

6. Anthropologist Renato Rosaldo ([1989] 1993) wrote about this process decades ago in "Grief and the Headhunter's Rage."

References

Barad, Karen. 2007. *Meeting the Universe Halfway: Quantum Physics and the Entanglement of Matter and Meaning.* Durham, NC: Duke University Press.

Daughtry, J. Martin. 2015. *Listening to War: Sound, Music, Trauma, and Survival in Wartime Iraq.* New York: Oxford University Press.

Eidsheim, Nina Sun. 2015. *Sensing Sound: Singing and Listening as Vibrational Practice.* Durham, NC: Duke University Press.

Harraway, Donna. 2016. *Staying with the Trouble: Making Kin in the Chthulucene.* Durham, NC: Duke University Press.

Kapchan, Deborah. 2016. "Slow Activism: Listening to the Pain and Praise of Others." *International Journal of Middle East Studies* 48:115–19.

———. 2017. "The Splash of Icarus: Theorizing Sound Writing/Writing Sound Theory." In *Theorizing Sound Writing*, edited by Deborah Kapchan, 1–22. Middletown, CT: Wesleyan University Press.

Kisliuk, Michelle. (1998) 2000. *Seize the Dance! BaAka Musical Life and the Ethnography of Performance.* New York: Oxford University Press.

———. 2017. "Writing the Magnified Musicking Moment." In *Theorizing Sound Writing*, edited by Deborah Kapchan, 86–113. Middletown, CT: Wesleyan University Press.

Kisliuk, Michelle, with Justin Serge Mongosso. 2003. "Representing a Real Man: Music, Identity, and Upheaval in Centrafrique." *Emergences: Journal for the Study of Media and Composite Cultures* 13 (1): 33–46.

Kuruvilla, Elizabeth. 2016. "Amitav Ghosh: We Are Living Our Lives as Though We Are Mad." *Live Mint*, E-paper. July 18. https://tinyurl.com/z8sqwjg.

Le Guin, Ursula K. 2004. *The Wave in the Mind: Talks and Essays on the Writer, the Reader, and the Imagination.* Boston: Shambala.

Nancy, Jean-Luc. 2002. *Listening.* New York: Fordham University Press.

Nixon, Rob. 2011. *Slow Violence and the Environmentalism of the Poor.* Cambridge, MA: Harvard University Press.

Rosaldo, Renato. (1989) 1993. *Culture and Truth: The Remaking of Social Analysis.* Boston: Beacon Press.

Sarno, Louis. 1995. *Bayaka: The Extraordinary Music of the BaBenzele Pygmies and the Sounds of Their Forest Home.* Produced by Bernie Krause. Ellipsis Arts CD3490, compact disc.

Schechner, Richard. 1977. *Essays on Performance Theory, 1970–1976.* Ann Arbor: University of Michigan Press.

Titon, Jeff Todd. 1980. "The Life Story." *Journal of American Folklore* 93 (369): 276–92.

———. 2015. "Thoreau's Ear." *Sound Studies* 1 (1): 144–54.

Tyler, Stephen. 1986. "On Ethnographic Surrealism." In *Writing Culture: The Poetics and Politics of Ethnography*, edited by James Clifford and George Marcus, 122–40. Berkeley: University of California Press.

Viveiros de Castro, Eduardo. 2014. *Cannibal Metaphysics for a Post-Structural Anthropology.* Translated and edited by Peter Skafish. Minneapolis: Univocal.

CHAPTER 18

Lament and Affective Cardiac Responses

MARGARITA MAZO

THIS CHAPTER CONSIDERS the funeral lament as an integral part of
the larger adaptive process regulating negative emotions at crucial moments of
life. Sustainability of the lament is understood here in the spirit of Jeff Titon's
pioneering approach to sustainability of music culture (2015). For centuries,
the lament retained its capacity to change not only in response to extremely
emotional situations and life transformations but also as a direct channel of their
productive management. Ethnographic studies of the lament have demonstrated
its role both in expressing emotions of grief and bereavement and in mobilizing
social support systems. By juxtaposing the earlier ethnographic studies with
new empirical research on the affective cardiac responses to Russian laments,
this chapter offers insight into the lament's role in preventing the physical and
cognitive breakdown of the grief-stricken body. As such, I pursue the lament as
a critical component of the involuntary regulation of emotion vital to sustaining
human life.

On Lament in General

In many cultures of the world, laments have been passed down since ancient
times as expressions of grief, bereavement, and suffering. Scholarly works are
known on laments from China (McLaren 2008) to Palestine (Racy 1985), Greece
(Caraveli-Chaves 1980), Ireland (Ó Laoire 2005), Karelia (Gomon and Konkka
1977; Tolbert 1990, 2007), Hungary (Kiss and Rajeczky 1966), Papua New Guinea

(Feld 1982, 1990), Amerindian Brazil (Urban 1988, 1996), and beyond. In Russia, written records mentioning laments go back to the tenth century, but they clearly existed in oral tradition much earlier. Usually, the lamenters (lament performers) are women.

While extremely emotional and personal, laments are nevertheless strongly regulated by local traditions. Notwithstanding the immense diversity and local specificity of lament's melodic and poetic forms, its sound is recognizable across cultures. It merges singing, spoken and recited phrases, or just snippets of words, as well as expressive shouts and exclamations. It also encompasses paralinguistic gestures of crying and wailing, such as voiced breathing, tremors, gasps, sobs, rapid oscillations of pitch, and a tearful nasal timbre (Mazo 1978, 1994a; Urban 1988; Vaughn 1990). Collectively, these combined vocalizations engender the unmistakable sonic production of the lament. While doing fieldwork in Russian villages, I was struck repeatedly by local women's comments that lamenting is extremely emotional and disturbing, yet soothing: "Lamenting breaks my heart, but I feel better afterward" (field notes, 1975, Sonduga, Vologda Province; see also Mazo 1994a, 164). Considered along these lines, lamenting serves as a cathartic alleviation of grief, not unlike a healing trance, which Thomas Csordas analogizes as "a biocultural black box" (1994, 3). The experiment on affective cardiac responses to Russian laments discussed later in this chapter takes an initial step in unlocking it.

Russian Village Lament: Contexts and Consequences

In order to contextualize both lament's sustainability and the findings of the experiment, I highlight here some foundational ethnographic and performative aspects of Russian laments. In this, I draw on my earlier research on the ritual's contexts, symbolic meanings, and performative processes, as well as lament's intersubjective, sonic, and stylistic features (Mazo 1978, 1994a, 1994b).

In Russian villages, lament is a rich and heterogeneous phenomenon. It can assume a varying intensity, from utter despair and desolation to compliance and acceptance. Representing a fluid spectrum of expression, laments might be introversive and subdued and thus uttered in a soft voice, or angry and agonized with anguish and shouts. Our focus here is on the funeral lament, but laments can also be commemorative or matrimonial (now rare). They continue be heard in response to wars, natural disasters, and social turmoil. They are also performed in private nonritual contexts of feeling extremely sad or disturbed as well as feeling excited and happy. In short, laments occur in any context that may induce an adult to cry (see Vingerhoets et al. 2001 for a review of research on crying).[1]

In Russia, lament is commonly called *плач* (crying), and as made clear in the sonic connections outlined above, lamenting and crying have indeed much in common (Karelian laments are called "crying with words" in Tolbert 1990, 2007). Yet lamenting is far more complex than crying alone, and most importantly here, it is part of an elaborate ritual. With its social and emotive associations having been established through generations, lament's idiosyncratic sound often triggers weeping among villagers immediately upon hearing it. A lament usually starts softly, as a direct communication with the deceased ("Why did you leave me? . . . How am I going to live now?" etc.), then moves into an array of often conflicting emotions, from feeling lost or powerless or angry to finding consolation in happy memories (cf. crying in Ochsner and Gross 2005; O'Connor et al. 2007). As lamenting evolves and the emotions intensify, so too does the sound: the muscles and the entire vocal tract of the lamenter tighten to the extent that she cannot control her vocalization (see images of the vocal folds while lamenting and singing in Mazo et al. 2010). Under these conditions, all sound qualities, as well as all other performative features of lamenting, gradually lose stability and become increasingly chaotic. This escalating instability of the sound is one of the lament's defining features; it effectively conveys the emotional state of the lamenter and the sensibilities of those around her.

Other participants in the ritual react to the escalating vocal expression of the lamenter with tears and crying. More than this, they also enter into a symbiotic relationship with her, responding with physical and verbal gestures that project their understanding and willingness to help and reinforce their social bonding (cf. Vingerhoets et al. 2001 on crying). These expressions of empathy become especially vital at the end of lamenting because habitually the lamenter cannot stop of her own accord. She must rather be stopped by bodily contact, such as an embrace or other caring gesture of a relative or friend. Believing that the lamenter might succumb to physiological harm if not interrupted in time, vigilant observers watch over and stop her at the appropriate moment to prevent her cathartic lament becoming a physiological disaster (cf. Vingerhoets and Scheirs 2001 on crying; Becker 2007 on trance).

In some local traditions, professional lamenters—women invited to lament on behalf of others—still exist today. They are known for their personal predisposition and expertise in expressing the meaning of the situation but also for their ability to affect others emotionally and to "make everyone around cry" (field notes, 1975, Sonduga, Vologda Province), that is, to incite compassion and tears, to watch out for the griever, and to make the social bond with her stronger. The very existence of this professional institution in village life is telling as to the significance of the lament both in sustaining personal well-being and in keeping up the good of the community.

In addition to the multifarious aspects of lamenting mentioned, the process also helps the griever to comprehend the present through verbalization and externalization, as if expelling negative emotions from the body. Such dislocation of the negative condition is known cross-culturally to render certain emotions less painful, whether mentally or corporeally, and thus more manageable (e.g., Becker 2007; Wolf 2007). Yet amid the turbulence of grief and distress, the ability to give voice to one's feelings and to articulate inner chaos and pain does not come easily. Enabling the process is the embodied experience of the ritual's beneficence, ingrained from childhood in all participants, who understand that real help is readily available through lamenting and the emotional and corporeal responses it incites.

Lament is always improvised. It is composed anew every time in connection with the situational context, cognitive cultural experience, as well as the personal story, psychology, and physiology. Lament always changes, and no two laments are the same, even by the same person (cf. continually emerging folklore in Baron and Walker, this volume). Yet like any improvisation, it relies on the lamenter's ability to internalize and freely operate within the patterns and rules established by local tradition (see Finnegan 1988; Feld 1990). The latter regulates the lament's entire template, from its formulaic melodic and verbal expressions to its repetitive structure, including not only the placement of the sonic gestures of crying but also their acceptable length and volume. Communal tradition thus provides a ready-made and multi-channeled mold to voice the pain, denial, confusion, and disorder of death, all with the aim of helping one accept reality and find peace within oneself.[2]

This brief excursus sheds light on the centuries-old praxes of the lament, pointing out that one crucial function of the funeral lament is to provide a shield against the harmful consequences of bereavement, including the so-called broken-heart phenomenon. Moreover, the focus on the intensity of the lament's sound and the heterogeneity of its meanings for an enculturated person prepares the groundwork necessary to understand the lament as a sustainable phenomenon with an overwhelmingly long history.

A New Study: Affective Heart Responses to Russian Lament

Since the beginning of the century, a pivotal shift in focus toward the culture-dependent and individual correlates can be observed in psychology, linguistics, and, still more recently, in social and cultural branches of neuroscience (e.g., Kashdan and Rottenberg 2010; Patel 2008; Fields 2007; Han and Northoff 2008; Chiao and Ambady 2007). Now, according to neuroscientist Howard Fields, "the study of the context-determined components is an inherently interdisciplinary idea and is in its infancy" (2007, 59). Simultaneously, interdisciplinary scientific and humanities approaches have been increasingly gaining ground in ethnomusicological research (e.g., Becker 2009a, 2009b; Clayton, Sager, and Will 2005; Will 2011).

My project was seeded by two preliminary studies, both using the same field recordings as the experiment discussed here: a perceptual experiment on the listeners' verbal responses to the sonic and formal aspects of Russian laments (Meyer, Palmer, and Mazo 1998), and an empirical pilot experiments on respiratory changes while listening to Russian laments as compared to singing and speaking (conducted 2001–3). The studies demonstrated stronger responses to the laments with gasps and other gestures of crying. Both studies also indicated lament's structural features as a culture-specific factor, while performative sonic qualities of laments, such as vocal timbre and gestures of crying, were shown as culture-invariant.

The current research pursues the potential of these findings. It merges ethnomusicological and scientific methodologies by gauging the cardiac responses of culturally diverse listeners to a culturally specific form of Russian lament. Going beyond the listeners' self-assessments of their experiences, we "listen to" their hearts with the aim of understanding the interrelationships between the verbal and the physiological responses. The interactions between these two sources foreground the confluence of ethnographic salience and scientific significance in this study. The interdisciplinary methodology enables the ethnomusicological study of laments to move into new territory, effectively demonstrating both opportunities and challenges presented by the current dialogue between the humanities and the scientific disciplines.

A novel attempt to understand the heterogeneity and complexity of the lament's significance to different people and in different contexts, this study raises multiple important questions. Here I consider whether the sustainability of lament practice can be indicative of going beyond coping, and whether the psychophysiological efficacy of the lament might lie in its contribution to the prevention of emotional—and therefore cognitive and physical—paralysis during trying times when the emotions of negative valence are prone to become unmanageable.

Experiment's Design and Participants

During the experiment, the participants listened to five excerpts of field recordings from the Russian villages of Novokumskaya and Levokumskaya, Stavropol Province, while respiration, pulse, and electrocardiogram (ECG) were recorded and sampled by BioPac Systems, Inc. At the end, the participants were asked to fill out a questionnaire and comment on their experience during the experiment. These verbal responses guided our data analyses, although only the heart responses can be discussed here.[3]

To overcome the lack of control over the variables in the field-recorded stimuli, unusual for scientific experiments because of this reason (see Becker 2009a), this study was set to compare the responses to lament and nonlament. For this purpose, three different vocal modes of expressing sadness and grief—lamenting, speaking, and singing—were recorded from the same lamenter and with approximately the same texts to keep control over the vocal timbre and verbal content. The subject pool provided another level of control: almost all listeners were American-born Ohio State University students; none had any direct experience with either Russian village culture or lament. Their backgrounds were thus similar in important ways, but some were born into Russian-speaking families and had a native or near-native level of familiarity with the Russian language, literature, arts, food, and general family practices. The participants were divided into two groups based on enculturation to Russian culture or lack thereof; the groups were conditionally named "Russians" and "Non-Russians."

The Stimuli

Three stimuli, coded as "Lament," "Speaking," and "Singing," were used to compare lament and nonlament. All three were performed at my request by Mrs. G., who was not in mourning at the time but agreed to lament for her mother, long passed-away. Emotionally well controlled, her Lament did not contain any voiced inhalations, with voiced exhalations present in moderation. She then agreed to "sing and say the same words."

The fourth stimulus was a spontaneous lament of Mrs. S, who was in actual mourning for her son, recently deceased in an accident. Her highly emotional lament was saturated with heavily voiced inhalations and other sonic gestures of crying. This stimulus was coded as "InEx" (with a strong presence of voiced inhalation). Unlike the Lament stimulus, InEx naturally did not have voiced exhalations. To test the effect of voiced breathing, a fifth stimulus was added: the very same excerpt as in InEx, but with all voiced inhalations replaced by silences (ambient noise). This was "NoInEx" stimulus. All five stimuli thus had distinctly different vocal modes and emotional intensity.

Each stimulus consisted of three two-minute sections, called periods: (1) Base, or Baseline (silence), (2) Task, or Challenge (sound), and (3) Recovery (post-stimulus silence), with Task being one of the five stimuli described above. Base and Recovery were filled with ambient noise, respectively preceding and following the Task to provide a comparative before-and-after paradigm of heart conditions. Only the responses to three lament stimuli will be addressed here.

Why Heart Rate Variability (HRV)?

This study relies on Julian F. Thayer and Richard D. Lane's model of "neurovisceral integration" (2000), which integrates flexible associations between different neural networks into responses to situational demands by the central and autonomic nervous systems. The model's complexity and nonlinearity are impossible to address here at length, but three general principles derived from this model have framed the understanding of the heart responses in this study.

First, heart rate variability (HRV) refers to the beat-to-beat changes in heart rate (HR) that occur naturally as a function of fluctuations in the vagal nerve activity and symptomatic outputs. Mediated by the vagal nerve, HRV is associated with autonomic flexibility and adaptive emotional self-regulation: HRV is higher at rest (Base and Recovery periods of the stimuli), with normal vagal withdrawal and lowering HRV during any challenge (Task), that is, listening to the recorded sound. A higher level of resting HRV allows a fast reaction to situational demands (fight or flight), a sign of good health. Decreased resting HRV is linked to poor autonomic, attentional, emotional, and cognitive processing; low resting HRV is usually associated with the organism's dysfunction.

Second, HR and HRV are negatively correlated. That is, at rest, the healthy HR would be relatively low, with HRV being relatively high. Performance of any task, including those requiring sustained attention and emotional engagement, produce an increase of HR and a reduction in HRV. At the end of processing a task, HR and HRV normally revert to their resting levels.

Finally, HR is the result of a complex interplay of two main branches of the autonomic nervous system, the sympathetic and the parasympathetic nervous systems. The former mediates cardiac systems at the level of seconds, while the latter operates in milliseconds, securing quick responses and adaptability. The high frequency (HF) component of the HRV power spectrum is a reliable index of parasympathetic activity. For that reason, our HRV analyses are based on the HF data.

To examine the dynamics of physiological change, HR was extracted from ECG, and HRV was calculated from interbeat interval (the distance between the high peaks of the consecutive heartbeats, measured in milliseconds), according to a highly sensitive and complex method.[4] Subsequent statistical analyses examined the relationships between cardiac responses, cultural background, and individual physiology (resting HRV level). All results were compared with the participants' self-evaluations and verbal comments.

Results and Discussion

Significant differences in behavior between the Russian and Non-Russian groups were observed in the course of the experiment: while Non-Russians exhibited a wide variety of reactions to the stimuli, ranging from boredom and laughter to extreme empathy and tears, the reactions of the Russians were largely uniform. The self-reported verbal responses were far apart as well. Initial statistical analyses of heart responses calculated as averages of all participants, however, showed no clearly identifiable leanings, with two exceptions: HR responses to Lament and InEx (figure 18.1) and HRV in responses to the spontaneous InEx only (figure 18.2), both with a high statistical significance of p-value <.01 (p-value < .05 indicates statistical significance of any test result). Both are important finds and will be discussed below. Still, all other cardiac responses showed no statistically significant difference, contradicting the observations and self-reported comments. I hypothesized that the statistical averaging of data had masked the differences in individual responses within each group.

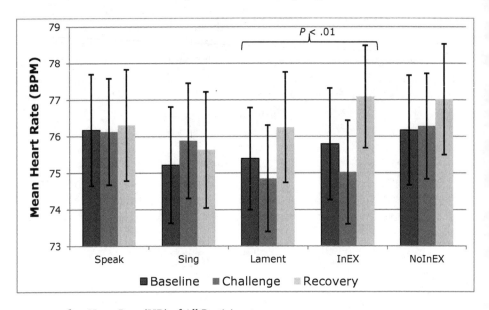

FIG. 18.1. Heart Rate (HR) of All Participants

There was a main effect of B_C_R—*Wilks' Lambda* = .018 F(2,49) = 5.46, $p < .006$, $\eta_p^2 = .18$, indicating HR change across the Base (Baseline), Task (Challenge), and Recovery. Follow-up Bonferroni-adjusted t-tests indicated that it was the Challenge (M = 75.63) and Recovery (M = 76.45) values ($p < .01$) that differed. There was a significant two-way interaction with Task and B_C_R—*Wilks' Lambda* = .020 F(8,43) = 3.36, $p < .001$, $\eta_p^2 = .38$. Planned interaction contrasts indicated that the patterns of response for the Lament and InEx Tasks were different from the other three Tasks F(1,50) = 7.62, $p < .01$. Statistical analyses showed that participants were more responsive to these two Tasks, even after the Task itself was finished, as compared to the three other Challenges (Sing, Speak, NoInEx) F(1,50) = 7.62, $p < .05$).

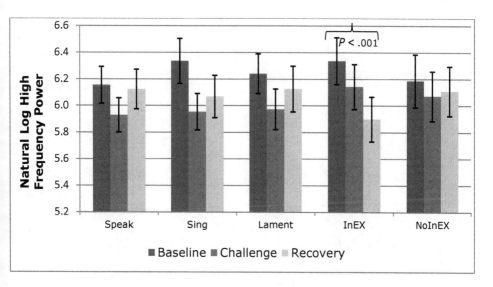

FIG. 18.2. Heart Rate Variability (HRV) of All Participants

There was a main effect of B_C_R—*Wilks' Lambda* = .84 F(2,49) = 36.30, $p < .02$, $\eta_p^2 = .16$, indicating HRV changed across the Baseline, Challenge, and Recovery phases. Follow-up Bonferroni-adjusted t-tests indicated that the difference was mainly Baseline (M = 6.25) to Challenge (M = 6.01) $p < .02$, but was also marginally different from Baseline (M = 6.25) to Recovery (M = 6.06) $p < .058$. In essence, vagally mediated HRV withdrew during the Challenges across all Tasks with a trend toward recovery subsequently.

There was a significant two-way interaction between Challenge × B_C_R—*Wilks' Lambda* = .71 F(8,43) = 2.21, $p < .05$, $\eta_p^2 = .29$. Planned interaction contrasts indicated that only InEx produced a pattern of vagal withdrawal that was linear, while the other Challenges produced quadratic effects indicating situationally appropriate processing and recovery F(1,39) = 11.44, $p < .001$.

To test this hypothesis, both the Russian and the Non-Russian groups were subdivided according to a median split of individual resting HRV level as an index of responsiveness (in line with the Thayer and Lane model). The split produced four subgroups to compare: Non-Russians higher HRV (n = 22), Non-Russians lower HRV (n = 20), Russians higher HRV (n = 6), and Russians lower HRV (n = 7). Introducing the resting HRV level as an additional between-subject factor became a fortuitous methodological solution with important results (figure 18.3). The new analyses showed that different stimuli produced clearly different patterns of heart responses. Both individual physiology (resting HRV level) and enculturation (e.g., understanding the meaning of words, and having the ability to contextualize the sound and connect it to previous experience) were shown to be consequential. The interactions of these two factors defined the potential for sustainable patterns of responses to laments.

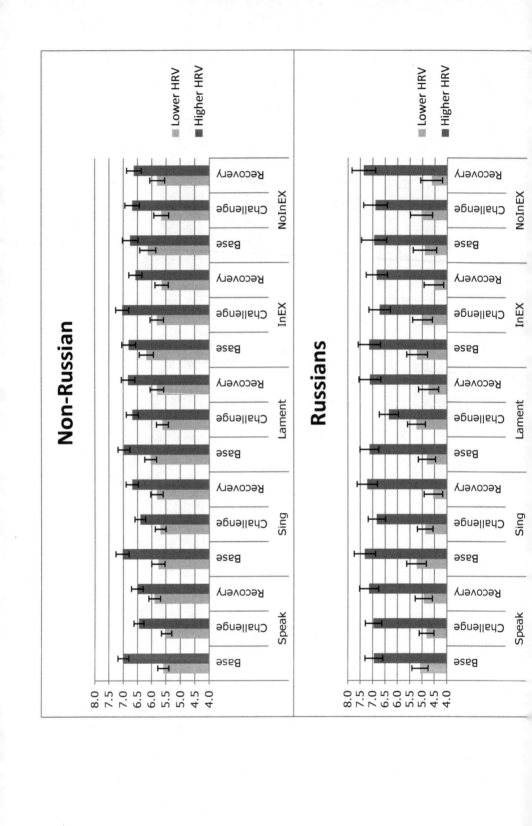

We now turn to the results of the statistical analyses to explain these conclusions. It may be worth remembering that both Lament and InEx stimuli were taken from emotional but distinct performances, with the sound of crying being unrestrained and raw in the spontaneous InEx, while subdued, albeit readily discernible, in Lament. This may explain the special patterns of physiological responses to these stimuli.

Figure 18.1 shows statistically significant HR responses of all participants to both Lament and InEx: the HR kept consistently rising during Recovery, meaning that the processing of the experience continued in the listeners' bodies even after the sound stopped (cf. Graham 1975). Figure 18.2, meanwhile, shows that the HRV responses to Lament were not overwhelming enough to keep HRV down in Recovery, whereas the spontaneous InEx produced a uniquely linear pattern of lowering HRV from Base through Recovery. No other stimuli show such a response in figure 18.2. This linear pattern indicates that InEx was truly propelling the heart responses in all groups to be not only strong but also prolonged: the participants were still ruminating on and processing what they had just heard beyond the time of listening per se.

The new analyses of the same data, now split according to individual resting HRV, yields meaningfully nuanced results (figure 18.3). In all groups, responses to Lament and InEx during the Task period confirm the results in figures 18.1 and 18.2, but the Recovery period appears to be conditioned by both individual physiology and enculturation. To wit, the linear pattern of lowering HRV in InEx seen for all participants in figure 18.2 now appears only in participants

FIG. 18.3. (Opposite Page) Heart Rate Variability by High- and Low-HRV-Level Participants of Russian and Non-Russian Groups

As expected, there was a between-subjects main effect for HRV level $F(1,50) = 36.30$, $p < .001$, $\eta_p^2 = .42$, indicating that the higher-HRV-level group did have higher HRV than the lower-level group. In addition, there was an interaction between Russian status × HRV level $F(1,50) = 5.521$, $p < .03$ $\eta_p^2 = .10$ characterized by higher-HRV individuals showing little difference between Russian and Non-Russian groups, while lower-HRV Russians had the lowest HRV of all the groups.

Finally, there was a significant three-way interaction of B_C_R × Russian Status × HRV level—*Wilks' Lambda* = .84 $F(2,49) = 4.80$, $p < .02$, $\eta_p^2 = .16$. Follow-up planned contrasts tests indicated that the Non-Russian lower-HRV group showed a significant quadratic pattern of response $F(1,50) = 5.03$, $p < .05$, while the corresponding Russian group showed a linear pattern of response $F(1,50) = 14.86$, $p < .003$. Importantly, the higher-HRV Russians showed a quadratic pattern $F(1,50) = 5.05$) $p < .03$, while the Non-Russians did not $F(1,50) = 2.16$, $p > .05$. To summarize, the higher-HRV Russians showed a pattern of vagal regulation consistent with good regulation, while the lower-HRV Russians showed continued vagal withdrawal at Recovery.

with a lower resting HRV, both Russian and Non-Russian. Moreover, Russians with a lower HRV level also showed the same pattern in Singing and a tendency toward it in their responses to Lament and NoInEx. The latter observation is not supported by statistical significance, although the trend of the prolonged processing in this group is apparent. The reasons could be multiple. For example, the stimuli are too complex or new and difficult to understand even for Russian participants; the nature of these stimuli is too intense and stressful; the individual physiology of these participants, namely, low resting HRV, required more time to process the experience even beyond the Task period. Citing Jos Brosschot, Suzanne Pieper, and Julian Thayer (2005) in a private electronic communication, John Sollers suggested that this pattern might also be viewed as "a perseverative process whereas threatening or uncertain events are replayed in the mind as rumination or prognosticated about via worry (worry and rumination have both been shown to affect HR and HRV)." The connection of this response pattern with perseverative cognition could indeed be a good explanation for this find, although it needs to be examined further in future studies. One thing is clear, I reiterate: the linear pattern of responses indicates that all lower HRV participants in both groups were strongly affected by the spontaneous lament InEx and were still overwhelmed, ruminating, and dealing with what they had just heard even after the sound was gone.

In contrast, this linear pattern did not occur in higher HRV level participants, whether Russian or Non-Russian. Instead, they showed an adaptive quadratic pattern of HRV responses across the stimuli, whereas HRV is higher at Base and Recovery with the normal HRV drop during Task (the change in high HRV Non-Russians is minimal for the last stimulus). Thus, the individuals with a higher resting HRV level completed the processing of all stimuli by the end of the Task period, according to a quadratic pattern considered in psychophysiology as a situationally appropriate regulation. As multiple articles have shown, a higher resting HRV level is associated with better emotion regulation and processing (Thayer and Lane 2000, 2009; Thayer et al. 2012).

The above comparison of the HRV responses between Russian and Non-Russian listeners highlights the most interesting interactions of enculturation, cognition, and individual physiology. Even though Russian participants had never heard a village lament before, they were aware of it from literature, films, and so on and could contextualize the sound. This, in addition to their ability to understand the conveyance of sadness and grief with the texts themselves, informed their listening such that each stimulus had an emotional relevance for Russian listeners—the finding supported by the verbal responses. Furthermore, their general cultural familiarity also helped them to process the stimuli—no matter how distressing—more effectively. Accordingly, their responses were more affected by all stimuli than were the responses of the Non-Russian listeners, who recognized and responded to the sonic gestures of crying in the "real" lament—not culture-specific features in InEx—but were not particularly affected by other stimuli.

Beyond InEx, the absence of noteworthy differences in the response patterns to other stimuli among Non-Russian participants suggests that—unlike in the Russian groups—the level of resting HRV did not play as significant a role in responses to the specificity of the stimuli. Rather, the HRV patterns indexed the significance of enculturation, or lack thereof in this case, by showing a relatively similar ability to recover to baseline levels after each stimulus. Alternatively, the Non-Russian individuals may have been less engaged in the tasks, with their physiological responses reflecting their inability to contextualize the sound.

The relatively small participant pool, the Russian group particularly, explains the lower statistical power of some results, yet the results nevertheless allow us to trace the patterns and trends of change in the responses to different stimuli by the participants of different cultural and resting HRV groups. Such findings are distinctly important at this stage of applying a controlled and methodologically sound approach to new experimental research.

To summarize, by analyzing the listeners' verbal and cardiac responses to excerpts from Russian laments, we observe that the heart "hears": the HRV systematically changes across three sonically different periods of each stimulus. Furthermore, backed by subjective verbal assessments, the HRV analyses suggest that the special sonic qualities of the laments determine the negative valence of the stimuli regardless of the listeners' cultural background. These are strong culture-invariant cues. Significantly, this observation holds true even if some of the Non-Russian listeners perceived the negative valence of crying as the positive-valence laughter, due to certain sonic features they share, the exhalatory gasps particularly. A discussion of this remarkable result, however, is beyond the scope of this paper.

The study isolated voiced breathing as a significant culture-invariant sonic marker of intense emotion. It was perceived as such independently of individual physiology or cultural familiarity. Voiced breathing in the spontaneous InEx was strongly affective cross-culturally, whereas in Lament it was significantly less, apparently due to the subtlety of this sonic gesture of crying in this particular performance.

We can now discern important multilevel interactions between different sonic expressions of grief, the listeners' cultural competence, individual physiology, and cardiac responses. Cultural intimacy renders cognitive connections with previous experiences possible, thus affecting the heart responses to emotions in the stimuli. At the same time, the individual's physiology plays an equally crucial role in the listener's ability to process emotions in line with the psychophysiological pattern of good regulation. These opposite trends in the results of the experiment suggest that listening to all modes of Russian lament elicit emotional arousal in enculturated listeners, but the ability to recover from negative emotions is significantly affected by the individual's physiological flexibility, as indexed by HRV. People with low resting HRV levels are likely to be particularly vulnerable during prolonged lamenting, and traditional lament practices seem to take steps to prevent potentially harmful consequences.

We should keep in mind that in a contextual performance of funeral laments the emotional recovery as indexed by HRV never depends on any single source, even as heterogeneous as the laments sound. The affective power of the lament is rebuilt every time in connection with the participant's own experience and personal correlates, and as much as the repeated exposure to laments constitutes a foundation of understanding them, the diversity and complexity of the lament's significance also come from beyond the lament itself. The elaborate ritual of which lament is an indispensable part provides appropriate situational contexts in which lamenting is called for and can be safely performed. These specific moments, as well as those when lamenting would not be appropriate, are well known and anticipated by everyone present. In addition to managing the timing of lamenting and limiting the contextual possibilities for spontaneous outbursts of emotions, potentially dangerous for the griever, the ritual guides the behavior of other participants as well, supports the ability of lamenting to induce their empathy, and provides comfort for a lament's cathartic ending. Lamenting as an entire phenomenon, then, is a well-regulated process that facilitates understanding and acceptance of the extreme situation, thereby introducing some order amid the disturbance, pain, and chaos of death. The totality of these factors may hold a clue to understanding the local reports of "feeling better afterward."

* * *

This study brings together ethnomusicological and psychophysiological paradigms to understand the effects of laments as expressions of grief, bereavement, suffering, and pain on enculturated and nonenculturated listeners. The multifarious evidence we considered here supports understanding of the lament far beyond its role as a coping mechanism. It helps regulate severe negative emotions by helping alleviate emotional tension, thus sustaining the health of a person in despair and detached from reality.

Pending the final confirmation by a larger study, this chapter proposes that for an enculturated listener, lamenting has a strong effect on emotion arousal, secures social comfort and the emotional support of others, and strengthens social and personal bonding within the entire community. For a grieving person, lamenting also advances an understanding and reassessment of the environment, the feelings, and the self in a critical moment of life. It externalizes pain and cognitive conflicts and plays an active role in preventing the "broken-heart phenomenon." The study also shows that only through convergence of physiological, cognitive-cultural, individual, and intersubjective factors is a person able to receive the full benefits of the affective power of lament to make one "feel better."

The heterogeneity and transformative power of the lament—and most plausibly other expressive forms for that matter—to effect change in the body, the heart rate variability in particular, can be considered a source of involuntary regulation of negative emotions in extreme situations. Collectively, all the praxes of the lament discussed here, coupled with the understanding of these praxes as widely known throughout human history and geography as a part of life-sustaining behaviors, point to the vital role of lament within the larger adaptive processes that sustain human life.

Notes

1. Sometimes women also start lamenting when they are happy and excited to the extent of being unable to control their emotions. This very interesting and little-known phenomenon cannot be deliberated here, but see a discussion of the vocal gestures of crying, especially the exhalatory gaps, at the end of this chapter.

2. Aaron Allen's thought-provoking chapter in this volume makes it tempting to examine lament within his sustainability-change/sustainability-maintain paradigm, taken as a continuum, rather than as a dichotomy.

3. The experiment was conducted in the Ohio State University Ethnomusicology Lab; the study's protocol was approved by the IRB of the Ohio State University. OSU graduate students Ursula Crosslin, Ken Archer, and Stafford Cole Harrison were my research assistants. Mr. Harrison was particularly involved during the last two years of the experiment, when in addition to administering the final stage of the experiment and data retrieval he participated in the preliminary data analyses and discussions. Initial statistical data analyses were done at the Department of Statistics by Christopher Holoman and the Department of Psychology Lab by La Barron Hill, then a PhD candidate. The completion of this project would not have been possible without the support and contribution of John J. Sollers III, professor of psychology at North Carolina Central University. He made the final high-level analyses of the statistical data and consulted my interpretation of the scientific results. Professor Sollers also prepared the figures with scientific annotations for this chapter.

4. According to Professor Sollers, the raw EKGs, sampled at 1,000 Hz, were preprocessed using a custom beat-detection utility to derive the interbeat interval series (in milliseconds), manually inspected, segmented, and exported in ASCII text format, then imported into the Kubios Heart Rate Variability Analysis Package (Tarvainen et al. 2009), and the estimates of HRV were derived. Using spectral analytic techniques (Task Force 1996), the natural log of absolute HF power was retained for present analyses.

References

Becker, Judith. 2007. "Music, Trancing, and the Absence of Pain." In *Pain and Its Trans-formations: The Interface of Biology and Culture*, edited by Sarah Coakley and Kay Kaufman Shelemay, 166–94. Cambridge, MA: Harvard University Press.

———. 2009a. "Ethnomusicology and Empiricism in the Twenty-First Century." *Ethnomusicology* 53 (3): 478–501.

———. 2009b. "Crossing Boundaries: An Introductory Essay." *Empirical Musicology Review* 4 (2): 45–48.

Brosschot, Jos F., Suzanne Pieper, and Julian F. Thayer. 2005. "Expanding Stress Theory: Prolonged Activation and Perseverative Cognition." *Psychoneuroendocrinology* 30 (10) (November): 1043–49.

Caraveli-Chaves, Anna. 1980. "Bridge between Words: The Greek Woman's Lament as Communicative Event." *Journal of American Folklore* 93 (368): 129–57.

Chiao, Joan Y., and Nalini Ambady. 2007. "Cultural Neuroscience: Parsing Universality and Diversity across Levels of Analysis." In *Handbook of Cultural Psychology*, edited by Shinobu Kitayama and Dov Cohen, 237–54. New York: Guilford Press.

Clayton, Martin, Rebecca Sager, and Udo Will. 2005. "In Time with the Music: The Concept of Entrainment and Its Significance for Ethnomusicology." *European Meetings in Ethnomusicology* 11:1–75.

Csordas, Thomas. 1994. *The Sacred Self: A Cultural Phenomenology of Charismatic Healing.* Berkeley: University of California Press.

Feld, Steven. 1982. *Sound and Sentiment: Birds, Weeping, Poetics, and Song in Kaluli Expression.* Philadelphia: University of Pennsylvania Press.

———. 1990. "Wept Thoughts: The Voicing of Kaluli Memories." *Oral Tradition* 5 (2–3): 241–66.

Fields, Howard. 2007. "Setting the Stage for Pain: Allegorical Tales from Neuroscience." In *Pain and Its Transformations: The Interface of Biology and Culture*, edited by Sarah Coakley and Kay Kaufman Shelemay, 36–61. Cambridge, MA: Harvard University Press.

Finnegan, Ruth. 1988. *Literacy and Orality: Studies in the Technology of Communication.* Oxford: Blackwell.

Gomon, Alla, and Unelma Konkka. 1977. "Karel'skie prichitaniya" [Karelian laments]. In *Musial Heritage of the Finnish-Ugric Peoples*, edited by Ingrid Rüütel, 323–53. Tallin: Eesti raamat.

Graham, Frances K. 1975. "The More or Less Startling Effects of Weak Prestimulation." *Psychophysiology* 12 (3): 238–48.

Han, Shihui, and Georg Northoff. 2008. "Culture-Sensitive Neural Substrates of Human Cognition: A Transcultural Neuroimaging Approach." *Nature Reviews Neuroscience* 8: 646–54.

Kashdan, Todd B., and Jonathan Rottenberg. 2010. "Psychological Flexibility as a Fundamental Aspect of Health." *Clinical Psychology Review* 30 (2): 865–78.

Kiss, Lajos, and Benjamin Rajeczky. 1966. *Siratók* [Laments]. Corpus Musicae Popularis Hungaricae 5. Budapest: Akadémiai Kiadó.

Mazo, Margarita. 1978. "Nikol'skie prichitaniia i ikh svyasi s drugimi zhanrami mestnoi pesennoi traditsii" [Nikol'sk laments and their relations with other songs of the local tradition]. In *Muzykal'naya folkloristika* [Musical folklore studies], edited by A. A. Banin, vol. 2, 213–35. Moscow: Sovetskii Kompozitor.

———. 1994a. "Lament Made Visible: A Study of Paramusical Features in Russian Laments." In *Theme and Variations: Writings on Music in Honor of Rulan Chao Pian*, edited by Bell Yung and Joseph Lam, 164–212. Cambridge, MA: Harvard University Press.

———. 1994b. "Wedding Laments in North Russian Villages." In *Music Cultures in Contact*, edited by Margaret Kartomi and Stephen Blum, 21–40. Basel: Gordon and Breach Science Publishers.

Mazo, Margarita, Ken-ichi Sakakibara, Hiroshi Imagawa, Niro Tayama, and Donna Erickson. 2010. "Vocal Fold Vibration in Lamenting, Speaking and Singing." In *Intersinging, University of Tokyo, 2010*, Conference Proceedings, 15–22. Tokyo: University of Tokyo.

McLaren, Anne E. 2008. *Performing Grief: Bridal Laments in Rural China*. Honolulu: University of Hawai'i Press.

Meyer, Rosalee, Caroline Palmer, and Margarita Mazo. 1998. "Affective and Coherence Responses to Russian Laments." *Music Perception* 16 (1): 135–50.

Ochsner, Kevin N., and James Gross. 2005. "The Cognitive Control of Emotion." *Trends in Cognitive Sciences* 9 (5): 242–49.

O'Connor, Mary-Frances, Harald Gunel, Kateri McRae, and Richard D Lane. 2007. "Baseline Vagal Tone Predicts BOLD Response during Elicitation of Grief." *Neuropsychopharmacology* 32 (10): 2184–89.

Ó Laoire, Lillis. 2005. "Irish Music." In *The Cambridge Companion to Modern Irish Culture*, edited by Joe Cleary and Claire Connoly, 267–303. Cambridge: Cambridge University Press.

Patel, Aniruddh D. 2008. *Music, Language, and the Brain*. New York: Oxford University Press.

Racy, Ali Jihad. 1985. *Laments of Lebanon*. New York: Ethnic Folkways Library FE 4046, LP.

Tarvainen, M. P., J. P. Niskanen, J. A. Lipponen, P. O. Ranta-Aho, and P. A. Karijalainen. 2009. Kubios HRV (software). Kubios Ltd.

Task Force. 1996. "Heart Rate Variability: Standards of Measurement, Physiological Interpretation, and Clinical Use." *European Heart Journal* 17:354–81.

Thayer, Julian F., Fredrik Åhs, Mats Fredrikson, John J. Sollers III, and Tor D. Wager. 2012. "A Meta-Analysis of Heart Rate Variability and Neuroimaging Studies: Implications for Heart Rate Variability as a Marker of Stress and Health." *Neuroscience & Biobehavioral Reviews* 36 (2): 747–56.

Thayer, Julian F., and Richard D. Lane. 2000. "A Model of Neurovisceral Integration in Emotion Regulation and Dysregulation." *Journal of Affective Disorders* 61 (3): 201–16.

———. 2009. "Claude Bernard and the Heart-Brain Connection: Further Elaboration of a Model of Neurovisceral Integration." *Neuroscience & Biobehavioral Reviews* 33 (2): 81–88.

Titon, Jeff Todd. 2015. "Sustainability, Resilience and Adaptive Management." In *The Oxford Handbook of Applied Ethnomusicology*, edited by Svanibor Pettan and Jeff Todd Titon, 157–98. New York: Oxford University Press.

Tolbert, Elizabeth. 1990. "Women Cry with Words: Symbolization of Affect in the Karelian Lament." *Yearbook for Traditional Music* 22:80–105.

———. 2007. "Pain and Transformation in the Finnish-Karelian Ritual Lament." In *Pain and Its Transformations: The Interface of Biology and Culture*, edited by Sarah Coakley and Kay Kaufman Shelemay, 147–65. Cambridge, MA: Harvard University Press.

Urban, Greg. 1988. "Ritual Wailing in Amerindian Brazil." *American Anthropologist* 90 (2): 385–400.

———. 1996. "Metaphysical Community." *The Interplay of the Senses and the Intellect.* Austin: University of Texas Press.

Vaughn, Kathryn. 1990. "Exploring Emotion in Sub-Structural Aspects of Karelian Lament: Application of the Time Series Analysis to Digitized Melody." *Yearbook for Traditional Music* 22:106–22.

Vingerhoets, Ad J. J. M., A. Jan Boelhouwer, Miranda A. L. Van Tilburg, and Guus L. Van Heck. 2001. "The Situational and Emotional Context of Adult Crying." In *Adult Crying: A Biopsychosocial Approach*, edited by Ad J. J. M. Vingerhoets and Randolph R. Cornelius, 71–90. Hove, UK: Brunner-Routledge.

Vingerhoets, Ad J. J. M, and Jan G. M. Scheirs. 2001. "Crying and Health." In *Adult Crying: A Biopsychosocial Approach*, edited by Ad J. J. M. Vingerhoets and Randolph R. Cornelius, 227–46. Hove, UK: Brunner-Routledge.

Will, Udo. 2011. "EEG Research Methodology and Brainwave Entrainment." In *Music, Science and the Rhythmic Brain: Cultural and Clinical Implications*, edited by J. Berger and G. Turow, 86–107. New York: Routledge.

Wolf, Richard K. 2007. "Doubleness, *Mātam*, and Muharram Drumming in South Asia." In *Pain and Its Transformations: The Interface of Biology and Culture*, edited by Sarah Coakley and Kay Kaufman Shelemay, 331–50. Cambridge, MA: Harvard University Press.

PART 5

Applying Sustainable Practices

CHAPTER 19

Resilience and Adaptive Management in Piano Pedagogy for Individuals with Autism Spectrum Conditions

DOTAN NITZBERG AND MICHAEL B. BAKAN

THE COAUTHORS OF THIS CHAPTER are a concert pianist who was diagnosed with the autism spectrum condition Asperger's syndrome (Nitzberg 2012) and an ethnomusicologist whose current research focuses on musicians with autism spectrum conditions, or ASCs (Bakan 2014a, 2014b, 2015a, 2015b, 2016a, 2016b, 2018).[1] We write as a collaborative pair of scholar-musician-teacher-activists interested in developing effective methods of music pedagogy for individuals with ASCs.[2] Our purpose is to advance pedagogical approaches that, beyond their specific musical uses, hold the potential for wider applications: improving quality of life for people on the autism spectrum, fostering better communication between them and their neurotypical peers, and cultivating a culture of increased mutual understanding across the expansive range of human neurodiversity.

We believe that such approaches have the capacity to foster *resilience*, which Jeff Todd Titon defines as "a system's capacity to recover and maintain its integrity, identity, and continuity when subjected to forces of disturbance and change" (Titon 2015, 158). ASC musical professionalism is the system at issue here, and our interest is in exploring how resilience may be fostered through strategies of *adaptive management*, that is, in Titon's terms, strategies that serve the system's "goal of sustainability" by "strengthening resilience and decreasing vulnerability in social groups facing undesirable change, and in individuals facing stress and trauma" (158).

We are well aware that these are unconventional interpretations and applications of Titon's resilience and adaptive management concepts, and also that Titon himself likely never envisioned a "system" along the lines of what we are calling ASC musical professionalism falling within their purview. Yet for us they do, both in the immediate terms of the case at hand and in the rather different light of a questioning orientation, specifically one that asks quite broadly what we might learn about the role of musical cultures in sustaining communities and (eco)systems (a guiding question for this book as a whole) from intimate and interpersonal pedagogical engagements such as those to be explored here.

Notes on Research Basis, Terminology, and the Perspective from Which We Write

This chapter is based principally on a series of online interviews that Bakan conducted with Nitzberg between May and July 2016. Additional material was drawn from an earlier set of such interviews that took place from February to June 2014. Quotations of Nitzberg from both sets of interviews appear throughout the text, with the date of the interview identified by a parenthetical in-text citation in each case. Additional quotations drawn from the script of a lecture titled "How to Teach Piano [to] People with Asperger," which Nitzberg wrote and delivered at the 2012 World Piano Teachers Association (WPTA) conference in Novi Sad, Serbia, also appear in the chapter. We use a parenthetical in-text citation, (Nitzberg 2012), to reference these quotations.

Some prefatory remarks concerning terminology are in order. We often used the terms "Asperger" and "Aspergers" as direct identifiers in place of more standard nomenclature (e.g., a pianist with Asperger's syndrome) during the dialogues leading to this chapter. This was not common linguistic practice, but it conformed to Nitzberg's parlance at the time. He stated, for example, "If you want an Asperger to succeed and develop, you have to instruct him and be specific" (May 13, 2016). He also used the common slang identifiers "Aspie" and "Aspies" in his discourse "to avoid over-formality," and we have included those terms here as well where appropriate. It is emphasized, however, that in light of incontrovertible recent evidence concerning the involvement of Hans Asperger—from whom "Asperger's syndrome" takes its name—in Nazi child euthanasia programs (Czech 2018), rejection of Asperger/Asperger's designations by individuals like Dotan Nitzberg who formerly identified with them is inevitable.

Yet Nitzberg resists identification as autistic, as *an* autistic, or as a person with autism, as well. "At times it can sound very rough to hear," he explains, adding that he feels "odd with the term 'autistic,'" mainly on account of hurtful "past experiences that lodged in [his] memory." He says, "Many musicians offended me by saying [that I was] 'emotionally handicapped,' 'playing like an autist,' and other derogatory comments as such. People who claim that are ignorant and should be ignored. They do not comprehend that at the moment Aspergers tackle a piece they recognize the character and 'emotion' right away. It's instilled there. Their intensity, concentration, and involvement [are] so high that it seems as if they are [just] 'doing their own thing,' [but that's a wrong impression]. . . . Only people with [a] sixth sense—that is, endowed with sensitivity beyond the average—can catch it" (June 19, 2014).[3]

Michael Bakan formerly served on Dotan's graduate supervisory committee in the College of Music at Florida State University (FSU), where Dotan was pursuing graduate studies in piano performance and pedagogy. Michael has heard Dotan perform in recital on multiple occasions. He regards Dotan as an exceptional musical artist and as a pianist who plays with deep expression and emotion. For him, the very idea that Dotan's playing could be judged as emotionally deficient is simply unfathomable. Perhaps only Dotan himself is more mystified by such appraisals. He states, "Throughout my life I had opportunities to play for fellow musicians, and whenever they were asked to give me their [assessments of my performance], many of them didn't manage to absorb my distinct way of expression and said I have an emotional shortage. To tell you frankly, it left me confused since Aspergers have [an] overdose of feelings, not a shortage!" (June 9, 2014).

As the coauthors of this chapter, we share the conviction that such criticisms are essentially groundless, emerging from misguided stereotypes about what people on the autism spectrum are like and what they are capable of. Subverting such stereotypes will not be our focus here, however. Our goal is to build bridges, not burn them. We draw on Dotan's own experiences and perspectives to do this, arguing for pedagogical approaches that compel teachers of ASC students—in piano and other areas—to develop an attuned sensitivity to their distinctive musical proclivities, an abiding commitment to accepting these proclivities as viable, and an eager willingness to work creatively, flexibly, and collaboratively toward their accommodation.

Adaptive Management and Strategies of Resilience

Pianists on the spectrum like Dotan face an untenable pair of options in the brutally competitive world of concert music performance: "pass" for neurotypical or be excluded from the ranks of "real" concert artists. Dotan's life story exemplifies this dilemma. Music has been at the center of his life since earliest childhood, serving as his main channel for artistic creation, personal expression, social connection, and self-identity. "I started talking fluently [in Hebrew] at the age of nine months," he reports, "and the first complete sentence I said was: 'That's what I want . . . Music! Music!' [Shortly] afterwards I was rushed to hospital due to an unknown cause, but my condition improved dramatically when my father placed a toy keyboard next to my pillow, and I was fascinated to discover that when I pressed a row of keys it produced a very pleasant sound" (June 9, 2014).

Dotan's formal piano studies began at age five. At ten he came under the tutelage of the Israeli pedagogue Yanina Kudlik and studied with her for the next twelve years. His progress under Kudlik was swift and impressive but was sometimes impacted by "panic attacks [that] originated from rough experiences and fears [he] kept within [him]self, [along] with [a] constant feeling of low self-esteem" (June 9, 2014). These problems compelled Dotan and his parents to seek professional help, ultimately leading to his Asperger's diagnosis. This had an immediate, positive effect: "At the moment I was diagnosed I felt relieved, that finally I have answers to all of those unsolved questions I carried within myself" (June 9, 2014).

Unfortunately, this quantum leap in self-understanding and acceptance did not necessarily translate into Dotan being better understood or appreciated by others. His talent and dedication to his art carried him to prestigious prizes in piano competitions in Israel and ultimately to winning large scholarships for university music studies in the United States. As he climbed higher on the rungs of the concert piano world's cut-throat competitive ladder, however, the very abilities for which he had been lauded early on—extraordinary feats of musical memory, dazzling technical brilliance, an attention to minute musical details to the point of apparent obsession—were turned against him by his critics, who were inclined to quickly relegate him to the status of an "autistic savant" (Straus 2014). According to their logic, fueled by a plethora of pervasive stereotypes, "autistics" like Dotan inherently lacked emotion, were deficient in empathy and creative capacity, and were impaired in most every area of social relations and communicative interaction. Thus "common sense" dictated that they could not be genuine musical artists at all, for how could true artistry emerge in the purported absence of the core emotional foundations that make people, and in turn the music they make, so quintessentially *human*?[4]

Such bigotry has damaged Dotan both professionally and personally, but he, like many on the spectrum, is nothing if not resilient. That resilience has enabled him to pursue the life he wants and deserves to have—the life of a concert pianist and a pedagogue—despite all obstacles (cf. Kisliuk on resilience in BaAka singing communities, this volume). He thrived in that pursuit under the mentorship of his two major professors in the FSU graduate piano program, Read Gainsford (performance) and Diana Dumlavwalla (pedagogy), and also on account of his own creativity and tenacious resourcefulness. "No matter how greatly I have benefited from my teacher's instructions," Dotan professes, "it never suffices [for] me. I feel this urge of trying things on my own. This is my nature" (July 27, 2016).

Dotan's spirit of adventure and commitment to advocating for people on the spectrum underlie his adaptive management strategies. While initially developed for his personal growth and professional advancement, they now form the basis of a committed effort to foster more-productive relationships between ASC pianists and their teachers, empowering both parties to more "creatively explore the possibilities of human thriving" through cultural partnership (see Turner, this volume). These strategies rest on a premise that Dotan describes as follows: "Many times Aspergers, and musicians [with this condition] in particular, know what they would like to achieve, but they cannot always define the means of how to achieve their goals. I am committed to defining and developing such means, both for my own sake and for others" (May 4, 2016).

Yet addressing this issue is only half of the equation. The other half concerns cultivating greater mutual understanding and more productive relationships between neurodiverse and neurotypical people, and in particular between neurotypical piano teachers and their non-neurotyptical students. Enabling teachers who work with ASC musicians to teach more effectively is central to this objective. The following list of "dos and don'ts" is directed toward that end.

Dotan's Dos and Don'ts of Teaching Piano Students with Asperger's Syndrome and other ASCs

1. Do work collaboratively with your student.

"Autistic brains are different from non-autistic brains—not better or worse, just different," proclaims Julia Bascom in her foreword to the landmark anthology *Loud Hands: Autistic People, Speaking* (Bascom 2012b, 10). The question of how and why has vexed scientists, philosophers, writers, artists, and activists for many decades. Theories abound, but we find the following one, proposed by the autistic self-advocate and scholar Nick Walker, to be especially germane: "Current evidence indicates that the central distinction is that autistic brains are characterized by particularly high levels of synaptic connectivity and responsiveness. This tends to make the autistic individual's subjective experience more intense and chaotic than that of non-autistic individuals: on both the sensorimotor and cognitive levels, the autistic mind tends to register more information, and the impact of each bit of information tends to be both stronger and less predictable" (Walker 2014).

The inner workings of the autistic mind, then, might be analogous to Charles Ives's song "The New River," as described by Denise Von Glahn in this volume.

"Whether intended as such or not," Von Glahn asserts, "Ives's song *responds to all that was happening around him at the time*" (emphasis mine). Dotan's cognitive experience is of a related order. As he explains, "Within my brain, zillions of thoughts are traveling at the speed of light, and sometimes it causes confusion, procrastination, stress, etc. . . . If I am trying to absorb and classify [all this] information at once, it's not going to work. The brain I possess can record a huge amount of knowledge; the absorption is quick but the classification process is slower, [and] this gap is hampering" (May 13, 2016).

Under such conditions of what Dotan calls "cognitive overload"—a condition that, left unchecked, may devolve into forms of "physical and cognitive breakdown" reminiscent of those described by Margarita Mazo (this volume)—pianists with ASC need their teachers to provide specific kinds of assistance in specific areas in order to achieve "utmost brilliance" (July 19, 2016) and also to avoid collapse. They require very clear guidance on, in Dotan's words, "efficient ways of learning pieces" to "develop [the] skill of knowing what and knowing how" (July 19, 2016). With so many thoughts swirling around in the mind at any given time—so many conflicting streams of information competing for attention—the task of determining which thoughts to attend to and which to "eject" can present daunting challenges. "I can and do collect all kinds of different information from all kinds of different sources," Dotan relates. "That is not a problem. The question is how to organize and prioritize it!" (July 19, 2016). He notes that some of his teachers, including Professor Gainsford, have been extremely helpful in this area while others have been anything but.

One might reasonably assume that the best kind of teacher for a pianist like Dotan would employ a highly directive approach, relieving the student of excessive responsibility for agency and decision making. Indeed, many prescribed "best practices" for teaching individuals with ASCs endorse such approaches (see Fein 2012, 69–70). Yet while Dotan claims that "if you want an Asperger to succeed and develop, you have to instruct him and be specific; otherwise it shall not work," he most values the teacher who is both willing and able to engage with him in a fully collaborative way:

> At the end of the line, only I know what works best for me. The teacher's task is to give me the tools to let it happen. That is what Dr. Gainsford does, among other things. Unlike many other teachers that merely 'tell you what to do,' [he creates an environment where in most situations] we both examine every problem that emerges (related to piano playing of course), and we both reach the best solution possible. On other occasions, he demonstrates for me a certain way of working out a difficulty [but then] gives me room to examine it and to perfect it according to my grasp. By doing so, and due to the fact I am able to implement things, it diminishes my dependence on him to the required

minimum. . . . Always remember, when it comes to teaching Aspies, [at least] in certain cases, if you want things to happen, [you must] either *make* them happen or *let* them happen. (July 19, 2016)

In Dotan's ideal pedagogical world, each piano lesson becomes an exercise in collaboration and dialogue, or, to use Robert Baron and Thomas Walker's terms (this volume), the product of a "sharing of authority, and dialogical, mutual engagement" between teacher and student. Dotan explains:

It is like learning how to cook with the instruction of a true chef. A true chef does not merely tell you what to do, but rather gives you the ingredients in order for you to examine, experiment, and prepare recipes of your own. The best way to learn is by being creative and using your creativity to cope better with your shortcomings and fill in your gaps. In fact, the more I think of it, the more I realize that many of the things I know nowadays are not necessarily due to what I learned formally, but are rather due to the opportunity I am having now of sitting with myself and finding effective solutions to my deficiencies. . . . Many things I have learned this year about piano playing are a result of self-research rather than [the] direct instructions of Dr. Gainsford. He teaches me to fish rather than just giving me fish. . . . By helping Aspergers with their 'fishing' rather than 'giving them fish' all the time, they naturally become much more encouraged and believe every problem related to piano playing is doable and solvable, and this confidence can extend into everyday life as well. (July 19, 2016)

2. Don't tell your student to "try harder."

Ambiguous statements that may be effective in motivating neurotypical piano students are ineffective with ASC students, Dotan claims. "Statements such as 'you are not trying hard enough' or 'I expect you to give me more' are both irritating and futile," he insists, "since we Aspies are very total [and thorough] in our work and naturally give of ourselves far beyond [the norm] in terms of trying to meet and also exceed expectations. Hence, teachers should direct their efforts with Aspergers—show them 'how to get it'—mainly by showing them methods of making their work more efficient" (July 19, 2016).

Far too often, this has not been Dotan's experience:

Many of my teachers have known "what" to require of me, but they couldn't always define the "how," and in order for me to succeed, the "how" has to be exactly clear. I'll give you the simplest example I can think of. I took a [combined course and practicum in piano pedagogy] and was assigned to teach an adult beginner piano student [as part of the practicum]. I was expected to implement everything we discussed in the course into the practicum, for example, regarding how to teach the inner subdivision of rhythm, how to count, how to use the whole apparatus [including] correct posture, etc.

Mainly due to the fact there were days [my student] did not even practice, [he did not make good progress] despite all the "recipes" I gave him of how to work out certain difficulties. When he came more or less prepared, things were all right, but when he came "out of shape" [having not practiced], it seemed to me nothing was helpful. I felt as if I was losing my mind. When I reported my difficulties, [the professor] told me (as far as I can remember): "You have to do a little bit more," "Try harder," "Be patient with him." [This advice was] futile to me, because no matter what I do, I do even far beyond what is required; therefore, to tell me things such as "You can do more" is empty and meaningless. The amount of effort is almost never the problem. Having a clear sense of where and how to *direct* one's effort is the key, and that is where the teacher can be most helpful. (July 19, 2016)

3. Do use humor and analogies in your teaching (but don't use sarcasm or vulgar humor).

"Aspergers most likely will not understand all sorts of humor, especially not sarcastic or vulgar humor," Dotan says. "As for double meanings, puns, it depends on the context. Yet musical humor is crystal clear for us, particularly if one uses it for pedagogical purposes" (July 27, 2016).

Dotan provides an example. While studying with Roberta Rust at Lynn University in Florida, he worked with her on Brahms's Paganini Variations, vol. 2, which he describes as "a work known for being notoriously difficult" (July 27, 2016). He played her the sixth variation. She listened, then suggested he try it again, but this time with more "lilt." Dotan did not know what this meant, so he asked Professor Rust. She did her best to explain and demonstrate, but he was still left unsure of the meaning.

Later, Dotan happened on a recording of "the signature song of the Swedish Chef from *The Muppets*" (July 27, 2016). Hearing the song's playful, gently swinging rhythm, he suddenly understood precisely what *lilt* meant. He applied this newfound knowledge to his performance of the Brahms sixth variation at his next lesson. The results were excellent. Rust was satisfied with the interpretation, Dotan was pleased, and they shared a good laugh joking about how this comical song had elevated Dotan's performance of such a difficult piece.

"So one essential lesson," Dotan summarizes. "When you teach, ease up!" (July 27, 2016).

4. Don't overwhelm your student with too many performance demonstrations.

Many of Dotan's teachers have had what he calls "a tendency to overflow the head with too many details" (July 27, 2016). Because people with ASCs tend to take in so much information at once, with "each bit of information" registering intensely and in relatively unpredictable ways (Walker 2014), it is important to teach in a manner that keeps the scope of the lesson manageable at all times. The teacher should resist demonstrating excessively long passages or multiple passages in quick succession and should always be precise in identifying the central purpose of the performance illustration.[5] Excessive demonstration "confuses the student and leads only to mental overflow," Dotan contends, following with a personal example. "My first teacher wasted half of the lesson on demonstrating fragments of pieces and singing the notes out loud simultaneously." It was too much for Dotan, and his brain would "shut down." He recalls, "No wonder when I was asked to do so, I couldn't read a single note! Hence, [to] those who teach Aspergers, no matter what level they are: Don't demonstrate too much; show only the specific passages that require special treatment and nothing more; otherwise the student will not get the main point" (July 27, 2016).

5. Do be patient, kind, and respectful toward your student.

Individuals with ASCs do not respond well to harsh methods. "It is very important for us to have a teacher that conveys [a] warm sense of familiarity and domestic treatment," Dotan emphasizes. "After all, that's the key that brings us to brilliant achievements. . . . Sometimes, Aspergers have to cope with obsessive-compulsive thoughts, particularly when bits and pieces within the pieces don't come along the way they want [them] to" (Nitzberg 2012). In such instances, he adds, they can gain much reassurance by consulting with their teacher between lessons. Therefore, teachers who take on an ASC student should always attempt to make themselves available outside the classroom or studio, at least within reasonable limits. In his own case, Dotan notes, when such channels of communication were closed, "no one has benefitted, neither me nor the teacher. It didn't bring any good result and only deepened the frustration. . . . So if being welcoming to other people is obvious, for us it's a necessity!" (Nitzberg 2012).

The teacher must be sensitive to the reality, too, that musicians on the spectrum, even those with exceptional abilities in areas such as musical memory and technical dexterity, tend to process information relatively slowly, largely because they are taking in so much information at every moment. Thus, they may need considerably more time and space to work things out than their neurotypical peers, and this can test the teacher's patience. Dotan insists that an emphasis on "pre-planning" or "pre-preparation" on the part of both student and teacher—whether for practice sessions, lessons, or recitals—is essential to nurturing good relations and avoiding problems. "Don't expect them to 'get things right' in an instant," he warns. "It might lead to further frustrations. Rather, expect them to write the 'recipes' [of the lesson] down, keep them in mind, and keep working and perfecting specific skills every day. Only thus can one vouchsafe their improvement" (July 19, 2016).

And remember, too, Dotan adds, that "being patient and kind means more than just being nice. It also means knowing *what* to demand and *how* to convey the material" (July 19, 2016). Teachers who have and share knowledge that way show respect to their students in doing so, and for Dotan, at least, showing that kind of respect demonstrates patience and kindness of the highest order.

This chapter has focused on teaching piano to students on the autism spectrum, but its lessons have great potential value in other settings as well, for example, in teaching piano students who are not on the spectrum; in the teaching of music generally, across the spectrum of neurodiversity, whether in applied lesson, ensemble, or academic settings; in teaching subjects outside music to autistic individuals and groups; and in fostering better relationships and mutual understandings overall.

Teaching is an art, not a science. There is no one-size-fits-all prescription, and we understand well that even within the relatively limited scope of this inquiry—teaching piano to individuals with ASCs—the approaches we suggest will not work in every case. That said, we are confident that the five "dos" and "don'ts" of teaching proposed here—work collaboratively with your students, give precise pedagogical instructions rather than vague comments like "try harder," use humor and analogy to enrich your students' learning experience, avoid overwhelming your students with too many demonstrations or too much information, and treat your students with patience, kindness, and respect—will prove useful as points of departure for establishing positive and productive teacher-student relationships.

There is one additional "do" we would like to share in closing as well, and we consider it to be at least as important as the others: when teaching neurodiverse students—indeed when teaching anyone—*do* always engage with your student as an individual, not as a "type" and not as a vessel of some label or diagnosis. Dotan Nitzberg is not, in the end, an Asperger pianist, an autistic pianist, or anything else of the sort. He is a pianist, and he is a person: unique, resolute, and possessed of his own way of being in the world. It is *his* resilience, *his* strategies of adaptive management, *his* insights into establishing and nurturing a sustainable culture of ASC musical professionalism, that form the heart of this chapter—and that perhaps offer points of departure on the micro level for productively approaching our engagements with larger and more multidimensional systems of musical culture and community as well. Dotan, the unique individual and not some monolith of Asperger's syndrome or autism that he "represents," is who we have heard and learned from here, and no matter how large the system, how diverse the musical culture, how multifaceted the community, or how complex the environment at issue, we will always do well to remember that the wants, needs, and actions of individual human beings are foundational to everything that they affect and everything that affects them.

We close now with some final words from Dotan, in particular with an assertion that for us captures the essence of sustainable resilience and of resilient sustainability as well: "I finally realized I am not handicapped AT ALL! I just need some extra help in certain things; otherwise I'm good! Those who claimed I am unable of accomplishing a task due to my 'DISABILITY' deserve my mercy because they are so full of prejudices. And those who said 'I AM NOT SUFFICIENTLY MATURE,' woe to them as well, since I grow up and develop, and I do it my way, with my own pace, and I do it with so much fun, pleasure, and grace. Every instant!" (July 2, 2016).

Notes

1. In *DSM IV-TR Casebook: A Learning Companion to the Diagnostic and Statistical Manual of Mental Disorders* (Spitzer et al. 2000), Asperger's disorder (Asperger's syndrome) was one of four separate diagnoses within the category of ASD, or autism spectrum disorder. The fifth edition of the *Diagnostic and Statistical Manual of Mental Disorders: DSM-5* (American Psychiatric Association 2013), however, brought major changes, folding all four of the formerly separate diagnostic categories into a single diagnosis: ASD. There has been considerable controversy over these changes (see Silberman 2015), and many individuals on the spectrum, including Dotan at the time of the dialogues leading to this chapter (2014, 2016), have insisted that they *are* Aspergers or individuals living with Asperger's syndrome, as opposed to autistics or people living with autism, or ASD. For this reason, we have used "Asperger" and its related terms in this chapter (at least in quotations from the dialogues), despite the disappearance of "Asperger's disorder" as an official diagnostic category in DSM-5.

2. We belong to a growing cohort of scholars and activists in the autistic advocacy and neurodiversity arenas who advocate for use of the designation "autism spectrum condition" (ASC) in place of "autism spectrum disorder" (ASD).

3. See also Straus (2011) and Headlam (2006) on distinctively autistic ways of listening to and hearing music.

4. A deeply unsettling issue that underlies much discourse and literature on autism concerns questioning assessments concerning the very humanity of people on the au-

tism spectrum. For insightful critical consideration of such discourse and its attendant debates, see, among other sources, Fein (2012), Silberman (2015), and numerous chapters in the anthology *Loud Hands: Autistic People, Speaking* (Bascom 2012a).

5. Compare to Jeffery Summit's enlightening discussion in this volume of Cantor Linda Sue Sohn's methods for teaching dyslexic students to chant Torah.

References

American Psychiatric Association. 2013. *Diagnostic and Statistical Manual of Mental Disorders: DSM-5.* 5th ed. Washington, DC: American Psychiatric Association.

Bakan, Michael B. 2014a. "Ethnomusicological Perspectives on Autism, Neurodiversity, and Music Therapy." *Voices: A World Forum for Music Therapy* 14 (3). https://voices. no/index.php/voices/article/view/799/660.

———. 2014b. "The Musicality of Stimming: Promoting Neurodiversity in the Ethno-musicology of Autism." *Musicultures* 41 (2): 133–61.

———. 2015a. "'Don't Go Changing to Try and Please Me': Combating Essentialism through Ethnography in the Ethnomusicology of Autism." *Ethnomusicology* 59 (1): 116–44.

———. 2015b. "Being Applied in the Ethnomusicology of Autism." In *The Oxford Hand-book of Applied Ethnomusicology*, edited by Svanibor Pettan and Jeff Todd Titon, 278–316. New York: Oxford University Press.

———. 2016a. "Music, Autism, and Disability Aesthetics." Colloquy: On the Disability Aesthetics of Music, convened by Blake Howe and Stephanie Jensen-Moulton. *Journal of the American Musicological Society* 69 (2): 548–53.

———. 2016b. "Toward an Ethnographic Model of Disability in the Ethnomusicology of Autism." In *The Oxford Handbook of Music and Disability Studies*, edited by Blake Howe, Stephanie Jensen-Moulton, Neil Lerner, and Joseph N. Straus, 15–36. New York: Oxford University Press.

———. 2018. Speaking for Ourselves: Conversations on Life, Music, and Autism. New York: Oxford University Press.

Bascom, Julia. 2012a. Foreword to Bascom 2012b.

———, ed. 2012b. *Loud Hands: Autistic People, Speaking.* Washington, DC: Autistic Press / Autistic Self Advocacy Network.

Czech, Herwig. 2018. "Hans Asperger, National Socialism, and 'Race Hygiene' in Nazi-Era Vienna." *Molecular Autism* 9: 29. doi.org/10.1186/s13229-018-0208-6.

Fein, Elizabeth. 2012. "The Machine Within: An Ethnography of Asperger's Syndrome, Biomedicine, and the Paradoxes of Identity and Technology in the Late Modern United States." PhD diss., University of Chicago.

Headlam, Dave. 2006. "Learning to Hear Autistically." In *Sounding Off: Theorizing Dis-ability in Music*, edited by Neil Lerner and Joseph N. Straus, 109–20. New York: Routledge.

Nitzberg, Dotan. 2012. "How to Teach Piano [to] People with Asperger." Lecture-demon-stration presented at the World Piano Teachers Association (WPTA) annual confer-ence, Novi Sad, Serbia. https://www.youtube.com/watch?v=g7LTFboZAqk.

Silberman, Steve. 2015. *NeuroTribes: The Legacy of Autism and the Future of Neurodiversity*. Foreword by Oliver Sacks. New York: Avery.

Spitzer, Robert L., Mariam Gibbon, Andrew E. Skodol, and Michael B. First, eds. 2000. *DSM-IV-TR Casebook: A Learning Companion to the Diagnostic and Statistical Manual of Mental Disorders*. 4th ed., text rev. Washington, DC: American Psychiatric Association.

Straus, Joseph N. 2011. *Extraordinary Measures: Disability in Music*. New York: Oxford University Press.

———. 2014. "Idiots Savants, Retarded Savants, Talented Aments, Mono-Savants, Autistic Savants, Just Plain Savants, People with Savant Syndrome, and Autistic People Who Are Good at Things: A View from Disability Studies." *Disability Studies Quarterly* 34 (3). http://dsq-sds.org/article/view/3407/3640.

Titon, Jeff Todd. 2015. "Sustainability, Resilience, and Adaptive Management for Applied Ethnomusicology." In *The Oxford Handbook of Applied Ethnomusicology*, edited by Svanibor Pettan and Jeff Todd Titon, 157–95. New York: Oxford University Press.

Walker, Nick. 2014. "What Is Autism?" *Neurocosmopolitanism: Nick Walker's Notes on Neurodiversity, Autism, and Cognitive Liberty* (blog), 1 March. http://neurocosmopolitanism.com/what-is-autism/.

CHAPTER 20

The Fiesta de la Bulería of Jerez de la Frontera

Music, Identity, and the Construction of Heritage

ROSHAN SAMTANI

MUSIC PLAYS A POWERFUL ROLE in the construction, articulation, and maintenance of ethnicity, identity, and belonging. A vital biocultural resource (Titon 2009, 5–6), music is strategically employed by humans both to define personal and group identity and to celebrate the fact of belonging to a family, a community, and a place. Ethnomusicologists have increasingly turned their attention to the musical construction of place, together with music's implication in the construction of identities and ethnicities (Feld and Basso 1996; Stokes 1994; Sugarman 1999; Rice 2003, 2007).

This chapter analyzes the relationship between music, emplacement, and the construction and maintenance of identity with particular reference to flamenco, a genre conventionally associated with the *gitano*, or Roma community in Spain.[1] Through analysis of a musical event dedicated to a song type known as the *bulería*, I describe how it has become a musical emblem of the city of Jerez, serving as a conduit for the expression of gitano identity and conferring prestige to a sanctified locality in flamenco history. My broader goal in this chapter is to illustrate how the environment, intangible culture, and economics felicitously come together through advocacy and adaptive management, resulting in the sustainability of people and the music that they practice.

Toponymy and topophilic sentiments are distinctive and distinguishing aspects of many music cultures, reflecting the importance of place and its influence on the construction of identity, the development of regional and local variations, and the shaping of classification schemes. As Lawrence Buell indicates, the notion of "place" encapsulates a spectrum of experience pertaining to "environmental materiality, toward social perception or construction, and toward individual affect or bond" (2005, 63). Music functions as a powerful catalyst for such experiential expression, serving to reinforce a group's sense of emplacement, identity, and collective being.

This chapter is organized in several sections. In the first, I briefly sketch the history of gitano settlers in Jerez, foregrounding the particular conditions that allowed for their integration. The second, third, and fourth sections focus on the bulería and examine its poetic and musical characteristics in order to understand its affective power, the process of meaning construction, and the construction of identity. The final part of the chapter employs the Fiesta de la Bulería as a framework to reflect on the invention of tradition and the construction of heritage.

A Brief History of the Gitanos of Jerez de la Frontera

Flamenco in Jerez de la Frontera (I will refer to it as Jerez henceforth) is characterized by ethnic associations with the gitano community. A branch of the broader diaspora known as the Roma, the gitanos arrived in Spain in the early fifteenth century and gradually settled in various regions of the peninsula (San Román Espinosa 1997, 7). After their arrival, the gitanos of Jerez played an important role in the adaptation and syncretization of the folk and popular musics that they encountered. This process intensified after their sedentarization and enabled the emergence of flamenco. The substantial presence of gitanos in the city of Jerez and its vicinity is linked to a high demand for agricultural labors and animal caretakers; ancillary activities connected with smithery also provided employment opportunities. The alternation and combination of various occupations, a characteristic of gitano society, has also been underscored by San Román Espinosa (50) as a fundamental strategy that contributed to their resilience and successful integration into the labor market. The *fragua*, or smithy, was a typical workplace where poetry was sung to accompany the tasks associated with the hammer and anvil. Gitanos also encountered a better reception from many inhabitants of the city, in marked contrast to their reception in other areas of Spain.

The settlement of gitano migrants in Jerez occurred in two important extramural neighborhoods, namely, the barrios of San Miguel and Santiago. Other

districts, such as La Albarizuela and San Telmo, also served as focal points for
their settlement and for the development of flamenco.

The Bulería and Its Poetic and Musical Characteristics

A brief overview of some pertinent aspects of the flamenco repertoire will enable us to better situate the bulería and to understand its association with Jerez.

The geographical location of the earliest strata of flamenco songs comprises
a region known as the Lower Guadalquivir, situated between Seville and Cádiz,
limited by the Atlantic Ocean to the south, the River Guadalquivir in the West,
and the western extremity of the Betic chain of mountains to the east.

The *tonás*, the earliest flamenco songs, were sung without instrumental accompaniment and represent the first expressions of a gitano style of poetry.
In addition to quotidian topics, solitude and suffering are recurrent themes in
the poetry of the earliest song types. Songs are constantly re-created and serve
as frameworks for new compositions. The *soleá* (plural *soleares*) is the most
important song type since its rhythmic framework, a twelve-beat cycle with a
characteristic accentuation scheme, is the basis for other song types, including
the bulería.

Songs in the flamenco repertoire may be grouped under a typology based
on *compás*, the fundamental referent in flamenco performance. In the case of
songs that are strictly measured, compás is conceptualized as a cyclical structure
containing a fixed number of pulses with a strict accentuation scheme, yielding
a groove pattern. It is a procedural device that encodes a set of rhythmic, melodic, and harmonic instructions crucial to the performance. The term *pre-form*,
coined by Jeff Titon in his analysis of the blues (Titon 1978), may be applied to
describe a compás pattern.

The bulería is traditionally classified as part of the festive repertoire. Historically, Jerez has been the nucleus for the development of the bulería and a
plaintive song type known as the *siguiriya*. Style is frequently associated with
family lineages, and this contributes to the stability of the repertoire and to the
conservation of stylistic nuances that identify the lineage. Voice quality, phras-
ing, poetic content, and rhythmic artifice are prominent features of the Jerez
style of interpretation. Performance style functions as "an important symbol of
identity, and indeed, traditional flamenco style can be seen to proclaim its class,
regional, and ethnic orientation fairly unambiguously" (Manuel 1989, 55).

Rhythmic support in flamenco is provided by *palmas* (hand claps) and a box-
like instrument known as the *cajón* (imported from Peru in the early 1970s).
The rhythmic pattern of the bulería is a timeline consisting of twelve pulses
that mixes ternary and binary structures (6/8 alternates with 3/4). The highest point of tension in the twelve-pulse cycle occurs on pulse number three,

marked by the B♭ chord. The point of resolution occurs on pulse number ten. In performance, chains of such cycles are developed during improvisation often employing secondary dominant chords, thus delaying the resolution and ensuring the audience's attention and engagement. Hocket-type constructions played by *palmeros*, or hand clappers, result in a dense polyrhythmic texture.

Flamenco poetry draws on a wealth of verbal art embodied in aphorisms and traditional sayings (*refranes*). The use of archaisms and local tropes often presents translation difficulties. Lyrics, or *letras*, are organized in *coplas* (verses). A rich reservoir of oral history and verbal art, flamenco lyrics have "served as persistent and ever-effective vehicles for the expression of the anxieties and vicissitudes of Andalusian and gypsy daily life" (Manuel 1989, 52). Formulaic constructions firmly established in the flamenco tradition are performed and re-created. Some coplas eulogize great performers, vividly demonstrating the role of performance in the transmission of tradition and historical memory. Notation is not a part of conventional flamenco practice, and skills are conventionally acquired through mimesis and memorization, processes that occur during the socialization of children.

A defining feature of flamenco harmony and melody is the extensive use of the Phrygian mode and the Phrygian cadence. This cadence may be represented by the descending progression D minor–C7–B♭ major–A (in the tonality of A). Major, minor, and chromatic scales are widely employed in passagework. Flamenco guitar music is characterized by a variety of textures, including single-note passages, arpeggios, rhythmic accompaniment, and percussion. In addition to the accompaniment of song and dance, the guitarist provides solo variations, or *falsetas*, at strategic moments.

I now turn my attention to sound quality, another vital component that imbues flamenco with its affective power and referential potency.

Sound and the Construction of Meaning

The explanation or elucidation of how musical sounds signify is essential to an understanding of the construction of meaning in the performance and reception of music. In her study of *qawwali* music, a multilayered performance tradition that flourishes in India and Pakistan, Regula Qureshi emphasizes the importance of "an understanding of the dynamic that motivates the production of music, i.e. the meaning or significance of the sound system in terms of the social use and cultural context—referential meaning in the widest sense of the word" (1987, 57).

Jesús Agarrado, one of my teachers, constantly emphasized the relationship between poetry, guitar accompaniment, and *la tierra* (the land). His attitude encapsulates knowledge, custom, and a worldview molded by a habitus where lifeways, geography, and historical memory shape the language of flamenco. His emphasis on possessing a feel for *cante* (poetry and songs) and the connection he made between song, guitar performance, and place offers us a good idea of referential meaning and music making.

The practice known as *jaleo*, an integral part of flamenco performance, refers to animatory interjections in the form of stock phrases, reacting and responding to tension and release patterns that occur at the structurally important points of the compás. The audience often joins in these cheers, and the significance of these interjections helps us better understand the construction of meaning in the reception and performance of music.

The following section explores some frameworks for examining the nexus between the performance and reception of music and the construction and reaffirmation of identity.

Music, Meaning, and Identity Construction

Many scholars in ethnomusicology have sought to illustrate the dialectical nature of the relationship between sound structures, social structures, and identity (e.g., Feld 1988; Peña 1985; Perlman 1998; Rice 1994, 2007; Seeger 1987; Sugarman 1997, 1999). In addition, theoretical orientations that privilege phenomenology as a conduit for understanding musical experience have in turn been expressed using a variety of methodologies, including bi-musicality (Hood 1960, 1971; Berliner 1978; Sudnow, 2001; Titon 1994, 1995).

Semiotics, developed by Charles Sanders Peirce (1839–1914) and Ferdinand de Saussure (1857–1913), has been a highly influential discipline for understanding human experience and the production and construction of meaning (Perman 2010; Turino 1999, 2014). Peirce's semiotics, expressed in a theory of signs, constitutes a powerful methodological tool for a better understanding of how music signifies. Thomas Turino regards Peircian semiotics as a core methodology for ethnomusicological training, research, analysis, and praxis. He argues: "If ethnomusicology is the study of the dialectical interplay of music making and social life, then Peircian theory is particularly suited for ethnomusicological work. Why? From a Peircian perspective: (1) every musical sound, performance or dance movement, and contextual feature that affects an actual perceiver is a sign, and (2) every perceiver is affected by signs in relation to his or her own personal history of experience, which is at once a partially unique but largely shared social experience" (2014, 188). Clearly, this enhances our understanding of how music creates the feeling described as "unisonance" (Anderson 1991, 145) or "social synchrony" (Turino 1999, 221).

The two categories of signs relevant to this discussion are the icon and the index. The icon is a type of sign that acquires its potency based on a resemblance between the sign and its object. The re-creation of coplas (verses), falsetas (guitar variations), and *pasos de baile* (dance gestures) distinguishes every flamenco event. Iconicity determines form recognition and enables the perception of rhymed patterns in poetry, motivic manipulation, repeated sections, and larger structural relationships. Yet another important function of icons is the rendering of imagined entities in a concrete perceptible form, what Turino considers "a basic social function of icons in art, ritual, and performance" (2014, 194).

The index acquires its potency through the co-occurrence of sign and object. The musical event is replete with indices that include the selection of the repertoire and other constitutive elements such as formulaic cadences, poetry, guitar solos, and rhythmic artifice. With reference to indices, Turino notes that

> one source for the affective power of musical indices is the fact that they are able to condense great quantities and varieties of meaning—even contradictory meanings within a single sign. Indices signify through co-occurrence with their object in real-time situations. Once such indexical relations have been established, however, actual co-presence of sign and object is no longer required; the index may still call to mind objects previously experientially attached. But when former indexically related objects are not present, or even when they are, new elements in the situation may become linked to the same sign. Of key significance to a theory of musical affectivity, indices continually take on new layers of meaning while potentially also carrying along former associations—a kind of semantic snowballing. . . . Indexical relations are grounded in personal experience; the members of social groups will share indices proportional to common experiences. (1999, 235)

An additional factor to be considered is that of sonic density or "the relative number of signs potentially operating together in any given medium" (Turino 2014, 189). The sonic mosaic of flamenco comprises a spectrum of elements that coalesce as a complex web of signs, the interpretation of which is an enactive process that is derived socially in the context of the family.

The socialization process is, therefore, a rewarding area for understanding how shared experiences are developed. Flamenco knowledge is an essential part of the socialization of children in gitano society. They grow up knowing their heritage. (Song and dance, an important part of this heritage, are essential to the process of identity construction.) Commenting on the transmission of gitano customs, flamencologist Juan de la Plata Franco Martínez notes that "the most natural of these customs, song and dance, is taught to children at a very early stage, when they are scarcely able to talk or walk—and to make them proud of belonging to the gitano race " (2001, 90, my translation).[2]

Occasionally, during encounters with Jesus Agarrado's children after lessons, I witnessed the process of transmission of flamenco knowledge in informal contexts within the environment of the immediate and extended family. Listening to a *nana*, or lullaby (a song type in the repertoire), is a ritual embedded in the daily lives of most children, functioning as an effective vehicle for the transmission of poetry, basic melodic profiles, and accentuation patterns.

In addition to the family, the local community plays an important role in the transmission process through neighborhood associations or social clubs known as *peñas*. These clubs are often named after historically significant artists or song types and promote a range of performances and didactic activities, thus fostering flamenco's transmission and sustenance. The peña serves both as a focal point for aficionados and as an informal conservatoire where local performers hone their skills.

The fiesta is a highly inclusive and socially agreeable context for flamenco performances. The freedom to eat, drink, and amble around contrasts with the etiquette and rules associated with theaters and concert halls. Aficionados interact at the bar, strengthening social relationships based on their affinity for flamenco. The local performers at the Fiesta de la Bulería, familiar to most aficionados, are representative of the region, embodying local knowledge and the nuances of the region's identifying repertoire. In many cases, the use of an *apodo*, or stage name, revealing the performer's city demonstrates a profound affiliation with her local origins. The event thus facilitates the expression of social roles and the construction of networks, all of which contribute to the reaffirmation of identity-based links.

Documenting the Invention of Tradition: The Fiesta de la Bulería

In a seminal volume on the invention of tradition, Eric Hobsbawm describes an invented tradition as "a set of practices, normally governed by overtly or tacitly accepted rules and of a ritual or symbolic nature, which seek to inculcate certain values and norms of behavior by repetition, which automatically implies continuation with the past" (Hobsbawm and Ranger 1992, 1).

The ritualization of the Fiesta de la Bulería as an annual celebration illustrates how music and notions of ethnicity, identity, belonging, and heritage coalesce in a collectively sociable context, ultimately ensuring the sustainability of the gitano community and its intangible cultural heritage. The association between song, city, and ethnic community has acquired an aura of timelessness with the celebration of the Fiesta de la Bulería. This aura is enhanced by the fiesta's synchronization with the autumn harvest, invoking emotional associations with the land and with the patron of Jerez, Saint Dionysius. In addition to the intensive cultivation of olives, viticulture has historically been an essential component of Andalusia's economy, most prominently in the region of the lower Guadalquivir. Fittingly, the celebrations commence with the *pisa de las uvas*, or the trampling of grapes, a ritual associated with the tasting of the year's wine. The fiesta, which celebrated its fiftieth anniversary in 2017, is a good example of how the natural environment, cultural practices, and economics constitute an ecosystem of culture that has been effectively configured through advocacy and adaptive management.

In this context, it is important to describe the activities of the Cátedra of Jerez, an academic institution founded by a group of aficionados spearheaded by Juan de la Plata Franco Martínez. A passionate and dedicated advocate of gitano culture, Franco Martínez was deeply concerned about the sustainability of flamenco culture in Jerez and sought to save and revalorize vanishing flamenco and folkloric treasures. In his memoirs, he recounts, "in the year 1967, we created the popular Fiesta de la Bulería, in order to exalt a song and dance that was typically Jerezano [from Jerez]," adding that "the fiesta was born with a philosophy which emphasized that while other festive songs could be performed during the fiesta the repertoire should predominantly consist of songs and dances using the bulerías song type" (Franco Martínez 2010, 85–86, my translation).[3]

The fiesta is programmed on a Saturday night at the bullring and draws many spectators. Attendance figures have increased significantly in recent years, reflecting its growing popularity among foreign tourists. In addition to *tapas*, or snacks, paper cones of fried fish typical of the region and a range of beverages are available at the venue.

The rules pertaining to performance are fluid: each singer chooses freely from the repertoire but must conclude with the bulerías of Jerez. Most (if not all) of the performers hail from the different barrios of Jerez or other towns in the vicinity. Various dance groups participate in the fiesta, thus accentuating the three components of flamenco: song, guitar music, and dance. Audience participation is expressed in rhythmic hand clapping and jaleo.

In his analysis, Hobsbawm groups invented traditions into three overlapping types based on function: "(a) Those establishing or symbolizing social cohesion or the membership of groups, real or artificial communities, (b) those establishing or legitimizing institutions, status or relations of authority, and (c) those whose main purpose was socialization, the inculcation of beliefs, value systems and conventions of behavior" (Hobsbawm and Ranger 1992, 9).

In addition to fulfilling these functions, the Fiesta de la Bulería consecrates the city of Jerez, legitimizing its historical status as the *cuna* (cradle) of flamenco. The significance of the fiesta may be appreciated on several levels since it is a collage of various realms of experience that constitute the heritage of Jerez: flamenco, viticulture, gastronomy, and collective sociability.

In this chapter I have sought to illustrate the relationship between identity, place, and expressive culture. Shared representations, enabled through collectively held conceptions of being, place, and music form the basis for a powerful meaning system that serves as a repository of the historical memory of the gitano community and its culture. The active transmission of cultural knowledge and values through flamenco is a constitutive and essential part of the daily lives of most gitanos and many Andalusians.

The transformation of the bulería into a musical emblem of the city of Jerez through the institutionalization of the Fiesta de la Bulería illustrates how expressive culture, identity, the environment, and regional gastronomic products are creatively juxtaposed with the broader goal of heritage building, ultimately fostering the sustainability of an ecosystem of culture.

Finally, it is necessary to reflect on the continued marginalization of gypsy populations and of the many others who suffer discrimination. As Timothy Cooley affirms in this volume, the "separation of peoples . . . is a historical myth. Segregations and apartheids are not sustainable." Sadly, negative stereotypes and xenophobic attitudes persist, and gitanos continue to be viewed as "exotic assets to some imaginary pluralist society" (Charnon-Deutsch 2004, 11).

The case of Jerez, an exception in the broader urban landscape of Spain, provides us with an example of how expressive culture, specifically song, music, and dance, can act as a catalyst for human well-being, interconnectedness, and conviviality, thereby contributing to the sustainability of a marginalized community and its heritage and to an ecosystem of culture.

Notes

It is a pleasure to acknowledge the assistance of the Graduate School at Brown University for funding my ethnographic research in Spain (2000–2006). I am deeply grateful to Jeff Todd Titon for his mentorship and encouragement during my doctoral studies. Thanks to the Centro Andaluz de Documentación del Flamenco (Jerez de la Frontera) for its collaboration. Finally, my sincere gratitude goes to Timothy Cooley for his comments and suggestions.

1. In Castilian Spanish the consonant *j* is pronounced as *h*. The consonant *g* is pronounced as a guttural *h* when followed by either an *e* or an *i*; thus, the word *gitano* is pronounced *hitano*. Stressed vowels are indicated by an accent above the vowel, as in *á, é, í,* and *ó*. Thus, José is pronounced *Ho-say*, and *soleá* is pronounced *sol-ay-a*. The use of an *apodo* (a name used for professional reasons) is extremely common in flamenco. In such cases, I append the apodo to the concerned person's name, e.g., Juan Moneo, "El Torta."

2. The original citation appears in a section titled "Algunas costumbres de los gitanos Jerezanos" (Some customs of the gitanos of Jerez) and reads: "Lo más natural de esas costumbres, es el cante y el baile, que se les enseña a los niños, apenas empiezan a hablar o mantenerse en pie. Y hacerse orgullo de pertenecer a la raza gitana."

3. In his detailed reminiscences regarding the fiesta, Franco Martínez notes that "en el año 1967 creamos la popularísima Fiesta de la Bulería en exaltación del cante y del baile por antonomasia jerezano. . . . La fiesta nació con una filosofía. En ella se podría

cantar otros cantes festeros, pero siempre predominando, en calidad y abundancia, los cantes y bailes por bulerías."

References

Anderson, Benedict. 1991. *Imagined Communities*. London: Verso.

Berliner, Paul. 1978. *The Soul of Mbira*. Berkeley: University of California Press.

Buell, Lawrence. 2005. *The Future of Environmental Criticism: Environmental Crisis and the Literary Imagination*. Oxford: Blackwell.

Charnon-Deutsch, Lou. 2004. *The Spanish Gypsy: The History of a European Obsession*. University Park: Pennsylvania State University Press.

Feld, Steven. 1988. "Aesthetics as Iconicity of Style, or 'Lift-Up-Over Sounding': Getting into the Kaluli Groove." *Yearbook for Traditional Music* 20:74–114.

Feld, Steven, and Keith H. Basso, eds. 1996. *Senses of Place*. Santa Fe: SAR Press.

Franco Martínez, Juan de la Plata. 2001. *Los gitanos de Jerez*. Jerez de la Frontera: Cátedra de Flamencología y Estudios Folklóricos Andaluces.

———. 2010. *El flamenco que he vivido: Vivencias, escritos, y recuerdos de un viejo aficionado*. Seville: Signatura Ediciones de Andalucia.

Hobsbawm, Eric, and Terence Ranger. 1992. *The Invention of Tradition*. London: Cambridge University Press.

Hood, Mantle. 1960. "The Challenge of Bi-Musicality." *Ethnomusicology* 4 (2): 55–59.

———. 1971. *The Ethnomusicologist*. New York: McGraw-Hill.

Manuel, Peter. 1989. "Andalusian, Gypsy, and Class Identity in the Contemporary Flamenco Complex." *Ethnomusicology* 35 (1): 47–65.

Peña, Manuel. 1985. "From *Ranchero* to *Jaiton*: Ethnicity and Class in Texas-Mexican Music (Two Styles in the Form of a Pair)." *Ethnomusicology* 29 (1): 29–55.

Perlman, Marc. 1998. "The Social Meanings of Modal Practices: Status, Gender, History, and *Pathet* in Central Javanese Music." *Ethnomusicology* 42 (1): 45–80.

Perman, Tony. 2010. "Dancing in Opposition: Muchongoyo, Emotion, and the Politics of Performance in Southeastern Zimbabwe." *Ethnomusicology* 54 (3): 425–51.

Qureshi, Regula Burckhardt. 1987. "Musical Sound and Contextual Input: A Performance Model for Musical Analysis." *Ethnomusicology* 31 (1): 56–86.

Rice, Timothy. 1994. *May It Fill Your Soul: Experiencing Bulgarian Music*. Chicago: University of Chicago Press.

———. 2003. "Time, Place, and Metaphor in Musical Experience and Ethnography." *Ethnomusicology* 47 (2): 151–79.

———. 2007. "Reflections on Music and Identity in Ethnomusicology." *Muzikologija/Musicology* (Journal of the Serbian Academy of Sciences and Arts) 7:17–38.

San Román Espinosa, Teresa. 1997. *La diferencia inquietante: Viejas y nuevas estrategias culturales de los gitanos*. Madrid: Siglo Veintiuno Editores.

Seeger, Anthony. 1987. *Why Suyá Sing: A Musical Anthropology of an Amazonian People*. Cambridge: Cambridge University Press.

Stokes, Martin, ed. 1994. *Ethnicity, Identity, and Music: The Musical Construction of Place*. London: Oxford/Berg.

Sudnow, David. 2001. *Ways of the Hand: A Rewritten Account*. Cambridge, MA: MIT Press.

Sugarman, Jane. 1997. *Engendering Song: Singing and Subjectivity at Prespa Albanian Weddings*. Chicago: University of Chicago Press.

———. 1999. "Imagining the Homeland: Poetry, Songs, and the Discourses of Albanian Nationalism." *Ethnomusicology* 43 (3): 419–58.

Titon, Jeff Todd. 1978. "Every Day I Have the Blues: Improvisation and Daily Life." *Southern Folklore Quarterly* 42:85–98.

———. 1994. "Knowing People Making Music: Toward a New Epistemology for Ethnomusicology." In *Etnomusikologianmuosikirja* [Yearbook of the Finnish Society for Ethnomusicology], vol. 6, 5–13. Helsinki: Suomenetnomusikologinenseura.

———. 1995. "Bimusicality as Metaphor." *Journal of American Folklore* 108:287–97.

———. 2009. "Economy, Ecology, and Music: An Introduction." *the world of music* 51 (1): 5–15.

Turino, Thomas. 1999. "Signs of Imagination, Identity, and Experience: A Peircian Semiotic Theory for Music." *Ethnomusicology* 43 (2): 221–55.

———. 2014. "Peircean Thought as Core Theory for a Phenomenological Ethnomusicology." *Ethnomusicology* 58 (2): 185–221.

CHAPTER 21

Fiddle-icious

A Community Model for Musical Sustainability

THOMAS FAUX

DON ROY IS, by most accounts, southern Maine's preeminent Franco-American fiddler. A many-time contest champion with, as he puts it, "a box of trophies in the attic waiting to be melted down into fishing sinkers," Don is an extraordinarily creative musician, steeped in regional practice, and sophisticated with regard to the commercial and cultural implications of "heritage production." He and his spouse and music partner, Cindy Roy, have toured extensively in the United States and Canada, represented "New England Francophone culture" on the Lincoln Center and Kennedy Center stages and at the Library of Congress, and have been returning guests on Garrison Keillor's *A Prairie Home Companion* radio program. Don was the Maine State fiddling champion in 1990, was nominated for a National Heritage Fellowship in 1994, and was awarded Maine Arts Commission Traditional Arts Fellowships in 1994 and 2001. He has received national and regional recognition for his fiddling, is a major draw at festivals and fiddle camps, and currently divides his time between performing, his longtime job with the Maine Department of Transportation, and building violins in his Gorham, Maine, woodshop.

Since 2001 Don has also directed Fiddle-icious, a community fiddling program that has expanded beyond its church-hall meeting space into the homes and daily lives of the participants. The program is rooted in Don's inherited sense of music as a participatory activity and stands in contrast to heritage industry notions of cultural preservation and revival. As such, Don's work demonstrates a strategy of selecting expressive elements in order to cultivate an emergent sense of community and makes a compelling case for what Jeff Titon has conceived of as cultural resilience: "Resilience . . . offers a strategy, a means toward the goal of sustainability. Resilience refers to a system's capacity to recover and maintain its integrity, identity, and continuity when subjected to forces of disturbance and change" (2015, 158).

Raised in the shadow of the now-defunct fish canneries and lime quarries of Rockland, Maine, Don gives credit for his earliest instruction, repertoire, and inspiration to his uncle and first fiddle teacher, Lucien Mathieu. In 1923 Lucien was born into a large French Canadian family in the small mill town of Winslow, Maine, where he learned to fiddle from his own uncle. Lucien performed throughout the northeast in the 1940s and 1950s with the well-known fiddler (and future grandfather of Cindy Roy) Alfie Martin and later with Don Doan's regionally popular group, the Old Time Katahdin Mountaineers (Lucien Mathieu, radio interview conducted by author, May 1999, WMPG-FM, Portland, Maine). In 1992 Lucien was inducted into the Maine Country Music Hall of Fame. In his eighties Lucien remained an active regional performer, popular at nursing homes and summer festivals. He passed away in 2011.

Under his celebrated uncle's guidance, Don began learning to fiddle as a teenager in the 1970s. Uncle Lucien's weekend-long musical house parties were local legend, and Don's musicianship was cultivated in a musical family and community that included musicians and step-dancers from all over New England and eastern Canada. Significantly, Lucien also introduced him to the recordings of older players such as the eminent Montreal fiddler Jean Carignan. Don says he "wore out the records" listening to and emulating Carignan's bowing style and inventiveness. With Lucien, Don traveled to contests throughout the region, becoming familiar with the competitive fiddling landscape and developing a reputation for his expressive playing and quiet demeanor. In northern competitive fiddling circles often dominated in the 1970s and early 1980s by ex-urbanites who were locally labeled as "hippies" or "back-to-the-landers," Don was a local guy. He drove a snowplow for the Maine Turnpike Authority, had learned his instrument at the knee of his uncle, retained a strong sense of his own working-class identity, and his Down East drawl contrasted with the sometimes more strident tones of cosmopolitan imports from Boston and other urban points south. Now in his fifties, Don is a powerful and imaginative player with a ringing tone that evokes Carignan and a vast stock of dance tunes and ornamental techniques from French Canada, New England, and the Maritimes.

During the 1980s Don and his uncle toured together as the core of the Maine French Fiddlers, a multigenerational group that also included Don's early inspirations Gerry Robichaud and Ben Guillemette. The Maine French Fiddlers quickly developed a presence in the American roots-music market: they were featured several times on *A Prairie Home Companion*, played a celebrated concert at Carnegie Hall in 1990, and by the early 1990s were a hot property on festival stages throughout the Northeast. Don's credentials as a regional tradition-bearer were as indisputable as his musicianship, and as his performing experience broadened he was increasingly in demand as a musician and as a unique Franco-American artistic voice rooted in regional music practice. During the 1990s Don was frequently called on by event producers to represent vanishing Maine Franco culture on music festival stages and in regional celebrations.

In 1994 he became associated with Portland Performing Arts, Inc. (PPA), a now-defunct public arts presenting organization partly dedicated to what its literature called "community-generated cultural programming" (Graves 1996, 2). In addition to producing public concerts, the organization contracted with tradition-bearing musicians and dancers to work within Portland's various immigrant and refugee communities, providing community members with access to culture-specific performances and local performers with professional instruction. These programs targeted a number of Portland's communities that were said to be underrepresented by mainstream arts programming, and one of the earliest programs involved marketing of traditional Franco-American music and dance in the region, in an effort both to provide visibility for this marginalized population and to fortify what was increasingly perceived as a fading culture. Musicians and dancers from Quebec's vibrant traditional music scene were contracted to come across the border to Maine to teach fiddling, step dance, and button accordion and to be the featured entertainment at community soirees held in the basement of Sainte-Hyacinth's Church, a center of social activity for the large Franco-American parish in Westbrook, a paper-mill town just inland of Portland.

Through the 1990s and into the next decade, Don worked closely with PPA. He was featured in public concerts and at sponsored community gatherings, he conducted fiddling workshops, and his work was highlighted in the organization's promotional literature. Through his close association with PPA and then other nonprofit presenting organizations, Don became increasingly known as a carrier of a fading Franco-American musical tradition, and his professional performing arena expanded beyond community dance halls onto national stages, where he was celebrated both as a musician and as a representative of southern Maine's French community. In a concert at the Kennedy Center in Washington, DC, in 2004, appearing with his trio in front of an Acadian flag as part of the Musical Celebration of French-Canadian Culture, Don was described as a quintessential musical representative of French New England: "the finest Franco fiddler in New England, whose playing exactly exemplifies what Franco-American fiddling is all about" (Kennedy Center 2016).

The public identification of Don Roy as a Maine Franco-American artist and the increase in performing opportunities beginning in the 1980s coincided with a late twentieth-century boom in ethnic performance presentation and was specifically linked to a rapidly growing regional demand for expressive francophone voices in northern New England. The deindustrialization of Maine's mill towns and the concomitant decline of the region's urban francophone culture have been well documented (Quintal 1996; Hareven and Langenbach 1978). In short, after nearly a century of social and political marginalization, a number of state agencies and nonprofit organizations were turning their attention to what was perceived as a cultural crisis in the state's French communities. Don Roy's combination of musical, cultural, and personal qualities made him particularly attractive to traditional music promoters and grant writers. Also as Maine's francophone community has succumbed in recent decades to mill closures, secularization, and assimilation, Don's appearances at high-profile performance venues has helped raise the visibility of Franco-American fiddling as an American vernacular musical genre and indirectly served to bring mainstream attention to Maine's dwindling French culture.

Nonetheless, in the late 1990s Don's direct professional link to the institutional arts funders was dissolved. Cindy Roy noted that while their work with the heritage industry had been rewarding, their community was aging, and the organization with which they were affiliated had shifted its priorities:

> Their original grant for us was for two years I think. Then they got it extended for a couple of years. But now it's gone. And Portland is a different place now. There [are] a lot of Somalis and other African refugees, and I think the Center [for Cultural Exchange, formerly PPA] is more geared toward those newer populations. There's not a lot of things going for the Franco-American community anymore. They still have the Asian things; the Cambodians still have their program, and the African program. But as far as the French community, the people who care about it anymore are older, sixty, seventy, eighty years old. Too old to come into town [to watch performances]. (interview, August 2005, Falmouth, ME)

It should be noted that Cindy Roy's expressed dismay at the fickleness of institutional support for the Franco-American project hardly reflects a success story for the revitalization of southern Maine French lifeways or expressive culture. By all accounts, the French in Maine are an aging population whose language, religion, music, and community bonds are increasingly frail, and the reassignment of limited funds in no way indicates a revitalized community. It should also be noted that Cindy Roy's comments do not imply a belief that that Maine Francos are inherently more or less deserving of support than any other regional population. Rather, she expresses recognition that in a finite underwriting environment, all such support is subject to the constraints of shifting demographics and marketing.

As institutional support for the Franco-American program dried up, perhaps overshadowed by the expressive culture of more recent or marketable immigrant and refugee communities, Don began developing a music project that would place his musical skill directly in the service of his own southern Maine community. The project that he named Fiddle-icious was partly an outgrowth of work begun with the heritage industry but, more crucially, grew out of Don's life experience with music as a binding social force. With the administrative experience gained from his work with the nonprofits, he began conducting monthly music sessions open to fiddlers at all skill levels. In 2001 he rented the basement of the Congregational Church near his home, and the project quickly became a congregation of players: "We went from playing once a month to weekly, and the group grew to over seventy people" (Don and Cindy Roy, interview, August 2005, Falmouth, ME). Although the music was central to the meetings and the ostensible reason for gathering, Don says there is something more at stake:

> [There were] friendships and sense of community that developed. I saw people who were strangers three months before offer their homes to those who were ailing. One lady told me that she had moved from a large city to become more involved in the community and that this was the first time she had felt that part of anything so positive. As for myself, the reward of seeing the personal growth and congealing of people gathering for a very positive reason is compensation way beyond any monetary value. (quoted in *Portland Press Herald* 2005)

While Fiddle-icious—at more than eighty members in 2015—is nominally a series of public music workshops, advertised weekly in the local newspaper, it is perhaps more fundamentally an expanding web of ongoing relationships around a core of participatory music. Don Roy is the big draw: as a well-known musician with a confident teaching manner, he is the central figure and the reason for the group's existence. He speaks of the project as something more than music instruction:

> I love what I'm seeing now, with people busting off, forming their own groups, going off to do things on their own. Good friendships have been made. That's really what I want . . . to get people doing things on their own. And getting the better players to teach the others. Now some of the more advanced players—who came here a few years ago for lessons, and would NEVER have gotten up in front of a crowd to play—now they're playing and teaching all over the place. They've started a group up in Freeport. And they are getting together for potluck suppers. That's what's in it for me. (personal communication, August 2005, Falmouth, ME)

Rhonda Bullock, a longtime violinist in the group, notes another value in Don's work with the group: "Not many people have the kind of background Don has. He gives us a connection to his musical family and heritage that some of us wish we had, growing up" (interview, Maine, 2015, Falmouth, ME).

A sense of warmth infuses the church on Monday nights. A folding card table holding an old-fashioned violin case is set up by the door to collect donations for the rental of the church building; it competes for space with flyers for upcoming local music and other events and with baskets of tomatoes, cookies, or other items that the musicians bring for collective distribution and consumption. The playing starts "after supper." Don and Cindy "grab something quick to eat together after work" and then drive directly to the church, to "make sure the heat is on." Beginners begin showing up around six in the evening for a special instruction session and are already playing as the more experienced musicians drift in slowly, open their cases, rosin their bows. People catch up with one another as they come in; there is laughing, touching—a hand on a shoulder, a handshake, a hug—and a palpable sense that the musicians are happy to be here, happy to see one another, ready to play together. At seven they split into small groups. One of the experienced fiddlers, an elderly woman, takes a group of beginners aside to work on bowing. Cindy teaches Quebecois step dancing to a group of women in one of the basement rooms, and they spend some time practicing their footwork and then just dancing. Cindy has worked closely with the celebrated Quebec step-dancer Benoit Bourque, and she demonstrates a mix of steps learned from Bourque and the Acadian dancing she learned from her aunts as a child. Don spends the first part of the evening coaching fiddlers and accordion players individually, trying to touch base with everyone at least briefly; people gather in small ensembles throughout the church building to work together on the latest repertoire or to refresh the more familiar. Sometime around eight the entire group convenes in the church's main parish hall. They play through their current repertoire together for an hour or so, and then Don teaches two or three new tunes by rote. They start slowly, working phrase by phrase. By nine everyone is playing steadily, if deliberately, and by the end of the evening "the waltzes and jigs are up to speed, but the reels are usually still slow for some of them" (Don Roy, personal communication, August 2005, Falmouth, ME).

Don posts recordings of the tunes on the Fiddle-icious website along with his transcriptions of the material, but the primary method of transmission is aural, by rote. There is an intimacy that is cultivated by the face-to-face transmission: a looking into the eyes, an attention to body language, a sense of sharing that perhaps sets this old-time fiddling apart from many other American community ensemble genres—community orchestras, municipal bands, barbershop ensembles, and choirs—and it seems clear that this music embodies and engenders sociability in a very direct manner. While there is some chatter as the fiddlers learn the tunes, talk is mainly limited to the task at hand. There is an ambiance of intense engagement in the room as tunes become familiar under the fingers. At around nine o'clock Don loosens his bow and gives a few last words, a signal that the formally structured part of the evening is over. Announcements are made, brownies eaten, fiddles put away, and conversations are picked up.

The group's material is drawn from Don's seemingly inexhaustible stock of 32-bar tunes, gathered over a thirty-five-year fiddling career. While he has an enduring interest in the dance music of eastern Canada, like many Franco New England players—and like Carignan himself—Don plays from a range of regional fiddle repertoires. For the purposes of Fiddle-icious, he makes little functional distinction between Quebecois, Maritime, British Isles, or for that matter southern American fiddle tunes, although he says his preference is for the dance numbers from Quebec and eastern Canada: "The French and Cape Breton stuff are similar in melodies, and the bottom line is that I like it." And while an apparently boundless reserve of potential new material is surely one of the things that keeps the sessions musically challenging for veteran players, the simplicity and brevity of the form (virtually all follow the AABB, 8 bars in a section form), the diatonicism of the melodies, the pool of accessible and interchangeable phrases and ornaments, and the relatively limited temporal vocabulary of the music, at least at the entry level, are elements that appeal to beginners and more casual players. Don says he chooses tunes that contain elements that invite participation at various levels of expertise: "I pick tunes that all levels can handle. And stuff that lends itself to orchestration" (Don Roy, personal communication, August 2005, Falmouth, ME).

Thomas Turino has suggested that musical genres fall along a participatory/presentational continuum in which participatory musics are characterized by their capacity to engage nonspecialists and specialists equally: "Participatory music is defined and shaped stylistically by the fundamental goal of inviting the fullest participation possible, and the success of an occasion is judged primarily by the amount of participation realized. In heightened participatory contexts there is little or no distinction between performers and audience—there are only participants and potential participants. Nonetheless, participatory events may, and should, allow for different types of roles (e.g. instrumentalists and dancers) and levels of specialization" (2000, 48). Fiddle tunes are often reducible to skeletal form for the inexperienced, and the largely diatonic melodies are limited to a couple of modes in a few keys. Still, there is rhythmic nuance enough and room for melodic creativity for advanced players, and while Don teaches particular melodic variations, he constantly makes the point that his versions are not definitive, and that creative musicians need to take liberties to bring the music to life. The combination of accessibility and challenge inherent in the music then provides a sense of flow for each participant, and there is a feeling in the church on Monday nights that everyone is engaged, together.

The success of Don's program is mirrored in other similar recently emerged fiddle communities around Maine and elsewhere. In Farmington, Maine, ninety miles north of Don's church basement, Steve Muise directs the Franklin County Fiddlers, a large group of young players that has become something of a social institution in that town, drawing musicians into one another's homes and providing impetus for a lively local calendar of dances, traditional-music sessions, and concerts. Much further north, in the heavily Francophone Saint John Valley border region between Maine and Canada, Lisa Ornstein, a noted fiddler—and director of the Acadian Archives at the University of Maine at Fort Kent—began collecting donated violins in 2001 and distributing them to any of the area's fourth graders interested in coming to fiddle class. In describing her effort to nurture a long-standing Acadian tradition of social music making, Ornstein notes the importance of face-to-face engagement: "Our region has a rich heritage of traditional fiddling, but while fiddle music is still very appreciated by local audiences, the informal transmission of this art has all but disappeared, leaving no up-and-coming generation to carry on the heritage" (University of Maine at Fort Kent 2002).

But while Don Roy's fiddling may be firmly embedded in a rich Franco-American tradition, Don himself is a somewhat reluctant culture hero. Indeed, until he began working with the nonprofit arts presenters, he had little sense of his role as a "carrier of tradition." He says he was not particularly conscious of his "Franco-ness," didn't think of himself as particularly "ethnic," and even now is ambivalent about such labeling. He and Cindy Roy spoke candidly about their respective relationships with notions of Franco ethnicity:

> TF: Growing up you felt the stigma of being French?
> CINDY ROY: I did. It was nothing that my family did, or passed upon it [sic]
> it was just me. I don't think my friends growing up would have looked too
> kindly on what went on in my grandfather's house every week. I mean, it
> was a party, why should they not look kindly on it? Not have good feelings
> about it? But to me, being a fourteen-, fifteen-, sixteen-year old person, it
> was "oh . . . that's what my Pepé does, not what I want to do." There was a
> stigma, but I didn't realize it at the time. Just thought it was my own thing.
> My aunt—the step dancer I was telling you about—she would tell you a
> whole different story. When she was a teenager growing up in the fifties.
> They'd be cruising around town on Saturday night, and she'd be with her
> friends saying, "I wish I was home, there's a party going on there!" And
> things would be winding down, and she'd say let's go to my house. And she'd
> get there with her friends, and the music would be going, and everybody
> would be having a great time and her friends would be like "what's with

this? This is weird stuff." 'Cause it's not what they'd grown up with. Now it's
cool to be French! When I was a kid it was only cool to be Irish.

TF: Don, did you have that sense too?

DON ROY: I never thought about being "Franco-American." I still don't, until
someone comes around asking questions about it. I never had to think about
heritage, until seven or eight years ago when I got involved in the [House
Island] project. Then I did. (interview, August 2005, Falmouth, ME)

As agents of cultural diversity it is, of course, necessary for administrators,
promoters, and cultural activists to establish and maintain boundaries of ethnicity with precision. Authentic cultural difference is valuable currency among
presenters who, in order to simplify messages of ethnic identity, may display aspects of heritage symbolically by hanging a flag on the back of a stage, publishing
bilingual concert programs, or simply marketing a performer as a "quintessential
musical representative." As the French in Maine have become increasingly as-
similated, increasingly invisible, presenting institutions have learned to capitalize
on the perception of cultural loss, effectively framing their offerings as well as
their funding applications in terms of preserving and cultivating ethnic identity.

But while Don and Cindy Roy's roles as music mentors and community
leaders are surely profoundly embedded in their particular French Canadian
cultural inheritance, and while there have been ample opportunities for them
to take professional advantage of their Franco-American identity, there is no
claim of ethnicity here, either in the conceiving and promoting of his fiddling
group or in the musical practices shared, and there is no claim of cultural revival.
Rather, the Roys have chosen to emphasize what they see as the substance of
their heritage, the cultivating of social ties through their music, and I believe
that their program is successful in terms of the intensity of learning and in the
relations being built, precisely because of that emphasis.

Don Roy's music sits at an intersection in which technique, repertoire,
transmission, and perhaps the cultural significance of vernacular fiddling as
a genre—associated in the collective American imagination with harvest parties, barn raisings, and other materially life-sustaining activities—converge
into an expressive form with remarkable potential for enabling the growth of
face-to-face relationships. And I submit that Don's approach, privileging collective engagement over bureaucratically promoted categories of ethnic identity,
presents a holistic and cogent model for the cultivation of community through
participatory music making.

Don speaks directly to the issue of sustainability:

TF: What will happen in the future as it expands?

DR: We'll just keep doing it. We do some concerts, but mainly we'll just keep
doing it every week. We went from thirty-five people to seventy over one

year, and then over a hundred. You've got to wonder how many fiddle players there are in southern Maine. Well, the last thing I want to do is discourage anybody, and if we get another forty next year, well, the church will hold them. (interview, August 2005, Falmouth, ME)

Note

This article is primarily based on interviews conducted by the author with Don and Cindy Roy in August 2005 and November 2015. I would like to gratefully acknowledge the Roys' generosity and hospitality.

References

Graves, James Bau. 1996. *House Island Project: Advancing the Cultural Heritage of Maine's Ethnic Communities*. Portland, ME: Portland Performing Arts.

Hareven, Tamara K., and Randolph Langenbach. 1978. *Amoskeag: Life and Work in an American Factory-City*. New York: Pantheon.

Kennedy Center. 2016. "Don Roy Trio." http://kennedycenter.com/artist/B10125#. Accessed May 30.

Portland Press Herald. 2005. "Traditional Fiddle Music and Much More When Fiddleicious Comes to Town." Mainetoday, October 17.

Quintal, Claire, ed. 1996. *Steeples and Smokestacks: A Collection of Essays on the Franco-American Experience in New England*. Worcester, MA: Editions de l'Institut francais.

Titon, Jeff Todd. 2015. "Sustainability, Resilience, and Adaptive Management for Applied Ethnomusicology." In *The Oxford Handbook of Applied Ethnomusicology*, edited by Svanibor Pettan and Jeff Todd Titon, 157–95. New York: Oxford University Press.

Turino, Thomas. 2000. *Nationalist, Cosmopolitans, and Popular Music in Zimbabwe*. Chicago: University of Chicago Press.

University of Maine at Fort Kent. 2002. https://www.umfk.edu/valleyvision/january-11–2002-director-of-umfks-acadian-archives-fiddle-program-receives-recognition/ (web page no longer available).

CHAPTER 22

Discovering Maine's Intangible Cultural Heritage

PAULEENA M. MACDOUGALL

AS CLIFFORD MURPHY HAS NOTED, "when we go looking for culture, no matter where we're from, we can find ourselves drawn towards people and traditions 'from away.' We can forget that culture resides in our own neighborhoods and even within each of us. If this becomes habit, we can fail to recognize when we are in the presence of greatness, simply because it doesn't look like we thought it might" (Murphy 2015). Indeed, most people think of cultural heritage as related to place. It is often understood as a site of some historical importance. Society values tangible culture, and often that is where it focuses preservation and conservation efforts. *Intangible cultural heritage* is a fairly recent term that encompasses all the nontangible aspects of culture. I decided to use the term *intangible cultural heritage* (ICH) instead of *folklore* because, as anthropologist Kristin Kuutma points out in her article on heritage politics, it is a universally inclusive term for culture that avoids references to social stratum or inferiority perceived to be present in terms like *folklore, traditional,* or *popular culture,* which many people find too limiting or proscriptive and thus lacking in value (Kuutma 2013). Intangible cultural heritage is defined in relation to tangible but also to natural heritage—the environment or a place that provides the resources used in cultural activities. For example, a lobsterman's gear and boat are part of his or her tangible culture, the territory where he or she fishes is the natural heritage, and his or her knowledge of how to use the gear and the boat and navigate the ocean to capture lobsters is the intangible culture. In my experience as a culture worker in Maine, I have observed that advocacy for the stewardship of the ecosystem is an important part of cultural work. When we recognize that cultural constructions are part of the ecosystem, we can demonstrate the necessary connectedness of human culture to the environment. By clarifying the role that humans play in the ecosystem, our cultural work can also strengthen arguments for environmental sustainability. Understanding ICH is critical to understanding the interrelationship of humans and the environment.

The term *intangible cultural heritage* was defined by UNESCO in 2001 after a survey of world organizations. ICH is "transmitted from generation to generation, constantly recreated by communities and groups, in response to their environment, their interaction with nature, and their history. It includes the practices, representations, expressions, as well as the knowledge and skills (including instruments, objects, artifacts, cultural spaces), that communities, groups, and in some cases, individuals recognize as part of their cultural heritage. It is sometimes called living cultural heritage, and is manifested as: oral traditions and expressions, including language, performing arts; social practices, rituals, and festive events; knowledge and practices concerning nature and the universe; and traditional craftsmanship" (UNESCO 2016).

My personal discovery of Maine's ICH began when I worked on Indian Island in the 1980s, assisting the Penobscot Nation in work that would eventually lead to my current project compiling a dictionary of the Penobscot language. There I learned that the Penobscots value their language as an enduring symbol of their personal and community heritage (see also Cooley, this volume). The Penobscot language and culture are a permanent part of all of Maine's ICH witnessed by the many place-names across the state, the use of Penobscot-styled canoes for recreation, the adoption by Mainers of the practice of eating fiddleheads in the spring and snowshoeing, and in many other ways.

My work on Indian Island and later at the University of Maine led to a personal recognition of the importance of Maine's cultural heritage to Maine citizens but also to an international audience interested in the many ways that humans create culture. This recognition led to a growing awareness of the need for conservation, advocacy, education, and stewardship. I realized that my contribution to knowledge could come in the form of research and writing about Maine's ICH, and once I began teaching at the university I wanted to provide students with opportunities for making their own discoveries by doing primary research, including fieldwork, which I believe is a key component of cultural sustainability.

Maine's ICH includes various genres of creative knowledge such as music, dance, occupational know-how, and various artistic ventures. Much of Maine's ICH results from the type of place that Maine is: largely rural, with mostly resource-based economies, international boundaries, and nearly 3,500 miles of coastline on the Atlantic Ocean. Here in Maine an interest in intangible heritage has historically inspired many individuals to record and preserve Maine's culture, from the earliest European visitors who attempted to describe the Native American languages and practices they observed to nineteenth- and twentieth-century writers who collected and wrote about Maine's culture.

Some of these writers and researchers include Joanna Colcord (1938), who, with her brother Lincoln, collected songs from sailors; Fannie Hardy Eckstorm (see Barry, Eckstorm, and Smyth 1929), who collected songs from woodsmen and seamen, as well as stories and other indigenous knowledge; anthropologist Frank Speck (1940), who worked with the Penobscot, the Passamaquoddy, and the Maliseet people in the early twentieth century; folklorist Horace Beck (1957); University of Maine professor and folklorist Edward D. "Sandy" Ives (1965); folklorists David Taylor (see MacDougall, Taylor, and Hedler 2000); Jeff Todd Titon (2000); Clifford Murphy (2014); and others. All have contributed to our knowledge of Maine's ICH and many to the Northeast Archives of Folklore and Oral History—the core of the Maine Folklife Center's research—and to various publications, including the *Maine History Journal* and the center's annual monograph series, Northeast Folklore.

Researchers uncovered Maine's knowledge of processes: how to fish, how to hunt, how to build a boat, how to weave a basket, how to find natural materials, observations on weather phenomenon, creativity—something not easily measured but universally understood—song making, storytelling, dialects and unique word usages, and personal experiences of important events, for example, the experiences of veterans in war; how students experienced the University of Maine in the 1940s, 1950s, and 1960s; what it is like to work in a paper mill or to go to school without knowing English or with a disability. These and many other topics have been covered by my predecessor Sandy Ives, me, and other faculty, staff, students, and researchers to create a collection of regional cultural materials housed in the Northeast Archives of Folklore and Oral History, founded by Ives in 1958. From this work, it becomes clear that the cultural life of Maine is intimately connected to the ecosystem and that preservation of the ecosystem is essential for cultural survival. Culture and environment thus become an ecosystem of culture, and stewardship of culture must include stewardship of the natural world. Because of the way humans perceive the world as outside themselves, they tend to think of the ecosystem as being human-less. Of course, that is not the case. But if we add the cultural constructs that humans create to the ecosystem it becomes clearer that humans are part of the ecosystem and the ecosystem is essential to human life and culture.

The following excerpts from interviews help to illustrate the interconnectedness of human culture and ecosystems.[1] The first excerpt is from an interview I conducted on January 28, 1993, with master basket maker and Penobscot lan-

guage speaker Madeline Tomer Shay at Indian Island, Maine. In it she is responding to a question I asked her: how and when did you learn to make baskets?

> I couldn't remember how old I was, I was little—very little—and my grand-
> mother gave me all the gauges and the material and everything and said, "Now
> you sit and you work; you learn how to make baskets," she said, "because
> sometime when you marry and have a family, it is going to come in handy."
> And believe me, it did.
>
> My husband and I, when there was no work, he and I sat up till two-three
> o'clock in the morning making big baskets. And those big shoppers and bar-
> rels we only got $1.50 a piece for one. So you can imagine how many we had
> to make to make any amount of money. (2383)

The second passage is from an interview conducted seven years later by
history graduate student Anu Dudley at the Common Ground Fair in Unity,
Maine, on September 20, 2002, with another master basket maker, Theresa
Hoffman Secord, who was responsible for organizing the Maine Indian Basket Makers Alliance—an organization that supports and helps basket makers
market their wares. She is also responding to the question, how did you learn
to make baskets?

> Well, I started working for my tribe in 1984, after I had earned my Master's
> Degree in Geology, and so [laughs]—this is connected—I became the staff
> geologist for the Penobscot Nation in 1984 and actually headed up the Mineral
> Assessment Program for our tribe, which was, of course, new after the land
> claims settlement in 1980. And I worked for my tribe for thirteen years actu-
> ally, but during that time was also reconnecting with family and elder basket
> makers in the community. And I actually started apprenticing to Madeline
> Tomah [Shay] as a, as a basket maker in 1988. But I, I, interestingly, my con-
> nection with her began because I was interested in learning our language, and
> within a couple of sessions I learned that I was going to be a much better basket
> maker than a speaker of our, you know, really complicated Penobscot language.
>
> And so, that's how I learned to make baskets, and gradually became involved
> with other basket makers in the state through the Traditional Arts Apprentice-
> ship Program and the Maine Arts Commission, and even brought together the
> first gathering of tribal basket makers in Maine who are from all four federally
> recognized tribes in 1992, ten years ago.
>
> So, we formed a corporation, Maine Indian Basket Makers' Alliance, in 1993,
> and started doing a lot of public outreach programming, and gradually found
> our way, you know, here [at the Common Ground Fair] through, I think, con-
> nections with you Anu and the Folk Arts Area, where you had been inviting
> basket makers to participate in programs and demonstration programs.

It would have been Richard Silliboy and Molly Neptune Parker, who are actually our president and vice-president today. And so we formed our own tent area, Native American Arts Area, to try to enhance the participation of members of all four tribes. . . . From our point of view that's been a critical thrust of our work—the preservation of ash and sweet-grass basketry in the four tribes. (3067)

The preservation of ash has become a critical issue in Maine as the emerald ash borer, which kills ash trees, is making its way east after being introduced to the West Coast. The Penobscot people are monitoring and working with policy makers in hopes of preserving this important natural and cultural resource since preservation of the environmental resource is critical to sustaining the cultural.

The next two selections relate to Maine's traditional boat-building culture. In the first, Lynn Franklin interviewed boat builder Phil Nichols in 1974 at his home in Round Pond, Maine, about building Friendship Sloops in the 1930s.

On Loud's Island I bought an old Friendship sloop for 10 dollars. We put some barrels in and towed it to Round Pond. Made some molds of the outside, the stern, the stem and started a new boat from the molds I had made. This was during the Depression.

The new sloop was 33 foot. Had just sold a 30-foot sloop that was built by Wilbur Morse. I'd put that money, $560, in the bank. (0915)

In this next interview, conducted on March 2, 2004, at boat builder Eric Dow's shop in Brooklin, Maine, I asked him how he learned to make boats.

I went to the marine trade center in well it was Washington County VTI at that point. They had a boat building division. The school was headquartered in Calais but they had just taken over the old coast guard station in Lubec and set that up into a boat building program. A two-year program. So I attended that and came back here and started right out. I was still young and didn't need to earn a whole lot of money, luckily because I would have starved. I was still single. This building was in the family. My grandfather had been a mechanic and this was his garage so it started out small and it's still that way really still just 3 or 4 of us working here.

There were two instructors. There was Doug Dodge. He is from Beal's Island. His family had been building lobster boats there for generations and he had grown up doing that. He had started out as a mechanics teacher at the vocational school and originated the boat building program there. . . . He knew his profession so well that it was a little bit hard for him to teach it. Things that just came naturally to him were a little hard to put across to somebody who had no idea what to do but still he was a good boat builder. I guess he's still

in business. He worked there for probably seven or eight years and then went
back to Beal's and went back into boat building again. (3288)

The two interviews, though more than thirty years apart, illustrate Maine's
ongoing traditional method of using molds to build wooden boats. Although
Eric attended a school to learn to make boats, his teachers represented generations of Maine's master boat builders. Boat building is a way of life in many of
Maine's coastal communities and rests firmly on the connection that people
have to the ocean for fishing and recreation.

These stories help us to make sense of ICH by placing it in the context of an
ecosystem of culture. The idea, originally proposed for music by William Kay
Archer in his essay "On the Ecology of Music" (1964) has been adopted by a
number of ethnomusicologists, most notably by Jeff Todd Titon, who has written
on the topic for some twenty-five years. In his 2009 article on music and sustainability, Titon proposed that those of us charged with stewardship of intangible
cultural heritage should look to the world of ecology for parallels to understand
the importance of stewardship in preserving and sustaining culture. In a recent
Journal of American Folklore article (2016), Titon calls for careful consideration
of ecosystems of culture and proposes the following list of factors that influence
cultural vitality: cultural rights and ownership, circulation and conservation,
internal vitality of culture, social organization, education and transmission, roles
of community scholars, tourism and the creative economy, preservation versus
revitalization, partnerships, and good stewardship of resources.

According to Titon, ecosystems of culture include economics, the natural
environment, and cultural practices and knowledge. These factors interrelate
in our region in a way that creates the region's unique sense of place. A good
example of an ecosystem of culture is the Penobscot River. Inhabited for thousands of years, the river area has continued to be home to the Penobscot Nation,
who utilize the river both for its natural resources—fresh water, fish, and other
foods—and for travel. The Penobscot people developed the birch bark canoe
for summer travel on the water and snowshoes and toboggans for winter travel.
The preservation of the river for clean water, fish, and other natural resources is
central to Penobscot Nation culture and its intangibles—the language, stories,
indigenous knowledge, and daily and seasonal way of living that are intimately
connected—thus creating an ecosystem of culture. This is a contested space as
the tribe struggles to steward the water in the river in the face of objections by
the State of Maine (Chavaree 2014). Stewardship of this ecosystem of culture,
to continue with this example, requires both stewardship of the clean water,
to preserve the health of the environment, and preservation of the cultural
knowledge needed to continue practices such as resource extraction, canoeing,
and snowshoe making as well as language and stories that underpin identity.

Understanding the interconnectedness of the intangible, tangible, and natural in an ecosystem requires more than just partnering with communities in preserving cultural items. The relationship between the natural environment and tangible and intangible culture impact the way practitioners and community scholars and others view cultural rights and responsibilities (see also Baron and Walker; Allen; and Hufford, this volume).

Cultural Rights and Ownership

Cultural rights did not get the attention of the international community until 1948, when the United Nations added cultural rights to its international policy in article 27 of the Universal Declaration of Human Rights. The UN article states in part that every human has the right to freely participate in the cultural life of the community to enjoy the arts and to benefit from the moral and material interests resulting from any scientific, literary, or artistic production that he or she authors. Policy in the United States provides copyrights and patents, but little public policy protects cultural rights.

In the United States, Native Americans have taken the lead in lobbying for cultural rights. Beginning in the 1970s the Native Rights organization, spearheaded by the American Indian Movement, brought attention to the issue of possession, sale, and display of human remains and cultural artifacts, picketing some sites and protesting in other ways. Its lobbying resulted in the passage of the Native American Graves Protection and Repatriation Act (NAGPRA), a United States federal law enacted on November 16, 1990. This act requires federal agencies and institutions that receive federal funding to return certain Native American cultural items to lineal descendants and culturally affiliated Native American tribes.

Swiss attorney and cultural law specialist Karolina Kuprecht (2014) has written about the impact of NAGPRA as a pioneer act and a model for regulating indigenous peoples' cultural property claims in other parts of the world as well, especially because NAGPRA requires considering indigenous peoples' perspectives and confirms the belief in their rights to control the fate and integrity of their cultural property. Cultural affiliation and repatriation turned out to be successful instruments in stimulating a vibrant exchange between scientists, museums, and tribes, adding value to many collections and objects. While the law does not address intangible cultural heritage directly, ICH has become a critical part of the NAGPRA process through the use of oral histories and traditional knowledge to provide important information to scientists, museums, and agencies for decisions about the treatment and transfer of Native American cultural property. These elements of intangible culture became invaluable as sources for testable hypotheses, even relating to prehistoric times. At least 308

NAGPRA cases have incorporated oral histories and oral traditions in determining cultural affiliation.

Locally I have witnessed archaeologists working with tribes on repatriation issues but also more expansively on research projects and new research questions as a result of the collaboration initiated by NAGPRA. These projects result in much new information about ICH and its relationship to the environment, for example, history of land use, the meaning of place-names, legends and stories relating to places and artifacts, and information about resource gathering and hunting. Here is a case where ensuring cultural rights has resulted in both better relationships between academics and Native communities and better scholarship (Kapchan 2014). For example, the late University of Maine archaeologist Brian Robinson (1953–2016) hired students and community members from the Penobscot and Passamaquoddy tribes to do fieldwork in archaeological sites in Machias, Maine (Soctomah 2010).

Scholars have realized slowly the importance of protecting the cultural rights of the people they work with. When researchers in Maine first began conducting oral histories and collecting information about songs, stories, ballads, and other intangible cultural heritage, there were no guidelines about how information should be gathered, how communities, and individuals, rights should be protected, or even how information should be preserved. Throughout the twentieth century, folklorists, anthropologists, and other researchers developed these guidelines. The Oral History Association, the American Folklore Society, and other professional organizations also develop guidelines and make them accessible to researchers.

In the United States, regulations protecting human subjects first became effective on May 30, 1974, when the Department of Health, Education and Welfare initiated regulations based on NIH's Policies for the Protection of Human Subjects, which were first issued in 1966. The regulations established the IRB as one mechanism through which human subjects would be protected. Although the Oral History Association has requested that oral histories be exempt from this process, they are not.

In spite of protections such as NAGPRA, which deals primarily with tangible culture, and the IRB, which protects individuals in research, there are still questions that need to be considered when conducting research on ICH and an ongoing debate among academics and community representatives about whether the results of research should be part of a commons or copyrighted or even secluded from use. In addition to individual rights community rights also must be considered as well as rights of authorship. Questions about ownership, copyrights, and cultural rights are critical to both academics and archivists who have to make decisions about access and use of their collections.

Determining cultural rights and ownership are important particularly when making decisions about using the materials on the internet (in an online exhibit, for example) or in a television or radio program. Good policy honors the depositors' copyright by seeking their permission (wherever possible). This is especially important for practitioners and community scholars.

Role of Practitioners and Community Scholars

Again, Native American communities over the last decade or so have taken the lead in advocating for and developing policies in the United States for regulating research on their culture, setting up tribal review boards, and requesting that academics respect their ownership and cultural rights. At first, academics were concerned that this development would mean that they would no longer be able to conduct research on tribal culture. What it has meant, instead, is that Native communities and academics have built partnerships and conducted projects that are beneficial to the community as well as to the scholar. Currently the University of Maine has a collaborative project with the Penobscot Nation and the American Philosophical Society to complete and publish a dictionary of the Penobscot language and to provide language curriculum to language teachers in the Penobscot community. Other efforts I know of here at the university include work on environmental problems that affect Native communities such as the emerald ash borer (University of Maine 2016). Archaeologists have been working with the Passamaquoddies to understand the cultural meaning of petroglyphs in Machias, Maine, which the tribe wants to preserve (Maine Coast Heritage Trust 2006). Given a chance, practitioners and community scholars can be essential partners with academics in research on Maine's ICH.

Working closely with communities in both the development of research projects and in providing some benefit to the community is essential to the kind of stewardship that is required to sustain Maine's ecosystems. Commodifying and selling culture are not sustainable practices. When an individual or company purchases an item, a photograph, or a recording and restricts access, the ecosystem of culture suffers. A better strategy includes finding ways to share the fruits of the research with the community involved. This type of strategy provides benefit to researchers as well as practitioners, artists, and cultural communities. It also has economic value in relation to tourism. Maine has had a tourism industry based primarily on its natural resources since the late nineteenth century. But some of what draws people to Maine includes the hunting camp owners and guides, the farmers and fishermen, local foods and drink, and fairs and festivals. These cultural and natural attractions all contribute to what outsiders see as Maine's unique culture.

Tourism and the Creative Economy:
Educating the Public about ICH

Cultural tourism benefits from educational programming at fairs, festivals, and other events. Beginning in 1998, the Maine Folklife Center began educational programming at the Common Ground Fair. One of Maine's twenty-four licensed agricultural fairs, the Common Ground Country Fair was established in 1971 by the Maine Organic Gardeners and Farmers Association (see Titon, this volume). Between 1998 and 2004 the Maine Folklife Center staff provided programming on Maine's traditions at the fair and also conducted several oral history projects, including a study of the founders of the Common Ground Fair and a number of leaders in the Maine Organic Farmers and Gardeners Association.

Expansion of public folklore efforts began in 2001, when the city of Bangor applied to the National Council for the Traditional Arts to bring the National Folk Festival to Bangor. In developing the folk arts area for the festival, and working with the Page Farm and Home Museum, the Hudson Museum, University Extension, and a number of departments, folklorists identified folk traditions, interviewed practitioners, invited them to participate, and facilitated interaction between the artisans and the public at the narrative stage. We also partnered with off-campus organizations, including the Bangor Historical Society and the Penobscot Nation's Department of Natural Resources.

Bringing artisans and natural-resource stewards to the narrative stage to talk about the community context of their art and associated environmental issues allows them to share their knowledge with the public and to answer questions. We have also recorded their stories and photographed the artistic processes. During the last fifteen years we have created a collection of Maine's ICH and preserved it for researchers. While the act of bringing artists and artisans to a public event in and of itself does not sustain those arts, it does provide artists with public exposure and an opportunity to educate the public about their work. In addition, the documentation from these events provides a record of practices that helps to sustain Maine's cultural ecosystem for future researchers and community members (see Turner, this volume).

Researching intangible cultural heritage, human environmental interactions, and tangible culture are the keys to understanding Maine's cultural heritage in relationship to the region and especially in relation to the rest of the world. Part of the plan of research should include preservation of that research and public educational programming that brings such research to citizens. Such work bolsters the state's tourism industry by providing knowledge needed by cultural tourism businesses. The cultural life of Maine is intimately connected to the ecosystem, and thus the preservation of that ecosystem is essential for cultural survival. The ecosystem of culture includes intangible culture, tangible culture, and the environment. As researchers, we need to advocate for the stewardship of the ecosystem. By recognizing the cultural constructs that humans create within the ecosystem we recognize the interconnectedness of human culture to the environment. If rather than seeing humans as separate from the environment, researchers instead clarify the role that humans play in the ecosystem, we can strengthen our understanding of how the ecosystem is essential to human life and culture.

Notes

1. All recorded and transcribed interviews cited in this chapter are housed in the Northeast Archives of Folklore and Oral History. The archival accession number is given in parentheses following each excerpt.

References

Archer, William Kay. 1964. "On the Ecology of Music." *Ethnomusicology* 8 (1): 28–33.

Barry, Phillips, Fannie Hardy Eckstorm, and Mary Winslow Smyth. 1929. *British Ballads from Maine: The Development of Popular Songs with Texts and Airs.* New Haven, CT: Yale University Press.

Beck, Horace. 1957. *The Folklore of Maine.* Philadelphia: Lippincott.

Chavaree, Mark. 2014. "Penobscot Nation Suing Maine to Fight for Namesake River." *Bangor Daily News*, August 19. https://tinyurl.com/y7w9cy2k.

Colcord, Joanna C. 1938. *Songs of American Sailormen.* Introduced by Lincoln Colcord. New York: W. W. Norton.

Ives, Edward D. 1965. "Folksongs from Maine." *Northeast Folklore* 7:1965.

Kapchan, Deborah. 2014. *Cultural Heritage in Transit: Intangible Rights as Human Rights.* Philadelphia: University of Pennsylvania Press.

Kuprecht, Karolina. 2014. *Indigenous Peoples' Cultural Property Claims: Repatriation and Beyond.* Cham, Switzerland: Springer International.

Kuutma, Kristin. 2013. "Concepts and Contingencies in Heritage Politics." In *Anthropological Perspectives on Intangible Cultural Heritage*, edited by Lourdes Arizpe and Cristina Amescua, 1–15. Cham, Switzerland: Springer International.

MacDougall, Pauleena, David Taylor, and Betsy Hedler, eds. 2000. "Essays in Honor of Edward D. Ives." *Northeast Folklore* 35:3–438.

Maine Coast Heritage Trust. 2006. "Machias, Maine Petroglyphs: 3,000 Year Old Petroglyph Site Regained by Passamaquoddy Tribe." http://www.mcht.org/news/2006/10/3000_year_old_petroglyph_site_1.shtml. Accessed October 30, 2016. (Web page no longer available.)

Murphy, Clifford. 2014. *Yankee Twang: Country and Western Music in New England.* Urbana-Champaign: University of Illinois Press.

———. 2015. "Inherently Local Greatness." National Endowment for the Arts. https://www.arts.gov/article/inherently-local-greatness. Accessed September 29, 2018.

Northeast Archives of Folklore and Oral History. Special Collections, Raymond Fogler Library, University of Maine, Orono.

Soctomah, Donald. 2010. "Machias Bay Archaeology." *Tribal Historic Preservation Office: Passamaquoddy Tribe* (newsletter) 1 (1): 2–3. https://tinyurl.com/y7buymdv.

Speck, Frank Gouldsmith. 1940. *Penobscot Maine: The Life History of a Forest Tribe in Maine.* Philadelphia: University of Pennsylvania Press.

Titon, Jeff Todd. 2000. "Albert Collins: Poet of South Blue Hill, Maine." *Northeast Folklore* 35: 383–404.

———. 2009. "Music and Sustainability: An Ecological Viewpoint." *the world of music* 51 (1): 119–37.

———. 2016. "Orality, Commonality, Commons, Sustainability, and Resilience." *Journal of American Folklore* 128 (514): 486–97.

UNESCO. 2016. "What Is Intangible Cultural Heritage?" http://www.unesco.org/culture/ich/index.php?lg=en&pg=00002. Accessed August.

University of Maine. 2016. "UMaine and Tribes Work to Protect Brown Ash." https://forest.umaine.edu/spotlights/umaine-and-tribes-work-to-protect-brown-ash/. Accessed October 30.

CHAPTER 23

Song, Surfing, and Postcolonial Sustainability

TIMOTHY J. COOLEY

COLONIZATION EXPLOITS the environmental resources of place as well people and cultural practices associated with that place. Likewise, any vision for a sustainable postcolonial world must account for decolonizing cultural practices at least as much as territory or place. Yet decolonization does not mean detachment, separation, segregation. An ecological approach reminds us that organisms live in relation to other organisms and to their environment. From the perspective of environmental humanities, human relations to other organisms and the environment are actualized through cultural processes: social, historical, economic, ethical, and so forth (Heise 2017, 2). In the twenty-first century, this suggests that the historically colonized and the historic colonizer must acknowledge the relations that bind them to a shared global environment. Recognizing this relationship does not diminish Indigenous peoples' claims to homelands but instead calls for radical empathy (Turner, this volume) that leaves no room for neocolonialisms, neoliberalisms, or even neotribalisms that exacerbate the plundering of global resources for the advantage of a few (Manuel 2017). To riff on Linda Tuhiwai Smith's challenge to decolonize the minds of the colonized (1999, 24), the colonizers too must escape the mental grip of logics that replicate patterns of exploitation (see Cary 2004, 76, 80). Thus it is a double bind, but bound we are as organisms on this fragile planet.[1]

In this chapter I begin with one cultural practice—surfing—that was developed to an extremely high level by Indigenous peoples of Hawai'i over several millennia before it was appropriated by settler colonialists and exported globally. I show how surfing and musicking associated with surfing informs us about colonization and in some cases is part of colonial processes. More to the point, I demonstrate that musical practices related to surfing over time mark significant changes in the geopolitical situation for Hawai'i and Hawaiians, as well as the ways that surfing was integrated (or not) with ecological practices. I propose that when surfing and musicking are well integrated with other cultural practices, they model, reflect, and are an integral part of broader strategies for ecological resilience and sustainability (see Titon 2015). Conversely, when surfing and musicking are decontextualized through appropriation and commoditization, they tend to lose links to ecological sustainability. I conclude with a case study of a project that grows out of the Hawaiian Renaissance that began in the 1970s and is even more active today. That postcolonial and decolonial project merges traditional practices with cutting-edge scientific developments to promote sustainable land and sea management. Focused on practice, it seeks first to encourage interactions between Indigenous peoples globally beginning with enacted exchanges of cultural practices including food, music, and dance.

I also grapple with my own position as a musician, scholar, and surfer who benefits from the very legacy of colonization and cultural appropriation that I critique. While I need to be very careful about assuming affinity with surfers before the 1970s and beyond coastal areas of the mainland United States, I do personally identify with what I call "new surfing" (to distinguish it from earlier surfing culture in Hawai'i; see Cooley 2014, 29–30). And the guitar playing and songwriting traditions that intersect prominently with at least USA, Australian, and UK surfing scenes also resonate with my own musicking. Indeed, surfing and this sort of musicking are stable foundations of my self-identity extending back in to my formative years as an adolescent. If I am to advocate for meaningful and sustainable decolonization, I must reflexively and critically evaluate these aspects of my self-identity and of the colonial legacies of the musicking and sporting that I enjoy.

Hawai'i, Surfing, and Songs

A key source of information about historical practices of surfing and related musicking are Hawaiian legends and *mele* (chants) documented primarily in the nineteenth and early twentieth centuries but which we believe reflect precontact cultural practices. From these sources, we find ample evidence that riding ocean waves standing on surfboards was highly refined and practiced by men and women, young and old, from the royal classes to commoners. Though surfing was ubiquitous, we know more about the surfing practices of the royal Hawaiian classes because they figure more often in legends and chants, including a whole genre of royal surfing chants. For example, here is a brief fragment of the chant for Queen Emma—the queen consort of King Kamehameha IV in the mid-nineteenth century—that hints at the integration of surfing with other aspects of Hawaiian cultural and ecological processes:

"HE NALU NO EMMALANI" (SURF CHANT FOR QUEEN EMMA)

He nalu ka holua no Waiakanonoula,
He nalu ka lio me ke kaa i uka o ka aina,
He nalu ke ola'i naueue ka honua
He nalu ke anuenue me ka punohu i ka moana,
He nalu ka awa kau a ka manu iluna o ka laau
He nalu ka popolo me ka laulele,
E kaha ana ke kane me ka wahine,
E hee ana ka luahine me ka elemakule,
Pae aku, pae i ka nalu o Mauliola.

The hōlua sledding is the surfing of Waiakanono'ula
The horse and buggy are surfing upon the land
The earthquake is surfing that shakes the earth
The rainbow is surfing and so is the low lying rainbow on the ocean,
The awa planted by the birds on a tree is a "surf,"
The pōpolo and the laulele weeds are "surfs,"
Upon which men and women glide,
The old women and old men surf,
And land on the surf of Mauliola.[2]

Elsewhere I interpret in more detail this and other fragments from this long chant (Cooley 2014, 24–25), but here I point out two things. Note that the first and last lines name locations related to surfing. This is a prominent feature in Hawaiian surfing chants; they lyrically map the Hawaiian coastlines, naming surfing spots that were invariably key settlements. In this mele fragment, the chanted mapping extends the meaning of surfing beyond ocean wave riding in several ways. The chant fragment begins at Waiakanono'ula, the side of a volcano where the very dangerous sport of sledding over volcanic rock was practiced— volcano surfing. While volcanoes present dangers, they also support life. After all, volcanic action created the Hawaiian Islands themselves, which now support billions of living organisms. The chant fragment ends at Mauliola, which is not a geographic location but a metaphoric place of life and healing. Thus surfing is sung into existence as playful risk taking while engaging natural forces that give and sustain life and health. Note also the third and fourth lines of this brief mele extract, which extend analogies of surfing to earthquakes and rainbows, other waveforms expressed through seismic vibrations and the electromagnetic spectrum that produces visible light—the rainbow spectrum. The mele draws an analogy between surfing and waveforms that are felt (earthquakes) and seen (all light). In Queen Emma's surf chant we have a glimpse of surfing as a cultural practice that is conceptually engaged in a profound ecology.

Reinventing Surfing with Song

The first big change in musicking about surfing came shortly after the reigning monarch of the Kingdom of Hawai'i, Queen Lili'uokalani, was illegally deposed in 1893 by a "committee of safety" consisting of non-Native individuals representing primarily US sugar planters, descendants of missionaries, and financiers, all backed by US troops (Boyle 2015, 123). The conspirators staged the queen's overthrow when she made clear her intention to review constitutional changes that her predecessor, King Kalākaua, had been forced to sign in 1887. That so-called Bayonet Constitution removed much of the king's power and instituted economic thresholds for voting rights that effectively disenfranchised most Hawaiians and Asian immigrant laborers on the islands while favoring the minority wealthy white community (Walker 2011, 51). Thus the annexation of Hawai'i was driven by paired capitalist and racial motivations. Still, Lili'uokalani held out hope that international and US courts would restore her lawful authority, but instead the United States illegally annexed the Hawaiian Islands in 1898 (see Boyle 2015, Sai 2008, N. K. Silva 2004).

With the economic and political colonization of Hawai'i put in motion, then came the task of the demographic and cultural colonization of Hawai'i (see Alfred 2009 for similar mechanisms of "colonially-generated cultural disruption" among First Nations in Canada). This included the reinvention of surfing, which earlier had been considered the special realm of Hawaiians. First, surfing was depicted as in decline since it was claimed that Hawaiians had effectively abandoned surfing. Second, surfing was promoted as something that white people could master after all. This narrative pairing soon became a white-male hero trope with all the hallmarks of colonial appropriation wherein Indigenous peoples are erased, leaving a blank canvas on which white men can paint heroic self-images (see Moser 2010, 2011).

The fact is, however, that surfing was not being neglected by Hawaiians, and any decline of Hawaiian presence in the surfing lineups had more to do with dramatically declining populations caused by disease introduced by Europeans and Americans to Hawaiians who had no immunity (Lemarié 2015). Still, the pleasures of surfing became part of a larger push by some influential settler colonialists in Hawai'i to attract tourists and white settlers to help offset what they perceived as the racial threat, not so much of Hawaiians but of agricultural laborers from the so-called and undifferentiated Orient. Chief among those promoting the view that surfing was now available to whites was Alexander Hume Ford, a globe-trotting journalist who settled in Hawai'i in 1907 and immediately took to surfing with what historian Scott Laderman calls "mission-ary zeal" (2014, 19). Ford actively promoted the myth that it was his obligation to enact a cultural rescue of surfing, which in his self-serving interpretation Hawaiians were neglecting. However, sports enthusiasm was not at the core of Alexander Hume Ford's promotion of surfing. His motivations were colonialist and racist with the ultimate objective, as he put it, to "repeople the islands with white men" (quoted in Laderman 2014, 22).

Ford had an unlikely ally in his efforts to promote surfing to whites in a con-temporaneous new music genre called *hapa haole*, meaning "half-foreign" but usually interpreted as "half-white." Beginning in the first decade of the twentieth century, hapa haole music was one of the greatest exports for Hawaiʻi globally during the first half of the century—becoming the best-selling genre for leading record companies up to the 1930s. Responding to increased US Tourism to the islands (Carr 2014, 175), hapa haole typically combined English texts with some Hawaiian words or phrases, and a Hawaiian musical aesthetic with then-popular mainland styles such as ragtime, jazz, blues, and so forth.

Analyzing the texts of some seven hundred hapa haole songs from the first half of the twentieth century, I found that direct references to surfing, or *heʻe nalu*, are relatively rare, but they do depict a distinct context for surfing (Cooley 2014, 35–43). First, much hapa haole music portrays a Hawaiʻi where the Ha-waiian male is unthreatening—if present at all—while the Hawaiian female is foregrounded, infantilized, and sexualized. Both surfing and Hawaiian women are presented as attractions to Hawaiʻi that the white visitor might master. Surf-ing is also represented as something at which Hawaiian women excel, which is consistent with Hawaiian chants from the eighteenth and nineteenth centuries. Achieving popularity when print was still an important means for distributing popular music, the covers of hapa haole sheet music often depict idyllic scenes with white male tourists being entertained by hula dancing and/or ukulele playing Hawaiian women. Published collections of Hawaiian popular music also included overt promotions of surfing and tourism. Striking examples are a page of text and photos headed "How to Ride a Surfboard: A Correspondence Course in the Hawaiian 'Sport of Kings,'" in *Johnny Noble's Book of Famous Hawaiian Melodies* (Noble 1935, 8), and another full page of text and photos promoting surfing particularly in Waikiki in *King's Book of Hawaiian Melodies* (King 1948, 101).

The era of Hawaiʻi as a colonial territory of the United States came to an end in 1959, when the former sovereign nation was made the fiftieth state. Already in 1961, a new genre of music had emerged that presented surfing in dramatically different ways: surf music. Created in and evocative of Southern California—not Hawaiʻi—surf music seemed to celebrate the reinvention of surfing itself in the image of mainland United States: no longer the precontact favorite pastime of all Hawaiians, men, women, young, old, rich, and poor, new surfing was now portrayed as hypermasculine, white, middle-class, and expressive of youth culture and consumerism. Surf music also marks the shift of the burgeoning industry associated with surfing from Hawai'i to California. Surf music (instrumental, guitar-driven rock à la Dick Dale and songs about surfing à la the Beach Boys—both Los Angeles–area phenomena) captured the essence of reinvented new surfing. For example, on 45 rpm records (one song on each side) the Beach Boys' songs about surfing were always paired with hot rod songs that glorify the mainland United States' uniquely automobile-driven consumerism. And their "Surfer Girl" did not actually surf but remained "on shore / standing by the ocean's roar." Dick Dale literally amped the hypermasculinity of new surfing with his robust guitar amplifiers and speaker boxes developed for him by the local Fender Electric Instrument Company, the manufacturer of the famous Fender guitar, his use of extremely heavy-gauge strings, and his aggressive drumming-derived techniques for playing the guitar (Cooley 2014, 56–58). While rock historian Reebee Garofalo called surf music the "unabashed celebration of consumption" (2008, 156), I have come to hear it also as an anthem for the colonial appropriation and commoditization of Hawaiian cultural practices, reinvented to reflect mainland cultural values.

Practices of Resistance and Resilience

If the 1960s were the decade when new surfing was popularized as a decontextualized sport in the wake of Hawaiian statehood, the 1970s saw the beginning of renewed Hawaiian resistance movements—the Hawaiian Renaissance—with key involvement of a coalition of Hawaiian and *haole* (white) surfers (Walker 2011, 104–7). I interpret this as a hopeful example where the colonizer and the colonized joined in support of shared environmental and cultural interests. Blending cutting-edge scientific research and traditional Hawaiian knowledge, the Hawaiian Renaissance advocates for a return to earlier Hawaiian attitudes about surfing that include an ecological decolonizing of Hawai'i itself. The Hawaiian Renaissance reinvigorated efforts to manage Hawaiian affairs foregrounding local and Indigenous principles. The ongoing achievements of the Hawaiian Renaissance include reviving the Hawaiian language and forms of musicking, including hula dance, and generally fostering pride in being Hawaiian after decades of denigration leading up to the deposition of Queen Lili'uokalani, the illegal US annexation of Hawai'i, and statehood in 1959. The revivals of traditional practices have not been slavish returns to historic models but have incorporated postcontact influences while retaining core Hawaiian concepts of culture, history, and identity (see Teves 2014). Drawing energy from other civil rights movements around the world at the time, the Hawaiian Renaissance is notable for its grassroots origins or possibly seaweed origins since, as historian Isaiah Helekunihi Walker claims, many of the activists in the movement were then and still are today surfers and sailors (2011, 105–26). Here I focus on one project of the Hawaiian Renaissance that weaves together many of the themes of this book, in particular scientifically informed environmental movements, ecology, activism, and musicking.

The Polynesian Voyaging Society (PVS) was formed in 1973 by Hawaiian artist Herb Kawainui Kāne; Californian surfer, anthropologist, and influential historian of surfing Ben Finney, who was then a professor at the University of Hawai'i, Manoa; and another haole surfer and sailor, Tommy Holmes (Walker 2011, 117). The PVS's objective was to build a replica of an ancient Polynesian long-distance voyaging canoe. For Kāne, the project was motivated by heritage and a desire to reconnect with his Hawaiian/Polynesian ancestry. Kāne also insisted that the vessel should be sailed primarily by Hawaiians. Finney's objectives were different but complementary: it was a cultural and scientific research opportunity to prove that traditional Polynesian sailing vessels and navigational techniques from centuries prior were capable and sophisticated beyond anything contemporary European sailors had achieved.

The successes of the PVS's project are—though not without setbacks—nothing short of spectacular, in part because of the slow, measured, and in a word, *sustainable* pace of their very ambitious global vision. The PVS launched its flagship vessel, *Hōkūle'a*, in 1975. The following year, *Hōkūle'a*—a sustainably built vessel, powered by wind (no fossil fuels), and navigated with traditional Polynesian techniques using the sun, stars, and ocean swell and wind patterns (no sextant, no GPS)—sailed the nearly three thousand miles of open ocean from Hawai'i to Tahiti. In the four decades since, *Hōkūle'a* has made numerous long-distance journeys. Here I focus on the PVS's most recent and ambitious effort, the Mālama Honua Worldwide Voyage, a three-year journey circumnavigating the earth. This journey began in May 2014, when *Hōkūle'a* sailed from Hawai'i; the vessel and its crew returned to their point of departure in June 2017 after calling on over 150 ports in eighteen nations.

As noted on hokulea.com, Mālama Honua can be translated simply as "to care for our Island Earth," but the meaning also expands to include taking care of and protecting everything making up our world: land, oceans, living organisms, cultures, communities. The PVS's Mālama Honua Worldwide Voyage embodies an overtly ecological mission, as articulated by PVS president and native Hawaiian navigator Nainoa Thompson: "We're not going to change the world; we're going to build a network of people around the Earth who are going to change it" (http://www.hokulea.com/malama-honua-ohana-hokulea-episode-2/). The crew's method was to interact with Indigenous peoples whenever possible when they came into ports, and these encounters almost invariably included ceremonies with chants, songs, dances, and the exchange of knowledge and symbolic objects. These encounters are documented on their blogs, web pages, and online newsletters. Take, for example, a blog posted by *Hōkūle'a* crew member and cultural protocol specialist Maya L. Kawailanaokeawaiki Saffery, on July 31, 2016. She wrote that as *Hōkūle'a* arrived at Pemetic, Maine, they were greeted by Wabanaki, Native American peoples from Maine, who paddled out to meet them in their birch-bark canoes. Then together these two groups of Indigenous peoples created a ceremonial space in the working boatyard where they docked so that they "could share prayers, speeches, songs, and dances in Hawaiian and Algonquin languages in honor of this historic coming together of our peoples" (Saffery 2016). But her most memorable day was when they traveled to Indian Island, the Penobscot Nation reservation, part of the Wabanaki Confederacy (see MacDougall in this volume for more on Indian Island and the Penobscot community). This was a day of sharing food, stories, song, and dance away from prying eyes and documenting cameras. In her blog post, Saffery wrote reflexively about her own "move away from the 'performance' of hula where the dances and songs become objects for display and consumption and . . . move toward the 'practice' of hula as a lifestyle and expression of aloha 'āina [love for one's land, ancestors, people, culture]." Ultimately Saffery's act of sharing during this meeting of Indigenous peoples was to offer a mele "'Umia ke Aloha i Pa'a i Loko," composed by the deposed Queen Lili'uokalani in 1895 while she was still under house arrest and not allowed to communicate with her subjects and supporters.[3] Containing what Kīhei de Silva has described as "political double entendre" (2008) that her imprisoners did not understand, this and several other mele composed by Lili'uokalani at this time were smuggled out and published in a Hawaiian-language newspaper.

I read Maya Saffery's focus on cultural "practice" rather than "performance" as an act of decolonization because she denies the economic exploitation of performances of traditional Hawaiian culture. "Practice," on the other hand, is about repetitively reconnecting with the very things that colonialism takes away: land, ancestors, people, culture. In her communications with me about a draft of this chapter (email, October 18, 2017), Saffery wanted to recognize her mentors, colleagues, and peers who have been part of her understanding this move from "performance to practice." In particular she noted her colleague and hula sister Kahikina de Silva, who is cited by Jeff Corntassel (Cherokee Nation and professor of Indigenous Governance at the University of Victoria) as stating that "decolonization praxis comes from moving beyond political awareness and/ or symbolic gestures to everyday practices of resurgence" (quoted in Corntassel 2012, 89). This act of recognition by Saffery is another act of aloha 'āina and is consistent with Corntassel's call for Indigenous resurgence and decolonization based on everyday actions (praxis) that reinforce one's relationships with one's community and the natural world (Corntassel 2012, 87, 92, 96, 97).

Everyday actions that reinforce profoundly integrated relationships with other organisms—whether human or not—and the environment form a model for ecology. They are a basis for cultural sustainability. While some of the scholars and activist engaged in this chapter are specifically concerned with Indigenous decolonization and self-determination (Alfred, Boyle, Corntassel, de Silva, Saffery, Sai, Silva, Smith, Teves, Walker), those of us who are not Indigenous and who have benefited from the spoils of colonization need to hear and honor their desires, models, and practices. (For discussions of ecological models among Indigenous peoples, see also Hurley-Glowa, Kisliuk, MacDougall, Post, and Tucker in this volume.) This involves rejecting the colonial and neoliberal paradigms built on economic-growth models and replacing them with ecological models centered on human cultural practices that are profoundly relational. For example, Saffery's "practice" is very similar to Rory Turner's notion of participation and empathy (this volume) and Jeff Todd Titon's call for "musical being-in-the-world" (Titon 2008, 31 and 32), all modes of human interaction that resist consumption and thus colonial exploitation.

I began this chapter stating that decolonization does not mean detachment, separation, segregation, but must be relational. I conclude by holding up the Polynesian Voyaging Society as a decolonizing intervention that starts with traditional ecological knowledge combined with cutting-edge science to enact a model of global exchange that overturns colonial and neoliberal models of resource exploitation. Powered by renewable and nonconsumable energies to literally carry their people and mission around the world, the PVS prioritized global networks and relations with Indigenous peoples when the crew came to port, yet the organization makes its message freely available to all. It delivers through practice the political and social message that sustainable systems work. The maps of the Mālama Honua journey depict a globe circumscribed by lines of decolonization; lines inscribed on those blue areas of our maps that account for 71 percent of the planet's surface and an astounding 99 percent of the living space, according to Hawaiʻi Pacific University's Oceanic Institute (http://www.oceanicinstitute.org/aboutoceans/aquafacts.html). Decolonizing Hawaiʻi does not mean retelling the myth of an isolated archipelago but rather calls for renewing the tradition of exchange of food, stories, songs, and dances between Indigenous peoples worldwide. This, in turn, provides a model of sustainable exchange without the exploitation of human and earth resources. Decolonizing Hawaiʻi is about broad connections on a global ecological scale, because isolation, separation of peoples, is a historical myth. Segregations and apartheids are not sustainable.

Notes

1. I am indebted to Gregory Barz and Maya L. Kawailanaokeawaiki Saffery, who read and commented on earlier versions of this chapter.

2. Fragment from "Surf Chant for Queen Emma," *Hawaiian Ethnological Notes*, 3:458, taken from HI.M.74, 234–238, both housed at the Bishop Museum Archives, Honolulu, Hawai'i. Reproduced without diacritics as found in the original manuscript. English adapted from Mary Kawena Pukui. Used with permission.

3. The significance of this particular mele was brought to my attention by Min Yen Ong and Jordan Kapono Bee after I presented an earlier version of this research at the 2017 British Forum for Ethnomusicology annual meeting in Sheffield, UK.

References

Alfred, Gerald Taiaiake. 2009. "Colonialism and State Dependency." *Journal of Aboriginal Health* 5:42–60.

Boyle, Francis A. 2015. *Restoring the Kingdom of Hawaii: The Kānaka Maoli Route to Independence*. Atlanta: Clarity Press.

Carr, James Revell. 2014. *Hawaiian Music in Motion: Mariners, Missionaries, and Minstrels*. Urbana-Champaign: University of Illinois Press.

Cary, Lisa J. 2004. "Always Already Colonizer/Colonized: White Australian Wanderings." In *Decolonizing Research in Cross-Cultural Contexts: Critical Personal Narratives*, edited by Kagendo Mutua and Beth Blue Swadener, 69–83. Albany: State University of New York Press.

Cooley, Timothy J. 2014. *Surfing about Music*. Berkeley: University of California Press.

Corntassel, Jeff. 2012. "Re-envisioning Resurgence: Indigenous Pathways to Decolonization and Sustainable Self-Determination." *Decolonization: Indigeneity, Education & Society* 1 (1): 86–101.

de Silva, Kīhei. 2008. "'Umia ke Aloha i Pa'a I Loko." Essay first published in Hālau Mōhala 'Ilima's Merrie Monarch Fact Sheet. http://www.halaumohalailima.com/HMI/Umia_Ke_Aloha.html.

Garofalo, Reebee. 2008. *Rockin' Out: Popular Music in the USA*. 4th ed. Upper Saddle River, NJ: Prentice Hall.

Heise, Ursula K. 2017. "Introduction: Planet, Species, Justice—and the Stories We Tell about Them." In *The Routledge Companion to the Environmental Humanities*, edited by Ursula K. Heise, Jon Christensen, and Michelle Niemann, 1–10. London: Routledge.

King, Charles E. 1948. *King's Book of Hawaiian Melodies*. Honolulu: printed by author.

Laderman, Scott. 2014. *Empire in Waves: A Political History of Surfing*. Berkeley: University of California Press.

Lemarié, Jérémy. 2015. "Debunking the Myth that Missionaries Nearly Killed Surfing in the 19th Century Hawai'i." *trim*, no. 4, 44–68.

Manuel, Peter. 2017. "World Music and Activism since the End of History." *Music and Politics* 11 (1): 1–16.

Moser, Patrick. 2010. "Revival." *Kurungabaa: A Journal of Literature, History and Ideas from the Sea* 3 (1): 46–69.

———. 2011. "The Reports of Surfing's Demise Have Been Greatly Exaggerated." *Bamboo Ridge: Journal of Hawai'i Literature and Arts*, no. 98, 195–204.

Noble, Johnny. 1935. *Johnny Noble's Book of Famous Hawaiian Melodies: Including Hulas and Popular Hawaiian Standards*. New York: Miller Music.

Saffery, Maya. 2016. "Everyday Acts of Aloha 'Āina." Crew blog, Hokulea.com, July 1. http://www.hokulea.com/crew-blog-maya-saffery-everyday-acts-aloha-aina/.

Sai, David Keanu. 2008. "A Slippery Path towards Hawaiian Indigeneity: An Analysis and Comparison between Hawaiian State Sovereignty and Hawaiian Indigeneity and Its Use and Practice in Hawai'i Today." *Journal of Law & Social Challenges* 10 (Fall): 68.

Silva, Noenoe K. 2004. *Aloha Betrayed: Native Hawaiian Resistance to American Colonialism*. Durham, NC: Duke University Press.

Smith, Linda Tuhiwai. 1999. *Decolonizing Methodologies: Research and Indigenous Peoples*. London: Zed Books.

Teves, Stephanie Nohelani. 2014. "Tradition and Performance." In *Native Studies Keywords*, edited by Stephanie Nohelani Teves, Andrea Smith, and Michelle H. Raheja, 257–69. Tucson: University of Arizona Press.

Titon, Jeff Todd. 2008. "Knowing Fieldwork." In *Shadows in the Field: New Perspectives for Fieldwork in Ethnomusicology*, edited by Gregory Barz and Timothy J. Cooley, 2nd ed., 25–41. New York: Oxford University Press.

———. 2015. "Sustainability, Resilience and Adaptive Management for Applied Ethnomusicology." In *The Oxford Handbook of Applied Ethnomusicology*, edited by Svanibor Pettan and Jeff Todd Titon, 157–98. New York: Oxford University Press.

Walker, Isaiah Helekunihi. 2011. *Waves of Resistance: Surfing and History in Twentieth-Century Hawai'i*. Honolulu: University of Hawai'i Press.

Contributors

AARON S. ALLEN is director of the Environment and Sustainability Program and an associate professor of music at the University of North Carolina at Greensboro. A fellow of the American Academy in Rome, he earned a PhD from Harvard University with a dissertation on the nineteenth-century Italian reception of Beethoven. His BA in music and BS in environmental studies are from Tulane University. He is coeditor with Kevin Dawe of the collection *Current Directions in Ecomusicology* (Routledge 2016), which the Society for Ethnomusicology awarded the 2018 Ellen Koskoff Edited Volume Prize..

MICHAEL BAKAN is a professor of ethnomusicology at Florida State University. His more than fifty publications include the books *Speaking for Ourselves: Conversations on Life, Music, and Autism; World Music: Traditions and Transformations;* and *Music of Death and New Creation,* as well as numerous articles on the ethnomusicology of autism. He serves as series editor for Routledge's Focus on World Music Series, has received grants from the National Endowment for the Arts for his music and autism research, and has spoken at institutions including Harvard, Columbia, and the Berklee College of Music. As a percussionist, he has performed with John Cage, Rudolf Serkin, George Clinton, and Tito Puente.

ROBERT BARON is the founding director of the Folk Arts Program of the New York State Council on the Arts and teaches in the Master's Program in Cultural Sustainability at Goucher College. He has been a Fulbright Senior Specialist in Finland, the Philippines, and Slovenia, a Smithsonian Museum Practice Fellow, and a Non-Resident Fellow of the W. E. B. Du Bois Institute for African and African American Research at Harvard University. Baron received the Benjamin A. Botkin award for significant lifetime achievement in public folklore from the American Folklore Society. His research interests include public folklore, cultural policy, creolization and museum studies. His publications include *Public Folklore*, edited with Nick Spitzer; *Creolization as Cultural Creativity*, edited with Ana Cara; and articles in *Curator*, the *International Journal of Heritage Studies*, the *Journal of American Folklore*, *Western Folklore*, and the *Journal of Folklore Research*. Baron holds a PhD in folklore and folklife from the University of Pennsylvania.

DANIEL CAVICCHI is the vice provost at Rhode Island School of Design. He is the author of *Listening and Longing: Music Lovers in the Age of Barnum* and *Tramps like Us: Music and Meaning among Springsteen Fans*, and coeditor of *My Music: Explorations of Music in Daily Life*. His public work has included curricula for the Experience Music Project and PBS; *Songs of Conscience, Sounds of Freedom*, the inaugural special exhibit for the Grammy Museum in Los Angeles; and the *Witness Tree Project*, a history and design curriculum with the National Park Service.

TIMOTHY J. COOLEY is a professor of ethnomusicology and global studies at the University of California, Santa Barbara. He teaches courses on vernacular and popular musics in Central European and the United States. His volume, co-edited with Gregory Barz *Shadows in the Field: New Perspectives for Fieldwork in Ethnomusicology*, now in its second edition, is a standard text for students of ethnomusicology. His second book, *Making Music in the Polish Tatras: Tourists, Ethnographers, and Mountain Musicians*, won the 2006 Orbis Prize for Polish Studies. Cooley's most recent book, *Surfing about Music*, considers how surfers musically express their ideas about surfing, and how surfing as a sport and lifestyle is represented in popular culture.

MARK F. DEWITT is the author of *Cajun and Zydeco Dance Music in Northern California: Modern Pleasures in a Postmodern World* (University Press of Mississippi, 2008). He holds the Dr. Tommy Comeaux Endowed Chair in Traditional Music at the University of Louisiana at Lafayette, where he directs an undergraduate curriculum and degree program in traditional music, especially Cajun and Creole French music. He completed his doctoral studies at the University of California, Berkeley in ethnomusicology. As an undergraduate at the Massachusetts Institute of Technology, he majored in urban planning, concentrating on energy and environmental policy.

BARRY DORNFELD is an organizational consultant, an ethnographer of communication, and a documentary filmmaker with a long-standing interest in music and expressive culture. His documentary work includes: "Eatala: A Life in Klezmer," "Gandy Dancers," portraying the expressive culture and history of African-American railroad workers in the US, and broadcast nationally on

PBS, and "Powerhouse for God," made with Jeff Titon and Tom Rankin. A principal at CFAR, Inc., he consults on organizational culture, change, and collaboration. Dornfeld has a PhD in communication from the Annenberg School at the University of Pennsylvania and has published articles and a book about social capital, digital media and public television. His most recent book, *The Moment You Can't Ignore*, coauthored with Mal O'Connor, was published by PublicAffairs Books in 2014.

THOMAS FAUX is an ethnomusicologist on the music faculty at Illinois State University. He has conducted fieldwork among francophone musicians in Québec, northern New England, and Louisiana, and among South American musicians in New England and Peru. He is coproducer of the ten-part radio documentary *Your Neighbor's Radio*, which explores music in immigrant and refugee communities in Portland, Maine, and is founder of a community music school in Urbana, Illinois. He earned a master's degree at Tufts University and is completing his doctoral studies at the University of Illinois.

BURT FEINTUCH was a professor of folklore and English and director of the Center for the Humanities at the University of New Hampshire. Feintuch published on traditional music, cultural conservation, and other topics in vernacular culture. From 1990 to 1995, he edited the *Journal of American Folklore*. He did ethnographic research in music cultures in Great Britain, the United States, and Canada. For many years he researched traditional music and culture on Cape Breton Island. His latest book, in collaboration with photographer Gary Samson, is *Talking New Orleans Music*. Feintuch produced sound recordings for Smithsonian Folkways and Rounder.

NANCY GUY is an ethnomusicologist whose broad interests include the musics of Taiwan and China, varieties of opera (including European and Chinese operas), music and politics, and the ecocritical study of music. Her first book, *Peking Opera and Politics in Taiwan* (University of Illinois Press, 2005), won the ASCAP Béla Bartók Award for Excellence in Ethnomusicology and was also named an "Outstanding Academic Title for 2006" by *Choice*. Guy's second book, *The Magic of Beverly Sills*, focuses on the artistry and appeal of the beloved American coloratura soprano and was published by University of Illinois Press in 2015. Guy is a professor of music at the University of California, San Diego.

MARY HUFFORD has worked over the past three decades in government, academic, and nonprofit sectors. As folklife specialist at the American Folklife Center, Library of Congress (1982–2002), she led regional team fieldwork projects in the New Jersey Pine Barrens and the southern West Virginia coalfields. From 2002 to 2012, she served on the graduate faculty of folklore and folklife at the University of Pennsylvania, directing the Center for Folklore and Ethnography from 2002 to 2008. She is associate director of the Livelihoods Knowledge Exchange Network (LiKEN), a link tank that nurtures collaboratories for the stewardship of place, culture, and land. A fellow of the American Folklore Society and a Guggenheim fellow, she is the author of *Chaseworld: Foxhunting and Storytelling in New Jersey's Pine Barrens* and numerous monographs and articles on folklore and the environment and the editor of *Conserving Culture: A New Discourse on Culture*. A complete list of her downloadable publications is available at http://vt.academia.edu/MaryHufford.

SUSAN HURLEY-GLOWA is an associate professor of ethnomusicology at the University of Texas Rio Grande Valley. She earned a PhD in ethnomusicology at Brown University. In 2007, she moved to Alaska with her family, where she taught music and played horn in local ensembles. In 2011, she began teaching musicology and applied horn at the University of Texas Brownsville, now UTRGV. Since then, she commutes between Texas and Alaska. Her research interests include Luso African, Latin American, and Alaskan music cultures. She has published numerous articles; hosts a radio show on 88FM, Rio Grande Valley Public Radio; and wrote, directed, and produced a documentary film on Cape Verdean music cultures.

PATRICK HUTCHINSON is an internationally recognized performer and teacher of the Irish uilleann pipes, the instrument on which he twice won the All-Ireland slow airs title, twenty-two years apart, most recently in 2014 in Sligo. With Paul Cranford and David Papazian, he is the coauthor of *Move Your Fingers: The Life and Music of Chris Langan* (Cranford, 2002). He holds a PhD in ethnomusicology from Brown, where he was fortunate to study with Jeff Titon, a man who shares his passion for neighborly music making.

MICHELLE KISLIUK, an associate professor of music at the University of Virginia, has a PhD in performance studies from New York University. Integrating theory and practice, her research specializations include the music, dance, daily life, and cultural politics of forest people (BaAka) in the Central African Republic. Her essays have appeared in collections including *Theorizing Sound Writing* (Wesleyan University Press), *Teaching Performance Studies* (University of Southern Illinois Press), *Performing Ethnomusicology* (University of California Press), *Shadows in the Field* (Oxford University Press), and *Music and Gender* (University of Illinois Press). Her book *Seize the Dance! BaAka Musical Life and the Ethnography of Performance* (Oxford University Press) won the ASCAP Deems Taylor Special Recognition Award.

PAULEENA M. MACDOUGALL, the director emerita of the Maine Folklife Center, received her PhD in American history from the University of Maine in 1995. She serves as a faculty associate in anthropology at the University of Maine, where she teaches courses in folklore. Since 1979, MacDougall has published numerous articles on Maine's Native American language, culture, and history and two books, *The Penobscot Dance of Resistance: Tradition in the History of a People* (University Press of New England, 2004) and *Fannie Hardy Eckstorm and Her Quest for Local Knowledge: 1865–1946* (Lexington Press, 2013). MacDougall edits the Maine Folklife Center's annual monograph series, Northeast Folklore. She is currently working in collaboration with the Penobscot Indian Nation in preparing "The Penobscot Indian Language Dictionary" for publication by the University of Maine Press in 2019.

MARGARITA MAZO, professor emerita at Ohio State University, is internationally known for her research and publications on Russian music. She has published widely on music making in Russian villages, music in cognate communities in Russia and the United States, emotion and vocal expression, lament as coping in grief, and music by Russian composers, including Igor Stravinsky's *Les Noces*. She is currently completing a project in cognitive ethnomusicology on the interaction of cultural experience and affective heart responses to laments. She is the founder of the programs in ethnomusicology and cognitive ethnomusicology at Ohio State University. Prior to her position at OSU, she taught at Harvard University, New England Conservatory, and Saint Petersburg Conservatory.

DOTAN NITZBERG is originally from Israel and currently resides in Canada, where he is a scholar of music, autism, and double-giftedness pursuing his PhD at the University of New Brunswick. He holds degrees from Tel Aviv's Buchmann-Mehta School of Music, Lynn University, and Florida State University. Nitzberg has performed at the Kennedy Center in Washington, DC, and in recital or as a concerto soloist throughout Israel, Italy, and the United States. He is a three-time laureate of the America-Israel Scholarship Contest and has presented his research at international conferences, including at the 2012 World Piano Teachers Association Conference in Novi Sad, Serbia. Dotan's collaborations with the ethnomusicologist Michael Bakan include a chapter in the book Speaking for Ourselves: Conversations on Life, Music, and Autism.

JENNIFER C. POST is an ethnomusicologist with recent research experience in the music and musical instruments of Central Asia and the Turkic world. Her current fieldwork in Mongolia considers the impact of social, economic, and ecological change on musical production of Mongolian Kazakh mobile pastoral herders. Published and forthcoming articles address music in connection with repatriation, traditional ecological knowledge, cultural and biological sustainability, and musical instrument production and use. She has taught at Middlebury College in Vermont and the New Zealand School of Music and is currently a senior lecturer at the School of Music, University of Arizona.

TOM RANKIN is a professor of the practice of art and documentary studies at Duke University, where he directs the MFA in Experimental and Documentary Arts Program. Formerly he was director of the Center for Documentary Studies at Duke. His books include *Sacred Space: Photographs from the Mississippi Delta* (1993); *Deaf Maggie Lee Sayre: Photographs of a River Life* (1995); *Faulkner's World: The Photographs of Martin J. Dain* (1997); and *One Place: Paul Kwilecki and Four Decades of Photographs from Decatur County, Georgia* (2013). His photographs have been collected and published widely and included in numerous exhibitions. A frequent writer and lecturer on photography, culture, and the documentary tradition, he is the general editor of the series Documentary Arts and Culture, published by the University of North Carolina Press.

ROSHAN SAMTANI is an ethnomusicologist specializing in flamenco history and guitar performance. He earned a PhD at Brown University. He currently teaches the history and theory of flamenco at the University Studies Abroad Consortium (Madrid) and at Stanford University's Bing Overseas Studies Program, Madrid.

JEFFREY A. SUMMIT, PhD, holds the appointment of research professor in the Department of Music at Tufts University. He also serves as a senior consultant to Hillel International: The Foundation for Jewish Campus Life. He is the author of *Singing God's Words: The Performance of Biblical Chant in Contemporary Judaism* (Oxford University Press) and *The Lord's Song in a Strange Land: Music and Identity in Contemporary Jewish Worship* (Oxford University Press). His CD *Abayudaya: Music from the Jewish People of Uganda* (Smithsonian Folkways Recordings) was nominated for a Grammy award. In 2013 his CD with video *Delicious Peace: Coffee, Music and Interfaith Harmony in Uganda* (Smithsonian Folkways Recordings) was named best world music CD by the Independent Music Awards. His research focuses on music and identity, music and spiritual experience, music and advocacy, and the impact of technology on the transmission of tradition.

JOSHUA TUCKER is an associate professor of music at Brown University and the author of *Gentleman Troubadours and Andean Pop Stars: Huayno Music, Media Work, and Ethnic Imaginaries in Urban Peru*. His work, which has been funded by the Wenner-Gren Foundation and the Social Science and Humanities Research Council of Canada, focuses largely on the social politics of popular music in Latin America. His current research centers on the intersection between indigenous activism, acoustic ecology, and instrument making among Quechua-speaking musicians in the southern Andes.

RORY TURNER, PhD (Indiana University Folklore Institute), is an assistant professor in Goucher College's Department of Sociology/Anthropology. He designed, launched, and continues to teach in Goucher College's Master of the Arts in Cultural Sustainability Program. Formerly director of the Folk and Traditional Arts Program and program initiative specialist at the Maryland State Arts Council, he cofounded and directed the Maryland Traditions Program from 2000 to 2007. He also launched and subsequently revived the Baltimore Rhythm Festival. His publications include articles, reviews, and creative writing in journals such as *Folklore Forum, Anthropology and Humanism,* and *TDR (The Drama Review).*

DENISE VON GLAHN is the Curtis Mayes Orpheus Professor and coordinator of the Musicology Area at Florida State University, where she also directs the Center for Music of the Americas. She has published two books on music and nature topics: *The Sounds of Place: Music and the American Cultural Landscape,* which won a 2004 ASCAP–Deems Taylor Award, and *Music and the Skillful Listener: American Women Compose the Natural World,* which won the Pauline Alderman Award of 2015. Her scholarship has appeared in *JAMS, JSAM,* and *American Music,* as well as journals and essay collections in the United States and abroad. Von Glahn coedits the series Music, Nature, Place at Indiana University Press with Sabine Feisst and has just completed a biography of Libby Larsen for the University of Illinois Press.

THOMAS WALKER directs the MA programs in Environmental Studies and Historic Preservation at Goucher College and previously served as a codirector of the MA in Cultural Sustainability Program. Trained in anthropology, history, and folklore at Indiana University, where he received his PhD, he has been an educator, ethnographer, event organizer, and advocate for issues concerning work and occupational culture. He is also a venture philanthropist, serving as trustee to a private foundation that funds research, policy initiatives, and projects addressing environmental economics in areas of climate change, energy policy, sustainable fisheries, carbon tax, ecosystem services, and ecotourism.

Index

Portney, Kent E., 131, 133
Post, Jennifer C., 5, 39, 77, 80
pragmatism, American, 19–20
Prairie Home Companion, A (radio show),
 273, 275
Pratt, Ray, 133
pre-form (term), 264
"Premonitions," 125n5
Presley, Elvis, 135
Primiano, Leonard, 34
Princen, Thomas, 4
public folklore, 36–38
Puckett, Anita, 24
Pukui, Mary Kawena, 304n2
Purcell, Al, 179
Purcell, Leo, 179–80
Putnam, Robert, 211
Pygmies of the Ituri Forest, The (Ethnic Folk-
 ways), 149

Qazanbaiuly, Minäp, 77
Quintal, Claire, 276
Quispillaccta. *See* Peru

Racy, Ali Jihad, 229
radical critical empathy: breaking the "more
 is better" axiom for, 39; category errors and,
 32; centrality of, in cultural sustainability,
 37–38; challenge of cultural sustainability
 and, 38–39; hybrid research collectives and
 alternative economies in, 39–40; politics of
 well-being and, 40–41; public folklore and,
 36–37; scholars in, 33–35
Radio Quispillaccta, 183–84, 191
Rafferty, Mike, 175–76
Rajeczky, Benjamin, 229
Raker, John E., 118
Ranger, Terence, 269
Rankin, Tom, 159, 162, 166–67, 170–73
Rappaport, Roy A., 39
Rawidowicz, Simon, 197
Rawls, Alex, 94
Recording Industry of America, 137
"Recycling Truck," 67–68
reforestation efforts, 11
Reganold, John, 55n6
Regier, Henry A., 212
Reid, Herbert, 28, 30n2
resilience, 4–5, 274, 296; and adaptive man-
 agement in piano pedagogy, 249–59; of
 Alaska Natives, 103; defined, 249; interven-
 tion and, 6–10; resistance and, 300–303;

in response to climate change in Western
 Mongolia, 82–84
resistance, and resilience, 300–303
Restoration, The (film), 94
restorative culture making, 40
Reyes-Garcia, Victoria, 10
Rhodes, Richard, 121
Rice, Timothy, 262, 266
Richard, Zachary, 93, 95, 97n4
Riley, Steve, 92, 93
Ritter, Jonathan, 188
Riverdance, 181
Robbins, Tim, 94
Robichaud, Gerry, 274
Robicheaux, Earl, 91–92
Roche, Francis, 177
Rodman, Gil, 133
Roma community. *See* gitanos
Rosaldo, Renato, 227n6
Ross, Alex, 109
Rothenberg, Jerome, 206
Rottenberg, Jonathan, 232
Rouch, Jean, 148
Roy, Cindy, 273–82
Roy, Don, 273–82
Ruby, Jay, 156n3
"Ruined River, The," 113
Russian village lament: contexts and conse-
 quences of, 230–32; emotional stimuli in,
 234; experimental design and participants
 on, 233–34; study of heart responses to,
 232–42; study results and discussion,
 236–42
Rust, Roberta, 256
Ryan, Robin, 56n11

Saad, Ali Mansour, 82
Saffery, Maya L. Kawailanaokeawaiki, 302–3,
 304n1
Sager, Rebecca, 233
Sai, David Keanu, 298, 303
Salcedo, Uriel, 186–92
Salomon, Frank, 185
Samson, Gary, 210, 214–16, 219n3
Sanchez, Paul, 94
Sand County Almanac (Leopold), 20
San Román Espinosa, Teresa, 263
Santa Fe American Folklore Society, 34
Sarno, Louis, 223
Sayre, Archie, *160*, 161
Sayre, Maggie Lee, 159–63, *160–63*
Schafer, R. Murray, xxiv, 69, 121
Schechner, Richard, 133, 221

The University of Illinois Press
is a founding member of the
Association of University Presses.

———————————————————

University of Illinois Press
1325 South Oak Street
Champaign, IL 61820-6903
www.press.uillinois.edu